Houghton
Mifflin
Harcourt

# collections

**Cover, Title Page Photo Credits:** ©AStock/Corbis

Printed in the U.S.A.

ISBN 978-0-544-04666-5

5 6 7 8 9 10    0868    21 20 19 18 17 16 15 14

4500501619        B C D E F G

# collections

**GRADE 6**

**Program Consultants:**

**Kylene Beers**

**Martha Hougen**

**Carol Jago**

**William L. McBride**

**Erik Palmer**

**Lydia Stack**

# About Our Program Consultants

**Kylene Beers**  Nationally known lecturer and author on reading and literacy; 2011 recipient of the Conference on English Leadership Exemplary Leader Award; coauthor of *Notice and Note: Strategies for Close Reading*; former president of the National Council of Teachers of English. Dr. Beers is the nationally known author of *When Kids Can't Read: What Teachers Can Do* and coeditor of *Adolescent Literacy: Turning Promise into Practice*, as well as articles in the *Journal of Adolescent and Adult Literacy*. Former editor of *Voices from the Middle*, she is the 2001 recipient of NCTE's Richard W. Halley Award, given for outstanding contributions to middle school literacy. She recently served as Senior Reading Researcher at the Comer School Development Program at Yale University as well as Senior Reading Advisor to Secondary Schools for the Reading and Writing Project at Teachers College.

**Martha Hougen**  National consultant, presenter, researcher, and author. Areas of expertise include differentiating instruction for students with learning difficulties, including those with learning disabilities and dyslexia; and teacher and leader preparation improvement. Dr. Hougen has taught at the middle school through graduate levels. Recently her focus has been on working with teacher educators to enhance teacher and leader preparation to better meet the needs of all students. Currently she is working with the University of Florida at the Collaboration for Effective Educator Development, Accountability, and Reform Center (CEEDAR Center) to improve the achievement of students with disabilities by reforming teacher and leader licensure, evaluation, and preparation. She has led similar efforts in Texas with the Higher Education Collaborative and the College & Career Readiness Initiative Faculty Collaboratives. In addition to peer-reviewed articles, curricular documents, and presentations, Dr. Hougen has published two college textbooks: *The Fundamentals of Literacy Assessment and Instruction Pre-K–6* (2012) and *The Fundamentals of Literacy Assessment and Instruction 6–12* (2014).

**Carol Jago**  Teacher of English with 32 years of experience at Santa Monica High School in California; author and nationally known lecturer; and former president of the National Council of Teachers of English. Currently serves as Associate Director of the California Reading and Literature Project at UCLA. With expertise in standards assessment and secondary education, Ms. Jago is the author of numerous books on education, including *With Rigor for All* and *Papers, Papers, Papers*, and is active with the California Association of Teachers of English, editing its scholarly journal *California English* since 1996. Ms. Jago also served on the planning committee for the 2009 NAEP Framework and the 2011 NAEP Writing Framework.

**William L. McBride**  Curriculum specialist. Dr. McBride is a nationally known speaker, educator, and author who now trains teachers in instructional methodologies. He is coauthor of *What's Happening?*, an innovative, high-interest text for middle-grade readers, and author of *If They Can Argue Well, They Can Write Well*. A former reading specialist, English teacher, and social studies teacher, he holds a master's degree in reading and a doctorate in curriculum and instruction from the University of North Carolina at Chapel Hill. Dr. McBride has contributed to the development of textbook series in language arts, social studies, science, and vocabulary. He is also known for his novel *Entertaining an Elephant*, which tells the story of a veteran teacher who becomes reinspired with both his profession and his life.

**Erik Palmer**  Veteran teacher and education consultant based in Denver, Colorado. Author of *Well Spoken: Teaching Speaking to All Students* and *Digitally Speaking: How to Improve Student Presentations*. His areas of focus include improving oral communication, promoting technology in classroom presentations, and updating instruction through the use of digital tools. He holds a bachelor's degree from Oberlin College and a master's degree in curriculum and instruction from the University of Colorado.

**Lydia Stack**  Internationally known teacher educator and author. She is involved in a Stanford University project to support English Language Learners, *Understanding Language*. The goal of this project is to enrich academic content and language instruction for English Language Learners (ELLs) in grades K-12 by making explicit the language and literacy skills necessary to meet the Common Core State Standards (CCSS) and Next Generation Science Standards. Her teaching experience includes twenty-five years as an elementary and high school ESL teacher, and she is a past president of Teachers of English to Speakers of Other Languages (TESOL). Her awards include the TESOL James E. Alatis Award and the San Francisco STAR Teacher Award. Her publications include *On Our Way to English, Visions: Language, Literature, Content,* and *American Themes*, a literature anthology for high school students in the ACCESS program of the U.S. State Department's Office of English Language Programs.

## Additional thanks to the following Program Reviewers

Rosemary Asquino
Sylvia B. Bennett
Yvonne Bradley
Leslie Brown
Haley Carroll
Caitlin Chalmers
Emily Colley-King
Stacy Collins
Denise DeBonis
Courtney Dickerson
Sarah Easley
Phyllis J. Everette
Peter J. Foy Sr.

Carol M. Gibby
Angie Gill
Mary K. Goff
Saira Haas
Lisa M. Janeway
Robert V. Kidd Jr.
Kim Lilley
John C. Lowe
Taryn Curtis MacGee
Meredith S. Maddox
Cynthia Martin
Kelli M. McDonough
Megan Pankiewicz

Linda Beck Pieplow
Molly Pieplow
Mary-Sarah Proctor
Jessica A. Stith
Peter Swartley
Pamela Thomas
Linda A. Tobias
Rachel Ukleja
Lauren Vint
Heather Lynn York
Leigh Ann Zerr

COMMON CORE

# COLLECTION 1
# Facing Fear

**KEY LEARNING OBJECTIVES**

Make inferences.
Describe characters and setting.
Describe plot.
Identify repetition and rhyme scheme.
Analyze structure of lyric poems.
Analyze point of view.

Cite evidence.
Determine central ideas and details.
Analyze text features and structure.
Analyze purpose in media.
Understand visual and sound elements.

Image credit: © Corbis

# Close Reader

**eBook** *Explore It!*

 ▶ **Video Links**   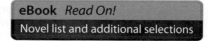 **eBook** *Read On!* Novel list and additional selections   **Visit hmhfyi.com** for current articles and informational texts.

# COLLECTION **2**
# Animal Intelligence

**KEY LEARNING OBJECTIVES**

Paraphrase ideas.
Describe character responses.
Identify and analyze imagery.
Identify and analyze personification.
Analyze point of view.
Summarize central ideas and details.

Analyze anecdotes.
Identify persuasive techniques.
Analyze text features and structure.
Determine author's purpose.
Integrate information in different media.
Trace and evaluate an argument.

Image credits: ©Doug Norman/Alamy

# Close Reader

**eBook**  *Explore It!*

 **Video Links**      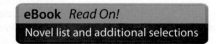 **eBook** *Read On!* Novel list and additional selections    **Visit hmhfyi.com** for current articles and informational texts.

# COLLECTION 3
# Dealing with Disaster

**KEY LEARNING OBJECTIVES**

Identify alliteration.
Identify figurative language.
Identify dialect.
Understand tone.
Compare and contrast poetic forms.
Analyze elements of narrative nonfiction.

Determine meanings of technical language.
Analyze author's style.
Analyze cause-and-effect organization.
Interpret elements of a documentary.
Integrate information in media.

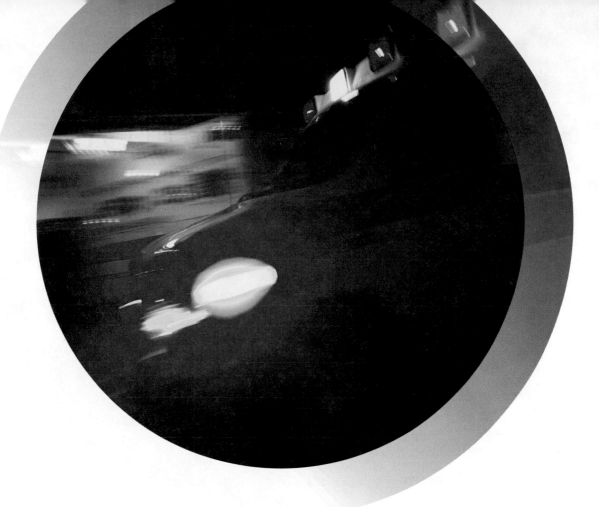

# Close Reader

**eBook** *Explore It!*

 **Video Links**     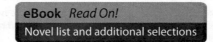 **eBook** *Read On!* Novel list and additional selections    **Visit hmhfyi.com** for current articles and informational texts.

COLLECTION **4**

# Making Your Voice Heard

## COLLECTION PERFORMANCE TASK

**KEY LEARNING OBJECTIVES**

Determine theme.
Identify internal and external conflicts.
Describe characterization.
Identify figurative language.
Analyze tone.

Analyze author's style.
Analyze persuasive techniques.
Trace and evaluate an argument.
Compare and contrast arguments.

# Close Reader

Image credits: © Fred de Noyelle/Godong/Corbis

**eBook** *Explore It!*

 **Video Links**

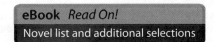 **eBook** *Read On!*
Novel list and additional selections

 **Visit hmhfyi.com**
for current articles and
informational texts.

# COLLECTION 5
# Decisions That Matter

**KEY LEARNING OBJECTIVES**

Determine theme in poetry.
Describe flashback.
Determine and analyze mood.
Analyze poetic structure.
Analyze narrative poetry.
Analyze elements of a news report.

Identify elements of a memoir.
Identify elements of a biography.
Compare and contrast genres.
Analyze primary and secondary sources.
Integrate information in different media.

# Close Reader

**BIOGRAPHY**
Community Hero: Chief Wilma Mankiller          Susannah Abbey

**AUTOBIOGRAPHY**
*from* Every Day Is a New Day          Wilma Mankiller

**POEM**
The Light—Ah! The Light (Marie Curie
discovered the principles of radioactivity.)          Joyce Sidman

**eBook** *Explore It!*

 **Video Links**     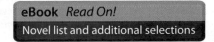 **eBook** *Read On!* Novel list and additional selections    **Visit hmhfyi.com** for current articles and informational texts.

**COMMON CORE**

COLLECTION **6**

# What Tales Tell

**KEY LEARNING OBJECTIVES**

Determine theme.
Describe foreshadowing.
Describe elements of myths.
Describe elements of folk tales.
Determine elements of parody.

Describe elements of drama.
Compare and contrast genres.
Cite textual evidence.
Analyze structure.

# Close Reader

**GREEK MYTH**
Medusa's Head                          *retold by* Olivia E. Coolidge

**POEM**
Medusa                                 Agha Shahid Ali

**NOVEL**
*from* The Prince and the Pauper:
Tom's Meeting with the Prince          Mark Twain

**DRAMA**                               Mark Twain
*from* The Prince and the Pauper        *dramatized by* Joellen Bland

**GRAPHIC STORY**
*from* The Prince and the Pauper        Marvel Comics

**eBook** *Explore It!*

 **Video Links**

**eBook** *Read On!*
Novel list and additional selections

 **Visit hmhfyi.com** for current articles and informational texts.

# Student Resources

# Connecting to Your World

Every time you read something, view something, write to someone, or react to what you've read or seen, you're participating in a world of ideas. You do this every day, inside the classroom and out. These skills will serve you not only at home and at school, but eventually (if you can-think that far ahead!), in your career.

The digital tools in this program will tap into the skills you already use and help you sharpen those skills for the future.

## Start your exploration at my.hrw.com

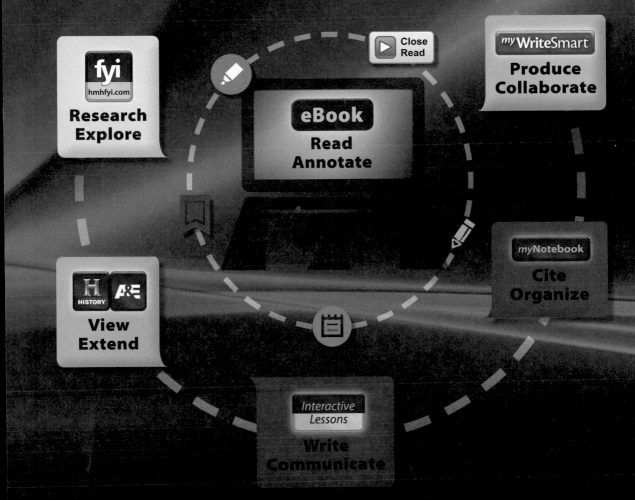

**fyi** hmhfyi.com
**Research Explore**

**eBook Read Annotate**

Close Read

*my* WriteSmart
**Produce Collaborate**

HISTORY A&E
**View Extend**

*my*Notebook
**Cite Organize**

Interactive Lessons
**Write Communicate**

# Writing and Speaking & Listening

Communication in today's world requires quite a variety of skills. To express yourself and win people over, you have to be able to write for print, for online media, and for spoken presentations. To collaborate, you have to work with people who might be sitting right next to you or at the other end of an Internet connection.

## Available Only in Your eBook

**Interactive Lessons**

**The interactive lessons in these collections will help you master the skills needed to become an expert communicator.**

### Choosing Relevant Evidence

Choose the pieces of evidence that support the reason shown and drag them into the box.

Tip

Reality stars are often placed in situations that cause them to grow or change in a positive way.

One contestant who participated in a fashion reality show remarked, "The show made me a better designer." ✓

The winner of one cooking show won a million dollars.

According to Nielsen ratings for this season, 17 of the top 50 most popular TV shows for viewers between the ages of 18-49 were reality shows.

68% of former contestants on a popular weight-loss show have maintained their goal weight for five years post-show.

You've got it! This quotation shows how one contestant experienced personal growth.

# Writing Arguments

**Learn how to build
a strong argument.**

COMMON CORE W 1, W 10

**Interactive
Lessons**

1. Introduction
2. What Is a Claim?
3. Support: Reasons and Evidence
4. Building Effective Support

5. Creating a Coherent Argument
6. Persuasive Techniques
7. Formal Style
8. Concluding Your Argument

# Writing Informative Texts

**Shed light on complex ideas
and topics.**

COMMON CORE W 2, W 10

**Interactive
Lessons**

1. Introduction
2. Developing a Topic
3. Organizing Ideas
4. Introductions and Conclusions

5. Elaboration
6. Using Graphics and Multimedia
7. Precise Language and Vocabulary
8. Formal Style

# Writing Narratives

**A good storyteller can
always capture an audience.**

COMMON CORE W 3, W 10

**Interactive
Lessons**

1. Introduction
2. Narrative Context
3. Point of View and Characters

4. Narrative Structure
5. Narrative Techniques
6. The Language of Narrative

# Writing as a Process

**Get from the first twinkle of an idea to a sparkling final draft.**

| **Interactive Lessons** | |
|---|---|
| **1.** Introduction | **4.** Revising and Editing |
| **2.** Task, Purpose, and Audience | **5.** Trying a New Approach |
| **3.** Planning and Drafting | |

# Producing and Publishing with Technology

**Learn how to write for an online audience.**

SUBMIT

| **Interactive Lessons** | |
|---|---|
| **1.** Introduction | **3.** Interacting with Your Online Audience |
| **2.** Writing for the Internet | **4.** Using Technology to Collaborate |

# Conducting Research

**There's a world of information out there. How do you find it?**

| **Interactive Lessons** | |
|---|---|
| **1.** Introduction | **5.** Conducting Field Research |
| **2.** Starting Your Research | **6.** Using the Internet for Research |
| **3.** Types of Sources | **7.** Taking Notes |
| **4.** Using the Library for Research | **8.** Refocusing Your Inquiry |

# Evaluating Sources
## Don't believe everything you read!

COMMON CORE W 8

**Interactive Lessons**

1. Introduction
2. Evaluating Sources for Usefulness
3. Evaluating Sources for Reliability

# Using Textual Evidence
## Put your research into writing.

COMMON CORE W 7, W 8, W 9

**Interactive Lessons**

1. Introduction
2. Synthesizing Information
3. Writing an Outline
4. Summarizing, Paraphrasing, and Quoting
5. Attribution

# Participating in Collaborative Discussions

COMMON CORE SL 1

### There's power in putting your heads together.

**Interactive Lessons**

1. Introduction
2. Preparing for Discussion
3. Establishing and Following Procedure
4. Speaking Constructively
5. Listening and Responding
6. Wrapping Up Your Discussion

# Analyzing and Evaluating Presentations

**Media-makers all want your attention.
What are they trying to tell you?**

COMMON CORE SL 2, SL 3, SL 6

| **Interactive Lessons** | 1. Introduction | 4. Tracing a Speaker's Argument |
| | 2. Analyzing a Presentation | 5. Rhetoric and Delivery |
| | 3. Evaluating a Speaker's Reliability | 6. Synthesizing Media Sources |

# Giving a Presentation

**Learn how to talk to a
roomful of people.**

COMMON CORE SL 4, SL 6

| **Interactive Lessons** | 1. Introduction | 3. The Content of Your Presentation |
| | 2. Knowing Your Audience | 4. Style in Presentation |
| | | 5. Delivering Your Presentation |

# Using Media in a Presentation

**If a picture is worth a thousand words,
just think what you can do with a video.**

COMMON CORE SL 5

| **Interactive Lessons** | 1. Introduction | 3. Using Presentation Software |
| | 2. Types of Media: Audio, Video, and Images | 4. Practicing Your Presentation |

# Supporting Close Reading, Research, and Writing

Understanding complex texts is hard work, even for experienced readers. It often takes multiple close readings to understand and write about an author's choices and meanings. The dynamic digital tools in this program will give you opportunities to learn and practice this critical skill of close reading—and help you integrate the text evidence you find into your writing.

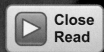

## Learn How to Do a Close Read

An effective close read is all about the details; you have to examine the language and ideas a writer includes. See how it's done by accessing the **Close Read Screencasts** in your eBook. Hear modeled conversations about anchor texts.

of the birds, how they soared and glided overhead. He pointed out the slow, graceful sweep of their wings as they beat the air steadily, without fluttering. Soon Icarus was sure that he, too, could fly and, raising his arms up and down, skirted over the white sand and even out over the waves, letting his feet touch the snowy foam as the water thundered and broke over the sharp rocks. Daedalus watched him proudly but

Soon Icarus was sure that he, too, could fly and, raising his arms up and down, skirted over the white sand and even out over the waves, letting his feet touch the snowy foam as the water thundered and broke over the sharp rocks.

There might be a sense of danger here.

Daedalus watched him proudly but with misgivings. He called Icarus to his side and, putting his arm round the boy's shoulders, said, 'Icarus, my son, we are about to make our flight. No human being has ever traveled through the air before, and I want you to listen carefully to my instructions.

# Annotate the Texts

Practice close reading by utilizing the powerful annotation tools in your eBook. Mark up key ideas and observations using highlighters and sticky notes.

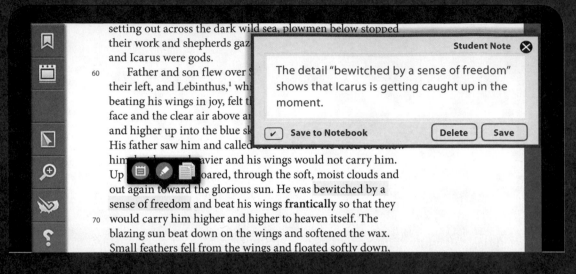

# Collect Text Evidence

Save your annotations to your notebook. Gathering and organizing this text evidence will help you complete performance tasks and other writing assignments.

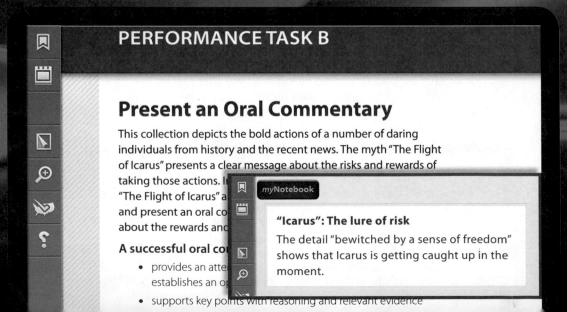

## Find More Text Evidence on the Web

Tap into the *FYI* website for links to high-interest informational texts about collection topics. Capture text evidence from any Web source by including it in your notebook.

## Integrate Text Evidence into Your Writing

Use the evidence you've gathered to formulate interpretations, draw conclusions, and offer insights. Integrate the best of your text evidence into your writing.

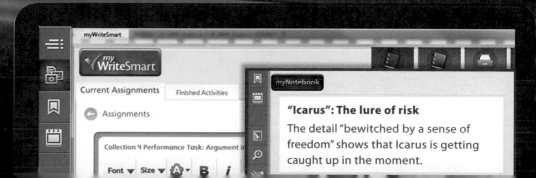

"Icarus": The lure of risk

The detail "bewitched by a sense of freedom" shows that Icarus is getting caught up in the moment.

# Complex Text:
## What It Is and What It Isn't … or Don't Let a Good Poem Get You Down

*By Carol Jago*

Do you sometimes think that what your teacher asks you to read is too hard? Let me tell you a secret. Those poems and passages can be tough for your teacher as well. Just because a text isn't easy doesn't mean there is something wrong with it or something wrong with the reader. It means you need to do more than skim across the words on the page. Reading complex text takes effort and focused attention. Do you sometimes wish writers would just say what they have to say simply? I assure you that writers don't use long sentences and unfamiliar words to annoy their readers or make readers feel dumb. They employ complex syntax and rich language in order to express complex ideas.

Excellent literature and nonfiction—the kind you will be reading over the course of the year—challenges readers in various ways. Sometimes the background of a story or the content of an essay is so unfamiliar that it is difficult to understand why characters are behaving as they do or to follow the argument a writer is making. By persevering, reading like a detective, and following clues in the text, you will find that your store of background knowledge grows. As a result, the next time you read about this subject, the text won't seem nearly as hard. The more you read, the better a reader you will become.

Good readers aren't put off by challenging text. When the going gets rough, they know what to do. Let's take vocabulary, a common measure of text complexity, as an example. Learning new words is the business of a lifetime. Rather than shutting down when you meet a word you don't know, take a moment to think about the word. Is any part of the word familiar to you? Is there something in the context of the sentence or paragraph that can help you figure out its meaning? Is there someone or something that can provide you with a definition? When reading literature or nonfiction from a time period other than our own, the text is often full of words we don't know. Each time you meet those words in succeeding readings you will be adding to your understanding of the word and its use. Your brain is a natural word-learning machine. The more you feed it complex text, the larger a vocabulary you'll have.

Have you ever been reading a long, complicated sentence and discovered that by the time you reached the end you had forgotten the beginning? Unlike the sentences we speak or dash off in a note to a friend, complex text is often full of sentences that are not only lengthy but also constructed in intricate ways. Such sentences require readers to slow down and figure out how phrases relate to one another as well as who is doing what to whom. Remember, rereading isn't cheating. It is exactly what experienced readers know to do when they meet dense text on the page. On the pages that follow you will find stories and articles that challenge you at the sentence level. Don't be intimidated. With careful attention to how those sentences are constructed, their meaning will unfold right before your eyes.

**"Your brain is a natural word-learning machine. The more you feed it complex text, the larger a vocabulary you'll have."**

Another way text can be complex involves the density of the ideas in a passage. Sometimes a writer piles on so much information that you think your head might explode if you read one more detail or one more qualification. At times like this talking with a friend can really help. Sharing questions and ideas, exploring a difficult passage together, can help you tease out the meaning of even the most difficult text. Poetry is often particularly dense and for that reason it poses particular challenges. A seemingly simple poem in terms of vocabulary and length may express extremely complex feelings and insights. Poets also love to use mythological and Biblical allusions which contemporary readers are not always familiar with. The only way to read text this complex is to read it again and again.

You are going to notice a range of complexity within each collection of readings. This spectrum reflects the range of texts that surround us: some easy, some hard, some seemingly easy but in fact hard, some seemingly hard but actually easy. Whatever their complexity, I think you will enjoy these readings tremendously. Remember, read for your life!

# Understanding the Common Core State Standards

## What are the English Language Arts Common Core State Standards?

The Common Core State Standards for English Language Arts indicate what you should know and be able to do by the end of your grade level. These understandings and skills will help you be better prepared for future classes, college courses, and a career. For this reason, the standards for each strand in English Language Arts (such as Reading Informational Text or Writing) directly relate to the College and Career Readiness Anchor Standards for each strand. The Anchor Standards broadly outline the understandings and skills you should master by the end of high school so that you are well-prepared for college or for a career.

## How do I learn the English Language Arts Common Core State Standards?

Your textbook is closely aligned to the English Language Arts Common Core State Standards. Every time you learn a concept or practice a skill, you are working on mastering one of the standards. Each collection, each selection, and each performance task in your textbook connects to one or more of the standards for English Language Arts listed on the following pages.

The English Language Arts Common Core State Standards are divided into five strands: Reading Literature, Reading Informational Text, Writing, Speaking and Listening, and Language.

©Jose Luis Pelaez Inc/Getty Images

| Strand | What It Means to You |
| --- | --- |
| **Reading Literature (RL)** | This strand concerns the literary texts you will read at this grade level: stories, drama, and poetry. The Common Core State Standards stress that you should read a range of texts of increasing complexity as you progress through high school. |
| **Reading Informational Text (RI)** | Informational text encompasses a broad range of literary nonfiction, including exposition, argument, and functional text, in such genres as personal essays, speeches, opinion pieces, memoirs, and historical and technical accounts. The Common Core State Standards stress that you will read a range of informational texts of increasing complexity as you progress from grade to grade. |
| **Writing (W)** | For the Writing strand you will focus on generating three types of texts—arguments, informative or explanatory texts, and narratives—while using the writing process and technology to develop and share your writing. The Common Core State Standards also emphasize research and specify that you should write routinely for both short and extended time frames. |
| **Speaking and Listening (SL)** | The Common Core State Standards focus on comprehending information presented in a variety of media and formats, on participating in collaborative discussions, and on presenting knowledge and ideas clearly. |
| **Language (L)** | The standards in the Language strand address the conventions of standard English grammar, usage, and mechanics; knowledge of language; and vocabulary acquisition and use. |

## Common Core Code Decoder

The codes you find on the pages of your textbook identify the specific knowledge or skill for the standard addressed in the text.

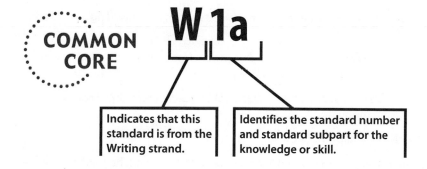

**COMMON CORE**

**W 1a**

Indicates that this standard is from the Writing strand.

Identifies the standard number and standard subpart for the knowledge or skill.

# English Language Arts
# Common Core State Standards

Listed below are the English Language Arts Common Core State Standards that you are required to master by the end of grade 6. To help you understand what is required of you, we have provided a summary of the concepts you will learn on your way to mastering each standard.

## College and Career Readiness Anchor Standards for Reading

| Common Core State Standards |
| --- |

**KEY IDEAS AND DETAILS**

1. Read closely to determine what the text says explicitly and to make logical inferences from it; cite specific textual evidence when writing or speaking to support conclusions drawn from the text.

2. Determine central ideas or themes of a text and analyze their development; summarize the key supporting details and ideas.

3. Analyze how and why individuals, events, and ideas develop and interact over the course of a text.

**CRAFT AND STRUCTURE**

4. Interpret words and phrases as they are used in a text, including determining technical, connotative, and figurative meanings, and analyze how specific word choices shape meaning or tone.

5. Analyze the structure of texts, including how specific sentences, paragraphs, and larger portions of the text (e.g., a section, chapter, scene, or stanza) relate to each other and the whole.

6. Assess how point of view or purpose shapes the content and style of a text.

**INTEGRATION OF KNOWLEDGE AND IDEAS**

7. Integrate and evaluate content presented in diverse formats and media, including visually and quantitatively, as well as in words.

8. Delineate and evaluate the argument and specific claims in a text, including the validity of the reasoning as well as the relevance and sufficiency of the evidence.

9. Analyze how two or more texts address similar themes or topics in order to build knowledge or to compare the approaches the authors take.

**RANGE OF READING AND LEVEL OF TEXT COMPLEXITY**

10. Read and comprehend complex literary and informational texts independently and proficiently.

# Reading Standards for Literature, Grade 6 Students

The College and Career Readiness Anchor Standards for Reading apply to both literature and informational text.

| Common Core State Standards | What It Means to You |
|---|---|
| **KEY IDEAS AND DETAILS** | |
| 1. Cite textual evidence to support analysis of what the text says explicitly as well as inferences drawn from the text. | You will use information from the text to support its main ideas—both those that are stated directly and those that are suggested. |
| 2. Determine a theme or central idea of a text and how it is conveyed through particular details; provide a summary of the text distinct from personal opinions or judgments. | You will analyze a text's main idea or theme by showing how it unfolds throughout the text. You will also summarize the main idea of the text as a whole without adding your own ideas or opinions. |
| 3. Describe how a particular story's or drama's plot unfolds in a series of episodes as well as how the characters respond or change as the plot moves toward a resolution. | You will describe the events that make up a story or drama's plot and how those events affect the characters. |
| **CRAFT AND STRUCTURE** | |
| 4. Determine the meaning of words and phrases as they are used in a text, including figurative and connotative meanings; analyze the impact of a specific word choice on meaning and tone. | You will analyze specific words, phrases, and patterns of sound in the text to determine what they mean and how they contribute to the text's larger meaning. |
| 5. Analyze how a particular sentence, chapter, scene, or stanza fits into the overall structure of a text and contributes to the development of the theme, setting, or plot. | You will analyze how a specific section of a text contributes to its larger meaning. |
| 6. Explain how an author develops the point of view of the narrator or speaker in a text. | You will analyze how an author shapes the narrator's point of view in a text. |

| Common Core State Standards | What It Means to You |
|---|---|
| **INTEGRATION OF KNOWLEDGE AND IDEAS** | |
| 7. Compare and contrast the experience of reading a story, drama, or poem to listening to or viewing an audio, video, or live version of the text, including contrasting what they "see" and "hear" when reading the text to what they perceive when they listen or watch. | You will compare and contrast how events and information are presented in visual and non-visual texts. |
| 8. (Not applicable to literature) | |
| 9. Compare and contrast texts in different forms or genres (e.g., stories and poems; historical novels and fantasy stories) in terms of their approaches to similar themes and topics. | You will analyze how different forms of texts treat the same themes and topics. |
| **RANGE OF READING AND LEVEL OF TEXT COMPLEXITY** | |
| 10. By the end of the year, read and comprehend literature, including stories, dramas, and poems, in the grades 6–8 text complexity band proficiently, with scaffolding as needed at the high end of the range. | You will read and understand grade-level appropriate literary texts by the end of grade 6. |

## Reading Standards for Informational Text, Grade 6 Students

| Common Core State Standards | What It Means to You |
|---|---|
| **KEY IDEAS AND DETAILS** | |
| 1. Cite textual evidence to support analysis of what the text says explicitly as well as inferences drawn from the text. | You will cite information from the text to support its main ideas—both those that are stated directly and those that are suggested. |
| 2. Determine a central idea of a text and how it is conveyed through particular details; provide a summary of the text distinct from personal opinions or judgments. | You will analyze the development of a text's main idea. You will also summarize the text without adding your own ideas or opinions. |
| 3. Analyze in detail how a key individual, event, or idea is introduced, illustrated, and elaborated in a text (e.g., through examples or anecdotes). | You will analyze how an author treats a key person, event, or idea throughout a text. |

| Common Core State Standards | What It Means to You |
|---|---|

## CRAFT AND STRUCTURE

| | |
|---|---|
| **4.** Determine the meaning of words and phrases as they are used in a text, including figurative, connotative, and technical meanings. | You will discover the meaning of specific words and phrases in the text. |
| **5.** Analyze how a particular sentence, paragraph, chapter, or section fits into the overall structure of a text and contributes to the development of the ideas. | You will examine the major sections of a text and analyze how each one adds to the whole. |
| **6.** Determine an author's point of view or purpose in a text and explain how it is conveyed in the text. | You will understand the author's point of view and explain how the author gets his or her point of view across. |

## INTEGRATION OF KNOWLEDGE AND IDEAS

| | |
|---|---|
| **7.** Integrate information presented in different media or formats (e.g., visually, quantitatively) as well as in words to develop a coherent understanding of a topic or issue. | You will use information from visual and non-visual sources to understand a topic or issue. |
| **8.** Trace and evaluate the argument and specific claims in a text, distinguishing claims that are supported by reasons and evidence from claims that are not. | You will evaluate the author's claims and reasoning and identify any weaknesses in them. |
| **9.** Compare and contrast one author's presentation of events with that of another (e.g., a memoir written by and a biography on the same person). | You will compare and contrast two different authors' treatments of the same subject. |

## RANGE OF READING AND LEVEL OF TEXT COMPLEXITY

| | |
|---|---|
| **10.** By the end of the year, read and comprehend literary nonfiction in the grades 6–8 text complexity band proficiently, with scaffolding as needed at the high end of the range. | You will demonstrate the ability to read and understand grade-level appropriate literary nonfiction texts by the end of grade 6. |

# College and Career Readiness Anchor Standards for Writing

## TEXT TYPES AND PURPOSES

1. Write arguments to support claims in an analysis of substantive topics or texts, using valid reasoning and relevant and sufficient evidence.

2. Write informative/explanatory texts to examine and convey complex ideas and information clearly and accurately through the effective selection, organization, and analysis of content.

3. Write narratives to develop real or imagined experiences or events using effective technique, well-chosen details, and well-structured event sequences.

## PRODUCTION AND DISTRIBUTION OF WRITING

4. Produce clear and coherent writing in which the development, organization, and style are appropriate to task, purpose, and audience.

5. Develop and strengthen writing as needed by planning, revising, editing, rewriting, or trying a new approach.

6. Use technology, including the Internet, to produce and publish writing and to interact and collaborate with others.

## RESEARCH TO BUILD AND PRESENT KNOWLEDGE

7. Conduct short as well as more sustained research projects based on focused questions, demonstrating understanding of the subject under investigation.

8. Gather relevant information from multiple print and digital sources, assess the credibility and accuracy of each source, and integrate the information while avoiding plagiarism.

9. Draw evidence from literary or informational texts to support analysis, reflection, and research.

## RANGE OF WRITING

10. Write routinely over extended time frames (time for research, reflection, and revision) and shorter time frames (a single sitting or a day or two) for a range of tasks, purposes, and audiences.

# Writing Standards, Grade 6 Students

| Common Core State Standards | What It Means to You |
|---|---|
| **TEXT TYPES AND PURPOSES** | |
| **1.** Write arguments to support claims with clear reasons and relevant evidence. | You will write and develop arguments with clear reasons and strong evidence that include |
|     **a.** Introduce claim(s) and organize the reasons and evidence clearly. | a clear introduction and organization of claims |
|     **b.** Support claim(s) with clear reasons and relevant evidence, using credible sources and demonstrating an understanding of the topic or text. | clear, accurate support for claims |
|     **c.** Use words, phrases, and clauses to clarify the relationships among claim(s) and reasons. | use of clear words, phrases, and clauses to link information |
|     **d.** Establish and maintain a formal style. | a formal style |
|     **e.** Provide a concluding statement or section that follows from the argument presented. | a strong concluding statement that connects to the argument |
| **2.** Write informative/explanatory texts to examine a topic and convey ideas, concepts, and information through the selection, organization, and analysis of relevant content. | You will write clear, well-organized, and thoughtful informative and explanatory texts with |
|     **a.** Introduce a topic; organize ideas, concepts, and information, using strategies such as definition, classification, comparison/contrast, and cause/effect; include formatting (e.g., headings), graphics (e.g., charts, tables), and multimedia when useful to aiding comprehension. | a clear introduction and organization, including headings and visuals (when appropriate) |
|     **b.** Develop the topic with relevant facts, definitions, concrete details, quotations, or other information and examples. | strong supporting details and background information |
|     **c.** Use appropriate transitions to clarify the relationships among ideas and concepts. | clear transitions to link ideas |
|     **d.** Use precise language and domain-specific vocabulary to inform about or explain the topic. | precise language and vocabulary |

| Common Core State Standards | What It Means to You |
|---|---|
| e. Establish and maintain a formal style. | a formal style |
| f. Provide a concluding statement or section that follows from the information or explanation presented. | a strong conclusion that connects to the topic |
| 3. Write narratives to develop real or imagined experiences or events using effective technique, relevant descriptive details, and well-structured event sequences. | You will write clear, well-structured, detailed narrative texts that |
| a. Engage and orient the reader by establishing a context and introducing a narrator and/or characters; organize an event sequence that unfolds naturally and logically. | draw your readers in with a clear topic that unfolds logically |
| b. Use narrative techniques, such as dialogue, pacing, and description, to develop experiences, events, and/or characters. | use narrative techniques to develop and expand on events and/or characters |
| c. Use a variety of transition words, phrases, and clauses to convey sequence and signal shifts from one time frame or setting to another. | use a variety of transition words to clearly signal shifts between time frames or settings |
| d. Use precise words and phrases, relevant descriptive details, and sensory language to convey experiences and events. | use precise words and sensory details that keep readers interested |
| e. Provide a conclusion that follows from the narrated experiences or events. | have a strong conclusion that connects to the topic |

## PRODUCTION AND DISTRIBUTION OF WRITING

| | |
|---|---|
| 4. Produce clear and coherent writing in which the development, organization, and style are appropriate to task, purpose, and audience. (Grade-specific expectations for writing types are defined in standards 1–3 above.) | You will produce writing that is appropriate to the task, purpose, and audience for whom you are writing. |
| 5. With some guidance and support from peers and adults, develop and strengthen writing as needed by planning, revising, editing, rewriting, or trying a new approach. | With help from peers and adults, you will revise and refine your writing to address what is most important for your purpose and audience. |

| Common Core State Standards | What It Means to You |
|---|---|
| 6. Use technology, including the Internet, to produce and publish writing as well as to interact and collaborate with others; demonstrate sufficient command of keyboarding skills to type a minimum of three pages in a single setting. | You will use technology to share your writing and to provide more information on your topic. You will also develop keyboarding skills to type at least three pages in a single setting. |

## RESEARCH TO BUILD AND PRESENT KNOWLEDGE

| Common Core State Standards | What It Means to You |
|---|---|
| 7. Conduct short research projects to answer a question, drawing on several sources and refocusing the inquiry when appropriate. | You will conduct short research projects to answer a question using multiple sources and altering your topic when needed. |
| 8. Gather relevant information from multiple print and digital sources; assess the credibility of each source; and quote or paraphrase the data and conclusions of others while avoiding plagiarism and providing basic bibliographic information for sources. | You will gather, quote, or restate information from different sources, and assess the strength of each source. You will also provide information for a bibliography. |
| 9. Draw evidence from literary or informational texts to support analysis, reflection, and research.<br>  a. Apply *grade 6 Reading standards* to literature (e.g., "Compare and contrast texts in different forms or genres [e.g., stories and poems; historical novels and fantasy stories] in terms of their approaches to similar themes and topics").<br>  b. Apply *grade 6 Reading standards* to literary nonfiction (e.g., "Trace and evaluate the argument and specific claims in a text, distinguishing claims that are supported by reasons and evidence from claims that are not"). | You will paraphrase, summarize, quote, and cite primary and secondary sources to support your analysis, reflection, and research. |

## RANGE OF WRITING

| Common Core State Standards | What It Means to You |
|---|---|
| 10. Write routinely over extended time frames (time for research, reflection, and revision) and shorter time frames (a single sitting or a day or two) for a range of discipline-specific tasks, purposes, and audiences. | You will write for many different purposes and audiences both over short and longer periods of time. |

# College and Career Readiness Anchor Standards for Speaking and Listening

| Common Core State Standards |
|---|
| **COMPREHENSION AND COLLABORATION** |
| 1. Prepare for and participate effectively in a range of conversations and collaborations with diverse partners, building on others' ideas and expressing their own clearly and persuasively. |
| 2. Integrate and evaluate information presented in diverse media and formats, including visually, quantitatively, and orally. |
| 3. Evaluate a speaker's point of view, reasoning, and use of evidence and rhetoric. |
| **PRESENTATION OF KNOWLEDGE AND IDEAS** |
| 4. Present information, findings, and supporting evidence such that listeners can follow the line of reasoning and the organization, development, and style are appropriate to task, purpose, and audience. |
| 5. Make strategic use of digital media and visual displays of data to express information and enhance understanding of presentations. |
| 6. Adapt speech to a variety of contexts and communicative tasks, demonstrating command of formal English when indicated or appropriate. |

# Speaking and Listening Standards, Grade 6 Students

| Common Core State Standards | What It Means to You |
|---|---|
| **COMPREHENSION AND COLLABORATION** | |
| 1. Engage effectively in a range of collaborative discussions (one-on-one, in groups, and teacher-led) with diverse partners on grade 6 topics, texts, and issues, building on others' ideas and expressing their own clearly. | You will actively participate in a variety of discussions in which you |
|    a. Come to discussions prepared, having read or studied required material; explicitly draw on that preparation by referring to evidence on the topic, text, or issue to probe and reflect on ideas under discussion. | have read any required material beforehand and have come to the discussion prepared |
|    b. Follow rules for collegial discussions, set specific goals and deadlines, and define individual roles as needed. | work with others to set goals and processes within the group |
|    c. Pose and respond to specific questions with elaboration and detail by making comments that contribute to the topic, text, or issue under discussion. | ask and respond to questions that relate to the topic |

| Common Core State Standards | What It Means to You |
|---|---|
| **d.** Review the key ideas expressed and demonstrate understanding of multiple perspectives through reflection and paraphrasing. | review and restate different points of view |
| **2.** Interpret information presented in diverse media and formats (e.g., visually, quantitatively, orally) and explain how it contributes to a topic, text, or issue under study. | You will analyze main ideas and details of various media and relate them to a topic under study. |
| **3.** Delineate a speaker's argument and specific claims, distinguishing claims that are supported by reasons and evidence from claims that are not. | You will evaluate a speaker's argument and identify any false reasoning or evidence. |

**PRESENTATION OF KNOWLEDGE AND IDEAS**

| Common Core State Standards | What It Means to You |
|---|---|
| **4.** Present claims and findings, sequencing ideas logically and using pertinent descriptions, facts, and details to accentuate main ideas or themes; use appropriate eye contact, adequate volume, and clear pronunciation. | You will organize and present information to your listeners in a logical sequence and style that is appropriate to your task and audience. |
| **5.** Include multimedia components (e.g., graphics, images, music, sound) and visual displays in presentations to clarify information. | You will use audio and/or visual materials to clarify and add to presentations. |
| **6.** Adapt speech to a variety of contexts and tasks, demonstrating command of formal English when indicated or appropriate. | You will adapt the formality of your speech appropriately. |

# College and Career Readiness Anchor Standards for Language

| Common Core State Standards |
| --- |

**CONVENTIONS OF STANDARD ENGLISH**

1. Demonstrate command of the conventions of standard English grammar and usage when writing or speaking.

2. Demonstrate command of the conventions of standard English capitalization, punctuation, and spelling when writing.

**KNOWLEDGE OF LANGUAGE**

3. Apply knowledge of language to understand how language functions in different contexts, to make effective choices for meaning or style, and to comprehend more fully when reading or listening.

**VOCABULARY ACQUISITION AND USE**

4. Determine or clarify the meaning of unknown and multiple-meaning words and phrases by using context clues, analyzing meaningful word parts, and consulting general and specialized reference materials, as appropriate.

5. Demonstrate understanding of word relationships and nuances in word meanings.

6. Acquire and use accurately a range of general academic and domain-specific words and phrases sufficient for reading, writing, speaking, and listening at the college and career readiness level; demonstrate independence in gathering vocabulary knowledge when considering a word or phrase important to comprehension or expression.

# Language Standards, Grade 6 Students

| Common Core State Standards | What It Means to You |
| --- | --- |
| **CONVENTIONS OF STANDARD ENGLISH** | |
| 1. Demonstrate command of the conventions of standard English grammar and usage when writing or speaking. | You will correctly understand and use the conventions of English grammar and usage, including |
| a. Ensure that pronouns are in the proper case (subjective, objective, possessive). | making sure pronouns are in the proper case |
| b. Use intensive pronouns (e.g., *myself, ourselves*). | using intensive pronouns |
| c. Recognize and correct inappropriate shifts in pronoun number and person. | correcting shifts in pronoun number and person |

| Common Core State Standards | What It Means to You |
|---|---|
| **d.** Recognize and correct vague pronouns (i.e., ones with unclear or ambiguous antecedents). | correcting unclear connections between pronouns and antecedents |
| **e.** Recognize variations from standard English in their own and others' writing and speaking, and identify and use strategies to improve expression in conventional language. | identifying your own and others' errors in speaking and writing and using strategies to improve expression |
| **2.** Demonstrate command of the conventions of standard English capitalization, punctuation, and spelling when writing. | You will correctly use the conventions of English capitalization, punctuation, and spelling, including |
| **a.** Use punctuation (commas, parentheses, dashes) to set off nonrestrictive/parenthetical elements. | punctuation to set off information that is not essential to the meaning of the sentence |
| **b.** Spell correctly. | spelling |

## KNOWLEDGE OF LANGUAGE

| | |
|---|---|
| **3.** Use knowledge of language and its conventions when writing, speaking, reading, or listening. | You will apply your knowledge of language in different contexts by |
| **a.** Vary sentence patterns for meaning, reader/listener interest, and style. | using various sentence patterns |
| **b.** Maintain consistency in style and tone. | keeping a consistent style and tone |

## VOCABULARY ACQUISITION AND USE

| | |
|---|---|
| **4.** Determine or clarify the meaning of unknown and multiple-meaning words and phrases based on grade 6 reading and content, choosing flexibly from a range of strategies. | You will understand the meaning of grade-level appropriate words and phrases by |
| **a.** Use context (e.g., the overall meaning of a sentence or paragraph; a word's position or function in a sentence) as a clue to the meaning of a word or phrase. | using context clues |
| **b.** Use common, grade-appropriate Greek or Latin affixes and roots as clues to the meaning of a word (e.g., *audience, auditory, audible*). | using Greek or Latin roots |

| Common Core State Standards | What It Means to You |
|---|---|
| **c.** Consult reference materials (e.g., dictionaries, glossaries, thesauruses), both print and digital, to find the pronunciation of a word or determine or clarify its precise meaning or its part of speech. | using reference materials |
| **d.** Verify the preliminary determination of the meaning of a word or phrase (e.g., by checking the inferred meaning in context or in a dictionary). | inferring and verifying the meanings of words in context |
| **5.** Demonstrate understanding of figurative language, word relationships, and nuances in word meanings. | You will understand figurative language, word relationships, and slight differences in word meanings by |
| **a.** Interpret figures of speech (e.g., personification) in context. | interpreting figures of speech in context |
| **b.** Use the relationship between particular words (e.g., cause/effect, part/whole, item/category) to better understand each of the words. | analyzing relationships between words |
| **c.** Distinguish among the connotations (associations) of words with similar denotations (definitions) (e.g., *stingy, scrimping, economical, unwasteful, thrifty*). | distinguishing among words with similar definitions |
| **6.** Acquire and use accurately grade-appropriate general academic and domain-specific words and phrases; gather vocabulary knowledge when considering a word or phrase important to comprehension or expression. | You will learn and use grade-appropriate vocabulary. |

# Facing Fear

"Do one thing every day that scares you."
—Eleanor Roosevelt

# Facing Fear

In this collection, you will explore how people experience fear and how fear affects the brain and the body.

# PERFORMANCE TASK Preview

After reading this collection, you will have the opportunity to complete two performance tasks:

• In one, you will write a short story in which a character faces a fear.

• In the second, you will write an expository essay about a fear using information found in selections from the collection and your own research.

# ACADEMIC VOCABULARY

Study the words and their definitions in the chart below. You will use these words as you discuss and write about the texts in this collection.

| Word | Definition | Related Forms |
|------|-----------|---------------|
| **evident** (ĕv´ĭ-dənt) *adj.* | easily seen or understood; obvious | evidence, evidently |
| **factor** (făk´tər) *n.* | someone or something that has an affect on an event, a process, or a situation | factorable |
| **indicate** (ĭn´dĭ-kāt´) *tr.v.* | to point out; also, to serve as a sign or symbol of something | indication, indicator, indicative |
| **similar** (sĭm´ə-lər) *adj.* | alike in appearance or nature, though not identical; having features that are the same | similarly, similarity |
| **specific** (spĭ-sĭf´ĭk) *adj.* | concerned with a particular thing; also, precise or exact | specifically, specifics, specification |

**Graham Salisbury** (b. 1944) *was born in Pennsylvania but grew up in Hawaii. Growing up with a distant mother and without a father, who was killed in World War II, Salisbury lacked guidance. His characters explore choices similar to those he faced—making and keeping friends and learning honesty and courage. Their struggles, like Salisbury's, also take place in a Hawaiian setting. Among his many writing awards are the Boston Globe/Horn Book award and a School Library Journal Best Book of the Year award.*

# The Ravine

Short Story by Graham Salisbury

**SETTING A PURPOSE** As you read, pay attention to how a tragic event affects Vinny. Write down any questions you have while reading.

When Vinny and three others dropped down into the ravine,[1] they entered a jungle thick with tangled trees and rumors of what might have happened to the dead boy's body.

The muddy trail was slick and, in places where it had fallen away, flat-out dangerous. The cool breeze that swept the Hawaiian hillside pastures above died early in the descent.

There were four of them—Vinny; his best friend, Joe-Boy; Mo, who was afraid of nothing; and Joe-Boy's *haole*[2]
10   girlfriend, Starlene—all fifteen. It was a Tuesday in July, two weeks and a day after the boy had drowned. If, in fact, that's what had happened to him.

---

[1] **ravine** (rə-vēn´): a deep, narrow valley made by running water.
[2] **haole** (hou´lē): in Hawaii, a white person or non-native Hawaiian.

Vinny slipped, and dropped his towel in the mud. He picked it up and tried to brush it off, but instead smeared the mud spot around until the towel resembled something someone's dog had slept on. "Tst," he said.

Joe-Boy, hiking down just behind him, laughed. "Hey, Vinny, just think, that kid walked where you walking."

"Shuddup," Vinny said.

"You prob'ly stepping right where his foot was."

Vinny moved to the edge of the trail, where the ravine fell through a twisted jungle of **gnarly** trees and underbrush to the stream far below. He could see Starlene and Mo farther ahead, their heads bobbing as they walked, both almost down to the pond where the boy had died.

"Hey," Joe-Boy went on, "maybe you going be the one to find his body."

"You don't cut it out, Joe-Boy, I going . . . I going . . . "

"What, cry?"

Vinny scowled. Sometimes Joe-Boy was a big fat babooze.

They slid down the trail. Mud oozed between Vinny's toes. He grabbed at roots and branches to keep from falling. Mo and Starlene were out of sight now, the trail ahead having cut back.

Joe-Boy said, "You going jump in the water and go down and your hand going touch his face, stuck under the rocks. *Ha ha ha . . . a ha ha ha!*"

Vinny winced. He didn't want to be here. It was too soon, way too soon. Two weeks and one day.

He saw a footprint in the mud and stepped around it.

The dead boy had jumped and had never come back up. Four search and rescue divers hunted for two days straight and never found him. Not a trace. Gave Vinny the creeps. It didn't make sense. The pond wasn't that big.

He wondered why it didn't seem to bother anyone else. Maybe it did and they just didn't want to say.

Butchie was the kid's name. Only fourteen.

Fourteen.

Two weeks and one day ago he was walking down this trail. Now nobody could find him.

The jungle crushed in, reaching over the trail, and Vinny brushed leafy branches aside. The roar of the waterfall got louder, louder.

**gnarly**
(när´lē) *adj.* Something that is *gnarly* has many knots and bumpy areas on its surface.

Starlene said it was the goddess that took him, the one that lives in the stone down by the road. She did that every now and then, Starlene said, took somebody when she got lonely. Took him and kept him. Vinny had heard that legend before, but he'd never believed in it.

Now he didn't know what he believed.

The body had to be stuck down there. But still, four divers and they couldn't find it?

Vinny decided he'd better believe in the legend. If he didn't, the goddess might get mad and send him bad luck. Or maybe take *him*, too.

*Stopstopstop! Don't think like that.*

"Come on," Joe-Boy said, nudging Vinny from behind. "Hurry it up."

Just then Starlene whooped, her voice bouncing around the walls of the ravine.

"Let's *go*," Joe-Boy said. "They there already."

Moments later, Vinny jumped up onto a large boulder at the edge of the pond. Starlene was swimming out in the brown water. It wasn't murky brown, but clean and clear to a depth of maybe three or four feet. Because of the waterfall you had to yell if you wanted to say something. The whole place smelled of mud and ginger and iron.

Starlene swam across to the waterfall on the far side of the pond and ducked under it, then climbed out and edged along the rock wall behind it, moving slowly, like a spider. Above, sun-sparkling stream water spilled over the lip of a one-hundred-foot drop.

Mo and Joe-Boy threw their towels onto the rocks and dove into the pond. Vinny watched, his muddy towel hooked around his neck. Reluctantly, he let it fall, then dove in after them.

The cold mountain water tasted tangy. Was it because the boy's body was down there decomposing?[3] He spit it out.

He followed Joe-Boy and Mo to the waterfall and ducked under it. They climbed up onto the rock ledge, just as Starlene had done, then spidered their way over to where you could climb to a small ledge about fifteen feet up. They took their time because the hand and footholds were slimy with moss.

---

[3] **decomposing** (dē´kəm-pōz´ĭng): starting to decay and fall apart.

Starlene jumped first. Her shriek echoed off the rocky cliff, then died in the dense green jungle.

Mo jumped, then Joe-Boy, then Vinny.

The fifteen-foot ledge was not the problem.

It was the one above it, the one you had to work up to, the big one, where you had to take a deadly zigzag trail that climbed up and away from the waterfall, then cut back and forth to a food-wide ledge something more like fifty feet up.

That was the problem.

That was where the boy had jumped from.

Joe-Boy and Starlene swam out to the middle of the pond. Mo swam back under the waterfall and climbed once again to the fifteen-foot ledge.

Vinny started to swim out toward Joe-Boy but stopped when he saw Starlene put her arms around him. She kissed him. They sank under for a long time, then came back up, still kissing.

Vinny turned away and swam back over to the other side of the pond, where he'd first gotten in. His mother would kill him if she ever heard about where he'd come. After the boy drowned, or was taken by the goddess, or whatever happened to him, she said never to come to this pond again. Ever. It was off-limits. Permanently.

But not his dad. He said, "You fall off a horse, you get back on, right? Or else you going be scared of it all your life."

His mother scoffed and waved him off. "Don't listen to him, Vinny, listen to me. Don't go there. That pond is
120 haunted." Which had made his dad laugh.

But Vinny promised he'd stay away.

But then Starlene and Joe-Boy said, "Come with us anyway. You let your mommy run your life, or what?" And Vinny said, "But what if I get caught?" And Joe-Boy said, "So?"

Vinny mashed his lips. He was so weak. Couldn't even say no. But if he'd said, "I can't go, my mother won't like it," they would have laughed him right off the island. No, he had to go. No choice.

So he'd come along, and so far it was fine. He'd even gone
130 in the water. Everyone was happy. All he had to do now was wait it out and go home and hope his mother never heard about it.

When he looked up, Starlene was gone.

He glanced around the pond until he spotted her starting up the zigzag trail to the fifty-foot ledge. She was moving slowly, hanging on to roots and branches on the upside of the cliff. He couldn't believe she was going there. He wanted to yell, *Hey, Starlene, that's where he* died!

But she already knew that.

140 Mo jumped from the lower ledge, yelling, "Banzaiiii!" An explosion of coffee-colored water erupted when he hit.

Joe-Boy swam over to where Starlene had gotten out. He waved to Vinny, grinning like a fool, then followed Starlene up the zigzag trail.

Now Starlene was twenty-five, thirty feet up. Vinny watched her for a while, then lost sight of her when she slipped behind a wall of jungle that blocked his view. A few minutes later she popped back out, now almost at the top, where the trail ended, where there was nothing but mud and a few plants
150 to grab on to if you slipped, plants that would rip right out of the ground, plants that wouldn't stop you if you fell, nothing but your screams between you and the rocks below.

Vinny's stomach tingled just watching her. He couldn't imagine what it must feel like to be up there, especially if you were afraid of heights, like he was. *She has no fear*, Vinny thought, *no fear at all. Pleasepleaseplease, Starlene. I don't want to see you die.*

Starlene crept forward, making her way to the end of the trail, where the small ledge was.

160      Joe-Boy popped out of the jungle behind her. He stopped, waiting for her to jump before going on.

     Vinny held his breath.

     Starlene, in her cutoff jeans and soaked T-shirt, stood perfectly still, her arms at her sides. Vinny suddenly felt like hugging her. Why, he couldn't tell. *Starlene, please.*

     She reached behind her and took a wide leaf from a plant, then eased down and scooped up a finger of mud. She made a brown cross on her forehead, then wiped her muddy fingers on her jeans.

170      She waited.

     Was she thinking about the dead boy?

     She stuck the stem end of the leaf in her mouth, leaving the rest of it to hang out. When she jumped, the leaf would flap up and cover her nose and keep water from rushing into it. An old island trick.

     She jumped.

     Down, down.

     Almost in slow motion, it seemed at first, then faster and faster. She fell feetfirst, arms flapping to keep balance so she
180 wouldn't land on her back, or stomach, which would probably almost kill her.

     Just before she hit, she crossed her arms over her chest and vanished within a small explosion of rusty water.

     Vinny stood, not breathing at all, praying.

     Ten seconds. Twenty, thirty . . .

     She came back up, laughing.

     *She shouldn't make fun that way,* Vinny thought. It was dangerous, disrespectful. It was asking for it.

     Vinny looked up when he heard Joe-Boy shout, "Hey,
190 Vinny, watch how a man does it! Look!"

     Joe-Boy scooped up some mud and drew a stroke of lightning across his chest. When he jumped, he threw himself out, face and body parallel to the pond, his arms and legs spread out. *He's crazy,* Vinny thought, *absolutely insane.* At the last second Joe-Boy folded into a ball and hit. *Ca-roomp!* He came up whooping and yelling, "*Wooo!* So *good!* Come on, Vinny, it's hot!"

     Vinny faked a laugh. He waved, shouting, "Naah, the water's too cold!"

200 　Now Mo was heading up the zigzag trail—Mo, who hardly ever said a word and would do anything anyone ever challenged him to do. *Come on, Mo, not you, too.*

Vinny knew then that he would have to jump.

Jump, or never live it down.

Mo jumped in the same way Joe-Boy had, man-style, splayed out in a suicide fall. He came up grinning.

Starlene and Joe-Boy turned toward Vinny.

Vinny got up and hiked around the edge of the pond, walking in the muddy shallows, looking at a school of small
210 brown-backed fish near a ginger patch.

Maybe they'd forget about him.

Starlene torpedoed over, swimming underwater. Her body glittered in the small amount of sunlight that penetrated the trees around the rim of the ravine. When she came up, she broke the surface smoothly, gracefully, like a swan. Her blond hair sleeked back like river grass.

She smiled a sweet smile. "Joe-Boy says you're afraid to jump. I didn't believe him. He's wrong, right?"

Vinny said quickly, "Of course he's wrong. I just don't
220 want to, that's all. The water's cold."

"Naah, it's nice."

Vinny looked away. On the other side of the pond Joe-Boy and Mo were on the cliff behind the waterfall.

"Joe-Boy says your mom told you not to come here. Is that true?"

Vinny nodded. "Yeah. Stupid, but she thinks it's haunted."

"She's right."

"What?"

"That boy didn't die, Vinny. The stone goddess took him.
230 He's in a good place right now. He's her prince."

Vinny scowled. He couldn't tell if Starlene was teasing him or if she really believed that. He said, "Yeah, prob'ly."

"Are you going to jump, or is Joe-Boy right?"

"Joe-Boy's an idiot. Sure I'm going to jump."

Starlene grinned, staring at Vinny a little too long. "He is an idiot, isn't he? But I love him."

"Yeah, well . . ."

"Go to it, big boy. I'll be watching."

Starlene sank down and swam out into the pond.
240 　*Ca-ripes.*

Vinny ripped a hank[4] of white ginger from the ginger patch and smelled it, and prayed he'd still be alive after the sun went down.

He took his time climbing the zigzag trail. When he got to the part where the jungle hid him from view, he stopped and smelled the ginger again. So sweet and alive it made Vinny wish for all he was worth that he was climbing out of the ravine right now, heading home.

But of course, there was no way he could do that.

250    Not before jumping.

He tossed the ginger onto the muddy trail and continued on. He slipped once or twice, maybe three times. He didn't keep track. He was too numb now, too caught up in the insane thing he was about to do. He'd never been this far up the trail before. Once he'd tried to go all the way, but couldn't. It made him dizzy.

When he stepped out and the jungle opened into a huge bowl where he could look down, way, way down, he could see there three heads in the water, heads with arms moving slowly

260    to keep them afloat, and a few bright rays of sunlight pouring down onto them, and when he saw this, his stomach fluttered and rose. Something sour came up and he spit it out.

It made him wobble to look down. He closed his eyes. His whole body trembled. The trail was no wider than the length of his foot. And it was wet and muddy from little **rivulets** of water that bled from the side of the cliff.

The next few steps were the hardest he'd ever taken in his life. He tried not to look down, but he couldn't help it. His gaze was drawn there. He struggled to push back an

270    urge to fly, just jump off and fly. He could almost see himself spiraling down like a glider, or a bird, or a leaf.

His hands shook as if he were freezing. He wondered, *Had the dead boy felt this way?* Or had he felt brave, like Starlene or Joe-Boy, or Mo, who seemed to feel nothing.

Somebody from below shouted, but Vinny couldn't make it out over the waterfall, roaring down just feet beyond the ledge where he would soon be standing, **cascading** past so close its mist dampened the air he breathed.

*The dead boy had just come to the ravine to have fun,*

280    Vinny thought. Just a regular kid like himself, come to swim

**rivulet**
(rĭv′yə-lĭt) *n.* A *rivulet* is a small brook or stream.

**cascade**
(kăs-kād′) *v.* Something that can *cascade* will fall, pour, or rush in stages, like a waterfall over steep rocks.

---

[4] **hank** (hăngk): a coiled or looped bundle of something, such as rope or yarn.

> **" The next few steps were the hardest he'd ever taken in his life. "**

and be with his friends, then go home and eat macaroni and cheese and watch TV, maybe play with his dog or wander around after dark.

But he'd done none of that.

Where was he?

Inch by inch Vinny made it to the ledge. He stood, swaying slightly, the tips of his toes one small movement from the **precipice**.

Far below, Joe-Boy waved his arm back and forth. It was dreamy to see—back and forth, back and forth. He looked so small down there.

For a moment Vinny's mind went blank, as if he were in some trance, some dream where he could so easily lean out and fall, and think or feel nothing.

A breeze picked up and moved the trees on the ridge-line, but not a breath of it reached the fifty-foot ledge.

Vinny thought he heard a voice, small and distant. Yes. Something inside him, a tiny voice pleading, *Don't do it. Walk away. Just turn and go and walk back down.*

"... I can't," Vinny whispered.

*You can, you can, you can. Walk back down.*

Vinny waited.

And waited.

Joe-Boy yelled, then Starlene, both of them waving.

Then something very strange happened.

Vinny felt at peace. Completely and totally calm and at peace. He had not made up his mind about jumping. But something else inside him had.

Thoughts and feelings swarmed, stinging him: *Jump! Jump! Jump! Jump!*

But deep inside, where the peace was, where his mind wasn't, he would not jump. He would walk back down.

**precipice**
(prĕs´ə-pĭs) *n.*
A *precipice* is an overhanging or extremely steep area of rock.

*No! No, no, no!*

Vinny eased down and fingered up some mud and made a cross on his chest, big and bold. He grabbed a leaf, stuck it in his mouth. *Be calm, be calm. Don't look down.*

After a long pause he spit the leaf out and rubbed the cross to a blur.

They walked out of the ravine in silence, Starlene, Joe-Boy, and Mo far ahead of him. They hadn't said a word since he'd come down off the trail. He knew what they were thinking. He knew, he knew, he knew.

At the same time the peace was still there. He had no idea what it was. But he prayed it wouldn't leave him now, prayed it wouldn't go away, would never go away, because in there, in that place where the peace was, it didn't matter what they thought.

Vinny emerged from the ravine into a brilliance that surprised him. Joe-Boy, Starlene, and Mo were now almost down to the road.

Vinny breathed deeply, and looked up and out over the island. He saw, from there, a land that rolled away like honey, easing down a descent of rich Kikuyu grass pasture-land, flowing from there over vast highlands of brown and green, then, finally, falling massively to the coast and flat blue sea.

He'd never seen anything like it.

Had it always been here? This view of the island?

He stared and stared, then sat, taking it in.

He'd never seen anything so beautiful in all his life.

**COLLABORATIVE DISCUSSION**  With a small group, discuss how Vinny's feelings and behavior are influenced by the boy's tragic death. Refer to events in the story to support your ideas.

# Describe Stories: Character and Setting

Like real people, characters have personalities, drive, and life-changing events. To describe characters in terms of how they appear in stories, you can use these terms:

- **Character traits** are the qualities shown by a character, such as physical traits (tall, brown eyes) or expressions of personality (kind, anxious).
- **Character motivation** is the reason or reasons a character acts, feels, or thinks in a certain way.
- **Character development** is how a character changes throughout a story.

Think about your impressions of the characters in "The Ravine." What traits and motivations does Vinny exhibit throughout the story?

In a story like "The Ravine," the setting is a key factor in the events of the story and how the characters react to it and each other. The **setting** is the time and place in which the action occurs. The time can be a particular time of day, season, year, or historical period. The place can be an outside location, a room, a building, or a country.

Setting can affect characters by influencing their values, beliefs, and emotions or by affecting the way they live and interact with other characters. What impact does the setting have on Vinny?

# Make Inferences

 COMMON CORE RL 1

Readers often make inferences to figure out something an author has not explained. An **inference** is a logical guess that is based on facts and one's own knowledge and experience. To support your inference, you may need to **cite evidence,** or provide examples and quotations from the story. For example, you can make an inference about Vinny and Joe-Boy's friendship.

| Evidence from the Story | My Own Knowledge | Inference |
|---|---|---|
| • Joe-Boy is Vinny's "best friend." <br> • Joe-Boy teases Vinny about finding the body. | Sometimes friends tease each other in a friendly way, but this teasing does not seem kind. | They may be friends, but Joe-Boy is not especially nice to Vinny. |

# Analyzing the Text

**Cite Text Evidence**   Support your responses with evidence from the text.

1. **Summarize**  Review lines 38–65. In your own words, describe what Vinny knows about the dead boy. Explain his thoughts and feelings about this past event.

2. **Draw Conclusions**  Review lines 71–100. What are some examples of language the author uses to describe the setting? Why is the setting important to the story?

3. **Cite Evidence**  Reread lines 110–132 and think about what the author wants us to understand about Vinny. What words would you use to describe Vinny's character traits?

4. **Make Inferences**  Before jumping, the characters perform certain rituals. Reread lines 163–206 to review how they prepare to jump. What inferences can you make about the characters' feelings and their reasons for these rituals?

5. **Analyze**  Consider Vinny's feelings and actions throughout the story. How is Vinny different by the end of the story? How is he the same?

6. **Critique**  Review the story's ending in lines 319–339 and examine the descriptions the author provides. Do you think the ending makes the story more powerful? Why or why not?

## PERFORMANCE TASK

**Writing Activity: Essay**  Write a two- or three-paragraph essay to compare and contrast the character traits of Vinny and Joe-Boy.

- Introduce your topic by briefly describing the characters and their relationship to each other.

- Next, tell about how their character traits are different. Use examples from the text to support your ideas.
- Then indicate the character traits that the boys share or that are similar. Include evidence from the text.

# Critical Vocabulary

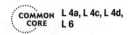

COMMON CORE   L 4a, L 4c, L 4d, L 6

gnarly          rivulet          cascade          precipice

**Practice and Apply**  With a partner, discuss the following questions. Then work together to write a sentence for each vocabulary word.

1. Which vocabulary word goes with *twisted*? Why?

2. Which vocabulary word goes with *edge*? Why?

3. Which vocabulary word goes with *trickle*? Why?

4. Which vocabulary word goes with *pouring*? Why?

## Vocabulary Strategy: Using Context Clues

When you encounter an unfamiliar word in your reading, one way to figure out the meaning is to use context clues. **Context clues** are hints about the meaning of an unknown word that may be found in the words, phrases, sentences, and paragraphs that surround that unknown word. Look at this example:

> **And it was wet and muddy from little rivulets of water that bled from the side of the cliff.**

To figure out the meaning of *rivulets*, look for clues in the surrounding words and ideas in the sentence. The sentence says that the rivulets of water "bled" from the cliff. This helps you imagine water flowing from the cliff in the same way that blood flows from a cut or scrape on your arm; the blood looks like a running stream. Combining this image with the word "little," you can imagine that rivulets might be little streams. Then use a dictionary to confirm your guess: A *rivulet* is "a small brook or stream."

**Practice and Apply**  Reread "The Ravine" and find the following words. Look at the surrounding words and sentences for clues to each word's meaning. Fill out a chart like the one shown.

| Word | Context Clues | My Guessed Definition | Dictionary Definition |
|---|---|---|---|
| **winced** (lines 35–39) | | | |
| **scoffed** (lines 116–120) | | | |
| **parallel** (lines 192–194) | | | |

# Language Conventions: Recognize Variations from Standard English

Writers often use words in dialogue that vary from Standard English to bring their characters to life. Writers may also use dialect to convey information about a community in which a character lives. **Dialect** is a form of language that is spoken in a particular region by the people who live there. In "The Ravine," the author uses the following sentences to give his characters an informal and conversational voice.

> **"Shuddup," Vinny said.**
> **"You prob'ly stepping right where his foot was."**
> **"Hey," Joe-Boy went on, "maybe you going be the one to find his body."**
> ***Stopstopstop! Don't think like that.***

Notice the informal spelling of *Shut up* and *probably* in the first two sentences. These variations indicate informal speech patterns that many people use every day. The phrase "maybe you going be the one" is an example of incorrect grammar that can be a part of dialect. In the last sentence, the words *Stopstopstop* are run together to indicate the urgency of Vinny's thoughts. A character's way of speaking can help you better understand that character.

**Practice and Apply**  Read the sentences and identify the variations from standard English. Then rewrite each sentence to show that you understand what is being said.

1.  "S'up, Denise? How's it goin'?" asked Claire.

2.  Jake did not want to answer. He shrugged his shoulders. "I dunno," he mumbled.

3.  I refuse. I quit. I will neverever go back to that sad old place again.

4.  "Gimme a break!" scoffed Tina. "I saw ya there with Jill, ya liar!"

5.  I was just hangin' out with some friends at the mall. We weren't lookin' for no trouble. Know what I'm sayin'?

**Margaret Peterson Haddix** (b. 1964) *dreamed about writing novels as a child. Her interest in writing was sparked by her father's imaginative tales; however, she did not think she could support herself writing stories. She worked as a newspaper reporter after college but never gave up her dream. Eventually, Haddix quit her job and began working on her first novel. Haddix has now written more than a dozen young adult novels.*

# Fine?

Short Story by Margaret Peterson Haddix

**SETTING A PURPOSE** As you read, pay attention to the clues that help you understand how Bailey feels and thinks about her life.

"Contrary to popular opinion," the MRI **technician** says, "this is not a torture device, it was not invented by aliens, and it does not enable us to read your thoughts."

Bailey looks doubtfully at the huge machine in front of her. She has already forgotten what MRI stands for. Does that mean there's really something wrong with her?

"Just joking," the man says. "But you wouldn't believe the questions I get. This won't be a problem for you at all unless . . . you're not claustrophobic, are you?"

10 "No," Bailey says. But she has to think about the question. Wearing a hospital gown, sitting in a wheelchair, she has a hard time remembering what and who she is. Bailey Smith, sophomore at Riverside High School, all-around ordinary kid.

*But I won't be ordinary if that machine finds something awful in my brain . . . .*

**technician**
(tĕk-nĭsh´ən) *n.* A *technician* is a person who does skilled practical work using specific equipment.

"Good," the technician is saying. "Because I have to admit, some people do go a little nutso in there." He's a short man with glasses; he seems amused that some people might not enjoy his precious machine.

20 "Bailey will be fine," Bailey's mother says firmly from behind the wheelchair.

"Mom," Bailey protests, shorthand for "Mom, you're embarrassing me," "Mom, you're bugging me," "Mom, you're driving me crazy." Bailey has said that word that way a thousand times in the past couple of years: When her mother said she shouldn't let her bra straps show. When her mother thought people went to homecoming *with dates*. When her mother asked why Bailey didn't like Hanson's music anymore. The complaint "Mom" was usually so perfect at conveying

30 Bailey's thoughts. But it sounds all wrong in this huge, hollow room.

"Well," the technician says, "time to get this over with."

Bailey lies down on a narrow pallet[1] sticking out of the machine like a tongue. The technician starts to pull a covering over her head, then stops.

"Almost forgot," he says. "Want to listen to the radio while you're in there?"

"Okay," Bailey says.

"What station?"

40 Bailey starts to say Z-98, the station everyone at school listens to, the only station Bailey ever turns on.

"Country 101?" the technician teases. "Want to hear cowboys crying in their beer?"

"No," Bailey says. She surprises herself by deciding, "Something classical."

As soon as she's in the tube, Bailey regrets her choice. All those throbbing violins, those crashing cymbals—Bailey knows next to nothing about classical music and cares about it even less. The slow, cultured voice of the announcer—

50 "And now we'll hear Mozart's finest concerto, at least in my humble opinion"—could drive anyone crazy. Or nutso, as the technician had said.

---

[1] **pallet** (păl′ĭt): a bed-like platform, sometimes covered with padding or cloth.

"All right," the technician's voice comes over her headphones. He's in the control room, but he sounds a million miles away. "Hold very still, and we'll get started."

There's a noise like the clip-clop of horses' hooves—not real horses, but maybe a mechanical kind someone might create if he'd never heard real ones. The noise drowns out the classical music, and in losing it, Bailey realizes why she asked
60 for it in the first place: She knew she'd never have to listen to it again. If she'd chosen Z-98, some song she liked might be ruined for her forever. She could imagine hearing an Ace of Base song six months from now and thinking, *That's the song that was playing the day they found out about my brain tumor—*

*But if there's a tumor, will I even be alive six months from now?*

Something catches in Bailey's throat and she has to swallow a cough.
70 *Silly*, she chides herself. *Nobody's said anything about a tumor.* The only real possibility the emergency room doctor mentioned, ordering all these tests, was a stroke, which was too ridiculous to think about. Old people had strokes. Bailey is only sixteen.

*Maybe they'll just find out I made the whole thing up.*

But she hadn't. Her arm had gone totally numb, right there in algebra class. She hadn't been able to feel the pencil in her fingers. And she hadn't been able to see right, she hadn't been able to hear much—Mr. Vickers's raspy voice had seemed to
80 come at her through a tunnel. Still, she might not have said anything about it if Mr. Vickers hadn't called on her to go work a problem on the board.

"I can't . . . ," she tried to say, but she couldn't seem to make her brain think the words right, she couldn't get her mouth to move. She tried to stand up but fell down instead. Mr. Vickers had Paula Klinely take her to the nurse, the nurse called her mother, and now she's in an MRI tube listening to the clip-clop of fake horses.

The clip-clopping stops and the violins come back.
90 "You moved," the technician says over the headphones with the same tone of exaggerated patience as the classical music announcer. "We'll have to do that one again. The less you move, the quicker we'll be done."

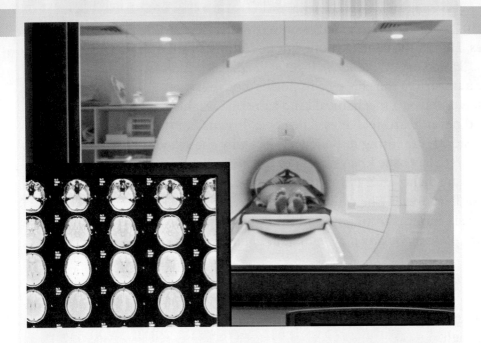

"I'm sorry," Bailey apologizes, though she's not sure he can hear her. If she's going to die at sixteen, she wants people to remember her as a nice person. She can imagine people giving testimonials at her funeral: *She was always so good, so kind to animals and people alike.* Her best friend, Allison, could **reminisce,** *And if she found a spider indoors, she was*
100 *always very careful about carrying it outside instead of killing it.* She hopes Allison would remember to say that. Maybe this technician would even come to the funeral.

*I never get close to the patients,* he might say. *I view everyone as just another brain scan. But here was a kid who was always so gracious and noble. She knew she was dying, but she was always concerned about other people. She always asked about my family, my pets, my—*

Bailey can't think what else the technician might be impressed by her asking about. She decides he should break
110 down in sobs at that point.

The clip-clopping starts again. Bailey concentrates on not moving. She's very glad the MRI can't read her thoughts.

When the MRI is finally done and the technician pulls her out of the tube, Bailey scans his face for some expression—of pity, maybe, or better yet, boredom.

"Well?" she says.

**reminisce**
(rĕm´ə-nĭs´) *v.*
When you *reminisce,* you remember past experiences or events.

"What?" he asks, looking down at the controls that lower her pallet.

"What did you find?" she asks, forgetting that she is supposed to be acting like she cares more about his dog than her life.

"Oh, I'm not allowed to discuss results with patients," the technician says. "Your doctor will review everything and then talk to you."

He's less chatty now. Does that mean anything?

Bailey climbs back into the wheelchair—something else that's ridiculous, because isn't she perfectly capable of walking now? The technician pushes her out to the waiting room, where Bailey's mother is intently reading *Golf Digest*. To the best of Bailey's knowledge, Bailey's mother has never played golf in her entire life.

"Well?" Bailey's mother asks. But she directs the question to Bailey, not the technician. "Are you all right?"

"I'm fine," Bailey insists.

Bailey's mother lays her hand on Bailey's shoulder, something she never would have done under normal circumstances. Bailey doesn't pull away.

The technician is on the phone.

"They have a room ready for you now," he reports. "An aide will be by in a few minutes to take you up there."

He leaves, and Bailey and her mother are alone.

"Do you really feel okay?" Bailey's mother asks. "You haven't had another . . . episode?"

"No. I've just got a little headache," Bailey says. But it's just the edge of a headache—nothing Bailey would mention if she weren't in the hospital. "Do I really have to stay all night?"

"That's what the doctor said. They can't schedule the other tests until tomorrow. And—" Mom stops and starts over. "Look at it as a chance to play hooky. To avoid biology class."

She smiles brightly at Bailey, and Bailey resists the urge to retort, "I'd rather dissect[2] frogs than die." But she realizes she'd said exactly the reverse only a week ago in the school cafeteria: "I'd rather die than dissect a frog." She remembers the exact moment she spoke the words: Sunlight had been streaming in the window behind Allison, grease was congealing on the school lunch tacos, all her friends were laughing.

---

[2] **dissect** (dĭ-sĕkt´): to cut apart or separate into pieces, especially to study more closely.

*Oh, God, did I bring this on myself?* Bailey wonders. *I didn't really mean that. God, I'll dissect a billion frogs if you want me to. If you let me live.* But she knows from TV disease-

160 of-the-week movies that bargaining with God never works.

"Mom, what do you think is wrong with me?" Bailey asks, and is amazed that the question comes out sounding merely conversational. She wants to whimper.

Mom keeps her smile, but it seems even less genuine now.

"I'm no doctor," she says. "But I think you blacked out because you skipped lunch to do your history report. That's all."

"I had a candy bar," Bailey says.

"My point exactly," Mom says, and laughs, and Bailey

170 feels much better. Mom wouldn't dare criticize Bailey's eating habits if she thought something was really wrong.

Would she?

Bailey's room is in the main part of the hospital, not the pediatric wing, a fact that worries Bailey's mom.

"Are you sure?" she asks the aide who is skillfully maneuvering Bailey's wheelchair past several carts of dinner trays. "She's only sixteen. Don't they—"

"Listen, lady, I just go where they send me," the aide responds. He's a thin man with sallow skin and a dark braid

180 hanging down his back. Bailey can't decide if he would have been considered cool or a scuzz in high school. Probably a scuzz if he ended up as a hospital aide. Then she decides she shouldn't think things like that, not if she wants people to remember her as a nice person.

The aide is explaining to Mom that lots of kids have checked in lately; the pediatric wing is full. He makes it sound like a hotel everyone wants to stay at.

"But if she's not in the pediatric wing, I can't spend the night with her," Mom frets.

190 "Nope. Not according to what they tell me," the aide agrees.

They arrive at the door of Bailey's room. At first glance Bailey thinks the mistake is even bigger than Mom feared: She's been given a bed in a nursing home. The room is crowded with people at least a decade or two older than Bailey's own grandparents. Then Bailey realizes that only one of the old people is actually in a bed. The rest are visitors.

"Coming through," the aide says, only barely missing knocking down one man's cane and another man's walker.

200      "Oh, look, Aunt Mabel's got a roommate," someone says. "Won't that be nice."

But they're all looking back and forth from Bailey to her mother, obviously confused.

"She fainted," Bailey's mother announces. "She's just in for a few tests."

It's a cue for Bailey to say, once more, "Mom!" This time she keeps her mouth shut and her head down.

The old people nod and smile. One woman says, "She looks just like my granddaughter. I'm sure she'll be fine," as if

210    the resemblance could save Bailey's life. Another woman adds, "You know those doctors. They just don't want to get sued."

As Bailey silently climbs from the chair to the bed she sees that her mother is smiling back at the old people, but the corners of her mouth are tighter than ever.

A nurse appears and whips a curtain between Bailey's bed and the old people. The aide fades away with a strange little wave, almost a salute. That one hand gesture makes Bailey want to call after him: *Wait! What happens to most of the people you wheel around? Do they die?*

220    But the nurse has begun asking questions.

"I know some of these won't apply to you," she apologizes, "but it's hospital policy . . . ."

Bailey can't help giggling at "Do you wear dentures?" and "Do you have any artificial limbs?" The nurse zips through the questions without looking up, until she reaches "Do you do recreational drugs?"

"No," Bailey says. They asked that in the emergency room, too.

"Are you sure?" The nurse squints suspiciously at Bailey.

230    "Yes," Bailey says. "I have never done drugs." She spaces the words out, trying to sound **emphatic**, but it comes out all wrong.

"My daughter," Bailey's mother interjects, "has never taken anything stronger than aspirin."

It's true, and Bailey's glad it's true, but she wants to sink through the floor with humiliation at her mother's words.

How can she care about humiliation at a time like this?

Someone comes and takes ten vials of blood from Bailey's arm. Someone else starts what he calls an IV port on the back

**emphatic**
(ĕm-făt′ĭk) *adj.*
If something is *emphatic*, it is expressed in a definite and forceful way.

240 of Bailey's left hand. It's basically a needle taped into her vein, ready for any injection she might need. Someone else takes her blood pressure and makes Bailey push on his hands with her feet, then close her eyes and hold her arms out straight.

"Good," the man says when Bailey opens her eyes.

*I did that right? So I'm okay?* Bailey wants to ask. But something about lying in a hospital bed has made Bailey mute. She can barely say a word to her own mother, sitting two feet away.

"Visiting hours are over," the man tells Mom in a flat voice.

250 "But my daughter—," Mom protests, and stops, swallows hard. Bailey is stunned. Mom is never at a loss for words. "She's only sixteen, and—"

"No visitors after five. Hospital policy," the man says, but there's a hint of compassion in his voice now. "We'll take good care of her. I promise."

"Well . . . " Still Mom hesitates. She looks at Bailey. "I know the Montinis didn't really want to take Andrew overnight, they were just being nice, and with your dad away . . . "

Andrew is Bailey's younger brother, seven years old
and, everyone agrees, a pure terror. Bailey's dad is away on
a business trip. Mom couldn't even reach him on the phone
from the emergency room. Bailey can't see why Mom is telling
her what she already knows. Then Bailey understands: Mom is
asking Bailey for permission to leave.

*They're going to make you leave anyway,* Bailey wants
to say. *What do you want me to do?* But it's strange. For a
minute Bailey feels like she's the mother and her mother is the
daughter.

"Go on," she says magnanimously.[3] "I'll be fine."

But as soon as her mother is out the door, Bailey wants to
run after her, crying, "Mom-mee! Don't go!" just like she used
to do at preschool, years and years and years ago.

Once they're alone together, Bailey's roommate, Mabel, gets
gabby.

"Ten days I've been lying in this hospital bed," she
announces, speaking to the TV as much as to Bailey. "First
they say it's my kidneys, then it's my bladder—or is that the
same thing? I forget. Then there's my spleen—"

Bailey can't imagine lying in any hospital bed for ten
days. She's already antsy, after just two hours. The sheets are
suffocating her legs. She hated that spring in junior high when
she signed up for track and Mom made her finish the whole
season. But now she longs to run and run and run, sprints and
relays and maybe even marathons.

*I've never run a marathon. What else will I never get to do
if I die now?*

Bailey is glad when Mabel distracts her by announcing
joyfully, "Oh good, dinner."

An aide slides  a covered tray in front of Mabel and one in
front of Bailey.

"We didn't know what you wanted, 'cause you weren't here
last night," the aide says accusingly.

Bailey lifts the cover. Dinner is some kind of meat covered
in brown gravy, green beans blanched to a sickly gray, mashed
potatoes that could pass for glue, gummy apples with a slab
of soggy pie dough on top—food Bailey would never eat in a

---

[3] **magnanimously** (măg-năn′ə-məs-lē):  to do something in a courageous, kind,
unselfish way.

million years. And yet, somehow, she finds that she can eat it, and does, every bite.

*See?* she wants to tell someone. *I'm healthy. So healthy I can eat this slop and not die.*

Beside her tray is a menu for the next day. Bailey studies it as carefully as a cram sheet for some major final exam. Hospital Food 101, maybe. If she were still here for dinner tomorrow night, she'd have a choice of meat loaf or fried chicken, chocolate cake or ice cream.

But of course she won't be here tomorrow night. Because they're going to find out, first thing tomorrow, that there's nothing wrong with her.

She hopes.

The aide comes back for Bailey's tray.

"You didn't fill that out," she says, pointing at Bailey's menu.

"I'm just here overnight. I don't need to—," Bailey protests.

"Fill it out anyway," the aide orders.

Meekly, Bailey puts check marks in little boxes. Pancakes for breakfast. Chicken salad for lunch. Meat loaf and chocolate cake.

It doesn't matter. If she's still here tomorrow night, she knows, she won't be hungry.

The aide glances out Bailey's window. "Man, look at that traffic," she moans.

Bailey looks up, puzzled, and the aide has to explain: "Rush hour."

It's five forty-five. Bailey is stunned that the rest of the world is going on outside this hospital room. She is stunned to realize that she should be at marching band practice, right now, with Mr. Chaynowski ordering them to do a final run-through of "Another Opening, Another Show," before marching back to the school, packing up her clarinet, joking with her friends.

It's too weird to think about. She's actually glad when Mabel flips on the local news.

Three hours later Bailey is ready to scream. She can't stand the TV. It's into sitcoms now, old-lady ones Bailey never watches. Bailey has never noticed before, but on TV everyone smiles all the time. Everyone laughs at everything.

How dare they?

Searching desperately for something to distract her, Bailey
notices her backpack, cast off in the corner. She pulls out her
340   algebra book.

She is a normal sixteen-year-old. Sixteen-year-olds do
homework on Tuesday nights.

Bailey missed the end of class, when Mr. Vickers assigns
the homework, but he always assigns the odd problems.
She takes out a pencil and paper, and imagines what Mr.
Vickers will say on Thursday: *Bailey, good to have you back.*
*Remember to make up the homework.*

Bailey will use her airiest voice: *Oh, it's already done. Here.*
And he'll stare in amazement.

350   *Why, Bailey*, he'll say, admiration creeping into his voice.
*You're such a* **conscientious** *student.*

Mr. Vickers is straight out of college, and a real hottie. Lots
of girls have crushes on him.

*Why, there you were on the verge of death,* he might say.
*And you still—*

Bailey doesn't want to think anymore about what
Mr. Vickers might say. The numbers swim in front of her eyes.

The phone rings. Mabel answers it and grunts
disappointedly, "It's for you."

360   Bailey picks up her phone.

"Oh, Bay-ley!" It's Allison.

Bailey is suddenly so happy she can't speak. She grins as
widely as someone on TV.

"Bailey?" Allison asks. "Are you all right?"

"I'm fine," Bailey says. But she's not happy anymore.
Allison's voice is all wrong, and so is Bailey's. She can't seem
to make her words come out right.

"Well," Allison says, and stops. It strikes Bailey that
Allison doesn't know what to say either. Allison—who usually
370   talks so much she could get a speeding ticket for her mouth.

"What'd you think? That I was going to be the dead
person in the yearbook for our class?" Bailey jokes desperately.
Their yearbook came out last week, and Allison had gone on
and on about how every year the senior class had someone die,
usually in a car wreck, and that person got a whole page of
the yearbook dedicated to him. Last year the dead person was
the head cheerleader, so there were lots of pictures. Allison
and Bailey and their friends had spent an entire lunch period

**conscientious**
(kŏn´shē-ĕn´shəs) *adj.*
If someone is
*conscientious*, that
person is very careful
and thorough.

imagining what a memorial page might say for everyone in their class.

380     "Imogene Rogers, world's biggest airhead, floated off into outer space . . . John Vhymes, biggest show-off, thought he had a better idea for running heaven than God does . . . Stanley Witherspoon, died two years ago but nobody noticed until now . . . "

It had been funny last week. It isn't now. Bailey hears Allison inhale sharply. Bailey tries to pretend she didn't say anything.

"So what happened after I left?" Bailey asks. "Anything
390 good?"

"Everyone was just talking about you," Allison says. "Do you know what's wrong yet?"

Suddenly Bailey can't talk to Allison. She just can't.

"Listen, Al, some nurse is coming in in a minute to take my blood pressure. I'll call you later, okay?"

It isn't really a lie. They're always coming in to take her blood pressure.

Allison hangs up. Bailey hopes Mabel's hearing is as bad as her kidneys.

400 Bailey is surprised that she can fall asleep. She's even more surprised when they wake her up at 6 A.M. for an electro-cardiogram.

"But my mom—," she protests groggily.

"They don't want to test your mom's heart," the aide says. "They want to test yours."

Bailey is climbing into the wheelchair when the phone rings.

"Oh, Bailey," her mother's voice rushes at her. "They said you were already up. I was just getting ready to come down
410 there, but something awful happened—the car won't start. I called Triple A, but it's going to be an hour before they get out here. I'm looking for someone to give me a ride or loan me a car. . . . I am so sorry. This is incredibly bad timing. Are you okay?"

It's easiest for Bailey to say automatically, like a robot, "I'm fine."

"I'll get there as soon as I can," Mom assures her.

"I know. That's fine," Bailey says. But the words have no meaning anymore.

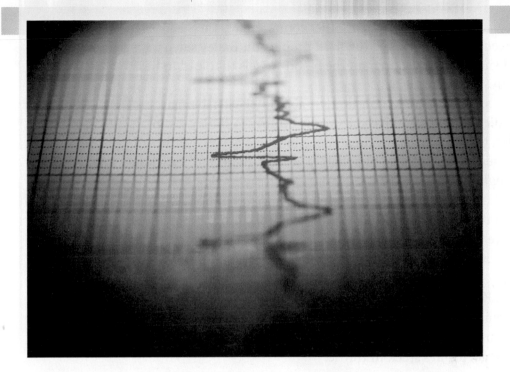

420    Down in the EKG room they put cold gel on Bailey's chest and the technician runs a probe[4] along Bailey's rib cage. Even though the technician is a woman, Bailey is embarrassed because the probe keeps running into her breasts.

"Um-hmm," the technician mutters to herself.

Bailey knows better now than to ask what the "Um-hmm" means. She can't see the TV screen the technician peers into. The technician pushes harder and harder on the probe, until it feels like an animal trying to burrow between Bailey's ribs. Bailey can't help crying out.

430    The technician looks up, surprised, as if she'd forgotten that Bailey is an actual human being, capable of feeling pain.

"Sorry," she says, and pushes the probe down even harder.

*I am just a body here,* Bailey thinks. *Nobody here knows or cares that I'm nice to animals and small children, that I do my homework on time. That I'm a person.* She wants to say something to make the technician really see her, but the longer Bailey lies on the cold table in her hospital gown, the more she feels like all her personality is leaching away. She is just a body.

Is that what it's like to die?

---

[4] **probe** (prōb): a small device or instrument used to gather information.

440 Another technician in another room repeats the procedure—the cold gel, the hard probe—on Bailey's neck and shoulders, checking out the blood vessels that lead to her brain.

This woman talks constantly—about her kids, her garden, her diet—but it's not like she's really talking to Bailey. Even when the woman asks a direct question, "Have you ever heard of a geranium growing like that?" the woman doesn't stop long enough for Bailey to answer.

Bailey is crying, and the woman doesn't even notice.

450 Bailey thinks she'll have to dry her tears and wipe her eyes before she sees her mother. She can't wait to see her mother. She wants Mom to think about all these horrible things so Bailey doesn't have to. She wants Mom there to remember what Bailey is really like, so Bailey can remember how to act normal.

But when Bailey gets back to her room, there's only a message. Mom's stuck in traffic.

> "Bailey is standing on the edge of something awful, balanced between two possible futures."

Mom left the number for the Montinis' car phone, but Bailey doesn't call it. She turns her head to the wall so her 460 roommate won't see, and lies in bed sobbing silently. She's not sure if she's crying about the stalled traffic or the painful probe or the shame of having made jokes about dead people in the yearbook. Or the fact that whatever made Bailey faint yesterday might also make her die. *It really could happen,* Bailey thinks. *People die of terrible diseases all the time. There's no reason that it shouldn't happen to me.*

For the first time Bailey realizes none of her fears have been real before. When she imagined the MRI technician speaking at her funeral, the memorial page in the yearbook, Mr. Vickers's response to her devotion to algebra, even her personality leaching away, it was just a fantasy to her. Role-playing. A game.

But Bailey is standing on the edge of something awful, balanced between two possible futures. On one side is the life she's always known: homework and marching band and jokes with Allison and groans at her mother. Health. A future just like her past. And on the other side, over the cliff into whatever her illness is, is more time in hospital beds, more technicians seeing her innards but not really seeing her, more time crying alone. And maybe—death. Bailey longs fervently for her normal life back. In her mind it positively glows, an utterly joyous existence. Ordinary never looked so good.

But it's not her choice which future she gets.

"Hello?" someone calls tentatively.

Bailey pauses to hide the evidence of her crying before she turns. But, strangely, she's not crying anymore.

A man pulls the curtain around her bed, to give some privacy from her roommate.

"I'm Dr. Rogers, your neurologist," he says. "I've looked at all your test results, and—"

Bailey's heart pounds. She can barely hear him for the surge of blood in her ears. She feels dizzier than she felt yesterday, when everyone said she fainted.

"Shouldn't my mom be here to hear this?" Bailey asks. "She's coming soon."

Dr. Rogers looks at his watch.

"No. I can't wait."

*He's treating me like I'm a grown-up*, Bailey marvels. But the thought has an echo: *Grown-up enough to die.*

"This is a classic case," Dr. Rogers is saying. "I'm surprised nobody caught it yesterday. They still would have wanted the tests, just to be sure. . . . What you had was a migraine headache."

A headache? Not a stroke? Not a tumor? As soon as Dr. Rogers has said the inoffensive word, all the possibilities Bailey feared instantly recede. She's a million miles away from that frightening cliff now. Of course she isn't going to die.

How silly she'd been, to think she might. How silly, to think he'd tell her she was dying without her mother there.

510  Dr. Rogers is still talking, about the link between chocolate and migraines, about how common migraines are for young girls, about how it was perfectly normal for Bailey to get the symptoms of a migraine headache before her head even began to hurt. But Bailey barely listens. She's thinking about getting her ordinary life back—ordinary life with maybe a headache every now and then. Bailey doesn't care—her head barely even hurt yesterday. She doesn't expect a mere headache to change anything at all. She waits for the glow to fade from her view of her ordinary life, and it does, but not entirely. Even with

520  headaches she has a pretty good life.

Bailey's mother rushes into the room just then, apologizing right and left.

"Doctor, you must think I'm a terrible mother, not to be here at a time like this. What did you find out? Please tell me—it was just a fluke, right?"

"Mom," Bailey protests, in humiliation, with perfect emphasis.

The complaint never sounded so wonderful before.

**COLLABORATIVE DISCUSSION**  Being hospitalized and waiting to hear about her test results is an emotional experience for Bailey. With a partner, discuss the events that take place during her stay. How does each event help you understand more about Bailey's thoughts and feelings?

# Describe Stories: Plot and Suspense

 RL 3, RL 5

Stories, such as "Fine?", follow a pattern called a **plot,** which is the series of events in the story. At the center of a good plot is a conflict. A **conflict** is a problem or struggle between opposing forces that triggers the action and events. Most plots have the following stages:

- **Exposition** provides background and introduces the setting and characters. The conflict is also introduced at this stage.
- **Rising action** includes events that develop and intensify the conflict.
- The **climax** is the story's most exciting part and a turning point for the main character.
- **Falling action** eases the tension, and events unfold as a result of the climax.
- The **resolution** is the final part of the plot and reveals how the problem is solved.

To keep you involved and excited about the plot, a writer will often create suspense. **Suspense** is a feeling of growing tension and excitement that makes a reader curious about what will happen next in a story. At the start of "Fine?", you learn about the story's conflict—Bailey is in a hospital undergoing tests—and you want to find out more.

# Explain Point of View

 RL 6

In literature, the **narrator** is the voice that tells the story. A writer's choice of narrator is known as **point of view.**

| First-Person Point of View | Third-Person Point of View |
| --- | --- |
| The narrator is a character in the story. | The narrator is not a character in the story but more like a voice that tells it. |
| The narrator uses the pronouns *I, me,* and *my* to refer to himself or herself. | The narrator uses the pronouns *he, she,* and *they* to refer to the characters. |
| The narrator tells about his or her thoughts and feelings, but does not know what other characters are thinking and feeling. | A narrator called **third-person omniscient** knows what ALL the characters think and feel. |
|  | A narrator called **third-person limited** knows the thoughts and feelings of just one person, usually the main character. |

Think about the following questions to help you analyze point of view:

- How does the author's choice of point of view affect the story?
- What does the choice of narrator help you learn about characters and events?

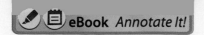 

# Analyzing the Text

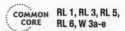
COMMON CORE    RL 1, RL 3, RL 5, RL 6, W 3a-e

**Cite Text Evidence**    Support your responses with evidence from the text.

1. **Identify** Reread lines 1–15. Identify the point of view of the story. Explain how you can tell which point of view is being used.

2. **Infer** An **external conflict** is a character's struggle against an outside force. An **internal conflict** takes place inside a character's mind. Go back through the story and record examples of the internal and external conflicts that Bailey faces.

3. **Draw Conclusions** Review lines 333–357. What does this passage tell you about Bailey's character?

4. **Evaluate** Reread the conversation Bailey has with her friend Allison in lines 371–395. How does the scene add suspense to the plot?

5. **Analyze** The plot of "Fine?" centers on Bailey's fear of what her illness is. Go back through the story and make a list of important events. Label each event to identify what happens at each stage of the plot—exposition, rising action, climax, falling action, and resolution. Explain how each event fits its plot stage.

6. **Connect** Reread lines 22–31 and 521–527. Explain why the author repeats Bailey's complaint. What does the author want you to know about Bailey at the end of the story?

7. **Analyze** How would the story be different if Bailey was the narrator? Name a detail that Bailey might leave out and explain why.

## PERFORMANCE TASK

**Writing Activity: Narrative** The story "Fine?" presents Bailey's thoughts and feelings about her impending diagnosis. Write a one- or two-page narrative that describes the situation from Bailey's mother's point of view.

- Think about and decide whether you will tell the story using first- or third-person point of view.
- Follow the actual story; do not change the events or plot.
- Include relevant details that Bailey shares with her mother.

# Critical Vocabulary

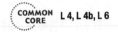 

**technician**　　**reminisce**　　**emphatic**　　**conscientious**

**Practice and Apply**  Complete the sentences with words that show that you understand the meaning of each vocabulary word.

1. We are going to have a TV **technician** come to our house because . . .

2. I like to hear old Uncle Al **reminisce** because . . .

3. The jury foreperson read the verdict in an **emphatic** voice because . . .

4. I am very **conscientious** when I do my chores because . . .

## Vocabulary Strategy: Greek Roots

You can often determine the meaning of an unfamiliar word by examining its root.  A **root** is a word part that contains the core meaning of the word. For example, *tech* comes from a Greek root that can mean "art," "skill," or "craft." You can find this root in the word *technician* and use its meaning to figure out that *technician* refers to someone who has a specific skill.

**Practice and Apply**  The Greek root *tech* is found in a number of English words. Choose a word from the web that best completes each sentence. Use your understanding of the root's meaning as well as context clues to figure out the meaning of each word.

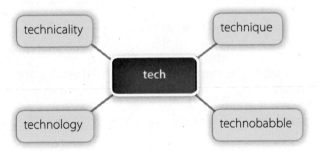

1. The artist has a special _____ that she uses to create her sculptures.

2. The audience wished that the scientist would use plain English instead of _____ to explain her latest invention.

3. Raul likes to be the first to purchase the latest _____ in computers.

4. The suspected thief was released from jail because of a _____.

# Language Conventions: Commas and Dashes

**Commas** can make the meaning of sentences clearer by separating certain words, phrases, or clauses. Commas can be used to set off nonrestrictive elements. A **nonrestrictive element** is a phrase or clause that can be removed from the sentence without changing the sentence's basic meaning. Notice how commas are used in the following sentence from the story "Fine?"

> **The only real possibility the emergency room doctor mentioned, ordering all these tests, was a stroke . . .**

If you remove the phrase *ordering all these tests*, the basic meaning of the sentence is still clear.

Like commas, **dashes** can also be used to set off nonrestrictive elements. Dashes are used most often when the nonrestrictive element indicates a more abrupt break in thought. Notice how dashes are used in this example from the story.

> **The slow, cultured voice of the announcer—"And now we'll hear Mozart's finest concerto, at least in my humble opinion"— could drive anyone crazy.**

Using commas and dashes to set off nonrestrictive elements helps to communicate meaning and information clearly. Look at the examples from the story again. If the commas and dashes were not included, the sentences would be confusing and difficult to follow.

**Practice and Apply** Use commas or dashes as indicated to set off the nonrestrictive element in each sentence.

1. The concert tickets I just bought them yesterday were expensive and nonrefundable. (dashes)

2. Mr. Jackson who moved here from Texas was introduced to us as the new principal. (commas)

3. Nola's voice never loud to begin with dropped to an airy whisper in the library. (commas)

4. Sharon eyed the sunrise deep red clouds and wispy flares of pink through the dining room window. (commas)

5. Our agreed-upon rule is that the drummer not the guitarist or the keyboardist is responsible for making sure the entire drum kit makes it to the show. (dashes)

**Maya Angelou** (b. 1928) *was born Marguerite Annie Johnson in St. Louis, Missouri. Though a childhood trauma led her to stop speaking for five and a half years, Angelou grew up to pursue a career as a singer and actor. She later turned to writing as her main form of expression, and in 1970, her best-selling autobiography* I Know Why the Caged Bird Sings *made her an international literary star. She is widely admired as a fearless and inspiring voice.*

# Life Doesn't Frighten Me

Poem by Maya Angelou

**SETTING A PURPOSE** As you read, think about the images and ideas that the poem brings to your mind.

Shadows on the wall
Noises down the hall
Life doesn't frighten me at all
Bad dogs barking loud
5 Big ghosts in a cloud
Life doesn't frighten me at all.

Mean old Mother Goose
Lions on the loose
They don't frighten me at all
10 Dragons breathing flame
On my counterpane[1]
That doesn't frighten me at all.

---

[1] **counterpane:** a bedspread.

I go boo
Make them shoo
15 I make fun
Way they run
I won't cry
So they fly
I just smile
20 They go wild
Life doesn't frighten me at all.

Tough guys in a fight
All alone at night
Life doesn't frighten me at all.

25 Panthers in the park
Strangers in the dark
No, they don't frighten me at all.

That new classroom where
Boys all pull my hair
30 (Kissy little girls
With their hair in curls)
They don't frighten me at all.

Don't show me frogs and snakes
And listen for my scream,
35 If I'm afraid at all
It's only in my dreams.

I've got a magic charm
That I keep up my sleeve,
I can walk the ocean floor
40 And never have to breathe.

Life doesn't frighten me at all
Not at all
Not at all.
Life doesn't frighten me at all.

**COLLABORATIVE DISCUSSION**  With a partner, discuss what the poem's main message might be, based on the images, words, and phrases in it. Why do you think the poet wrote this poem?

# Analyze Structure

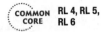

"Life Doesn't Frighten Me" is a lyric poem. **Lyric poetry** is a poetic form in which a single speaker expresses his or her thoughts and feelings. Lyric poetry can take many different forms and can address all types of topics, including complex ideas or everyday experiences.

Similar to a narrator in fiction, a **speaker** in poetry is the voice that "talks" to the reader. The speaker may be the poet or a fictional character. Even if a poem uses the pronouns *I* or *me*, it does not mean that the poet is the speaker. Clues in the title and in individual lines can help you determine the speaker and his or her situation.

To analyze the speaker in a lyric poem, ask yourself:

- Who is speaking? How do I know?
- What ideas does the speaker want to communicate? Why?

Poets use structure and poetic elements to create mood, express ideas, and reinforce meaning in their work. Most poems are meant to be heard, not just read. A poem's sounds are as carefully chosen as its words. The following elements are often present in lyric poetry as well as other forms of poetry.

> A **stanza** is a group of two or more lines that form a unit in a poem.
>
> **Repetition** is a technique in which a sound, word, phrase, or line is repeated.
>
> A **rhyme scheme** is a pattern of rhymes at the ends of lines. A rhyme scheme is noted by assigning a letter of the alphabet, beginning with *a*, to each line. Lines that rhyme are given the same letter.
>
> A **couplet** is a rhymed pair of lines.

As you read a poem, either silently or aloud, look at and listen to its different elements. Ask yourself:

- How does repetition add to the poem's meaning or emphasize its ideas?
- What patterns can I find in the poem's rhyme scheme? What rhythms do they add to the poem?
- What sounds are emphasized in the poem's rhyme scheme? Why might this be?

# Analyzing the Text

COMMON CORE — RL 1, RL 2, RL 4, RL 5, RL 6, SL 4, SL 6

**Cite Text Evidence**    Support your responses with evidence from the text.

1. **Infer**   Review lines 1–9 and lines 37–40. What conclusions can you draw about the speaker's age and personality?

2. **Analyze**   Examine and identify the different rhyme schemes the poet uses. What general statement could you use to describe the poem's rhyme scheme?

3. **Draw Conclusions**   Reread lines 1–21. Which scary things are clearly imaginary? Which are possibly real? What effect does this variety of things create in the poem?

4. **Evaluate**   Read aloud lines 1–24. Notice the change to couplets and shorter line lengths in the third stanza. What effect does this change have on your reading?

5. **Synthesize**   Explain how the structure of the poem and the repetition of the line "Life doesn't frighten me at all" help convey the meaning of the poem. Do you think the speaker of the poem is truly not afraid? Why or why not?

---

## PERFORMANCE TASK

**Speaking Activity: Oral Reading**
Different people can read the same poem aloud in very different ways. Prepare an oral reading of all or a part of "Life Doesn't Frighten Me."

- Every person finds his or her own meanings in a poem. Review the poem and write a statement that summarizes its meaning to you.

- Next, practice reading the poem aloud. At first, focus on the different rhythms, repetition, and sounds.
- Try giving different "personalities" to your reading until you find one that you like.
- Practice until you can read the poem smoothly. Then read it aloud to a small group.

**Background**  *Most people experience fear now and then; fear is an ordinary part of life. Some fears may be overcome quickly; others may continue, in varying degrees, for a lifetime. Science provides knowledge and insight into why we experience fear and why sometimes our fears seem out of control. Whether it is a fear of spiders, a fear of the dark, or a fear of flying, using science to understand the physical and emotional responses that we call fear is the first step toward conquering it.*

# Fears and Phobias

Online Article by kidshealth.org

**SETTING A PURPOSE**  As you read, pay attention to the details that explain the nature of fear and how fear can affect everyday life, both physically and emotionally.

The roller coaster hesitates for a split second at the peak of its steep track after a long, slow climb. You know what's about to happen—and there's no way to avoid it now. It's time to hang onto the handrail, palms sweating, heart racing, and brace yourself for the wild ride down.

## What Is Fear?

Fear is one of the most basic human emotions. It is programmed into the nervous system and works like an instinct. From the time we're infants, we are equipped with the survival instincts necessary to respond with fear when we
10    sense danger or feel unsafe.

Fear helps protect us. It makes us alert to danger and prepares us to deal with it. Feeling afraid is very natural—and helpful—in some situations. Fear can be like a warning, a signal that cautions us to be careful.

Like all emotions, fear can be mild, medium, or intense, depending on the situation and the person. A feeling of fear can be brief or it can last longer.

## How Fear Works

When we sense danger, the brain reacts instantly, sending signals that **activate** the nervous system. This causes physical
20  responses, such as a faster heartbeat, rapid breathing, and an increase in blood pressure. Blood pumps to muscle groups to prepare the body for physical action (such as running or fighting). Skin sweats to keep the body cool. Some people might notice sensations in the stomach, head, chest, legs, or hands. These physical sensations of fear can be mild or strong.

This response is known as "fight or flight" because that is exactly what the body is preparing itself to do: fight off the danger or run fast to get away. The body stays in this state of fight-flight until the brain receives an "all clear" message and
30  turns off the response.

Sometimes fear is **triggered** by something that is startling or unexpected (like a loud noise), even if it's not actually dangerous. That's because the fear reaction is activated instantly—a few seconds faster than the thinking part of the brain can process or evaluate what's happening. As soon as the brain gets enough information to realize there's no danger ("Oh, it's just a balloon bursting—whew!"), it turns off the fear reaction. All this can happen in seconds.

**activate**
(ăk´tə-vāt´) v. To *activate* something means to cause it to start working.

**trigger**
(trĭg´ər) v. To *trigger* something means to cause it to begin.

## FEAR OR FUN?

Some people find the rush of fear exciting. They might seek out the thrill of extreme sports and savor the scariest horror flicks. Others do not like the experience of feeling afraid or taking risks. During the scariest moments of a roller coaster ride one person might think, "I'll never get on this thing again—that is, if I make it out alive!" while another person thinks, "This is awesome! As soon as it's over, I'm getting back on!"

# Fears People Have

Fear is the word we use to describe our emotional reaction to
40 something that seems dangerous. But the word "fear" is used
in another way, too: to name something a person often feels
afraid of.

People fear things or situations that make them feel unsafe
or unsure. For instance, someone who isn't a strong swimmer
might have a fear of deep water. In this case, the fear is helpful
because it cautions the person to stay safe. Someone could
overcome this fear by learning how to swim safely.

A fear can be healthy if it cautions a person to stay safe
around something that could be dangerous. But sometimes a
50 fear is unnecessary and causes more caution than the situation
calls for.

Many people have a fear of public speaking. Whether it's
giving a report in class, speaking at an assembly, or reciting
lines in the school play, speaking in front of others is one of
the most common fears people have.

People tend to avoid the situations or things they fear. But
this doesn't help them overcome fear—in fact, it can be the
reverse. Avoiding something scary reinforces a fear and keeps
it strong.

60 People can overcome unnecessary fears by giving
themselves the chance to learn about and gradually get used
to the thing or situation they're afraid of. For example, people
who fly despite a fear of flying can become used to unfamiliar
sensations like takeoff or **turbulence**. They learn what to
expect and have a chance to watch what others do to relax
and enjoy the flight. Gradually (and safely) facing fear helps
someone overcome it.

**turbulence**
(tûr´byə-ləns) *n.* In
flying, *turbulence*
is an interruption
in the flow of wind
that causes planes to
rise, fall, or sway in a
rough way.

# Fears During Childhood

Certain fears are normal during childhood. That's because fear
can be a natural reaction to feeling unsure and vulnerable—
70 and much of what children experience is new and unfamiliar.

Young kids often have fears of the dark, being alone,
strangers, and monsters or other scary imaginary creatures.
School-aged kids might be afraid when it's stormy or at a first
sleepover. As they grow and learn, with the support of adults,
most kids are able to slowly conquer these fears and outgrow
them.

Some kids are more sensitive to fears and may have a tough time overcoming them. When fears last beyond the expected age, it might be a sign that someone is overly fearful, worried, or anxious. People whose fears are too intense or last too long might need help and support to overcome them.

## Phobias

A phobia is an intense fear reaction to a particular thing or a situation. With a phobia, the fear is out of proportion to the potential danger. But to the person with the phobia, the danger feels real because the fear is so very strong.

Phobias cause people to worry about, dread, feel upset by, and avoid the things or situations they fear because the physical sensations of fear can be so intense. So having a phobia can interfere with normal activities. A person with a phobia of dogs might feel afraid to walk to school in case he or she sees a dog on the way. Someone with an elevator phobia might avoid a field trip if it involves going on an elevator.

A girl with a phobia of thunderstorms might be afraid to go to school if the weather forecast predicts a storm. She might feel terrible distress and fear when the sky turns cloudy. A guy with social phobia experiences intense fear of public speaking or interacting, and may be afraid to answer questions in class, give a report, or speak to classmates in the lunchroom.

It can be exhausting and upsetting to feel the intense fear that goes with having a phobia. It can be disappointing to miss out on opportunities because fear is holding you back. And it can be confusing and embarrassing to feel afraid of things that others seem to have no problem with.

Sometimes, people get teased about their fears. Even if the person doing the teasing doesn't mean to be unkind and unfair, teasing only makes the situation worse.

## What Causes Phobias?

Some phobias develop when someone has a scary experience with a particular thing or situation. A tiny brain structure called the **amygdala** (pronounced: uh-mig-duh-luh) keeps track of experiences that trigger strong emotions. Once a certain thing or situation triggers a strong fear reaction, the amygdala warns the person by triggering a fear reaction every

time he or she encounters (or even thinks about) that thing or situation.

Someone might develop a bee phobia after being stung during a particularly scary situation. For that person, looking at a photograph of a bee, seeing a bee from a distance, or even walking near flowers where there *could* be a bee can all trigger the phobia.

120     Sometimes, though, there may be no single event that causes a particular phobia. Some people may be more sensitive to fears because of personality traits they are born with, certain genes[1] they've inherited, or situations they've experienced. People who have had strong childhood fears or anxiety may be more likely to have one or more phobias.

Having a phobia isn't a sign of weakness or **immaturity**. It's a response the brain has learned in an attempt to protect the person. It's as if the brain's alert system triggers a false alarm, generating intense fear that is out of proportion to the

**immaturity**
(ĭmʹə-tyo͝orʹĭ-tē) *n.*
*Immaturity* is the state of not being fully developed or grown.

---

[1] **genes** (jēnz): the parts of cells that give a living thing its physical characteristics and make it grow and develop; a person's genes come from their parents and other blood relatives.

situation. Because the fear signal is so intense, the person is convinced the danger is greater than it actually is.

## Overcoming Phobias

People can learn to overcome phobias by gradually facing their fears. This is not easy at first. It takes willingness and bravery. Sometimes people need the help of a therapist[2] to guide them through the process.

Overcoming a phobia usually starts with making a long list of the person's fears in least-to-worst order. For example, with a dog phobia, the list might start with the things the person is least afraid of, such as looking at a photo of a dog. It will then work all the way up to worst fears, such as standing next to someone who's petting a dog, petting a dog on a leash, and walking a dog.

Gradually, and with support, the person tries each fear situation on the list—one at a time, starting with the least fear. The person isn't forced to do anything and works on each fear until he or she feels comfortable, taking as long as needed.

A therapist could also show someone with a dog phobia how to approach, pet, and walk a dog, and help the person to try it, too. The person may expect terrible things to happen when near a dog. Talking about this can help, too. When people find that what they fear doesn't actually turn out to be true, it can be a great relief.

A therapist might also teach relaxation practices such as specific ways of breathing, muscle relaxation training, or soothing self-talk. These can help people feel comfortable and bold enough to face the fears on their list.

As somebody gets used to a feared object or situation, the brain adjusts how it responds and the phobia is overcome.

Often, the hardest part of overcoming a phobia is getting started. Once a person decides to go for it—and gets the right coaching and support—it can be surprising how quickly fear can melt away.

**COLLABORATIVE DISCUSSION** Fears and phobias are related, but they are quite different in some ways. With a partner, use evidence from the text to discuss these differences. Which response can be useful? Which one can be harmful, and why?

---

[2] **therapist** (thĕr´ə-pĭst): a person who is skilled in treating mental or physical illness.

# Cite Evidence

To support analysis of any text that you read, you need to be able to **cite evidence,** or provide specific information from the text. Evidence can include details, facts, statistics, quotations, and examples. The chart shows different ways to cite evidence from an informational text such as "Fears and Phobias."

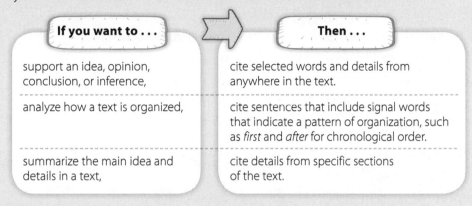

**If you want to . . .**

**Then . . .**

| If you want to . . . | Then . . . |
|---|---|
| support an idea, opinion, conclusion, or inference, | cite selected words and details from anywhere in the text. |
| analyze how a text is organized, | cite sentences that include signal words that indicate a pattern of organization, such as *first* and *after* for chronological order. |
| summarize the main idea and details in a text, | cite details from specific sections of the text. |

After reading "Fears and Phobias," imagine that you came to the conclusion that when we are afraid, our bodies respond in many ways. To support your conclusion, you could cite lines 18–25 as examples from the text.

# Analyze Structure

**Text features** are design elements such as boldface type and headings that highlight the organization and important information in a text. You can use text features to get an idea of the topics in a text. They can also help you locate particular topics or ideas after reading. Text features include:

- A **heading** is a kind of title that identifies the topic of the content that follows it. Headings often appear at the beginning of a chapter or article.
- A **subheading** is a kind of title that usually indicates the beginning of a new topic or section within a chapter or article. A subheading helps you identify the main idea of the text that follows.
- A **sidebar** is additional information that is usually set in a box alongside or within an article.

Analyze text features by asking yourself these questions:

- What text features does the text include?
- Which features help me preview and locate main ideas in the text?
- How does information under a particular heading fit into the whole text? What important ideas does it contain?

# Analyzing the Text

 COMMON CORE   RI 1, RI 3, RI 5, RI 6, W 2, W 4

**Cite Text Evidence**   Support your responses with evidence from the text.

1. **Cause/Effect**  Events are often related by **cause and effect**: one event brings about the other. The event that happens first is the **cause**; the one that follows is the **effect**. Reread lines 18–38. Examine the text and identify examples of cause-and-effect relationships.

2. **Cite Evidence**  What causes phobias? Cite evidence from the text that explains where phobias come from.

3. **Draw Conclusions**  Review lines 132–162. What factors are important in helping people overcome phobias? Explain whether the author believes it is worthwhile to try to overcome phobias and why.

4. **Compare**  Explain how a fear is different from a phobia. Identify examples of each that the author presents.

5. **Interpret**  What additional information does the sidebar provide? How does it add to your understanding of the article?

6. **Analyze**  Use the headings in "Fears and Phobias" to examine the main ideas the author presents. In your own words, describe the way the author orders the information.

# PERFORMANCE TASK

**Writing Activity: Summary**  Write a summary of "Fears and Phobias." A **summary** is a brief retelling of a text in your own words. You should cover only the main ideas and most important details. Your summary should be no more than one-third the length of the original text.

- Review the article to identify the main ideas.

- Introduce the summary by writing a topic sentence that explains the main purpose of the article.
- Tell what a fear is, what a phobia is, and how they are different. Cite evidence from the text.
- Conclude your summary by telling why the article is useful or important.

# Critical Vocabulary

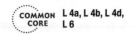 

**activate**     **trigger**     **turbulence**     **immaturity**

**Practice and Apply**  Answer each question and explain your response.

1. Which of the following is an example of **activate**? Why?
   unplugging a computer    pressing the power button on a computer

2. Which of the following is most likely to **trigger** an allergy? Why?
   getting stung by a bee    watching a movie about bees

3. Which of the following involves **turbulence**? Why?
   a canoe trip on a quiet lake    a canoe trip on a rushing, rocky river

4. Which of the following is an example of **immaturity**? Why?
   explaining why you are upset    crying when you don't get your way

## Vocabulary Strategy: Prefixes That Mean "Not"

A **prefix** is a word that appears at the beginning of a base word to form a new word. Many prefixes that mean "not" come from Latin, the language of ancient Rome. One example is the vocabulary word *immaturity* (*im* + *maturity*). To figure out the meaning of a word that contains a prefix and a base word, follow these steps.

- Think of the meaning of each word part separately.
- Use this information as well as context clues to define the word.

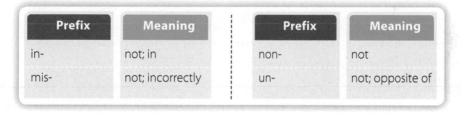

| Prefix | Meaning | | Prefix | Meaning |
|--------|---------|---|--------|---------|
| in- | not; in | | non- | not |
| mis- | not; incorrectly | | un- | not; opposite of |

**Practice and Apply**  Use the prefixes in the chart and context clues to help you determine a meaning for the boldface word in each sentence.

1. Not having Sunday hours at the library is **inconvenient** for people who work during the week.

2. The group agreed that their protest would be a **nonviolent** one.

3. Being late to the party was **unintentional;** we were stuck in traffic!

4. The careless reporter **misquoted** the mayor's remarks.

# Language Conventions:
# Subjective and Objective Pronouns

A **pronoun** is a word that takes the place of a noun or another pronoun. Personal pronouns take different forms, or cases, depending on how they are used in a sentence. A pronoun in the **subjective case** is one that is used as the subject of a sentence. A pronoun in the **objective case** is one that is used as an object of a verb or preposition. Here are some examples from "Fears and Phobias."

> **Subjective Case:** *It is programmed into the nervous system.*
> **Objective Case:** *Fear helps protect us.*

Pronouns can also be singular or plural in number. This chart shows the singular and plural forms of the subjective and objective case.

|          |               | Subjective | Objective    |
|----------|---------------|------------|--------------|
| Singular | First person  | I          | me           |
|          | Second person | you        | you          |
|          | Third person  | she, he, it | her, him, it |
| Plural   | First person  | we         | us           |
|          | Second person | you        | you          |
|          | Third person  | they       | them         |

Pronouns can be misused, especially in compound subjects and objects. Use a **subject pronoun** if the pronoun is part of a compound subject. Use an **object pronoun** if the pronoun is part of a compound object.

**Practice and Apply**  Choose the correct pronoun to complete each sentence.

1. Carlos took swimming lessons to help (him, it) overcome a fear of deep water.

2. When some people experience extreme fear, (you, they) may feel sick or dizzy.

3. I do not like small spaces. Being in an elevator makes (her, me) very anxious.

4. Danielle and Ramon explained how (he, they) use breathing exercises to help stay relaxed.

5. Leia and (I, me) are sometimes teased about our fears.

**Glenn Murphy** *is an expert in explaining science concepts for kids, teenagers, and adults. After receiving his Masters in Science Communication from London's Imperial College of Science, Technology and Medicine, Murphy managed the Explainer team at the Science Museum in London, England. This experience led to his first book,* Why Is Snot Green? *With the sequel,* How Loud Can You Burp?, *and several more books, Murphy continues to explain science topics with humor and energy.*

# In the Spotlight

*from* Stuff That Scares Your Pants Off!

Informational Text by Glenn Murphy

**SETTING A PURPOSE** As you read, focus on the science facts that explain why some people are afraid of speaking in public and how this fear may be overcome.

THE FEAR   Some of us are fine with the idea of standing in front of huge crowds of people. But others would happily bungee off a 200-foot bridge, or dive into a shoal of circling sharks, rather than experience the sheer terror of facing an audience. Shoved out onstage, or to the front of a class, people like this will quite literally lose their voice. The mouth may open, but the words won't come out. They just stand there gaping like helpless goldfish pulled out of water, their weak limbs quaking with fear, feeling like they want to run, hide, or cry. If that sounds like you, then you are one of the world's many, many sufferers of glossophobia—the fear of speaking (or trying to speak) in public.

10

# The Reality

Glossophobia is amazingly common—there are usually at least four or five kids in every grade who have it, and it's very common in adults too because you generally don't "grow out" of glossophobia. It takes help or practice to get over it. This is because it's basically a type of social phobia—a fear of being watched, judged, or sized up by other people (especially strangers, and especially large numbers of them).

20 So where does it come from, and what use is it? I mean, if fear of the dark, heights, and dangerous animals helped keep our ancestors from being **ambushed**, what good is a fear of speaking to people? Wouldn't being able to speak to big groups have helped those early humans to communicate? The ones who were best at it, you'd think, could become chiefs, kings, and emperors. If speaking is that useful, what is this fear trying to protect us from? Being booed and pelted with rotten vegetables if we do badly?

Well, the answer is—nothing, really. There's no real danger involved in speaking to people. But the action of standing 30 there and being watched can trigger a much older and more useful fear—the fear of being surrounded, threatened, and attacked by other people.

Throughout the animal world, and especially in primates (the group that includes humans, gorillas, and chimpanzees), staring at someone is a signal of fighting or **aggression**. Even when we chat with people we trust and like, we don't stare them down while we talk. Instead, we shift the focus of our eyes around the other person's face—from their eyes to their 40 mouth and nose and back again—and we glance away every so often during the conversation. (If you don't believe me, try it with a friend. Sit close to each other and just stare while you talk, without looking away, for one minute. You'll probably find you both start to feel really uncomfortable very quickly!) All of this helps to break up the eye contact, and reassures each person that the other is still friendly. Without it, a long burst of eye contact feels like the buildup to a fight.

Now multiply that one staring pair of eyes by thirty, and you have some idea of why standing up to speak in front of 50 a class can feel so unnerving. Multiply it by 500 or 1,000, and you see why it takes a lot of **confidence** to be onstage in a packed theater. Even though the audience is (probably)

**ambush**
(ăm´bŏŏsh) v. Some animals *ambush* their prey by hiding and then attacking as the prey comes near them.

**aggression**
(ə-grĕsh´ən) n. Angry, violent behavior or action is called *aggression*.

**confidence**
(kŏn´fĭ-dəns) n. A person who has *confidence* believes in his or her abilities or ideas.

friendly, the sensation is like being surrounded by an angry tribe, and all your brain wants to do is get you out of there. So that's what it prepares you to do. The "fight-or-flight" system kicks in, making your heart rate increase, your breathing tight and rapid, your muscles tense, and your guts feel queasy[1] (as blood is directed away from them). The whole time you're trying to speak or perform, your brain is saying,

60 "OK—any minute now we make a run for it, right? Get ready ... readyyy ... readyyyyyyyyyy ... "

For some people, this feels quite thrilling. But for glossophobics, it's absolutely terrifying.

But if you think about it, there really is nothing to be afraid of this time. Unlike the fear of water, heights, and the dark, there's no real danger present at all. Even if you speak or perform really badly, it's not like the audience is going to kill you—the worst response you'll get is silence, booing, or rotten fruit and veggies. None of these are pleasant, but none of them

70 can actually harm you either.

Happily, this also makes glossophobia a perfect example of a fear you can beat with simple practice. Since there's no real danger, it's much easier to work up from speaking to one, to two, to ten, to thirty people. Believe it or not, you can go from stage-phobic to star performer in no time!

## The Chances

The odds of being killed by a classroom or theater full of people just because you're speaking to or performing for them? Zero. Unless you're really, really bad ...

No, really—it's zero. Just kidding.

## The Lowdown

80 The fear of being "in the spotlight" is extremely common and, to those who suffer from it, extremely powerful. But it's also extremely easy to work through, given a bit of effort. Since there's no real danger involved, it's just a matter of convincing your brain that you don't need the "fight-or-flight" system to kick in when you're speaking or performing before people. How do you do that? Practice!

---

[1] **queasy** (kwē´zē): nauseated; sick to your stomach.

There are lots of ways of working through your fears and building your confidence before audiences. The most direct (and powerful) way is to join a school, church, or community speaking group, where you can be coached on how to give speeches. At first, you may practice alone or with one or two people. Then, as you get more confident, you can work up to larger and larger groups, until before you know it you're speaking to whole school assemblies, church congregations, or community groups! The best thing is that in many cases you get to talk about whatever you want, whether it's "Ten Ways to Make a Better World" or "My Love of Dinosaurs."

If that doesn't sound like any kind of fun, then you can get experience with speaking in front of audiences without speaking directly to them. In acting or debating clubs, you can practice talking to small groups of people while being watched by an audience, but without having to look straight at them. Plus the act of concentrating on your lines or on the argument will help **distract** you from the many watching eyes. When you get really good at it, you might even forget the audience is there!

**distract**
(dĭ-străkt´) v. To *distract* is to pull attention away from something or someone.

And if you really can't imagine speaking in front of crowds at all, then you can work up to it (or at the very least gain a lot more confidence) by trying other types of performance instead. Ever wanted to dance? How about play guitar, or sing? Learning a performing art of any kind will help you get over your fears of an audience if you eventually take it to the stage.

So if you're one of the world's many perform-o-phobes, don't worry—the "treatment" for it may turn out to be the most fun you've ever had. The prescription looks like this: take a handful of guitar, acting, or dance lessons, rock a roomful of people with your mad new skills, and call me in the morning!

**COLLABORATIVE DISCUSSION** With a partner, discuss the facts and ideas that explain glossophobia and why it is a fear that people must work at overcoming.

# Determine Central Idea

In informational text, the **central idea,** or **main idea,** is the most important idea that an author of a text wants you to know about the topic. You can look for the central idea of the entire text and you can look for the central idea in each paragraph.

The **topic sentence** of a paragraph states the paragraph's central idea. In informational text, the topic sentence is often the first sentence in a paragraph. However, it may appear anywhere in the paragraph. Sometimes the central idea is not directly stated but implied, or suggested by details. To identify an **implied** central idea, you need to examine the details to determine what the writer intends.

To find the central idea, follow these steps:
- Identify the specific topic of each paragraph or section.
- Examine all the details the author includes.

Ask what idea or message the details convey about the topic.

| Stated Central Idea | Implied Central Idea |
|---|---|
| Lines 87–97: Central idea at the beginning of a paragraph<br>Lines 13–19: Central idea at the end of a paragraph | Lines 48–61: Implied central idea<br>People who have glossophobia when speaking in public experience increased heart rate, rapid breathing, and queasiness. |

# Determine Details

**Supporting details** are words, phrases, or sentences that tell more about the central idea. Facts, opinions, examples, statistics, and anecdotes are all supporting details that writers may use depending on the type of writing.
- A **fact** is a statement that can be proved.
- An **opinion** is a statement that expresses a person's beliefs, feelings, or thoughts. An opinion cannot be proved.
- An **example** is a specific instance that helps to explain an idea, such as a personal story or experience.
- A **statistic** is a fact that is expressed in numbers.
- An **anecdote** is a short account of an interesting incident.

Reread lines 87–97. Ask yourself these questions:
- What is the central idea of this paragraph?
- What details, such as facts and examples, support the main idea?

# Analyzing the Text

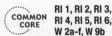 COMMON CORE RI 1, RI 2, RI 3, RI 4, RI 5, RI 6, W 2a-f, W 9b

**Cite Text Evidence**   Support your responses with evidence from the text.

1. **Interpret**   Reread lines 1–12. What words and phrases does the author use to create a vivid image of glossophobia? Explain why this description is important.

2. **Infer**   What is the central idea of lines 20–33 in "In the Spotlight"? Explain why this is an important idea in the article.

3. **Draw Conclusions**   Reread lines 34–47. Explain why the experiment the author proposes is valuable to the reader.

4. **Analyze**   The author states that glossophobia is ". . . extremely easy to work through, given a bit of effort" (lines 80–82). What examples support this idea? List one fact and one opinion about this idea.

5. **Summarize**   What is the central idea of "In the Spotlight"? Explain how each section of the article supports this central idea.

6. **Evaluate**   The author uses an informal, humorous writing style. What examples in the text show this style? Tell why the author probably used this style here and how well you think it works.

## PERFORMANCE TASK

 my WriteSmart

**Writing Activity: Letter**   Imagine that you are an advice columnist. Answer a letter from a reader who would like advice on how to cure glossophobia.

- Review "In the Spotlight." Identify the main ideas about curing glossophobia.

- Decide which suggestions you will advise the reader to use. Cite explicit evidence from "In the Spotlight" to support your suggestions.
- Create an alias, or a fake name, for the reader you are responding to.
- Read your letter aloud to a partner to see if it is clear and helpful.

# Critical Vocabulary

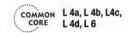 

**ambush**          **aggression**          **confidence**          **distract**

**Practice and Apply**  Answer each question and explain your response.

1. Which situation is an example of an **ambush**?
   **a.** a person who is hiding suddenly jumps out
   **b.** a dog runs out from a yard to greet someone walking by

2. Which situation shows **aggression**?
   **a.** a friend gives you a pat on the back
   **b.** a dog growls at someone walking by

3. Which group shows **confidence**?
   **a.** a debate team that is eager to begin a contest
   **b.** a marching band that decides not to be in a parade

4. Which of these would be a way to **distract** someone?
   **a.** waiting quietly while the person talks to someone else
   **b.** waving at a person who is giving a speech

## Vocabulary Strategy: Suffixes That Form Nouns

A **suffix** is a word part that appears at the end of a root or base word to form a new word. Some Latin suffixes, such as -*ance*, -*ence*, and -*ant*, can be added to verbs to form nouns. If you can recognize the verb that a suffix is attached to, you can often figure out the meaning of the noun formed from it.

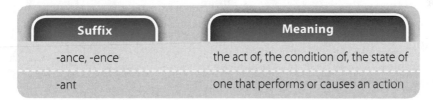

| Suffix | Meaning |
|---|---|
| -ance, -ence | the act of, the condition of, the state of |
| -ant | one that performs or causes an action |

For example, -*ence* is added to *confide* to make *confidence*. One meaning of *confide* is "to tell in secret." *Confidence* means "trust or the act of confiding."

**Practice and Apply**  Identify the verb in each underlined word. Use context clues to define the noun. Use a dictionary to confirm your definitions.

1. The <u>performance</u> was sold out in only one hour.

2. We celebrated my uncle's <u>emergence</u> as a great writer.

3. Mrs. Lowenstein is the attorney for the <u>defendant</u> in the trial.

4. She won her case because an <u>informant</u> testified at the trial.

# Language Conventions: Possessive Pronouns

**Pronouns** are words that take the place of nouns or other pronouns. Personal pronouns change form to show how they function in a sentence. A **possessive pronoun** shows ownership. Here are some examples from "In the Spotlight":

> **Instead, we shift the focus of <u>our</u> eyes around the other person's face—from <u>their</u> eyes to <u>their</u> mouth and nose and back again . . .**

In this sentence, both *our* and *their* are examples of possessive pronouns. Both are used to indicate ownership: *our* refers to the subjective pronoun *we*, and *their* refers to the "other person."

The chart shows possessive pronouns in either singular (one person) or plural (more than one person) form.

| | | Use Before Nouns | Use in Place of Nouns |
|---|---|---|---|
| | **Singular** | | |
| | **First person** | my | mine |
| | **Second person** | your | yours |
| | **Third person** | her, his, its | hers, his, its |
| | **Plural** | | |
| | **First person** | our | ours |
| | **Second person** | your | yours |
| | **Third person** | their | theirs |

**Practice and Apply**  Complete the sentences with the correct possessive pronoun. Remember that pronouns must agree with the noun they refer to in number, gender, and person.

1. The team felt confident; they felt _____ chances of winning were high.

2. Jenna was worried; _____ fear of heights made riding the roller coaster scary for her.

3. Kevin and I worked together on that project. That project is _____.

4. I speak next week. I need to practice _____ speech.

5. The dog pressed _____ face against the window.

**Background**  *The study and science of fear involves the work of many scientists over many years. These scientists have explored exactly how the body deals with fear as a nervous impulse. They have conducted research and used computer-generated brain imaging to study activity in the brain. Their work has revealed different brain structures, paths, and cells that help to explain fear and how the whole body responds to the fear alarm.*

## MEDIA ANALYSIS

# Wired for Fear

Online Science Exhibit by The California Science Center

**SETTING A PURPOSE**  "Fear is a full-body experience." This is how the website Goosebumps! The Science of Fear introduces its topic "Fear and the Brain." This website includes a collection of videos, articles, and images that covers several aspects of how the body, especially the brain, processes sensory information (what we see, hear, feel, smell, touch) and alerts us to what might be harmful to us.

The section of the website titled "Wired for Fear" provides information on the specific areas and cells of the brain that activate our responses to scary situations. This web page includes a video that you can access to watch an animated version of how the brain processes fear reactions. As you watch the video, note how these pathways connect to the brain's threat center and show why fear can be a good thing. Write down any questions you have during viewing.

**Format:** Online science exhibit
**Running Time:** 4:05

**AS YOU VIEW**  As you view the animated video, consider how the information is presented. Notice how the video introduces and explains new terms and ideas using text, sound, and visuals.

Consider how the use of these three elements helps you understand the scientific terms and ideas presented. As needed, pause the video to make notes about what impresses you or about ideas you might want to talk about later. Replay or rewind so that you can clarify anything you do not understand.

**COLLABORATIVE DISCUSSION**  With a small group, discuss how the brain pathways of our body's fear response work. What new ideas or information did you learn about fear and the brain from the video? Cite specific terms and segments from the video and tell what you learned from them.

# Interpret Information

Like other media, the video "Wired for Fear" was created for a specific purpose. The **purpose,** or intent, of any video or form of media is usually to inform, entertain, persuade, or express the feelings or thoughts of the creator. In meeting the purpose, the creator uses words as well as visual and sound elements to convey information.

**Visual elements** that can be used in animated videos include:

 **Stills** — images that are motionless, such as illustrations or photographs. In "Wired for Fear," a still of an illustration of the brain is used to point out where the amygdala is located.

 **Animation** — the process of creating images that appear to move and seem alive. Animation can be created through drawings, computer graphics, or photographs. For example, the hiking scenes in "Wired for Fear" are an animation cycle of drawings.

Visual elements can help viewers understand **technical terms,** which are the words and phrases used in a particular profession or field of study. For example, by showing the amygdala as a kind of master computer that processes information, the animated model in "Wired for Fear" helps viewers better understand the amygdala and what it does. Using light to highlight brain pathways is another way that the video's visuals help to explain the content in a memorable way.

**Sound elements** include what you hear in a video:

 **Music** — sounds created by singing, playing instruments, or using computer-generated tones. Music is often included in videos to create a mood.

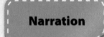 **Narration** — the words as well as the expression and quality of voice used by the narrator. In "Wired for Fear," the narrator uses emphasis and expression to connect the words to the visuals being shown.

To interpret visual and sound elements in a video, ask questions such as the following:

- Does the video use stills or animation? What purpose do they serve? How do they aid my understanding of the topic?
- How does the music match the video's topic or content? How does the music create or add to a mood?
- What does the narration add to the video?

# Analyzing the Media

COMMON CORE RI 1, RI 2, RI 3, RI 4, RI 5, RI 6, RI 7, W 6, SL 2, SL 5

**Cite Text Evidence** Support your responses with evidence from the media.

1. **Summarize** What situation does the hiker face in "Wired for Fear"? Describe how the video explains what the hiker experiences.

2. **Cause/Effect** Review the sequence that uses the animated model. What are some ways our bodies respond when the amygdala senses danger? What parts of the brain activate these responses?

3. **Infer** Explain the title "Wired for Fear." Why does the video use flashing lights and graphics that show movement in the animated model of how the brain processes potential danger?

4. **Integrate** Describe the music and narration used in the video. In what ways do they support the purpose of the video?

5. **Critique** Think about the purpose of this video. Consider the techniques that are used to support the information presented. Do you think "Wired for Fear" is an effective informational video? Why or why not?

## PERFORMANCE TASK

**Media Activity: Podcast** Create an audio recording for a podcast movie review of the video "Wired for Fear." You can work alone or with a partner.

- Focus on a few elements of the video that particularly impressed you. Include both positive and negative impressions that you think are relevant. Write notes about these impressions.

- Explain how each element you have chosen clarifies the topic, using examples from the video. Present ideas for additional information that could be included in this type of video. Write notes about these elements and examples.

- Use your notes to create an outline or draft of your podcast review.

- Create the recording of your review alone or with a partner, using a conversational approach. Share your review with a larger group.

# Write a Short Story

Like Vince in "The Ravine" and Bailey in "Fine?," many people face fear in their everyday lives. Look back at these short stories and use them as a model for writing your own short story in which a main character experiences a personal fear.

**COMMON CORE**

**W 3a–e** Write narratives.
**W 4** Produce clear and coherent writing.
**W 5** Strengthen writing as needed.

## A successful short story

- contains a plot
- establishes and resolves a conflict
- introduces and develops characters and a setting
- uses dialogue and descriptive details
- provides an exciting climax that flows from the story events and reflects a theme, or message, about life

## PLAN

*my* **Notebook**

Use the annotation tools in your eBook to record key details you might want to include. Save each detail to your notebook.

**Establish Story Elements** A short story is a narrative that describes experiences and events that you imagine but that seem realistic. In order to write your story, plan your characters and events by following these steps.

- First, think about a character in one of the short stories in this collection. Write down a description of that character and the events that happened to the character. How did the story depict the character facing a fear and resolving it?

- Next, brainstorm your own main character. What does your main character look like? How does the character act, speak, and relate to other characters? What is the character's fear?

- Determine the setting—the time and place where the story occurs—and brainstorm ideas for events that will take place to cause your character to confront his or her fear.

- Finally, determine the conflict—the problem or struggle that triggers the fear the main character must face. How does the main character face the fear and resolve the conflict? Write your ideas in short sentences, such as, "The boy is afraid of water but wants to go canoeing with his friends."

**ACADEMIC VOCABULARY**

As you plan, write, and review your draft, try to use the academic vocabulary words.

*evident*
*factor*
*indicate*
*similar*
*specific*

**Develop the Plot** Fill out a plot diagram to plan your story.

- In the exposition, introduce the main character, setting, and conflict.
- In the rising action, introduce obstacles that the character must overcome. Think about how these obstacles help build suspense and cause the character to face his or her fear.
- At the climax, describe the most important or exciting event.
- In the falling action, show how the conflict is resolved and convey the lesson the character learns.

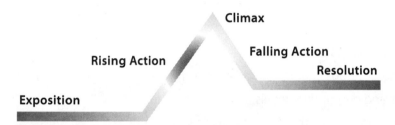

**Decide on a Point of View** Think about the point of view you want to use in your narrative. In first-person point of view, the narrator is a character in the story and uses first-person pronouns, such as *I, me,* and *we.* In third-person point of view, used in "The Ravine," the narrator is not a character. The narration is told using pronouns such as *he, she, it,* and *they.*

**Consider Your Purpose and Audience** Who will read or listen to your short story? What are their ages and gender? What effect do you want the story to have on readers? Do you want to entertain them with humor or scare them with mystery or tragedy? Keep your audience in mind as you prepare to write.

**PRODUCE**

*my* **WriteSmart**

Write your rough draft in *my*WriteSmart. Focus on getting your ideas down, rather than perfecting your choice of language.

**Write Your Short Story** Review your plot diagram as you begin your draft.

- Introduce the main character, setting, and conflict. Engage your audience with action and dialogue that sets up the conflict.
- Establish your point of view quickly, making it clear who is telling the story.
- Use your plot diagram to create the sequence of events. Use transitions such as *later that day* or *the following week* to keep the action moving.

- Use descriptive words and phrases and sensory language to create a vivid picture and build suspense.
- Make sure the story has an exciting climax.
- Tell how the conflict is resolved. Clearly show how the main character faces his fear, how this makes him feel, and how other characters respond.
- Leave the audience with a message to reflect on—a life lesson, for example.

## REVISE

*my*WriteSmart

Have your partner or a group of peers review your draft in *my*WriteSmart. Ask your reviewers to note any dialogue that doesn't sound real.

**Review Your Draft** Use the chart on the next page to evaluate your draft. Work with a partner to determine if you have effectively told your story to your audience. Consider the following:

- Make sure the beginning grabs the reader's attention.
- Examine the development of your characters. Are they believable? Do their actions and speech seem authentic?
- Add sensory details to more fully describe the story's time and place.
- Check that the conflict is clear and that the plot builds to an exciting climax.
- Examine the pacing to make sure the action moves in a smooth sequence of events. Delete any unnecessary events or reorganize events in a way that makes sense.
- Replace pronouns that change the story's point of view.
- Add details to show how the conflict was resolved. Make sure the resolution makes sense and ends in a satisfying way.
- Check that the resolution contains a message or life lesson such as the importance of overcoming one's fears.

## PRESENT

**Create a Finished Copy** Finalize your short story and choose a way to share it with your audience. Consider these options:

- Present your short story in an author's reading to the class.
- Submit your story to the school literary magazine or other online or print student literary publications.

| | Ideas and Evidence | Organization | Language |
|---|---|---|---|
| **ADVANCED** | • Conflict is skillfully established, developed, and resolved.<br>• Setting is skillfully established and developed and helps shape the conflict.<br>• Characters are compelling and believable.<br>• Dialogue and description are used effectively. | • Event sequence is smooth, is well structured, and creates suspense.<br>• The plot builds to a strong, satisfying conclusion.<br>• Pacing is clear and effective.<br>• The conclusion clearly reflects a theme, or message, about life. | • The story has a consistent and effective point of view.<br>• Words and phrases are precise and vivid. Sensory language reveals the setting and characters.<br>• Spelling, capitalization, and punctuation are correct.<br>• Grammar and usage are correct. |
| **COMPETENT** | • Conflict is introduced, developed, and resolved.<br>• Setting is established but could be more developed to shape the characters and conflict.<br>• Characters have some believable traits but may need development.<br>• Dialogue and description could be more interesting. | • Event sequence is generally well structured but includes some extraneous events.<br>• The plot builds to a conclusion.<br>• Pacing is somewhat clear.<br>• The conclusion could more clearly reflect a theme, or message, about life. | • The story has a consistent point of view.<br>• Descriptive words and phrases are used but could be more vivid and revealing of characters.<br>• Some spelling, capitalization, and punctuation errors occur.<br>• Some grammatical and usage errors are repeated in the story. |
| **LIMITED** | • Conflict is introduced but not developed or resolved.<br>• Setting is unclear and does not affect the characters or conflict.<br>• Characters are somewhat clear but undeveloped.<br>• Dialogue and description are insufficient or uninteresting. | • Events are not well structured, are too numerous, or distract from the plot.<br>• The plot is confusing and the conclusion is unsatisfying.<br>• Pacing is distracting or choppy.<br>• The conclusion does not reflect a theme, or message, about life. | • The story's point of view is inconsistent.<br>• Precise words and phrases and sensory language are mostly lacking.<br>• Spelling, capitalization, and punctuation are often incorrect but do not make reading the story difficult.<br>• Grammar and usage are incorrect in many places, but the writer's ideas are still clear. |
| **EMERGING** | • Conflict is not identifiable.<br>• Setting is not described.<br>• Characters are unclear and underdeveloped.<br>• Dialogue and descriptions are not included. | • Event sequence is not evident.<br>• There is no clear conclusion to the story.<br>• There is no evidence of pacing.<br>• The conclusion is missing. | • The story's point of view is never clearly established.<br>• Precise language and sensory words are lacking.<br>• Spelling, capitalization, and punctuation are incorrect throughout, making reading difficult.<br>• Many grammatical and usage errors change the meaning of the writer's ideas. |

COLLECTION 1
PERFORMANCE TASK B

Interactive Lessons
If you need help . . .
• **Writing Informative Texts**
• **Using Textual Evidence**

# Write an Expository Essay

In "Fears and Phobias" and other lessons in this collection, you learned about fear and the important role it plays in our lives. In the following activity, you will choose a fear and write an expository essay about it, using the texts you have read in this collection and adding your own research.

## A successful expository essay

- provides an introduction that catches the reader's attention and clearly states the topic
- logically organizes main ideas and supporting evidence
- includes evidence such as facts, definitions, examples, and quotations
- uses appropriate transitions to connect ideas
- provides a conclusion that supports the topic

COMMON CORE

**W 2a–e** Write informative texts.
**W 4** Produce clear and coherent writing.
**W 5** Strengthen writing as needed.
**W 8** Gather relevant and credible information from multiple print and digital sources while avoiding plagiarism and providing basic bibliographic information.

## PLAN

*my* Notebook

Use the annotation tools in your eBook to find evidence to support your ideas. Save each piece of evidence to your notebook.

**Determine Your Topic** Review the selections in the collection. Make a list of the different types of fears you read about. Choose the fear that you want to learn more about.

**Gather Information** Look for information about the type of fear you are investigating. Jot down important facts, examples, and definitions, including

- what causes this type of fear
- what happens to our bodies and emotions in response to this fear
- what methods can be used to overcome this fear

**Do Research** Use print and digital sources to find additional definitions, information, and quotations from experts.

- Search for unique or little-known facts. Make sure facts are credible. If possible, back up facts with research or endorsements from experts.

**ACADEMIC VOCABULARY**

As you write about fear, be sure to use the academic vocabulary words.

*evident*
*factor*
*indicate*
*similar*
*specific*

- Cite real-life examples of people living with this fear and explain how they overcame it.

- Explore and provide links to websites that can be used as resources for understanding this fear.

- Identify any visuals, such as pictures or graphs, that illustrate your ideas.

**Organize Your Ideas** Think about how you will organize your essay. Create an outline showing the information you will present in each paragraph. Organize your ideas in a logical sequence, making sure each idea follows from the previous idea and leads into the next idea.

> **I.** Use Roman numerals for main topics.
>     A. Indent and use capital letters for subtopics.
>         1. Indent and use numbers for supporting facts and details.
>         2. Indent and use numbers for supporting facts and details.
> **II.** Use Roman numerals for main topics.
>     B. Indent and use capital letters for subtopics.
>         1. Indent and use numbers for supporting facts and details.

**Consider Your Purpose and Audience** Think about who will read or listen to your essay and what you want them to understand. Keep this in mind as you prepare to write.

**PRODUCE**

**Write Your Essay** Review your notes and your outline as you begin your draft.

- Begin with an attention-grabbing introduction that defines your topic. Include an unusual comment, fact, quote, or personal anecdote. Be sure your topic is well defined so readers will understand what it is.

- Develop your main idea with supporting facts, details, examples, and quotations from experts. Group supporting information and ideas into paragraphs.

- Use transitions such as *in addition to* and *also* to connect ideas.

- Include website links and multimedia to add depth to your essay.

*my* **WriteSmart**

Write your rough draft in *my*WriteSmart. Focus on getting your ideas down, rather than perfecting your choice of language.

- In your conclusion, restate your main idea and summarize supporting details and facts to leave the reader with a lasting impression.

**Prepare Visuals**  Add charts, graphs, photos, or statistical data to your essay. These can be included in a sidebar to help clarify and further explain your ideas.

## REVISE

*my*WriteSmart

Have your partner or a group of peers review your draft in *my*WriteSmart. Ask your reviewers to note any details that do not support your ideas.

**Review Your Draft**  Use the chart on the next page to evaluate your draft. Work with a partner to determine if you have explained your topic clearly and if the information you presented supports your main ideas.  Consider the following:

- Does the introduction grab the reader's attention?
- Are the main idea and supporting evidence clearly defined?
- Does each paragraph have one distinct, main point? Is each point supported with facts, details, examples, or quotations from experts?
- Are facts, details, examples, and quotations accurate?
- Are ideas organized in a logical sequence? Do transitions help the reader follow along?
- Does the conclusion support the information presented?

## PRESENT

**Create a Finished Copy**  Finalize your essay and choose a way to share it with your audience. Consider these options:

- Present your essay as a speech to the class.
- Post your essay as a blog on a personal or school website.
- Record your essay as a news report and share it on a school website.

# COLLECTION 1  TASK B
## EXPOSITORY ESSAY

| | Ideas and Evidence | Organization | Language |
|---|---|---|---|
| **ADVANCED** | • The introduction is appealing, is informative, and catches the reader's attention; the topic is clearly identified.<br>• The topic is well developed with clear main ideas supported by facts, details, definitions, and examples from reliable sources.<br>• The conclusion effectively summarizes the information presented. | • The organization is effective and logical throughout the essay.<br>• Transitions logically connect related ideas. | • A consistent, formal writing style is used throughout.<br>• Language is strong and precise.<br>• Sentences vary in pattern and structure.<br>• Spelling, capitalization, and punctuation are correct.<br>• Grammar, usage, and mechanics are correct. |
| **COMPETENT** | • The introduction could be more appealing and engaging; the topic is clearly identified.<br>• One or two important points could use more support, but most main ideas are well supported by facts, details, definitions, and examples from reliable sources.<br>• The conclusion summarizes the information presented. | • The organization of main ideas and details is confusing in a few places.<br>• A few more transitions are needed to connect related ideas. | • The writing style is inconsistent in a few places.<br>• Language is too vague or general in some places.<br>• Sentences vary somewhat in pattern and structure.<br>• Some spelling, capitalization, and punctuation mistakes occur.<br>• Some grammar and usage errors are repeated. |
| **LIMITED** | • The introduction is only partly informative; the topic is unclear.<br>• Most important points could use more support from relevant facts, details, definitions, and examples from reliable sources.<br>• The conclusion is unclear or only partially summarizes the information presented. | • The organization of main ideas and details is logical in some places, but it often doesn't follow a pattern.<br>• More transitions are needed throughout to connect related ideas. | • The writing style becomes informal in many places.<br>• Language is too general or vague in many places.<br>• Sentence pattern and structure hardly vary; some fragments or run-on sentences occur.<br>• Spelling, capitalization, and punctuation are often incorrect but do not make reading difficult.<br>• Grammar and usage are often incorrect, but the writer's ideas are still clear. |
| **EMERGING** | • The introduction is missing or confusing.<br>• Supporting facts, details, definitions, or examples are unreliable or missing.<br>• The conclusion is missing. | • The organization is not logical; main ideas and details are presented randomly.<br>• No transitions are used, making the essay difficult to understand. | • The style is inappropriate for the essay.<br>• Language is too general to convey the information.<br>• Sentence structure is repetitive and monotonous; fragments and run-on sentences make the essay hard to follow.<br>• Spelling, capitalization, and punctuation are incorrect and distracting throughout.<br>• Many grammatical and usage errors change the meaning of the writer's ideas. |

©Doug Norman/Alamy

# Animal Intelligence

> **"** Each species, however inconspicuous and humble, . . . is a masterpiece. **"**
>
> —Edward O. Wilson

# Animal Intelligence

In this collection, you will explore various perspectives on the intelligence of animals.

COLLECTION

## PERFORMANCE TASK Preview

After reading this collection, you will have the opportunity to complete two performance tasks:

• In one, you will write a literary analysis in which you analyze an animal as the narrator or main character of a story.

• In the second, you will write an expository essay in which you explore how animals show intelligence.

## ACADEMIC VOCABULARY

Study the words and their definitions in the chart below. You will use these words as you discuss and write about the texts in this collection.

| Word | Definition | Related Forms |
|---|---|---|
| **benefit** (běn´ə-fĭt) *n.* | something that provides help or improves something else | beneficial |
| **distinct** (dĭ-stĭngkt´) *adj.* | easy to tell apart from others; not alike | distinctly, distinctness, distinctive, distinction |
| **environment** (ĕn-vī´rən-mənt) *n.* | surroundings; the conditions that surround someone or something | environmental, environmentalism |
| **illustrate** (ĭl´ə-strāt´) *v.* | to show, or clarify, by examples or comparing | illustratable, illustrator, illustration, illustrative, illustrational, illustratively |
| **respond** (rĭ-spŏnd´) *v.* | to make a reply; answer | responder, response |

**P. G. Wodehouse** (1881–1975) *was born in England. Although Wodehouse always wanted to be a writer, as a young man he was forced to work at a London bank to make a living. This career did not last long. After only two years, Wodehouse left the bank and began writing full time. In 1904, Wodehouse left England for New York. There, Wodehouse began writing plays and musicals in addition to novels and short stories. Wodehouse later added many movie screenplays to his long list of writing accomplishments.*

# The Mixer

Short Story by P. G. Wodehouse

**SETTING A PURPOSE** As you read, pay attention to how a dog's actions affect his master's plans. Write down any questions you have while reading.

Looking back, I always consider that my career as a dog proper really started when I was bought for the sum of half a crown[1] by the Shy Man. That event marked the end of my puppyhood. The knowledge that I was worth actual cash to somebody filled me with a sense of new responsibilities. It sobered me. Besides, it was only after that half-crown changed hands that I went out into the great world; and, however interesting life may be in an East End public-house,[2] it is only when you go out into the world that you really broaden your

10    mind and begin to see things.

---

[1] **half a crown:** another name for a *half-crown*, a British coin that is no longer in use; was worth two shillings and sixpence, or about 30 pennies (pence).

[2] **public-house:** a place, such as a bar, that is allowed to sell alcoholic beverages.

Within its limitations, my life had been singularly full and vivid. I was born, as I say, in a public-house in the East End, and however lacking a public-house may be in refinement and the true culture, it certainly provides plenty of excitement. Before I was six weeks old, I had upset three policemen by getting between their legs when they came round to the sidedoor, thinking they had heard suspicious noises; and I can still recall the interesting sensation of being chased seventeen times round the yard with a broom-handle

20  after a well-planned and completely successful raid on the larder. These and other happenings of a like nature soothed for the moment but could not cure the restlessness which has always been so marked a trait in my character. I have always been restless, unable to settle down in one place and anxious to get on to the next thing. This may be due to a gipsy[3] strain in my ancestry—one of my uncles traveled with a circus—or it may be the Artistic Temperament,[4] acquired from a grandfather who, before dying of a **surfeit** of paste in the property-room of the Bristol Coliseum, which he was

30  visiting in the course of a professional tour, had an established reputation on the music-hall stage as one of Professor Pond's Performing Poodles.

I owe the fullness and variety of my life to this restlessness of mine, for I have repeatedly left comfortable homes in order to follow some perfect stranger who looked as if he were on his way to somewhere interesting. Sometimes I think I must have cat blood in me.

The Shy Man came into our yard one afternoon in April, while I was sleeping with Mother in the sun on an old sweater

40  which we had borrowed from Fred, one of the barmen. I heard Mother growl, but I didn't take any notice. Mother is what they call a good watch-dog, and she growls at everybody except Master. At first when she used to do it, I would get up and bark my head off, but not now. Life's too short to bark at everybody who comes into our yard. It is behind the public-house, and they keep empty bottles and things there, so people are always coming and going.

**surfeit**
(sûr´fĭt) *n.* A *surfeit* is an excessive amount of something, such as food or drink.

---

[3] **gipsy** (jĭp´sē): also *gypsy* or *Gypsy*; a member of a race of people who travel from place to place, rather than living in one place.

[4] **Artistic Temperament:** a manner of thinking or acting said to be common among artists (painters, musicians, writers, actors); often used to explain traits such as sensitivity, odd or unusual behavior, or nervousness.

Besides, I was tired. I had had a very busy morning, helping the men bring in a lot of cases of beer and running into the saloon to talk to Fred and generally looking after things. So I was just dozing off again when I heard a voice say, "Well, he's ugly enough." Then I knew that they were talking about me.

I have never disguised it from myself, and nobody has ever disguised it from me, that I am not a handsome dog. Even Mother never thought me beautiful. She was no Gladys Cooper herself, but she never hesitated to **criticize** my appearance. In fact, I have yet to meet anyone who did. The first thing strangers say about me is "What an ugly dog!"

I don't know what I am. I have a bull-dog kind of a face, but the rest of me is terrier. I have a long tail which sticks straight up in the air. My hair is wiry. My eyes are brown. I am jet black with a white chest. I once overheard Fred saying that I was a Gorgonzola cheese-hound,[5] and I have generally found Fred reliable in his statements.

When I found that I was under discussion, I opened my eyes. Master was standing there, looking down at me, and by his side the man who had just said I was ugly enough. The man was a thin man, about the age of a barman and smaller than a policeman. He had patched brown shoes and black trousers.

"But he's got a sweet nature," said Master.

This was true, luckily for me. Mother always said, "A dog without influence or private means, if he is to make his way in the world, must have either good looks or **amiability**." But, according to her, I overdid it. "A dog," she used to say, "can have a good heart without chumming with every Tom, Dick, and Harry he meets. Your behavior is sometimes quite undog-like." Mother prided herself on being a one-man dog. She kept herself to herself, and wouldn't kiss anybody except Master—not even Fred.

Now, I'm a mixer. I can't help it. It's my nature. I like men. I like the taste of their boots, the smell of their legs, and the sound of their voices. It may be weak of me, but a man has only to speak to me, and a sort of thrill goes right down my spine and sets my tail wagging.

**criticize**
(krĭt´ĭ-sīz´) *v.* To *criticize* is to tell someone what you think is wrong with them.

**amiable**
(ā´mē-ə-bəl) *n.* To be *amiable* is to be good-natured and friendly.

---

[5] **Gorgonzola cheese-hound:** Gorgonzola is a bumpy, crumbly cheese with many swirls of blue mold in it; based on this phrase, the dog probably has a bumpy, sort of wrinkly face or body.

I wagged it now. The man looked at me rather distantly. He didn't pat me. I suspected—what I afterwards found to be the case—that he was shy, so I jumped up at him to put him at his ease. Mother growled again. I felt that she did not approve.

"Why, he's took quite a fancy to you already," said Master.

The man didn't say a word. He seemed to be brooding on something. He was one of those silent men. He reminded me of Joe, the old dog down the street at the grocer's shop, who lies at the door all day, blinking and not speaking to anybody.

Master began to talk about me. It surprised me, the way he praised me. I hadn't a suspicion he admired me so much. From what he said you would have thought I had won prizes and ribbons at the Crystal Palace. But the man didn't seem to be impressed. He kept on saying nothing.

When Master had finished telling him what a wonderful dog I was till I blushed, the man spoke.

"Less of it," he said. "Half a crown is my bid, and if he was an angel from on high you couldn't get another ha' penny out of me. What about it?"

A thrill went down my spine and out at my tail, for of course I saw now what was happening. The man wanted to buy me and take me away. I looked at Master hopefully.

"He's more like a son to me than a dog," said Master, sort of wistful.

"It's his face that makes you feel that way," said the man, unsympathetically. "If you had a son that's just how he would look. Half a crown is my offer, and I'm in a hurry."

"All right," said Master, with a sigh, "though it's giving him away, a valuable dog like that. Where's your half-crown?"

The man got a bit of rope and tied it round my neck.

I could hear Mother barking advice and telling me to be a credit to the family, but I was too excited to listen.

"Good-bye, Mother," I said. "Good-bye, Master. Good-bye, Fred. Good-bye, everybody. I'm off to see life. The Shy Man has bought me for half a crown. Wow!"

I kept running round in circles and shouting, till the man gave me a kick and told me to stop it.

So I did.

I don't know where we went, but it was a long way. I had never been off our street before in my life and didn't know the whole world was half as big as that. We walked on and on, and the man jerking at my rope whenever I wanted to stop and

look at anything. He wouldn't even let me pass the time of the
130 day with dogs we met.

When we had gone about a hundred miles and were just
going to turn in at a dark doorway, a policeman suddenly
stopped the man. I could feel by the way the man pulled at my
rope and tried to hurry on that he didn't want to speak to the
policeman. The more I saw of the man, the more I saw how
shy he was.

> ❝He's more like a son
> to me than a dog," said
> Master, sort of wistful.❞

"Hi!" said the policeman, and we had to stop.

"I've got a message for you, old pal," said the policeman.
"It's from the Board of Health. They told me to tell you you
140 needed a change of air. See?"

"All right!" said the man.

"And take it as soon as you like. Else you'll find you'll get it
given you. See?"

I looked at the man with a good deal of respect. He was
evidently someone very important, if they worried so about
his health.

"I'm going down to the country tonight," said the man.

The policeman seemed pleased.

"That's a bit of luck for the country," he said. "Don't go
150 changing your mind."

And we walked on, and went in at the dark doorway, and
climbed about a million stairs, and went into a room that
smelt of rats. The man sat down and swore a little, and I sat
and looked at him.

Presently I couldn't keep it in any longer.

"Do we live here?" I said. "Is it true we're going to the
country? Wasn't that policeman a good sort? Don't you like
policemen? I knew lots of policemen at the public-house. Are

there any other dogs here? What is there for dinner? What's in that cupboard? When are you going to take me out for another run? May I go out and see if I can find a cat?"

"Stop that yelping," he said.

"When we go to the country, where shall we live? Are you going to be a caretaker at a house? Fred's father is a caretaker at a big house in Kent. I've heard Fred talk about it. You didn't meet Fred when you came to the public-house, did you? You would like Fred. I like Fred. Mother likes Fred. We all like Fred."

I was going on to tell him a lot more about Fred, who had always been one of my warmest friends, when he suddenly got hold of a stick and **walloped** me with it.

"You keep quiet when you're told," he said.

He really was the shyest man I had ever met. It seemed to hurt him to be spoken to. However, he was the boss, and I had to humor him, so I didn't say any more.

We went down to the country that night, just as the man had told the policeman we would. I was all worked up, for I had heard so much about the country from Fred that I had always wanted to go there. Fred used to go off on a motor-bicycle sometimes to spend the night with his father in Kent, and once he brought back a squirrel with him, which I thought was for me to eat, but Mother said no. "The first thing a dog has to learn," Mother used often to say, "is that the whole world wasn't created for him to eat."

It was quite dark when we got to the country, but the man seemed to know where to go. He pulled at my rope, and we began to walk along a road with no people in it at all. We walked on and on, but it was all so new to me that I forgot how tired I was. I could feel my mind broadening with every step I took.

Every now and then we would pass a very big house which looked as if it was empty, but I knew that there was a caretaker inside, because of Fred's father. These big houses belong to very rich people, but they don't want to live in them till the summer so they put in caretakers, and the caretakers have a dog to keep off burglars. I wondered if that was what I had been brought here for.

"Are you going to be a caretaker?" I asked the man.

"Shut up," he said.

**wallop**
(wŏl´əp) v. To *wallop* is to hit or strike with a hard blow.

200    So I shut up.

After we had been walking a long time, we came to a cottage. A man came out. My man seemed to know him, for he called him Bill. I was quite surprised to see the man was not at all shy with Bill. They seemed very friendly.

"Is that him?" said Bill, looking at me.

"Bought him this afternoon," said the man.

"Well," said Bill, "he's ugly enough. He looks fierce. If you want a dog, he's the sort of dog you want. But what do you want one for? It seems to me it's a lot of trouble to take, when
210    there's no need of any trouble at all. Why not do what I've always wanted to do? What's wrong with just fixing the dog, same as it's always done, and walking in and helping yourself?"

"I'll tell you what's wrong" said the man. "To start with, you can't get at the dog to fix him except by day, when they let him out. At night he's shut up inside the house. And suppose you do fix him during the day, what happens then? Either the bloke[6] gets another before night, or else he sits up all night with a gun. It isn't like as if these blokes was ordinary blokes. They're down here to look after the house. That's their job,
220    and they don't take any chances."

It was the longest speech I had ever heard the man make, and it seemed to impress Bill. He was quite humble.

"I didn't think of that," he said. "We'd best start in to train this tyke at once."

Mother often used to say, when I went on about wanting to go out into the world and see life, "You'll be sorry when you do. The world isn't all bones and liver." And I hadn't been living with the man and Bill in their cottage long before I found out how right she was.

230    It was the man's shyness that made all the trouble. It seemed as if he hated to be taken notice of.

It started on my very first night at the cottage. I had fallen asleep in the kitchen, tired out after all the excitement of the day and the long walks I had had, when something woke me with a start. It was somebody scratching at the window, trying to get in.

Well, I ask you, I ask any dog, what would you have done in my place? Ever since I was old enough to listen, Mother had

---

[6] **bloke** (blōk): a British term for a man or a fellow.

told me over and over again what I must do in a case like this.
It is the ABC of a dog's education. "If you are in a room and
you hear anyone trying to get in," Mother used to say, "bark. It
may be some one who has business there, or it may not. Bark
first, and inquire afterwards. Dogs were made to be heard and
not seen."

I lifted my head and yelled. I have a good, deep voice, due
to a hound strain in my pedigree,[7] and at the public-house,
when there was a full moon, I have often had people leaning
out of the windows and saying things all down the street.
I took a deep breath and let it go.

"Man!" I shouted. "Bill! Man! Come quick! Here's a
burglar getting in!"

---

[7] **pedigree** (pĕd´ ĭ-grē´): an animal's list of ancestors, or family members; a
family tree.

Then somebody struck a light, and it was the man himself. He had come in through the window.

He picked up a stick, and he walloped me. I couldn't understand it. I couldn't see where I had done the wrong thing. But he was the boss, so there was nothing to be said.

If you'll believe me, that same thing happened every night. Every single night! And sometimes twice or three times before morning. And every time I would bark my loudest, and the man would strike a light and wallop me. The thing was baffling. I couldn't possibly have mistaken what Mother had said to me. She said it too often for that. Bark! Bark! Bark! It was the main plank of her whole system of education. And yet, here I was, getting walloped every night for doing it.

I thought it out till my head ached, and finally I got it right. I began to see that Mother's outlook was narrow. No doubt, living with a man like Master at the public-house, a man without a trace of shyness in his composition, barking was all right. But circumstances alter cases. I belonged to a man who was a mass of nerves, who got the jumps if you spoke to him. What I had to do was to forget the training I had had from Mother, sound as it no doubt was as a general thing, and to adapt myself to the needs of the particular man who had happened to buy me. I had tried Mother's way, and all it had brought me was walloping, so now I would think for myself.

So next night, when I heard the window go, I lay there without a word, though it went against all my better feelings. I didn't even growl. Someone came in and moved about in the dark, with a lantern, but, though I smelt that it was the man, I didn't ask him a single question. And presently the man lit a light and came over to me and gave me a pat, which was a thing he had never done before.

"Good dog!" he said. "Now you can have this."

And he let me lick out the saucepan in which the dinner had been cooked.

After that, we got on fine. Whenever I heard anyone at the window I just kept curled up and took no notice, and every time I got a bone or something good. It was easy, once you had got the hang of things.

It was about a week after that the man took me out one morning, and we walked a long way till we turned in at some big gates and went along a very smooth road till we came to a great house, standing all by itself in the middle of a whole lot of country. There was a big lawn in front of it, and all round there were fields and trees, and at the back a great wood.

The man rang a bell, and the door opened, and an old man came out.

"Well?" he said, not very cordially.

300 "I thought you might want to buy a good watch-dog," said the man.

"Well, that's queer, your saying that," said the caretaker. "It's a coincidence. That's exactly what I do want to buy. I was just thinking of going along and trying to get one. My old dog picked up something this morning that he oughtn't to have, and he's dead, poor feller."

"Poor feller," said the man. "Found an old bone with phosphorus on it, I guess."

"What do you want for this one?"

310 "Five shillings."[8]

"Is he a good watch-dog?"

"He's a grand watch-dog."

"He looks fierce enough."

"Ah!"

So the caretaker gave the man his five shillings, and the man went off and left me.

At first the newness of everything and the unaccustomed smells and getting to know the caretaker, who was a nice old man, prevented my missing the man, but as the day

320 went on and I began to realize that he had gone and would never come back, I got very depressed. I pattered all over the house, whining. It was a most interesting house, bigger than I thought a house could possibly be, but it couldn't cheer me up. You may think it strange that I should pine for the man, after all the wallopings he had given me, and it is odd, when you come to think of it. But dogs are dogs, and they are built like that. By the time it was evening I was thoroughly miserable. I found a shoe and an old clothes-brush in one of the rooms, but could eat nothing. I just sat and **moped**.

330 It's a funny thing, but it seems as if it always happened that just when you are feeling most miserable, something nice

**mope**
(mōp) *intr.v.* To *mope* is to be gloomy, miserable, and not interested in anything.

---

8 **five shillings:** a shilling is a coin of the United Kingdom that is no longer in use; it was worth 12 pennies (pence).

happens. As I sat there, there came from outside the sound of a motor-bicycle, and somebody shouted.

It was dear old Fred, my old pal Fred, the best old boy that ever stepped. I recognized his voice in a second, and I was scratching at the door before the old man had time to get up out of his chair.

Well, well, well! That was a pleasant surprise! I ran five times round the lawn without stopping, and then I came back and jumped up at him.

"What are you doing down here, Fred?" I said. "Is this caretaker your father? Have you seen the rabbits in the wood? How long are you going to stop? How's Mother? I like the country. Have you come all the way from the public-house? I'm living here now. Your father gave five shillings for me. That's twice as much as I was worth when I saw you last."

"Why, it's young Blackie!" That was what they called me at the saloon. "What are you doing here? Where did you get this dog, Father?"

"A man sold him to me this morning. Poor old Bob got poisoned. This one ought to be just as good a watch-dog. He barks loud enough."

"He should be. His mother is the best watch-dog in London. This cheese-hound used to belong to the boss. Funny him getting down here."

We went into the house and had supper. And after supper we sat and talked. Fred was only down for the night, he said, because the boss wanted him back next day.

"And I'd sooner have my job than yours, Dad," he said. "Of all the lonely places! I wonder you aren't scared of burglars."

"I've got my shot-gun, and there's the dog. I might be scared if it wasn't for him, but he kind of gives me confidence. Old Bob was the same. Dogs are a comfort in the country."

"Get many tramps here?"

"I've only seen one in two months, and that's the feller who sold me the dog here."

As they were talking about the man, I asked Fred if he knew him. They might have met at the public-house, when the man was buying me from the boss.

"You would like him," I said. "I wish you could have met."

They both looked at me.

"What's he growling at?" asked Fred. "Think he heard something?"

The old man laughed.

"He wasn't growling. He was talking in his sleep. You're nervous, Fred. It comes from living in the city."

"Well, I am. I like this place in the daytime, but it gives me the pip[9] at night. It's so quiet. How you can stand it here all the time, I can't understand. Two nights of it would have me seeing things."

His father laughed.

"If you feel like that, Fred, you had better take the gun to bed with you. I shall be quite happy without it."

"I will," said Fred. "I'll take six if you've got them."

And after that they went upstairs. I had a basket in the hall, which had belonged to Bob, the dog who had got poisoned. It was a comfortable basket, but I was so excited at having met Fred again that I couldn't sleep. Besides, there was a smell of mice somewhere, and I had to move around, trying to place it.

I was just sniffing at a place in the wall when I heard a scratching noise. At first I thought it was the mice working in a different place, but, when I listened, I found that the sound came from the window. Somebody was doing something to it from outside.

If it had been Mother, she would have lifted the roof off right there, and so should I, if it hadn't been for what the man had taught me. I didn't think it possible that this could be the man come back, for he had gone away and said nothing about ever seeing me again. But I didn't bark. I stopped where I was and listened. And presently the window came open, and somebody began to climb in.

I gave a good sniff, and I knew it was the man.

I was so delighted that for a moment I nearly forgot myself and shouted with joy, but I remembered in time how shy he was, and stopped myself. But I ran to him and jumped up quite quietly, and he told me to lie down. I was disappointed that he didn't seem more pleased to see me. I lay down.

It was very dark, but he had brought a lantern with him, and I could see him moving about the room, picking things up and putting them in a bag which he had brought with him.

---

9 **pip:** a slang term for a minor illness; here, probably an upset stomach from being nervous or worried.

Every now and then he would stop and listen, and then he would start moving round again. He was very quick about it, but very quiet. It was plain that he didn't want Fred or his father to come down and find him.

I kept thinking about this peculiarity of his while I watched him. I suppose, being chummy myself, I find it hard to understand that everybody else in the world isn't chummy too. Of course, my experience at the public-house
420 had taught me that men are just as different from each other as dogs. If I chewed Master's shoe, for instance, he used to kick me, but if I chewed Fred's, Fred would tickle me under the ear. And, similarly, some men are shy and some men are mixers. I quite appreciated that, but I couldn't help feeling that the man carried shyness to a point where it became **morbid**. And he didn't give himself a chance to cure himself of it. That was the point. Imagine a man hating to meet people so much that he never visited their houses till the middle of the night, when they were in bed and asleep. It was silly. Shyness had always
430 been something so outside my nature that I suppose I have never really been able to look at it sympathetically. I have always held the view that you can get over it if you make an effort. The trouble with the man was that he wouldn't make an effort. He went out of his way to avoid meeting people.

I was fond of the man. He was the sort of person you never get to know very well, but we had been together for quite a while, and I wouldn't have been a dog if I hadn't got attached to him.

**morbid**
(môr´bĭd) *adj.* A *morbid* quality or feeling is one that is unhealthy or unwholesome, like an illness or disease.

As I sat and watched him creep about the room, it
440 suddenly came to me that here was a chance of doing him a
real good turn in spite of himself. Fred was upstairs, and Fred,
as I knew by experience, was the easiest man to get along with
in the world. Nobody could be shy with Fred. I felt that if only
I could bring him and the man together, they would get along
splendidly, and it would teach the man not to be silly and
avoid people. It would help to give him the confidence which
he needed. I had seen him with Bill, and I knew that he could
be perfectly natural and easy when he liked.

It was true that the man might object at first, but after a
450 while he would see that I had acted simply for his good, and
would be grateful.

The difficulty was, how to get Fred down without scaring
the man. I knew that if I shouted he wouldn't wait, but would
be out of the window and away before Fred could get there.
What I had to do was to go to Fred's room, explain the whole
situation quietly to him, and ask him to come down and make
himself pleasant.

The man was far too busy to pay any attention to me.
He was kneeling in a corner with his back to me, putting
460 something in his bag. I seized the opportunity to steal softly
from the room.

Fred's door was shut, and I could hear him snoring.
I scratched gently, and then harder, till I heard the snores stop.
He got out of bed and opened the door.

"Don't make a noise," I whispered. "Come on downstairs.
I want you to meet a friend of mine."

At first he was quite peevish.[10]

"What's the idea," he said, "coming and spoiling a man's
beauty-sleep? Get out."

470 He actually started to go back into the room.

"No, honestly, Fred," I said, "I'm not fooling you. There *is*
a man downstairs. He got in through the window. I want you
to meet him. He's very shy, and I think it will do him good to
have a chat with you."

"What are you whining about?" Fred began, and then he
broke off suddenly and listened. We could both hear the man's
footsteps as he moved about.

---

[10] **peevish** (pē´vĭsh):  discontented or ill-tempered; cranky.

Fred jumped back into the room. He came out, carrying something. He didn't say any more but started to go
480 downstairs, very quiet, and I went after him.

There was the man, still putting things in his bag. I was just going to introduce Fred, when Fred gave a great yell.

I could have bitten him.

"What did you want to do that for, you chump?"[11] I said. "I told you he was shy. Now you've scared him."

He certainly had. The man was out of the window quicker than you would have believed possible. He just flew out. I called after him that it was only Fred and me, but at that moment a gun went off with a tremendous bang, so he
490 couldn't have heard me.

I was pretty sick about it. The whole thing had gone wrong. Fred seemed to have lost his head entirely. Naturally the man had been frightened with him carrying on in that way. I jumped out of the window to see if I could find the man and explain, but he was gone. Fred jumped out after me, and nearly squashed me.

It was pitch dark out there. I couldn't see a thing. But I knew the man could not have gone far, or I should have heard him. I started to sniff round on the chance of picking
500 up his trail. It wasn't long before I struck it.

Fred's father had come down now, and they were running about. The old man had a light. I followed the trail, and it ended at a large cedar tree, not far from the house. I stood underneath it and looked up, but of course I could not see anything.

"Are you up there?" I shouted. "There's nothing to be scared at. It was only Fred. He's an old pal of mine. He works at the place where you bought me. His gun went off by accident. He won't hurt you."
510 There wasn't a sound. I began to think I must have made a mistake.

"He's got away," I heard Fred say to his father, and just as he said it I caught a faint sound of someone moving in the branches above me.

"No he hasn't!" I shouted. "He's up this tree."

"I believe the dog's found him, Dad!"

"Yes, he's up here. Come along and meet him."

---

[11] **chump:** a stupid or silly person.

Fred came to the foot of the tree.

"You up there," he said, "come along down."

520 Not a sound from the tree.

"It's all right," I explained, "he *is* up there, but he's very shy. Ask him again."

"All right," said Fred, "stay there if you want to. But I'm going to shoot off this gun into the branches just for fun."

And then the man started to come down. As soon as he touched the ground I jumped up at him.

"This is fine!" I said. "Here's my friend Fred. You'll like him."

But it wasn't any good. They didn't get along together at 530 all. They hardly spoke. The man went into the house, and Fred went after him, carrying his gun. And when they got into the house it was just the same. The man sat in one chair, and Fred sat in another, and after a long time some men came in a motor-car, and the man went away with them. He didn't say good-bye to me.

When he had gone, Fred and his father made a great fuss of me. I couldn't understand it. Men are so odd. The man wasn't a bit pleased that I had brought him and Fred together, but Fred seemed as if he couldn't do enough for me having 540 introduced him to the man. However, Fred's father produced some cold ham—my favorite dish—and gave me quite a lot of it, so I stopped worrying over the thing. As Mother used to say, "Don't bother your head about what doesn't concern you. The only thing a dog need concern himself with is the bill of fare.[12] Eat your bun, and don't make yourself busy about other people's affairs." Mother's was in some ways a narrow outlook, but she had a great fund of sterling common sense.

**COLLABORATIVE DISCUSSION** What was the Shy Man's plan? How does the plan go wrong and why? With a partner, discuss these questions and whether the plan made sense.

---

[12] **bill of fare:** a list of items that are available, as on a menu.

# Describe Characters' Responses

Every good story has strong characters and an interesting plot. A **character** is a person, animal, or even an imaginary creature who takes part in a story. A **plot,** as you already know, is the series of events in a story.

When you read a story, it is interesting to see how characters respond to events or change as the plot moves toward its resolution. Authors illustrate characters' responses through their actions, thoughts, feelings, and interactions with other characters. When Blackie, the main character in "The Mixer," is sold to the Shy Man, he is thrilled, saying that he's "'off to see life.'" Blackie's response to this event tells you that he enjoys new experiences.

Look for more examples of characters' responses to the plot as you analyze "The Mixer." Ask yourself: How does the character respond when something happens to him or her? What does that tell me about the character?

# Explain Point of View

A story's **narrator** is the voice that tells the story. Point of view is the perspective from which the story is told. A **first-person** point of view means a character from the story is the narrator. When a story is told in first-person point of view, the narrator

- may be a major or minor character
- tells the story using first-person words like *I, me*, and *my*
- tells about his or her thoughts and feelings
- does not know what other characters are thinking or feeling

Sometimes point of view can be used to create irony and humor. **Irony** is a contrast between what is expected and what actually exists or happens. For example, it is ironic that Blackie calls his new owner "the Shy Man," because the man turns out not to be shy at all.

In "The Mixer," look for ways the narrator and point of view shape the way the story is told and how the narration creates irony. Ask yourself:

- Does the narrator understand everything that is happening?
- How is my understanding of the story limited by what the narrator knows or decides to tell?
- What events in the story are surprising?

# Analyzing the Text

COMMON
CORE
RL 1, RL 3, RL 5,
RL 6, RL 10,
W 2a-f

**Cite Text Evidence**   Support your responses with evidence from the text.

1. **Identify**   Reread lines 1–10. Identify clues that help you explain the story's point of view. What is the point of view and who is the narrator?

2. **Infer**   Reread lines 72–86. Describe the dog's character. How is his personality the same as or different from any other dog's personality?

3. **Interpret**   Review the events in lines 232–286. How does Blackie respond to his training? Explain what this tells you about his character.

4. **Draw Conclusions**   Review lines 334–355, when Fred appears at the country house. Explain why this event helps you understand the attempted burglary.

5. **Analyze**   How is Blackie affected by events in the story?

6. **Analyze**   Review lines 416–438. Tell what Blackie says that illustrates how he views the Shy Man. What is ironic about Blackie's view?

7. **Analyze**   What effect does Blackie's role as the narrator have on the story?

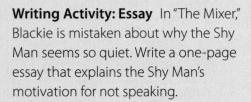

# PERFORMANCE TASK

**Writing Activity: Essay**   In "The Mixer," Blackie is mistaken about why the Shy Man seems so quiet. Write a one-page essay that explains the Shy Man's motivation for not speaking.

- Review the story. Make notes about events and situations that help you understand the man's character.
- Describe the man's character, using evidence from the text.

- Tell how the man responds to Blackie and to other characters in the story.
- Give concrete examples that illustrate why the man does not speak.
- Use appropriate transitions such as *furthermore, one reason,* and *in addition* to clarify relationships among your ideas.
- Provide a concluding statement that supports your explanation.

# Critical Vocabulary

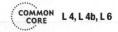 

| surfeit | criticize | amiable | wallop | mope | morbid |
|---|---|---|---|---|---|

**Practice and Apply**  Answer each question.

1. Have you ever consumed a **surfeit** of sweets? How did you feel afterwards?

2. When did you ever **criticize** someone? Why?

3. Have you ever been impressed by an **amiable** person? Why?

4. Have you ever wanted to **wallop** something? What was the result?

5. Do you ever **mope** about a situation? Tell when and why.

6. Have you ever felt that someone was being **morbid**? Tell how that person acted.

## Vocabulary Strategy: Greek Suffix *-ize*

The Greek suffix *-ize* often creates a verb when it is added to a noun. For example, the vocabulary word *criticize* means "to find fault with"—in other words, to act as a critic. In this case, the suffix *-ize* means "to become or be like." If you can recognize the noun that the suffix *-ize* is attached to, you can often figure out the meaning of the verb that is formed. The chart shows some meanings of the suffix *-ize*.

| Suffix | Meanings |
|---|---|
| *-ize* | to cause to be or to become; to cause to resemble; to treat as |

**Practice and Apply**  Complete each sentence with one of the following words. Then identify the noun in each word and its meaning. Use the information in the chart to write a definition for each boldface word.

| dramatize | idolize | authorize | equalize | jeopardize |
|---|---|---|---|---|

1. The store walls were plastered with posters of singers that teens _____.

2. Poor judgment and rash behavior could _____ our secret mission.

3. This note will _____ you to spend lunchtime in the library.

4. I am writing a play to _____ my grandmother's life story.

5. You need to sit on the other end of the seesaw to _____ the weight.

# Language Conventions: Intensive Pronouns

**Intensive pronouns** are formed by adding *-self* or *-selves* to certain personal pronouns and are used to intensify, or emphasize, the nouns or pronouns to which they refer. Like other pronouns, they also change their form to express person, number, and gender.

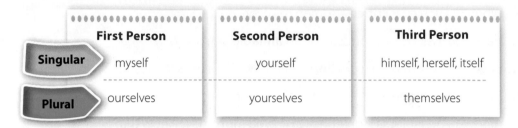

|  | First Person | Second Person | Third Person |
|---|---|---|---|
| **Singular** | myself | yourself | himself, herself, itself |
| **Plural** | ourselves | yourselves | themselves |

Here is an example of an intensive pronoun from "The Mixer."

**Then somebody struck a light, and it was the man <u>himself</u>.**

The intensive pronoun *himself* emphasizes Blackie's surprise at seeing his new owner breaking into his own home. Here are some more examples:

**The dog <u>itself</u> hid the bone.**
**He took the car home <u>himself</u>.**
**You ate the whole cake <u>yourself</u>!**
**The scouts will clean the room <u>themselves</u>.**

Keep in mind that standard English does not include forms such as *hisself* and *theirselves*, even though *his* and *their* are common possessive pronouns. The correct forms in these cases are *himself* and *themselves*.

**Practice and Apply**  Complete each sentence with the correct intensive pronoun.

1. The students _____ made all the refreshments.

2. I _____ had the best audition.

3. Judith _____ is to blame.

4. You _____ have to take responsibility for this.

5. Rico will finish the diorama _____.

**Background** *As a young lawyer,* **George Graham Vest** (1830–1904) *represented a man seeking payment for his dog, which had been shot by a sheep farmer. In this closing speech of the trial, Vest ignores the evidence given at trial; instead, he gives a moving tribute to dogs in general. Some said it was a perfect piece of oratory; others exclaimed that the jury was moved to tears. Vest's client won the case. Eight years later, Vest was elected to the U.S. Senate. His speech is now regarded as a classic tribute to "man's best friend."*

# TRIBUTE TO THE DOG

## Speech by George Graham Vest

**SETTING A PURPOSE** As you read, look for details and ideas the author uses to convince the reader/listener of a dog's value to people.

Gentlemen of the Jury: The best friend a man has in the world may turn against him and become his enemy. His son or daughter that he has reared[1] with loving care may prove ungrateful. Those who are nearest and dearest to us, those whom we trust with our happiness and our good name may become traitors to their faith. The money that a man has, he may lose. It flies away from him, perhaps when he needs it most. A man's reputation may be sacrificed in a moment of ill-considered action. The people who are prone to fall on
10 their knees to do us honor when success is with us, may be the first to throw the stone of **malice** when failure settles its cloud upon our heads.

**malice**
(măl´ĭs) *n. Malice* is a desire to harm others or to see someone suffer.

---

[1] **reared:** raised; guided to grow into an adult.

The one absolutely unselfish friend that man can have in this selfish world, the one that never deserts him, the one that never proves ungrateful or **treacherous** is his dog. A man's dog stands by him in **prosperity** and in poverty, in health and in sickness. He will sleep on the cold ground, where the wintry winds blow and the snow drives fiercely, if only he may be near his master's side. He will kiss the hand that has
20  no food to offer. He will lick the wounds and sores that come in encounters with the roughness of the world. He guards the sleep of his pauper² master as if he were a prince. When all other friends desert, he remains. When riches take wings,³ and reputation falls to pieces, he is as constant in his love as the sun in its journey through the heavens.

If fortune drives the master forth, an outcast in the world, friendless and homeless, the faithful dog asks no higher privilege than that of accompanying him, to guard him against danger, to fight against his enemies. And when the last
30  scene of all comes, and death takes his master in its **embrace** and his body is laid away in the cold ground, no matter if all other friends pursue their way,⁴ there by the graveside will the noble dog be found, his head between his paws, his eyes sad, but open in alert watchfulness, faithful and true even in death.

**treacherous**
(trĕch´ər-əs) *adj.* A *treacherous* person is untrustworthy and likely to betray others.

**prosperity**
(prŏ-spĕr´ĭ-tē) *n.* *Prosperity* means having success, particularly having enough money.

**embrace**
(ĕm-brās´) *n.* An *embrace* is a hug or encirclement, showing acceptance.

**COLLABORATIVE DISCUSSION**  The author of this speech argues that a dog is more faithful to its owner than the owner's friends and family. With a small group, identify text evidence and other details that support this argument.

---

² **pauper** (pô´pər):  someone who is extremely poor.
³ **take wings:**  disappear; vanish.
⁴ **pursue their way:**  continue with their lives; move on.

# Trace and Evaluate an Argument

"Tribute to the Dog" is a **persuasive speech,** which is a talk or public address that has a clear argument. An **argument** expresses a position and supports it with reasons and evidence. To analyze how an argument is constructed, you can **trace,** or follow the reasoning of, an argument as follows:

- Identify the **claim,** which is the speaker's position on the issue or problem.
- Look for **support,** which consists of reasons and evidence to prove the claim. **Reasons** are statements made to explain an action or belief. **Evidence** includes specific facts, statistics, and examples.
- Notice whether the author includes a **counterargument,** an argument made to address opposing viewpoints.

To find these elements, identify and analyze particular sentences or paragraphs that contribute to the development of the speaker's argument. After you trace an argument, you can **evaluate,** or judge, its effectiveness or whether or not the evidence is logical and convincing. Ask yourself:

- Has the speaker included enough reasons and evidence to support the claim?
- Do the ideas make sense? Do they flow in a logical way?
- Has the speaker thought about opposing ideas and provided counterarguments?

# Analyze the Meanings of Words and Phrases

"Tribute to the Dog" was written to persuade listeners to agree with the speaker's opinion. To convince an audience, a speaker can use a variety of **persuasive techniques,** which are methods used to influence others. One effective persuasive technique is the **emotional appeal,** which is a message that uses language or images that create strong feelings in the listener.

Identifying emotional appeals helps the audience understand how a speaker is trying to persuade them. In "Tribute to the Dog," when the speaker says that a dog "will kiss the hand that has no food," he is making an emotional appeal to the audience's feelings about their pets. Look for more examples of emotional appeals as you analyze "Tribute to the Dog."

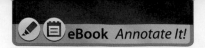
# Analyzing the Text

COMMON CORE RI 1, RI 2, RI 4, RI 5, RI 8, SL 1a, SL 4

**Cite Text Evidence** Support your responses with evidence from the text.

1. **Identify** What claim does Vest make in his speech?

2. **Infer** Reread lines 1–12. Identify the counterargument Vest presents. Why might he have chosen to begin the speech with a counterargument?

3. **Summarize** Reread lines 13–25. Summarize the reasons and evidence Vest uses to support his claim. Explain whether he successfully supports his claim.

4. **Analyze** Review lines 26–34. What is Vest's final appeal to his audience? What emotion does he appeal to? What words and phrases does Vest use to represent this appeal?

5. **Evaluate** Review Vest's claim and how he supports it. Do his ideas make sense to you? Do you find his argument persuasive? Why or why not?

## PERFORMANCE TASK

**Speaking Activity: Discussion** In a small-group panel discussion, tell why you agree or disagree with the speech "Tribute to the Dog," providing your own claim with support for your opinion.

- Prepare for the discussion by reviewing the speech and listing evidence from the text to support your opinion.

- When it's your turn to speak, present your claims and support in a logical way. Be sure to make eye contact with members of the panel, speak at an appropriate volume, and pronounce words clearly.

- Appoint a group leader to begin the discussion.

- Make sure each person on the panel has a chance to speak.

# Critical Vocabulary

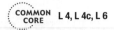 

malice      treacherous      prosperity      embrace

**Practice and Apply**  Answer each question.

1.  If someone shows **malice,** is he or she acting kind or cruel? Explain.

2.  If someone was **treacherous,** would you share a secret with that person? Explain.

3.  If a country has **prosperity,** how do its citizens feel? Why?

4.  Which would you rather have in your **embrace**—a dog or a porcupine? Explain.

## Vocabulary Strategy: Using a Print or Digital Dictionary

When you come across an unfamiliar word in a text, you can use strategies, such as context clues, to help you determine the meaning. If those strategies do not work, you should use a print or digital dictionary to find the correct definition. Here is an example of a dictionary entry.

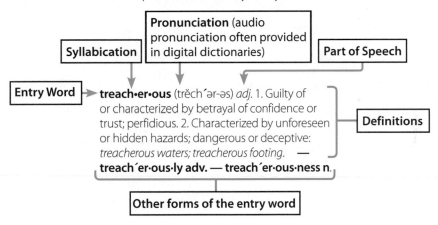

**Practice and Apply**  Use a print or digital dictionary to explore words found in "Tribute to the Dog."

1.  Reread lines 9–12. Look up *prone*. How many meanings are shown? Which meaning is used in the sentence?

2.  Reread lines 22–23. Look up *desert*. How many entries for *desert* are shown? Which entry and meaning is used in the speech?

3.  Reread lines 23–25. Look up *constant*. What is the meaning of *constant* in the sentence? What other form of *constant* do you find?

# Language Conventions:
# Relative Pronouns *who* and *whom*

The relative pronouns *who* and *whom* relate, or connect, adjective clauses to the words they modify in sentences. Deciding when to use *who* or *whom* can be confusing. Here are two simple rules:

- The relative pronoun *who* is used with subjects.
- The relative pronoun *whom* is used with objects.

Take a look at how *who* and *whom* are used in these sentences.

**Those who are nearest and dearest to us may betray us.**
**People with whom we trust our happiness may become traitors.**

The relative pronoun *who* is used in the first sentence because it relates the adjective clause to the subject, *those (people)*. In the second sentence, the relative pronoun *whom* is used because it is the object of the preposition *with*.

**Practice and Apply** Complete each sentence with the correct relative pronoun *who* or *whom*.

1. My brother, _____ lives in Florida, owns a potbellied pig.

2. My uncle, for _____ I have the highest regard, needs my help.

3. The owner hired the woman _____ he interviewed last week.

4. I have a friend _____ walks dogs for a living.

5. My sister, with _____ I share a room, is not an especially tidy person.

6. Tanya knows a doctor _____ specializes in caring for injured birds.

7. Darius is the one _____ will buy food for our pets.

8. The person to _____ I spoke was Dr Nash, the vet.

**Background** *People and animals are in constant interaction with each other. It is not surprising, then, that animals have long been a favorite focus of poets and storytellers. In particular, Native American literature and culture express a strong reverence for animals and the land, air, and water they share with us. Many Native American poems are prayers, thanking animals for food, clothing, and shelter, as well as the intelligence they seem to possess about the natural world.*

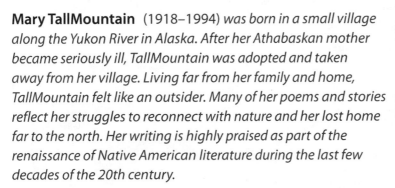

# Animal Wisdom

Poem by Nancy Wood

# The Last Wolf

Poem by Mary TallMountain

**Nancy Wood** (b. 1936) *is a poet, novelist, and photographer who lives on the edge of the natural wilderness that inspires her. Her artistic work focuses on the people of the Southwest, including the Native American people of the Taos Pueblo near her home in Santa Fe, New Mexico. Wood has produced more than 25 photography books. She has also published numerous books of poetry and fiction for adults and children.*

**Mary TallMountain** (1918–1994) *was born in a small village along the Yukon River in Alaska. After her Athabaskan mother became seriously ill, TallMountain was adopted and taken away from her village. Living far from her family and home, TallMountain felt like an outsider. Many of her poems and stories reflect her struggles to reconnect with nature and her lost home far to the north. Her writing is highly praised as part of the renaissance of Native American literature during the last few decades of the 20th century.*

**SETTING A PURPOSE** As you read, look for details and ideas that illustrate each poet's understanding of wild animals, their intelligence, and the environment.

# Animal Wisdom
by Nancy Wood

At first, the wild creatures were too busy
to explore their natural curiosity until
Turtle crawled up on land. He said:
What's missing is the ability
5    to find contentment in a slow-paced life.

As the oceans receded, fish sprouted whiskers.
Certain animals grew four legs and were able
to roam from shore to shore. Bear stood
upright and looked around. He said:
10   What's missing is devotion
to place, to give meaning to passing time.

Mountains grew from fiery heat, while
above them soared birds, the greatest
of which was Eagle, to whom penetrating
15   vision was given. He said: What's missing
is laughter so that arguments
can be resolved without rancor.[1]

After darkness and light settled their
differences
20   and the creatures paired up,
people appeared in all the corners of
the world. They said: What's missing
is perception.[2] They began to notice
the beauty hidden
25   in an ordinary stone,
the short lives of snowflakes,
the perfection of bird wings, and

---

[1] **rancor** (răng´kər): long-lasting resentment or anger.
[2] **perception** (pər-sĕp´shən): the ability to understand something, usually
through the senses; also insight, intuition.

the way a butterfly speaks
through its fragility.[3] When they realized
they had something in common with animals,
people began saying the same things.
They defended the Earth together,
though it was the animals who insisted
on keeping their own names.

30

---

[3] **fragility** (frə-jĭl´ ĭ-tē):  easily broken, damaged, or destroyed; frail.

## The Last Wolf
by Mary TallMountain

the last wolf hurried toward me
through the ruined city
and I heard his baying echoes
down the steep smashed warrens[1]
5  of Montgomery Street and past
the few ruby-crowned highrises
left standing
their lighted elevators useless

passing the flickering red and green
10  of traffic signals
baying his way eastward
in the mystery of his wild loping gait
closer the sounds in the deadly night
through clutter and rubble of quiet blocks
15  I heard his voice ascending[2] the hill
and at last his low whine as he came
floor by empty floor to the room
where I sat
in my narrow bed looking west, waiting
20  I heard him snuffle[3] at the door and
I watched
he trotted across the floor
he laid his long gray muzzle
on the spare white spread
25  and his eyes burned yellow
his small dotted eyebrows quivered

Yes, I said.
I know what they have done.

**COLLABORATIVE DISCUSSION** The authors of these poems have
a deep appreciation for wildlife. In what ways do the different
animals they write about demonstrate their intelligence?

---

[1] **warrens** (wôr´ənz): overcrowded living areas.
[2] **ascending** (ə-sĕnd´ĭng): rising up.
[3] **snuffle** (snŭf´əl): sniff.

# Determine Meanings of Words and Phrases

**Imagery** is the use of words and phrases in a way that allows readers to picture, or imagine, how something looks, feels, sounds, smells, or tastes. Effective imagery helps create a picture, or image, in the mind of the reader. To find imagery in a piece of writing, ask yourself, "What details help me picture what the author is describing?" In "The Last Wolf," the author uses imagery to describe a wolf entering the city:

> and I heard his baying echoes
> down the steep smashed warrens
> of Montgomery Street and past
> the few ruby-crowned highrises
> left standing

The sensory details in these lines help the reader imagine how the wolf sounds and what he sees as he runs. The phrase, "the few ruby-crowned highrises" illustrates the use of **figurative language,** or language that is not literally true, as part of the poem's imagery.

Figurative language is often used to create imagery. **Personification** is a type of figurative language in which an object or an animal is given human qualities. In "Animal Wisdom," a turtle talks the way a person would.

> Turtle crawled up on land. He said:
> What's missing is the ability
> to find contentment in a slow-paced life.

As you analyze "Animal Wisdom" and "The Last Wolf," look for more examples of imagery and personification in their language.

One way to clarify the meanings of words and phrases in a poem is to paraphrase them. **Paraphrasing** is restating text in your own words. An effective paraphrase is written in simpler language and is about the same length as the original text. The chart shows a paraphrase of a stanza from "The Last Wolf."

| Original Text | Paraphrase |
| --- | --- |
| he laid his long gray muzzle on the spare white spread and his eyes burned yellow his small dotted eyebrows quivered | The wolf laid his head on the bed and stared with intense emotion at the person there. |

Be sure to avoid using exact wording from the original text when you paraphrase. If you use exact words, you would need to enclose the words with quotation marks, but generally, quotes are not part of paraphrasing.

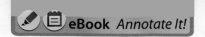
# Analyzing the Text

COMMON CORE  RL 1, RL 2, RL 4, RL 10, W 2a-f, W 4, W 9a

**Cite Text Evidence**    Support your responses with evidence from the text.

1. **Identify**   Reread lines 6–11 of "Animal Wisdom," noticing the use of personification. What is being personified?

2. **Analyze**   Examine lines 12–17 of "Animal Wisdom." Find two examples of imagery and describe the image that each suggests.

3. **Interpret**   Paraphase lines 28–34 of "Animal Wisdom." Why do you think the animals "insisted/on keeping their own names"?

4. **Identify**   Reread lines 9–19 of "The Last Wolf." Identify the imagery the author uses here, and explain which senses it appeals to.

5. **Analyze**   What opinion does author TallMountain have of the wolf and of people and their effect on the environment?

---

## PERFORMANCE TASK

**Writing Activity: Essay**   Write a one-page essay in which you compare and contrast how the writer of each poem feels about wildlife.

- In what ways are both writers' attitudes about animals alike?
- In what ways is the imagery in these poems the same? In what ways is it distinct, or different?
- Compare and contrast the way each author presents the idea of animal intelligence and how this wisdom can benefit people.

- Support your ideas with the imagery each author uses.
- Use appropriate transitions to clarify the relationships among your ideas.
- Provide a concluding statement.
- Share your essay by reading it aloud in a small group.

**Dorothy Hinshaw Patent** (b. 1940) *was born in Minnesota. As a child, Patent loved animals and being outdoors, spending much of her time exploring the woods near her home. Her love of animals led her to study animals when she went to college. After college, Patent worked as a scientist for several years. Then she decided to start writing nature books for children so she could share her love of the natural world with others. Patent has now published over 100 books for children and young adults.*

*from*

# How Smart Are Animals?

## Science Writing by Dorothy Hinshaw Patent

**SETTING A PURPOSE** As you read, focus on the distinct characteristics that indicate intelligence and how scientists try to discover these traits in animals.

## How Smart Is Smart?

The blizzard came on suddenly, with no warning. Eleven-year-old Andrea Anderson was outside near her home when the storm struck. The sixty- to eighty-mile-an-hour winds drove her into a snowdrift, and the snow quickly covered her up to her waist. Unable to get out, she screamed desperately for help. Through the swirling wind, Villa, a year-old Newfoundland dog[1] belonging to Andrea's neighbors, heard her cries. Villa had always been content to stay inside her dog run, but now she leapt over the five-foot fence and rushed to Andrea's side.

10 First she licked the girl, then began circling around her,

---

[1] **Newfoundland dog** (nōō′fən-lənd): a large strong dog bred in Newfoundland, Canada, and having a thick, usually black coat.

packing down the snow with her paws. Next, Villa stood still as a statue in front of the girl with her paws on the packed snow. The dog waited until Andrea grabbed her, then strained forward, pulling the girl from the drift. As the storm raged around them, Villa led the way back to Andrea's home.

Villa won the Ken-L Ration Dog Hero of the Year award in 1983 for her bravery, loyalty, and intelligence. Her feat was truly impressive—understanding that Andrea needed help and performing the tasks necessary to save her. We can all admire Villa and envy Andrea for having such a loyal friend. But did Villa's heroic behavior exhibit intelligence? Some scientists would say that, while Villa certainly is a wonderful animal, her behavior was unthinking, perhaps an instinctive holdover from the protective environment of the wolf pack, where the adult animals defend the pups against danger. After all, dogs **evolved** from wolves, which are highly social animals. They would say that Villa just acted, without really understanding the concept of danger or thinking about what she was doing. Up until the 1960s, this view of animals prevailed among scientists studying animal behavior. But nowadays, a variety of experiments and experiences with different creatures are showing that some animals have impressive mental abilities.

**evolve**
(ĭ-vŏlv´) v. When animals and plants *evolve,* they gradually change and develop into different forms.

## Do Animals Think?

If dogs might think, what about bees, rats, birds, cats, monkeys, and apes? How well do animals learn? How much of their experiences can they remember? Can they apply what they may have learned to new challenges in their lives? Are animals aware of the world around them? How might it be possible to learn about and evaluate the intelligence of different animals?

It is easy to confuse trainability with thinking. But just because an animal can learn to perform a trick doesn't mean that it knows what it is doing. In the IQ Zoo in Hotsprings, Arkansas, for example, animals perform some amazing tasks. A cat turns on the lights and then plays the piano, while a duck strums on the guitar with its bill. Parrots ride tiny bicycles and slide around on roller skates. At John F. Kennedy Airport in New York, beagles work for the Food and Drug Administration, sniffing at luggage and signaling when they

perceive drugs or illegal foods in the baggage. Dolphins and
50 killer whales at marine parks perform some spectacular feats,
and their behavior is often linked into a story line so that it
appears they are acting roles, as humans would in a movie or
play. These animals may seem to be behaving in an intelligent
fashion, but they are just repeating behavior patterns they
have been trained to perform for food rewards. The drug-
sniffing beagle has no concept of drug illegality, and the duck
doesn't understand or appreciate music. They aren't thinking
and then deciding what to do.

Studying the intelligence of animals is very tricky. During
60 the nineteenth and early twentieth centuries, people readily
**attributed** human emotions and mental abilities to animals.
Even learned scientists had great faith in animal minds—
"An animal can think in a human way and can express
human ideas in human language," said the respected Swiss
psychiatrist[2] Gustav Wolff in the early 1900s.

Wolff's statement was inspired by Clever Hans, a horse
that appeared to show remarkable intelligence. A retired
schoolteacher trained Hans as he would a child, with
blackboards, flash cards, number boards, and letter cards.
70 After four years of training, Hans was ready to perform in
public. When asked to solve a numerical problem, Hans would
paw the answer with his hoof. He shook his head "yes" and
"no," moved it "up" and "down," and turned it "right" or "left."
Hans would show his "knowledge" of colors by picking up a
rag of the appropriate shade with his teeth. Many scientists
of the time came to watch Hans and tried to figure out how
he performed his amazing feats; they went away impressed.
Hans appeared to understand human language and to have
mastered arithmetic.
80 Then Oskar Pfungst, a German experimental
psychologist,[3] uncovered Hans's secret by using what is now a
standard scientific method—the double blind experiment.[4]

**attribute**
(ə-trĭb´yo͞ot) *tr.v.* If you
*attribute* something
to a person, thing, or
event, you believe
that they cause it or
have it.

---

[2] **psychiatrist** (sĭ-kī´ə-trĭst): a doctor who deals with mental illness.

[3] **experimental psychologist** (sī-kŏl´ə-jĭst): a person trained to do research and
testing that deals with the processes of the human mind and human behavior.

[4] **double blind experiment:** an experiment in which neither the research subjects
nor the scientists know the correct responses; both sides of the experiment are
kept "in the dark" about the phenomena in question until the study ends.

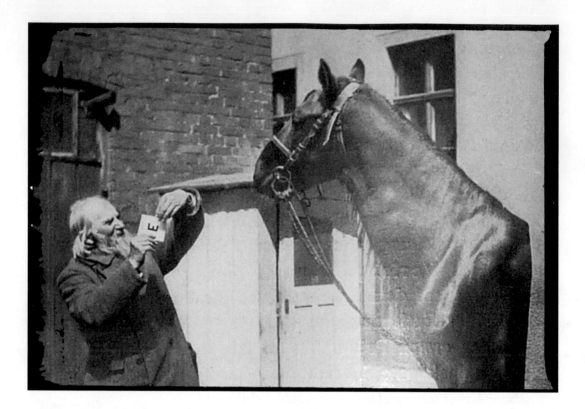

When the horse was asked a question, no one in his presence knew the answer. Under these conditions, Clever Hans was no longer so "smart"; he couldn't come up with the correct responses. By observing the horse and the audience when the answer was known, Pfungst discovered that Hans was very sensitive to the smallest movements of the people watching. They would lean ever so slightly forward until he had pawed 90 the correct number of times, then relax. He watched for that sign of relief, then stopped pawing. His trainer unknowingly moved his head from side to side or up and down just enough for Hans to take a cue as to what to do. At the end of his investigation, Pfungst was able to prove his point. He stood in front of Hans without asking any question. He nodded his head slightly, and the horse began to tap his hoof. When Pfungst straightened his head, Hans stood at attention.

    Ever since the embarrassment of Clever Hans, psychologists have been extremely wary of falling into the 100 same trap. They are ready to call upon the "Clever Hans **phenomenon**" whenever an animal seems to be exhibiting intelligent behavior. Clever Hans taught psychology some important lessons, but the incident may also have made

**phenomenon**
(fĭ-nŏm´ə-nŏn´) *n.*
A *phenomenon*
is an unusual or
remarkable fact or
event.

behavioral scientists[5] too cautious about the mental abilities of animals.

Animals that are easy to train may also be very intelligent. Some of the most trainable creatures, such as dolphins, are also the most likely candidates for genuine animal thinking. But finding ways to get at animals' real mental capacity can be very difficult.

## What Is Intelligence?

We humans recognize a "smart" person when we meet one; we know who is a "brain" and who is not. In school, we take IQ tests, which are supposed to give a numerical measure of our "intelligence." But these days, the whole concept of intelligence is being reevaluated. The older, standard IQ tests measure only a limited range of mental abilities, concentrating on mathematics and language skills. Creativity, which most people would agree is a critical element in the meaningful application of intelligence, has not traditionally been evaluated by such tests, and other important mental skills have also been ignored. But things are changing. Many scientists believe that dozens of different talents are a part of intelligence. In fact, more than a hundred factors of intelligence have been written about in scientific literature. Psychologists are now developing tests that measure intelligence more accurately and more broadly. The SOI (Structure of Intellect) test, for example, evaluates five main factors of intelligence: cognition (comprehension), memory, evaluation (judgment, planning, reasoning, and critical decision making), convergent production (solving problems where answers are known), and divergent production (solving problems creatively). Each of these is broken down further into many subcategories.

But what about animals? We can't hand them a pencil and paper and give them a test, and we can't ask them what they're thinking. We must find other ways of measuring their "smarts." And that's not the only problem. Since the lives of animals are so different from ours, we can't apply human standards to them. We must develop different ideas of what animal intelligence might be.

---

[5] **behavioral scientists:** researchers who study human and animal behavior and mental processes.

140    The concept of intelligence was thought up by humans, and our thinking about it is tied up with our own human system of values. The things that are important to animals can be different from those that matter to humans. When studying animals, we must test them in situations that have meaning for their lives, not ours, and not just look to see how much they resemble us.

## Studying Animal Thought

Many pitfalls await the scientist trying to interpret animals' behavior and make inferences about their intelligence. One is **inconsistency**. An animal might breeze through what we

150    consider a difficult learning task and then fail when presented with what seems obvious to us. When an animal can't perform well, we don't know if it really cannot solve the problems put to it or if it just doesn't want to. Sometimes the difficulty lies in the perceptive abilities of the animals. The animal may have the mental ability and the desire to solve the problem but is unable to make the discriminations[6] being asked of it. For example, a researcher using colored objects to compare learning in a cebus monkey and in a rhesus monkey first found that the rhesus scored much better than the cebus.

160    But rhesus monkeys have color vision that is essentially the same as ours, while the cebus's is significantly different. When the design of the experiment was changed and gray objects were substituted for the colored ones, the cebus monkeys actually did a little better than the rhesus.

Scientists studying animals in nature can run into difficulties in interpreting their results if they don't pay very close attention to what they see and hear. C. G. Beer of Rutgers University in New Jersey spent long hours studying laughing gull behavior. Early on, he interpreted what he called

170    the "long call" as a signal that was the same for each bird and that was made on all occasions. But when he recorded a variety of long calls and played them back to the gulls, he noticed that the birds didn't always respond in the same way. There were differences in the calls that were hard for a human researcher to hear. Beer then realized that the long call was actually so individualized that it helped distinguish one bird from another! The more carefully he listened to the calls and

**inconsistency**
(ĭn´kən-sĭs´tən-sē) *n.*
If something shows *inconsistency*, it does not always behave or respond the same way every time.

---

[6] **discriminations** (dĭ-skrĭm´ə-na´shəns): fine distinctions; small differences.

watched the gulls' reactions to them, the more **complexity** and variety he found in both the calls and the responses. From this
180  work Beer concluded: "We may often misunderstand what animals are doing in social interaction because we fail to draw our distinctions where the animals draw theirs."

## Measuring Animal Intelligence

Keeping all these concerns in mind, we can list some factors of intelligence that might be measurable or observable in animals—speed of learning, complexity of learned tasks, ability to retrieve information from long-term memory, rule learning, decision-making and problem-solving capacity, counting **aptitude**, understanding of spatial relations, and ability to learn by watching what others do. More advanced
190  signs of intelligence are tool manufacture and use, symbolic communication, and ability to form mental concepts.

With such a list of capabilities that might be involved with intelligence, it seems that scientists should be able to analyze and compare the intelligence of animals. But it's one thing to decide to test intelligence and another to design experiments that will measure it. You may read somewhere that rats, for example, are smarter than pigeons. But finding ways to compare the accomplishments of different species is virtually impossible. Animals are just too varied in their physical
200  makeup and in their life styles. Scientists have found that different kinds of animals learn better under different sorts of conditions, so the same experiment usually can't be used meaningfully on a rat and a pigeon. In addition, some animals have evolved special mental skills to deal with their particular environments. They might appear especially intelligent on one measure of brain power and very dull on another.

Dealing with wild animals presents new problems. Laboratory pigeons and rats have been bred for many generations in captivity. They are used to cages and to
210  humans, and large numbers are easy to acquire. Wild animals may not perform well in the laboratory because they are afraid or because the setting is so strange to them. And because wild animals are often hard to come by, the experimenter must usually work with only a small number of individuals. Variations of "intelligence" from one individual to the next can significantly affect the results. Primates—apes and monkeys—are among the most intelligent animals, and apes

**complexity**
(kəm-plĕkʹsĭ-tē) *n.*
*Complexity* is the state of having many different parts that are connected in a tangled or layered way.

**aptitude**
(ăpʹtĭ-to͞odʹ) *n.*
An *aptitude* for something is an ability to easily and quickly learn how to do it.

seem closer to our idea of "smart" than monkeys. But a bright
monkey may score as well on a test as an ape, while a dull
220   one may be outclassed by a rat. For these reasons, behavioral
scientists have realized that trying to compare the intelligence
of different animals is a very challenging problem.

That doesn't mean, however, that trying to find out how
animal minds function is not worth the effort. We can learn
a great deal through studying how various kinds of animals
solve problems and how they use their mental abilities to
survive in their natural environments.

**COLLABORATIVE DISCUSSION**  Can we know for certain whether
an animal is showing intelligence, or whether it is simply highly
trainable? What are some challenges scientists face in trying to
determine animal intelligence? Discuss these questions with a
small group. Be sure to cite evidence from the text.

# Summarize Text

One way to check your understanding of what you are reading is to summarize it. When you **summarize,** you briefly restate in your own words the central ideas and important details of a text. A **central idea** is the most important point in a paragraph, section, or an entire work. **Details** are the support for the central idea.

This chart shows how to summarize the section "Measuring Animal Intelligence" in *How Smart Are Animals?* The central idea and a sample detail from each paragraph is recorded.

| Central Idea | Detail |
|---|---|
| There are many ways intelligence in animals could be measured. *(lines 183–191)* | Tests might include creating and using tools. |
| It is difficult to design useful tests and to compare different species. *(lines 192–206)* | An experiment used on a rat might not be useful for testing a pigeon. |
| Using wild animals in a lab is problematic. *(lines 207–222)* | They might not perform well in a strange setting. |

**Summary**  The section "Measuring Animal Intelligence" focuses on how animal intelligence might be tested. While there are many ways animal intelligence could be measured, testing is also problematic. Designing useful tests, comparing different species, and using wild animals are some of the challenges scientists face.

Generally, a summary is no more then one-third the length of the original text and includes just the facts—not your personal opinions. Try summarizing other sections of the selection as you analyze *How Smart Are Animals?*

# Determine Author's Purpose

A writer's main reason for writing a text is called the **author's purpose.** The purpose may be to inform, entertain, persuade, or express thoughts and feelings. Most writers do not state their reason for writing. Their purpose is suggested through the information they present. A text can also have more than one purpose. To determine an author's purpose for writing, ask yourself these questions:

- Why is the writer telling me this?
- What does the writer want me to think about this topic?

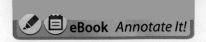
## Analyzing the Text

COMMON CORE · RI 1, RI 2, RI 3, RI 5, RI 6, RI 10, W 2, W 9

**Cite Text Evidence**   Support your responses with evidence from the text.

1. **Infer**   Reread lines 1–32 of *How Smart Are Animals?* What is the author's main purpose for writing? Explain how you know this.

2. **Infer**   The author introduces the topic with an **anecdote,** a short account of an event. Explain the author's purpose for including this event.

3. **Evaluate**   Review lines 33–110. Why does the author include the information about Clever Hans? Tell whether or not this example is effective and why.

4. **Summarize**   Review lines 147–182. What main ideas and details does the author present? Write a summary of the section.

5. **Analyze**   Review the main ideas the author discusses in each section of the excerpt. Tell whether or not the author answers the question "How smart are animals?" and explain why.

## PERFORMANCE TASK

**Writing Activity: Essay**   Write a one-page essay to explain the author's purpose in writing *How Smart Are Animals?*

- Review the selection. Note clues that help you determine the author's purpose in writing it.

- Summarize important ideas from the text. Cite relevant textual evidence to support your analysis, such as facts, definitions, details, and examples that help show the author's purpose.

# Critical Vocabulary

COMMON CORE · L 4a, L 4c, L 4d, L 6

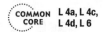

| evolve | attribute | phenomenon |
|--------|-----------|------------|
| inconsistency | complexity | aptitude |

**Practice and Apply**  Answer each question.

1. Which Vocabulary word goes with *complicated*? Why?

2. Which Vocabulary word goes with *irregular*? Why?

3. Which Vocabulary word goes with *change*? Why?

4. Which Vocabulary word goes with *event*? Why?

5. Which Vocabulary word goes with *assign*? Why?

6. Which Vocabulary word goes with *talent*? Why?

## Vocabulary Strategy: Verify Word Meaning

When you encounter an unfamiliar word in text, there are several ways you can **verify,** or check, its meaning. One way is to look for context clues in words, sentences, or paragraphs that surround the unfamiliar word. When you can't figure out the meaning of a word using context clues, you can look it up in a dictionary. Try to figure out the meaning of *aptitude* in this text.

> **Lin is so intelligent. She has an aptitude for solving difficult problems.**

If you are unfamiliar with the meaning of the word *aptitude,* you can tell from the surrounding text that it has something to do with intelligence, even though the text doesn't state the word's exact meaning. When you consult a dictionary, you will find that *aptitude* means "an inherent ability, as for learning; a talent."

**Practice and Apply**  Complete the chart for the words listed. First, record context clues that give clues about each word's meaning. Consult a dictionary to verify the word's meaning and then write the definition.

| Word | Context Clues | Dictionary Definition |
|------|---------------|----------------------|
| feat (lines 16–19) | | |
| wary (lines 98–100) | | |
| virtually (lines 196–199) | | |

# Language Conventions: Pronoun Number

A **pronoun** is a word used in the place of one or more nouns or pronouns. An **antecedent** is the noun or pronoun to which a pronoun refers. A pronoun must agree with its antecedent in number. In other words, if an antecedent is singular, you should use a singular pronoun. If an antecedent is plural, you should use a plural pronoun. Read this passage from *How Smart Are Animals?*

> **But what about animals? We can't hand them a pencil and paper and give them a test, and we can't ask them what they're thinking. We must find other ways of measuring their "smarts."**

The antecedent, *animals*, is plural, so the pronouns *them* and *their* are also plural.

It is important to recognize and correct shifts in pronoun number. Read this sentence:

> **Marcus gave his dog some treats. His dog gobbled it up.**

The pronoun *it* is singular, and does not match its plural antecedent, *treats*. This shift in number makes the sentence confusing. The correct pronoun to use is *them*.

Here's another example of a shift in pronoun number:

> **A scientist has to be careful when designing an experiment so that their results will be valid.**

The pronoun *their* is plural, and does not match its antecedent, *scientist*, which is singular. The correct pronoun to use is *his* or *her*.

**Practice and Apply**  Correct the shift in pronoun number in each sentence. Some sentences have more then one mistake.

1. At the aquatic park, my uncle trains dolphins to retrieve objects. The dolphins learn quickly and bring the objects back to them.

2. The puppy ran around the park, howling, looking for their owner.

3. Mother blue jays are fiercely protective of her young and will chase away any predators that might threaten it.

4. Barry and Mitch groomed the horse, Princess, after they fed them. Princess whinnied softly as if to say goodnight to him.

5. Zoo visitors are enthusiastic when you see the big cats.

**Peter Christie** (b. 1962) *loved exploring nature in the fields and streams of his native Canada as a child. As a freelance science author and editor, he enjoys writing for young people because they are naturally curious. Young people also love a good story, and for Christie, the best science writing is about telling a story. In his explorations of animal behavior and intelligence, Christie continues to find many stories to tell.*

*from*

# ANIMAL SNOOPS:
## The Wondrous World of Wildlife Spies

Informational Text by Peter Christie

**SETTING A PURPOSE** As you read, pay attention to the distinct ways animals snoop and spy on other animals in their environment and the reasons why they do this.

## Presenting: The Bird-Brained Burglar Bust

The house in Memphis, Tennessee, sat empty: the coast was clear for a robbery. Quickly and secretively, the three young burglars checked the windows and doors and found a way in. They piled up computers, DVD players, and other electronic equipment.

The thieves talked as they worked, paying no attention to the parrot, nearly motionless in its cage. Only when the crooks were ready to make their getaway did the bird finally pipe up. "JJ," it said plainly. "JJ, JJ."

10   Marshmallow—a six-year-old green parrot—had been quietly **eavesdropping**. And the private-eye parrot had learned a thing or two, including the nickname of one of the robbers: J.J.

**eavesdrop**
(ēvz´drŏp´) *intr.v.* To *eavesdrop* is to listen secretly to others' private conversations.

The burglars fled but soon realized that the parrot knew too much. "They were afraid the bird would stool[1] on them," said Billy Reilly, a local police officer. When the thieves returned to the crime scene to nab the bird, police captured them.

The Memphis crooks hadn't counted on Marshmallow's talents as an eavesdropper. Why would they? Few people imagine that animals can be highly skilled spies and snoops. Yet nature is filled with them.

More and more, scientists are discovering that creatures—from bugs to baboons—are experts at watching, listening, and prying into the lives of other animals. While Marshmallow's eavesdropping helped to **foil** human criminals, wild spies work for their own benefit. Spying can be the best or fastest way to find food or a mate, or get early warning of a **predator**.

Until recently, researchers preferred to think of communication between animals as similar to two people talking privately. But wildlife sounds and signals are often loud or bright enough that it is easy for others to listen in. It's like having conversations on social media that every one of your friends—and maybe some of your enemies—can read.

Animal messages are often detected by audiences that were not meant to get wind of[2] them. Hungry gopher snakes, for example, use foot-drumming signals between kangaroo rats to locate a snaky snack. Female chickadees listen in on singing contests of territorial[3] males when choosing a mate.

Biologists call it eavesdropping. It sounds sneaky, but it works well. And some animals are doubly sneaky, changing their behavior when they expect to be overheard. The animal communication network is far more complicated than researchers used to believe.

The **stakes** in wild spy games are high. Eavesdropping can determine whether animals mate, find a home, or enjoy a sneaky life instead of meeting sudden death. It can reveal

**foil**
(foil) *tr.v.* If you *foil* someone, you stop that person from being successful at something.

**predator**
(prĕd´ə-tər) *n.* A *predator* is an animal that survives by eating other animals.

**stake**
(stāk) *n.* A *stake* is something that can be gained or lost in a situation, such as money, food, or life.

---

[1] **stool:** a slang term meaning to tell on someone else, especially to spy on someone or to inform the police; to be a stool pigeon.

[2] **get wind of:** to learn of or find out about.

[3] **territorial** (tĕr´ĭ-tôr´ē-əl): displaying the behavior of defending an area, or territory, from other animals.

whom they should trust and even affect the evolution of songs and signals.

50     Naturally clever secret agents learn things from snooping that help them survive and pass their genes to the next generation. It's one more tool that crafty creatures use to understand the world around them.

## The Hungry Spy: Spying and Prying Predators

The path home was one the eastern chipmunk had traveled a hundred times before: under the ferns to the narrow tunnel into his burrow. The small animal ran briskly through the quiet Pennsylvania forest.

    Suddenly, a flash and a sting. The startled chipmunk jumped. Dried leaves scattered. A sharp pain seared his
60 haunches.[4] Scrambling away, he glimpsed the motionless length of a timber rattlesnake.

    The ambush had succeeded. The deadly serpent had lain coiled and still for many hours, waiting. Even now, after striking, the snake was in no hurry. She would track down the chipmunk's lifeless body after her venom had done its work.

    Patience is among the most practiced skills of a rattlesnake. Snooping is another. Before choosing an ambush site, timber rattlesnakes study the habits of their prey. Using their highly sensitive, flickering tongues, the snakes use scent
70 clues to reveal the routines of rodents and other tasty animals.

    Their tongues are so remarkable that they also pry into the hunting habits of other rattlesnakes. Scenting the difference between a recently fed rattlesnake and a hungry one, they use the clues to hide where another snake has dined and the hunting is likely to be successful.

For many animals, snooping and spying can mean the difference between a full stomach and starvation. Some creatures, like the rattlesnake, spy on the habits of their prey. Others **intercept** private communication—and think of the
80 signals as a call to supper.

    *Photinus* fireflies, for instance, broadcast their mating messages with a light show. These plant-eating beetles flash

**intercept**
(ĭn´tər-sĕpt´) *v.* To *intercept* is to stop or interrupt something.

---

[4] **haunches** (hônch´əz):  the hips, buttocks, and upper thighs of an animal.

luminescent[5] abdomens to wow potential mates on warm North American summer nights.

A bigger relative is named *Photuris*. They also blink biological tail lights during courtship, but are not always looking for a mate. These fireflies are predators that eat their smaller *Photinus* cousins. They spy on their blinking prey and follow the flashing beacon to a nighttime meal.

90 In the still-frigid early spring of northern Europe, a male moor frog begins his tuneless chorus: *Waug, waug, waug.*

Not minding that the ice has barely loosed its grip on the pond edge, the frog has emerged from wintering beneath marsh-bottom muck. He's all set to attract female moor frogs the moment they wake from chilly months of sleep.

*Waug, waug, waug…* **WHAM!**

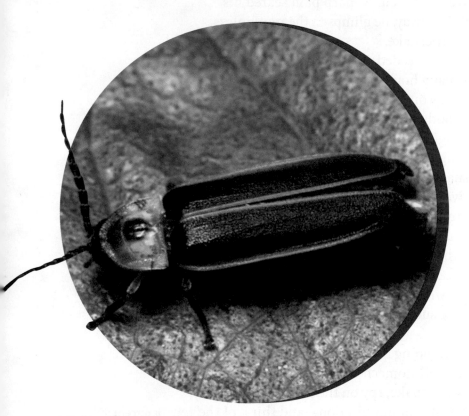

A flashing **Photinus** firefly looks good to his mate—but he looks delicious to his **Photuris** cousin!

---

[5] **luminescent** (loo´mə-nĕs´ənt): brightly lit up.

With a lightning strike, the long, lance-like bill of a white stork jabs through the marsh grass and snatches up the singing frog. In an instant, the tireless music-maker becomes the dinner of a spy.

White storks are master eavesdroppers. They rely on the songs of moor frogs to guide them when they're hunting. The birds are so skillful that they can stealthily follow frog sounds to within two or three strides of an unsuspecting singer.

Some spies can intercept signals sent by plants. Bright flowers invite bees and other animals to come for a meal of pollen or nectar (and to pollinate the plants at the same time). Scientists believe that the most symmetrical flowers—where each half mirrors the other like two sides of a face—help bees and birds recognize them as healthy, with top-quality pollen and nectar.

But crab spiders are deadly spies: they love to eat honeybees and know all about this flower-bee communication system. These sneaky spiders build their bee-trapping webs next to good-looking, symmetrical blooms that bees are more likely to visit.

## Deep Secrets Overheard

*Tick, tick, creak.*

In the eerie, deep-water gloom off the coast of Norway, an enormous sperm whale makes mysterious noises before it abruptly rakes its toothy mouth through a school of swimming squid.

Scientists believe the whale is using echolocation[6]—in the same way bats use echoes of their ultrasonic[7] chirps to "see" in the dark. The whale's ticks and creaks help it zero in on prey.

But the sounds may also help distant sperm whales to find a good meal. The whales' echolocation sounds travel far, farther than the length of Manhattan Island. Sly sperm whales may eavesdrop to learn where another whale is hunting successfully, and drop by for lunch.

---

[6] **echolocation** (ĕk´ō-lō-kā´shən): a system used by some animals to locate objects around them; the animals produce high-pitched sounds and "listen" for the sounds to come back.

[7] **ultrasonic** (ŭl´trə-sŏn´ĭk): not able to be heard by humans; above the range of sound waves that humans can hear.

## Live and Let Die: Spying and Prying to Stay Alive

The tiny antelope jerked his head up to listen.

He was a Gunther's dik-dik, a miniature antelope no larger than a Labrador dog. The tall grasses of the East African savannah[8] surrounded him like a curtain: he was well hidden from leopards and hyenas, but predators were also concealed from him. Through the chattering of birds and insects, the dik-dik recognized a familiar sound: *Gwaa, gwaa, gwaa.*

The insistent cry had an electric effect on the dik-dik. He leaped and bolted through the grass. The fleeing animal glimpsed the source of the sound—on a nearby tree sat a white-bellied go-away bird, sentinel of the savannah. Beyond it, barely visible above the grass, were the large black ears of a hunting wild dog.

Go-away birds are known for their noisy alarm call; the *gwaa* is thought by some to sound like a person shouting "g'away." These social birds feed together in chattering groups. A loud, urgent *gwaa* cry is a signal to other go-away birds that an eagle, wild dog, or other predator has been spotted nearby.

Many of these dangerous hunters also eat dik-diks. The wary antelopes use every trick in the book to avoid becoming a meal—including eavesdropping on go-away bird communication. Unable to see far on the grassy savannah, dik-diks rely on the birds, which spot approaching predators from treetop lookouts.

For many animals, spying is a life-and-death business. Creatures that catch warning signals meant for others may stay one step ahead of enemies. Iguanas on the Galápagos Islands, for instance, keep their ears open even though they never utter a sound themselves.

Galápagos marine iguanas feed on algae in the sea. When they're basking on rocks along the shore, young iguanas are a prime target for hungry Galápagos hawks. Another favorite hawk meal is the Galápagos mockingbird, but these birds have something to say about it: a distinctive chirp warns other mockingbirds a hawk is approaching. Marine iguanas

---

[8] **savannah** (sə-văn´ə):  a flat grassland environment, located in or near the tropics.

eavesdrop on mockingbird conversations. They can tell the alarm from other songs and calls and will dash for cover when they hear it.

Some animal snoops are born recognizing the warning signals of different creatures; others, such as bonnet macaques, have to learn. These monkeys of southern India often pal around with langur monkeys. Langurs are good lookouts, and
170 macaques will quickly scramble up a tree when they overhear a langur warning cry—as long as the macaques have learned the correct langur language.

Scientists say bonnet macaques at one animal reserve[9] respond to recorded Nilgiri langur alarm shrieks but are slower to flee after a similar cry by Hanuman langurs—which would rarely be seen there. Farther north, only Hanuman langurs are common and bonnet macaques there have learned the opposite langur language. They jump at the sound of Hanuman warnings but are less bothered by Nilgiri cries.

180 Eavesdropping on the alarm signals of other animals is useful, but spying on predators directly also has advantages. Geometrid moths, for instance, are slow, night-flying moths that can be easily overtaken by hunting bats. To make up for their sluggish speed, the moths have espionage skills—they can track bat radar.

Many moths are stone deaf, but geometrid moths have ears that tune into the ultrasonic frequency bats use when navigating by echolocation. Not only can they hear a bat approaching, geometrid moths can also tell how close it is.
190 If a bat is nearer than two bus lengths away, a moth will begin evasive zigzag flying. Closer than one bus length and the moth folds its wings and **plummets** to the ground, where the bat won't follow.

**plummet**
(plŭm´ ĭt) *v.* If you *plummet*, you fall straight down, suddenly and steeply.

# Pop and Stop

The seagrass is alive with the sound of music.

Singing fish—male Gulf toadfish—are performing their bizarre courtship serenade in the azure waters off the coast of Florida: *Grunt, grunt, trrrrrrt.* It's a song only a female

---

[9] **animal reserve:** an area of land that is protected to preserve wild animals that are often rare or endangered.

toadfish could like… unless an appreciative bottlenose dolphin is also in the audience.

200    Dolphins love to eat toadfish, and they eavesdrop on the singing fish to find their dinner. But the dolphins aren't the only spies in the sea: the toadfish spy on the dolphins, too. Dolphins make a low-frequency "pop" sound when they use sonar to reveal toadfish hidden under dense seagrass. The fish listen for popping from hunting dolphins, and stop singing when the sound gets near.

**COLLABORATIVE DISCUSSION**  With a partner or a small group, discuss facts and examples in the text that illustrate animals' abilities to snoop on other animals. Discuss whether or not these examples prove that animals have intelligence.

# Analyze Text: Anecdote

COMMON CORE RI 3

Peter Christie begins *Animal Snoops* with an anecdote about a parrot that helped police officers catch some burglars. An **anecdote** is a short account of an event that is usually intended to entertain or make a point. Authors often use an anecdote to introduce or give an example of an important idea in a way that is easy to understand and remember. Think about how the anecdote in *Animal Snoops* introduces animals' observation of other animals and the issue of animal intelligence. Look for more anecdotes as you analyze *Animal Snoops*.

# Integrate Information

COMMON CORE RI 5, RI 7

Authors of nonfiction texts often include features that draw the readers' attention or provide information in visual ways. For example, a text may contain larger or darker type that highlights certain ideas. These are **text features,** or elements such as boldface type, headings, and subheadings, that help organize and call attention to important information. Text features help readers better understand a text and its topic. Text features also include:

| Photographs | Captions |
| --- | --- |
| visual records of real people and objects in real settings. Photographs help readers understand exactly what something looks like. | brief explanations of what is in a photograph. Captions can indicate how the photographs relate to the text. |

Good readers integrate the information in text features, such as photos and captions, with the information in the text. To **integrate,** or synthesize, information means to take individual pieces of information and combine them in order to develop a coherent understanding of a topic. Think about the new or important ideas you learned as you read this text. How does the author use photographs and captions to help clarify those ideas?

Look for more examples of text features, including photographs and captions, as you analyze *Animal Snoops*. Be sure to synthesize the information in the text and in each text feature to gain a better understanding of what you read.

# Analyzing the Text

COMMON CORE
RI 1, RI 2, RI 3, RI 4, RI 5, RI 7, W 2, W 6, W 7, SL 5

*Cite Text Evidence*   Support your responses with evidence from the text.

1. **Analyze** The author uses an anecdote to introduce the topic. What important ideas are illustrated in the anecdote?

2. **Infer** The author refers to the animals in the text as spies and snoops. What does he mean by this?

3. **Interpret** In line 45, the author says "The stakes in wild spy games are high." What does this statement mean?

4. **Summarize** Review lines 128–193. What is the central idea of this section? Explain how the author elaborates on this idea.

5. **Compare** A rattlesnake and a sperm whale find their prey in different ways. Review lines 54–75 and lines 116–127. How does each animal gather information? How does each use that information?

6. **Synthesize** What important idea does the photograph and caption of the firefly (below line 96) help you understand?

# PERFORMANCE TASK

**Media Activity: Presentation** Do research to find out more about an animal mentioned in *Animal Snoops*.

- Choose one animal from the text.
- Do research to find more information about the animal, including its environment and its behavior.

- Use both print and digital sources for your research.
- Synthesize the information from the text with your research to present a slideshow presentation that describes the animal and how it lives. Include photographs with captions in your presentation.

# Critical Vocabulary

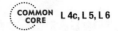 

**eavesdrop**     **foil**     **predator**     **stake**     **intercept**     **plummet**

**Practice and Apply**  Describe what is alike and different about the two words in each pair.

1. *eavesdrop* and *listen*

2. *foil* and *intercept*

3. *stake* and *reward*

4. *predator* and *enemy*

5. *plummet* and *fall*

## Vocabulary Strategy: Synonyms

A **synonym** is a word that has the same meaning or similar meaning as another word. However, the words are not all interchangeable. For example, the word *big* has many synonyms, such as *large, bulky, huge*, and *enormous*. You can have a big appetite, but you would not have a bulky appetite. You can use a **thesaurus,** or a book of synonyms, to find the precise word to describe *appetite*. Thesauruses are available in print and digital versions.

Look at how *eavesdrop* and its synonyms—*overhear* and *snoop*—are used in these sentences.

**The parrot decided to eavesdrop when it heard the burglars talking.**

**The parrot happened to overhear the burglars.**

**The neighbors decided to snoop in the backyard to see if the burglars dropped any valuables.**

Does the sentence completed with *eavesdrop* mean exactly the same as the sentences completed with *overhear* and *snoop*? How are the meanings of the three sentences different?

**Practice and Apply**  Read each sentence. Think about the meaning of the underlined word in each one. Then look up the word in a print or digital thesaurus. Choose a synonym that gives the sentence a more precise meaning. Discuss your choices with a partner.

1. Gopher snakes <u>notice</u> foot-drumming signals between kangaroo rats.

2. Some birds give out <u>noisy</u> warning signals when a predator is nearby.

3. Hunting bats can easily overtake the <u>slow,</u> night-flying geometrid moth.

# Language Conventions: Capitalization

In your writing, you will need to apply the rules of capitalization to proper adjectives. **Proper adjectives** are formed from **proper nouns**, which name specific people, places, and things. Proper adjectives are always capitalized and often end in the letters *n, an, ian, ese*, and *ish*. Many proper adjectives describe cultural references or locations.

In the following sentence from *Animal Snoops*, note how the proper adjective is capitalized.

> **The tall grasses of the East African savannah surrounded him like a curtain: he was well hidden from leopards and hyenas, but predators were also concealed from him.**

The chart shows two types of proper adjectives that require capitalization.

| Type | Example |
|---|---|
| cultural references | *The Chinese dumplings were delicious. Erin is taking African dance lessons.* |
| location | *We live close to the Canadian border. During our trip, we visited many Midwestern cities.* |

**Practice and Apply**  Identify the proper adjectives that should be capitalized in each sentence. Then write the sentences correctly.

1. My sister and I love italian cooking.

2. Jamaica is formerly a british colony.

3. The pacific northwest region of the United States has many national forests.

4. We visited the english countryside.

5. We enjoyed strolling through the quaint austrian village.

*Interactive Lessons*

If you need help . . .
• **Writing Informative Texts**
• **Using Textual Evidence**

# Write a Literary Analysis

In "The Mixer" you read a story from a dog's perspective. In other selections in this collection, you learned about various aspects of animal intelligence and behavior, suggesting that animals are smarter than we think. In "Tribute to the Dog," George Graham Vest observed that the dog is the one friend who "never deserts man" and "never proves ungrateful or treacherous." In the following activity, draw from the ideas and examples in these selections to help you write an analysis of the dog as the main character and narrator in "The Mixer."

**COMMON CORE**

**W 2a–f** Write explanatory texts.
**W 4** Produce clear and coherent writing.
**W 5** Develop and strengthen writing as needed.
**W 9a** Draw evidence from literary or informational texts to support analysis, reflection, and research.
**W 10** Write routinely over extended time frames.

## A successful literary analysis

- provides an introduction that captures the reader's attention and clearly states the topic

- clearly organizes ideas and concepts

- presents examples and quotations to support ideas

- provides a conclusion that leaves the reader with a question, insight, or memorable impression

**PLAN**

**Gather Information** Review "The Mixer." Jot down information about the dog's personality and character traits and how these influence how he narrates the story.

- Describe the personality of the dog in "The Mixer." What character traits are revealed through the dog's thoughts and actions?

- How does the dog view the other characters in the story?

- Explain the struggle or conflict that the dog faces. Tell how the dog responds to the conflict.

- Analyze the dog's actions. What influences these actions? What do the actions tell you about the dog?

- Identify whether the dog changes or grows as a result of the story's events. How is the dog different at the end of the story?

*my*Notebook

Use the annotation tools in your eBook to mark up key details that you might want to include. Save each detail to your notebook.

**ACADEMIC VOCABULARY**

As you plan and present your writing, be sure to use the academic vocabulary words.

*benefit*
*respond*
*environment*
*distinct*
*illustrate*

**Organize Your Ideas** Think about how you will organize your ideas. A three-column chart can help you present your ideas effectively.

| Character Traits | Quote or Example | Your Reflection |
|---|---|---|
| What the Character Says | | |
| What the Character Thinks | | |
| What the Character Does | | |

**Consider Your Purpose and Audience** Think about who will read or listen to your analysis, and what you want them to understand. Keep this in mind as you prepare to write.

PRODUCE

**Write Your Analysis** Review your notes and the information in your chart as you begin your draft.

- Begin by introducing "The Mixer," including your interpretation of the main character and his narration.

- Focus on the events in the story. Tell how the character changes and grows. Include evidence, such as examples and quotations, to support your ideas.

- Use the information in your chart to help you organize your ideas and evidence logically.

- Write a conclusion that summarizes your interpretation and focuses on the most important ideas you want to convey.

*my*WriteSmart

Draft the text for your analysis in *my*WriteSmart. Focus on listing and developing your ideas, rather than perfecting your choice of language.

*my* WriteSmart

Have your partner or a group of peers review your draft in *my*WriteSmart. Have them note if any ideas do not follow a logical sequence.

**Review Your Draft** Use the chart on the following page to evaluate your draft. Work with a partner to determine if you have explained your ideas clearly. Consider the following:

- Check that the introduction clearly states your main ideas.
- Examine each paragraph. Is each idea clearly stated and supported with evidence from the story?
- Be sure that the ideas are organized in a logical sequence. Do transition words help the reader follow along?
- Check that your conclusion summarizes your points and leaves the reader with a lasting impression.

**PRESENT**

**Create a Finished Copy** Finalize your analysis and choose a way to share it with your audience. Consider these options:

- Present your analysis as a speech to the class.
- Post your analysis as a blog on a personal or school website.
- Share your analysis with a magazine or website that focuses on animals.

# COLLECTION 2 TASK A
## LITERARY ANALYSIS

| Ideas and Evidence | Organization | Language |
|---|---|---|
| **ADVANCED** • The introduction is engaging, tells the title and author of the work, and presents a unique idea about one or two literary elements.<br>• Important points are supported by specific, relevant details.<br>• The conclusion effectively summarizes the analysis and gives an original idea or insight about the work. | • The organization of important points and supporting details is effective and logical throughout the analysis.<br>• Transitions logically connect related ideas. | • The analysis reflects an appropriately formal style.<br>• Language is precise and presents ideas in an original way.<br>• Sentences vary in structure and have a rhythmic flow.<br>• Spelling, capitalization, and punctuation are correct.<br>• Grammar, usage, and mechanics are correct. |
| **COMPETENT** • The introduction tells the title and author of the work but could be more engaging; it presents an idea about one literary element.<br>• One or two important points need more support.<br>• The conclusion summarizes most of the analysis but does not give an original idea or insight to think about. | • The organization of important points and supporting details is confusing in a few places.<br>• A few more transitions are needed to connect related ideas. | • The writing style is inconsistent in a few places.<br>• Most language is precise.<br>• Sentences vary somewhat in pattern and structure.<br>• Some spelling, capitalization, and punctuation mistakes occur.<br>• Some grammar and usage errors are repeated. |
| **LIMITED** • The introduction tells the title and author of the work, but is vague about the idea or literary elements the writer wishes to present and analyze.<br>• Most important points could use more supporting details; details are often too general.<br>• The conclusion is incomplete or unclear and does not present a new idea or insight. | • The organization of most important points is logical, but many supporting details are misplaced.<br>• More transitions are needed throughout to connect related ideas. | • The writing style becomes informal in many places.<br>• Language is repetitive or too general in many places.<br>• Sentence structures hardly vary; some fragments or run-on sentences occur.<br>• Spelling, capitalization, and punctuation are often incorrect but do not make reading difficult.<br>• Grammar and usage are often incorrect, but the writer's ideas are still clear. |
| **EMERGING** • The introduction is missing or confusing.<br>• Supporting details are irrelevant or missing.<br>• The conclusion is missing. | • The organization is not logical; important ideas are presented randomly.<br>• No transitions are used, making the analysis difficult to understand. | • The style is inappropriate for the analysis.<br>• Language is inaccurate, repetitive, and too general.<br>• Sentence structure is repetitive and monotonous; fragments and run-on sentences make the analysis hard to follow.<br>• Spelling, capitalization, and punctuation are incorrect and distracting throughout.<br>• Many grammatical and usage errors change the meaning of the writer's ideas. |

*Interactive Lessons*

If you need help...
• **Writing Informative Texts**
• **Conducting Research**

# Write an Expository Essay

In the excerpt from "How Smart Are Animals?" you learned that although studying animal behavior and intelligence can be tricky, scientists are coming up with new ways to measure it. In the following activity, draw from the ideas and examples in this text and others in this collection as well as any appropriate print and digital sources you research, to help you write a well-crafted essay on how animals exhibit intelligence.

**COMMON CORE**

**W 2a–f** Write explanatory texts.
**W 4** Produce clear and coherent writing.
**W 5** Develop and strengthen writing as needed.
**W 7** Conduct short research projects.
**W 8** Gather relevant and credible information from multiple print and digital sources.
**W 9b** Draw evidence from literary or informational texts to support analysis, reflection, and research.
**W 10** Write routinely over extended time frames.

## A successful expository essay

• provides an introduction that catches the reader's attention and clearly states the topic

• uses an organizational strategy to present main ideas

• includes evidence such as facts, definitions, quotations, and examples to support ideas

• uses appropriate transitions to connect ideas

• provides a conclusion that supports the information presented

## PLAN

*my*Notebook

Use the annotation tools in your eBook to find evidence to support your ideas. Save each detail to your notebook.

**Gather Information** Review the excerpts from "How Smart Are Animals?" and "Animal Snoops: The Wondrous World of Wildlife Spies." Look for information and ideas about how intelligence in animals can be determined.

• Distinguish different ways that animals show intelligence.
• Identify how scientists measure animal intelligence.
• Consider how an animal's environment can affect intelligence.
• Jot down facts, definitions, quotations, and examples that support these ideas.

**ACADEMIC VOCABULARY**

As you write about animal intelligence, be sure to use the academic vocabulary words.

*benefit*
*respond*
*environment*
*distinct*
*illustrate*

**Do Research** Use print and digital sources to gain a better understanding of how animals show intelligence.

• Search for facts that support your ideas. If possible, back up facts with research or endorsements from experts.

- Use relevant sources. Find sources online using appropriate keywords. Also use your school library to research books and magazines.

- Cite real-life examples of animal intelligence from credible sources.

- Check that the information you find is supported by the information you read in the collection.

**Organize Your Ideas** Think about how you will organize your essay. A hierarchy chart can help you present your ideas logically.

**Consider Your Purpose and Audience** Think about who will read or listen to your essay, and what you want them to understand. Keep this in mind as you prepare to write.

## PRODUCE

**Write Your Essay** Review your notes and the information in your hierarchy chart as you begin your draft.

- Begin by introducing the topic. Include an attention-grabbing lead, such as a question, real-life account, surprising fact, or quote. Be sure your topic is well defined.

- Develop your main idea with supporting facts, details, examples, and quotations from experts. Group supporting information and ideas into paragraphs.

- Make sure the paragraphs transition from one logical point to another.

- Write a conclusion that supports your main ideas, and leaves the reader with a lasting impression.

*my***WriteSmart**

Write your rough draft in *my*WriteSmart. Focus on getting your ideas down rather than perfecting your choice of language.

**Review Your Draft** Use the chart on the following page to evaluate your draft. Work with a partner to determine if you have explained your ideas clearly. Consider the following:

Have your partner or group of peers review your essay in *my*WriteSmart and note any main ideas that are not supported.

- Check that the topic is clearly defined.

- Examine each paragraph. Does each have one distinct idea? Is each idea supported with facts, details, quotations, or examples?

- Be sure that ideas are organized in a logical sequence. Do transitions help the reader follow along?

- Check that your conclusion supports the information presented.

**PRESENT**

**Create a Finished Copy** Finalize your essay and choose a way to share it with your audience. Consider these additional options:

- Present your essay as a speech to the class.

- Post your essay as a blog on a personal or school website.

- Convert your essay into a multimedia presentation.

| | Ideas and Evidence | Organization | Language |
|---|---|---|---|
| **ADVANCED** | • The introduction is appealing, is informative, and catches the reader's attention; the topic is clearly identified.<br>• The topic is well developed with clear main ideas supported by facts, details, definitions, and examples from reliable sources.<br>• The conclusion effectively summarizes the information presented. | • The organization of main ideas and details is effective and logical throughout the essay.<br>• Transitions logically connect related ideas. | • The essay reflects a formal writing style.<br>• Language is strong and precise.<br>• All sources are correctly cited.<br>• Sentences vary in pattern and structure.<br>• Spelling, capitalization, and punctuation are correct.<br>• Grammar, usage, and mechanics are correct. |
| **COMPETENT** | • The introduction could be more appealing and engaging; the topic is clearly identified.<br>• One or two important points could use more support, but most main ideas are well supported by facts, details, definitions, and examples from reliable sources.<br>• The conclusion summarizes the information presented. | • The organization of main ideas and details is confusing in a few places.<br>• A few more transitions are needed to connect related ideas. | • The writing style is inconsistent in a few places.<br>• Language is too vague or general in some places.<br>• Most sources are correctly cited.<br>• Sentences vary somewhat in pattern and structure.<br>• Some spelling, capitalization, and punctuation mistakes occur.<br>• Some grammar and usage errors are repeated. |
| **LIMITED** | • The introduction is only partly informative; the topic is unclear.<br>• Most important points could use more support from relevant facts, details, definitions, and examples from reliable sources.<br>• The conclusion is unclear or only partially summarizes the information presented. | • The organization of main ideas and details is logical in some places, but it often doesn't follow a pattern.<br>• More transitions are needed throughout to connect related ideas. | • The writing style becomes informal in many places.<br>• Language is too general or vague in many places.<br>• Many sources are incorrectly cited.<br>• Sentence pattern and structure hardly vary; some fragments or run-on sentences occur.<br>• Spelling, capitalization, and punctuation are often incorrect but do not make reading difficult.<br>• Grammar and usage are often incorrect, but the writer's ideas are still clear. |
| **EMERGING** | • The introduction is missing or confusing.<br>• Supporting facts, details, definitions, or examples are unreliable or missing.<br>• The conclusion is missing. | • The organization is not logical; main ideas and details are presented randomly.<br>• No transitions are used, making the essay difficult to understand. | • The style is inappropriate for the essay.<br>• Language is too general to convey the information.<br>• Source citations are incorrect or not included.<br>• Sentence structure is repetitive and monotonous; fragments and run-on sentences make the essay hard to follow.<br>• Spelling, capitalization, and punctuation are incorrect and distracting throughout.<br>• Many grammatical and usage errors change the meaning of the writer's ideas. |

©13/Corbis

# Dealing with Disaster

❝ Through every kind of disaster and setback and catastrophe. We are survivors. ❞

—Robert Fulghum

# Dealing with Disaster

In this collection, you will discover how people react in the face of disaster.

hmhfyi.com

COLLECTION

## PERFORMANCE TASK Preview

After reading this collection, you will have the opportunity to complete two performance tasks:

• In one, you will create a multimedia presentation with a partner or small group.

• In the second, you will write a narrative about what happens after a ship hits an iceberg.

## ACADEMIC VOCABULARY

Study the words and their definitions in the chart below. You will use these words as you discuss and write about the texts in this collection.

| Word | Definition | Related Forms |
|---|---|---|
| **circumstance** (sûr´kəm-stăns´) *n.* | a condition or fact that affects an event | circumstantial, circumstantially |
| **constraint** (kən-strānt´) *n.* | something or someone that limits or restricts another's actions | constrain |
| **impact** (ĭm´păkt´) *n.* | something striking against another; also, the effect or impression of one thing on another | impaction |
| **injure** (ĭn´jər) *tr.v.* | to hurt or cause damage | injurer, injurious, injury, injuriously, injuriousness |
| **significant** (sĭg-nĭf´ĭ-kənt) *adj.* | meaningful; important | significantly, significance |

**Brenda Z. Guiberson** *wanted to be a jungle explorer when she was a child. Much of her childhood was spent swimming, watching birds and salmon, and searching for arrowheads near her home along the Columbia River in the state of Washington. After volunteering at her child's school, Guiberson became interested in writing nature books for children. She says that she writes for the child in herself, the one who loves adventure, surprises, and learning new things—a jungle explorer in words.*

# MAMMOTH SHAKES AND MONSTER WAVES,
## Destruction in 12 Countries

Informational Text by Brenda Z. Guiberson

**SETTING A PURPOSE** As you read, pay attention to how earthquakes affect people, animals, the land, and the ocean, and think about how people explain and deal with the impact of these damaging events.

## Head for the Hills! It's Earth Against Earth

For centuries, a big chunk of earth under the Indian Ocean known as the India plate has been scraping against another chunk of earth, the Burma plate. At eight o'clock in the morning on December 26, 2004, this scraping reached a breaking point near the island of Sumatra in Indonesia. A 750-mile section of earth snapped and popped up as a new 40-foot-high cliff. This created one of the biggest earthquakes ever, 9.2 to 9.3 on the Richter scale.[1] At a hospital, oxygen tanks tumbled and beds lurched. At a mosque, the dome crashed to the floor. On the street, athletes running a race fell

10

---

[1] **Richter scale** (rĭk´tər): a scale ranging from 1 to 10 that expresses the amount of energy released by an earthquake; named after Charles Richter, an American seismologist.

to the ground and a hotel crumbled. Houses on stilts swayed and collapsed. A man tried to grab a fence that jumped back and forth, up and down, and side to side. The quake, the longest ever recorded, lasted 10 minutes. Some islands rose up, and others sank, leaving "fish now swimming around in once idyllic, palm-fringed villages," wrote Madhusree Mukerjee. The shaking was so severe that it caused the entire planet to vibrate one half inch. And that was just the beginning.

20 Maslahuddin Daud, a fisherman, said, "I had barely started fishing when the earthquake struck. The earth shook violently, coconut trees crashed noisily against each other, and people fell down in prayer. . . . I lingered at the beach to talk with an older fisherman. We watched the water drain from the beach, exposing thousands of fish." He saw a huge wave filling the horizon. Someone yelled, *"Air laut naik"*—"The sea is coming"—but tourists stayed on the beach, and locals collected flopping fish stranded by the receding water. Few seemed to understand that destruction was rolling their way at the speed of a jetliner.

## The Sea Is Coming?

30 All along the shorelines of a dozen countries, villagers, tourists, royalty, and soldiers were in the path of monster waves able to cross the entire ocean. People near the epicenter[2] of the earthquake were swallowed up in less than 30 minutes. The tsunami[3] didn't reach others for an hour, two hours, even six hours or more. Without a warning system, hundreds of thousands of people were caught unawares, many so far away from the source of the wave that they never even knew there had been an earthquake.

Yet earth against earth was the cause of all their problems.
40 When the sea floor **ruptured**, trillions of tons of water were

**rupture**
(rŭp′chər) *v.* To *rupture* means to break open or burst.

---

[2] **epicenter** (ĕp′ĭ-sĕn′tər): the point of the earth's surface directly above the focus of an earthquake.

[3] **tsunami** (tsōō-nä′mē): a huge ocean wave caused by an underwater earthquake or volcanic eruption.

instantly pushed up 40 feet by the rising land. Then the water came back down, and the collapse created a series of waves. These were not wind-whipped waves moving along at a few miles per hour. They were tsunami waves, racing out at 500 miles per hour. In deep water, the waves caused hardly a blip, but whenever one reached a coastline, the bottom slowed in the shallow water while the top kept coming, higher and higher, until massive walls of water, some over 100 feet high, smashed into land with the strength of many hurricanes.

50     The waves just kept coming, salty and polluted, with the second more powerful than the first, then the third and fourth, all so cluttered with debris that they became moving piles of concrete and cars, boats and coconuts, wood and tin, nails and glass, survivors and corpses. A shopkeeper said the noise was "like a thousand drums." As wave after wave smashed through villages, children were pulled from the arms of parents, clothing was ripped from bodies, and people and their possessions were flipped over, cut, and punched. Some were swept two miles inland, while others were caught in the

60 backwash[4] and carried out to sea. When the water started to drain, survivors shimmied down from coconut trees or other high places feeling dazed and confused. Weak voices called out to them from vast piles of debris. It was a changed world, soggy and broken; nothing looked familiar, nothing at all.

    This was the scene in many countries around the Indian Ocean. The waves swamped the Aceh Province of Indonesia, surged through Sri Lanka, Thailand, Myanmar (Burma), Bangladesh, Malaysia, and India, flooded the Maldives and Seychelles, and eventually reached Africa. In Aceh,

70 169,000 died quickly, but death was also reported 16 hours and 5,300 miles away in South Africa. The tsunami left 225,000 dead, 500,000 injured, and millions without homes or jobs. One-third of the dead were children, and 9,000 were tourists. Plain luck helped some to survive. Only a few received a warning.

---

[4] **backwash** (băk´wôsh´): a backward flow of water.

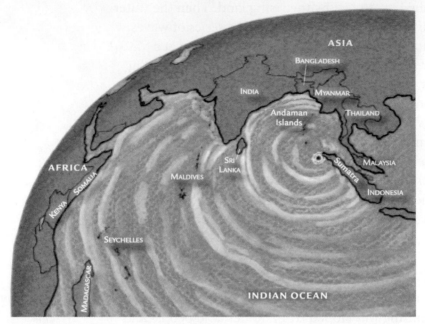

Racing at 500 miles per hour, the first wave took 20 minutes to reach Sumatra, 2 hours to Sri Lanka, 3½ hours to the Maldives, and 7½ hours to reach Africa. Traveling across the ocean at just two feet high, the waves piled up in shallow water to form great surges that reached 20 feet, 40 feet, and even much higher.

## Trumpeting Elephants, Skittering Crabs, and the Power of Story

On a beach in Thailand, 10-year-old Tilly Smith was enjoying Christmas vacation and building sand castles with her sister. She noticed hundreds of tiny crabs scuttling out of the water. Then she saw the sea retreat far back into the ocean, like some great monster was slurping it up with a straw. No one seemed to notice, so she started to play again but then stood up in alarm as the sea turned white, churning with bubbles. A great wave was building up on the horizon as far as she could see. Fishermen's longboats were bobbing up and down like toys in a bathtub. Tilly remembered a geography lesson two weeks earlier at her school in England. These were the warning signs she had just learned. A tsunami was coming! Her mother wasn't convinced, but Tilly persuaded her father to get the hotel staff to evacuate guests while she alerted those

80

90 on the beach. With this warning, they became some of the few survivors in the area.

On another beach, an eight-year-old named Amber Mason was riding on an elephant called Ning Nong. The elephant started to trumpet loudly and paw the ground with feet able to sense low vibrations. The mahout[5] riding with her tried to calm the animal, but the elephant charged up a hill. While the girl, elephant, and mahout made it safely to high ground, others on the beach couldn't outrun the tsunami waves that soon followed.

100 Before the waves hit Sri Lanka, all the animals in a national park started to behave strangely. Monkeys chattered with terror, snakes went rigid, cattle bolted, and flamingos took flight. All of them scrambled to the highest places they could reach, and the keepers, who had never seen such behavior, decided to follow.

Near the Similan Islands off the western coast of Thailand, local divers saw dolphins jump madly around them and then torpedo far out to sea. "Quick, follow them," they urged the captain. They knew stories of animals that help and thought 110 these dolphins could sense something unusual that the divers could not detect. Because, along with several other boats, they followed the dolphins to deep water, they were spared the smashing blow of the tsunami.

Closer to shore, Wimon, a fisherman, was eating watermelon when the strangeness began. The water turned murky with rocks bubbling at the top. He looked up to see the beach stretching out five times its normal width. Had there ever been such a low tide? Suddenly he was thrown off his bench and felt weightless. His boat bobbed up and down 120 in a strange wave that surged past to flood his village to the tops of the coconut trees. He worried about his wife and two daughters, who couldn't swim. Then he saw the second wave, spitting, rising even higher than the first. Should he head straight into it? He watched other fishermen try, and their boats split apart. He decided to go sideways, was lifted 20 feet, 30 feet, until he was surrounded by a hazy mist and felt weightless again. He fell with a slam but survived. Of the 24 longboats in the area, his was the only one still intact.

---

[5] **mahout** (mə-hout´):  a keeper and driver of an elephant.

The ancient tribes on the remote Andaman and Nicobar
130   Islands have lived close to nature for centuries. They are said
to detect changes by the smell of the wind and **gauge** the
depth of the sea with the sounds of their oars. Every minute
they pay close attention to the cries of birds and the behavior
of animals. These natural clues warned them that something
big was about to occur, and the stories of the forefathers told
them what to do. "When the earth shakes, the sea will rise up
onto the land. . . . Run to the hills or get into a boat and go far
out to sea."

Some members of aboriginal[6] groups survived the tsunami
140   because they read the signs of nature; heeded ancient stories;
packed up their children, baskets, nets, arrows, and embers;
and headed for the hills. Most people, however, lost their
homes and precious possessions. Almost all wild animals,
including tigers, elephants, water buffalo, monkeys, and birds,
survived in good shape. Endangered orangutans and other
creatures that live in the rain forests of Sumatra were not
affected by the tsunami until it was all over. The trees are an
easy source of timber, and forest creatures are losing vast acres
of habitat as people rebuild.

## Swamped and Scared

150   People caught in the tsunami suffered many injuries. After the
waves receded, some were caught under deep piles of debris. A
trapped deliveryman named Romi called and called for help
but received no response. After two days, rain fell, and he was
able to collect water for drinking. Mosquitoes feasted on him
at night. On the third day, more people were trudging through
the murky water to look for survivors. Four men tried to
rescue Romi, but they failed. Finally on the fifth day, 25 men
worked four hours and were finally able to haul him through
miles of debris. All around, tens of thousands of corpses
160   needed to be buried quickly. Elephants and bulldozers were
brought in to help with the wreckage.

As survivors returned to their villages, they often found
that nothing remained—no familiar landmarks, no driveway,
car, or motorbike. The house was gone and everything in it,
including toothbrush, comb, lipstick, and frying pan. Power

**gauge**
(gāj) *tr.v.* To *gauge*
something is to
measure it or judge
it, as in to make an
estimate.

---

[6] **aboriginal** (ăbˊə-rĭjˊə-nəl):  having lived in an area from the beginning; earliest
known.

was out, and phones were dead. According to one survivor, "Many people were literally left with nothing—not even coins in their pockets or clothes on their backs." They suffered from breathing problems after swallowing mud, sand, and toxic water. Before starting to rebuild, many spent days, and then weeks, looking for lost relatives.

On the first day, those nearest the earthquake were **traumatized** by 37 more tremors. During the next days, there were more earthquakes: 18 on Monday, 5 on Tuesday, 7 on Wednesday, 7 on Thursday, 9 on Friday. Each time the ground trembled, people who still had shelter scampered outside, "joining the others who feared that the walls and ceiling would fall in on them," wrote Barry Bearak.

**traumatize**
(trôˊmə-tīzˊ, trouˊ-) *tr.v.*
To *traumatize* means to upset or shock someone, causing emotional and mental pain.

The tsunami left a huge problem of contaminated water. In Sri Lanka, for instance, 40,000 wells were destroyed and the freshwater aquifer[7] became toxic. In the Maldives, 16 coral reef atolls[8] lost their freshwater and may be uninhabitable until decades of monsoons can refresh the supply. Other countries had similar problems as the salty waves mixed with freshwater and sewers. Thousands of banana, rice, and mango plantations were destroyed by thick layers of salty sludge. For drinking, Spain and Australia delivered gigantic water purifying machines. Military ships from the United States and Singapore made freshwater from the sea, and several companies sent water purifiers, including one that could turn raw sewage into drinking water in seconds. Some purifiers were lightweight and could be flown in by helicopter to areas that lost all road and bridge access.

As people sought help for severe injuries, supplies were scarce. At one hospital only 5 of 956 health workers were available. Barry Bearak wrote, "Little in the way of supplies was kept in the emergency room—no IVs, no painkillers, few bandages. As in many poor nations, new patients were examined and then their families were sent to buy drugs, syringes, and other items needed for treatment." When health workers ran out of anesthetic, ice cubes were used to deaden the pain. When they ran out of suture threads, wounds were wrapped in plastic snipped from seat covers or left open. The

---

[7] **aquifer** (ăkˊwə-fər): an underground layer of earth, sand, or gravel that holds and can release water.

[8] **atolls** (ătˊôlzˊ): ringlike coral islands and reefs that nearly or entirely enclose a body of water.

ones who had wounds cleaned but not stitched were actually lucky. After three days, those with stitches often developed fatal infections when contaminated water was trapped inside their injury.

Relief workers from around the world eventually arrived with vaccines, **antibiotics**, food, blankets, tents, field hospitals, 210 building supplies, and mosquito nets. In general, health care was well planned and prevented the outbreak of diseases, but the number of dead and wounded could be overwhelming. Sometimes tourists were treated before villagers. Villagers were treated before Burmese immigrant workers. Friends and family were treated before strangers. In India, people called Dalits, "untouchables," traditionally judged to be "less than human," were denied aid, even fresh drinking water. Social problems that exist before a disaster get magnified or changed afterward.

**antibiotic**
(ăn´tĭ-bī-ŏt´ĭk) *n.* An *antibiotic* is a drug used in medicine to kill bacteria and to cure infections.

# Rebuilding

220 Parts of India, Sri Lanka, and Indonesia were war zones before the tsunami, and these situations complicated relief efforts. In Indonesia, for instance, no foreigners had been allowed into Aceh Province for years because of the fighting. After so many died, however, foreign help was welcomed. Later, peace talks were held to aid the relief efforts because workers were afraid to go into war zones. Groups felt it was time for Muslims, Hindus, Christians, and Buddhists to work together as members of a world community.

In many areas it was both the custom and law that women 230 could enter the water only if fully clothed and wearing a head scarf. Therefore, most of them had never learned to swim, and the waves killed three times more women than men. Before the tsunami, women in Aceh Province had a hard time finding spouses because large numbers of men had died fighting in the long guerrilla[9] war. After the tsunami, thousands of men were left without wives and children, and there were many new marriages.

In some areas, unscrupulous people saw a chance to increase their wealth during the chaos. A powerful

---

[9] **guerrilla** (gə-rĭl´ə):  irregular military; a guerrilla war is one fought by small, irregular bands of soliders that try to undermine the enemy.

240   corporation, the Far East Company, for instance, tried to take land from villagers in Laem Pom, Thailand, who had lived on a beautiful beach for many years. With all documents gone, it was hard to prove ownership of the land. A local woman named Dang decided to fight when the company posted a bodyguard to keep them out. Not only did the survivors want to rebuild, but they were desperate to search through the debris for bodies. Dang told her story to Parliament, but nothing changed. Finally she asked her neighbors to bring whatever documents they had; as a group, they would

250   challenge the bodyguard. "He might be able to stop one of us, or even a few or us, but he can't stop all of us," she said. Twenty-seven families gathered together and were able to walk past the bodyguard. They set up a camp on a concrete slab.

An official offered Dang a bribe of five furnished houses plus a scooter and telephone if she would leave. Dang refused and eventually received donations of 30,000 baht (about $830); 10,000 bricks; 5,000 tiles; and help from Thai students. Erich Krauss wrote, "It reminded her that there were still good people in this world—people whose hearts were large enough

260   to care about the people of Laem Pom."

A man named Wichien missed the tsunami because he was inland diving for river sand used to make ceramics. His wife, Nang, tried to escape on a truck but got caught in a traffic jam. She had worked since the age of six and once learned how to harvest coconuts, so she was able to shimmy up a tree. She managed to hold on at the top even as ants swarmed over her body. As she called out to Buddha, she could hear what sounded like "a thousand children calling out for their parents and a thousand parents calling out for their children."

After spending several days in a hospital, she and her husband discovered that part of their house remained standing but needed much repair. Some materials were provided by a group who also brought Bibles and instructions to read certain sections. "Our God will help you," they said, and then sent a van to take them to church. This was confusing to Nang because, according to Erich Krauss, "She was a Buddhist. She loved going to the temple to pray with the monks. When the wave had taken her under, she had called out to the great Buddha."

The church group never really provided the help Nang wanted, so she took a job cleaning the house of a local official. She then discovered "rice cookers, gas stoves, dishes, bowls" stored in a room instead of being distributed to villagers who needed them. When Nang asked for a rice cooker, "the leader's assistant would say she would get something tomorrow but the tomorrow they talked about never came," said Erich Krauss.

Wonderful assistance was donated to the tsunami survivors but many of them also had to deal with theft, deception, and disappointment. Relief workers had the best success when they found out what the local people needed, included them in the planning, and then made sure necessary materials were delivered. For example, when villagers wanted to rebuild using traditional methods, engineers gave them a demonstration showing that a similar but stronger house design would hold up better in the next earthquake. Models were made of both types of houses and put on a "shake table" to imitate an earthquake. When the traditional house crumbled and the reinforced house did not, all agreed the new design would be better. Then they worked together to include features that fit the lifestyle of the village.

## Tree Zones

Many people noticed that some shorelines were damaged much more than others, even though they were close together. A study in October 2005 by seven nations that included ecologists, botanists, geographers, a forester, and a tsunami wave engineer found that "areas with trees suffered less destruction than areas without trees." They calculated that 30 trees per 100 square meters could reduce the maximum flow of the waves by more than 90 percent. "Just like the **degradation** of wetlands in Louisiana almost certainly increased Hurricane Katrina's destructive powers," they concluded, "the degradation of mangroves in India magnified the tsunami's destruction." They found similar results in areas where coral reefs had been destroyed to make shrimp farms. Houses with landscaping also experienced much less scouring and water damage.

**degradation**
(dĕg´rə-dā´shən) *n.* Damage done to something in nature, by weather or water for example, is called *degradation.*

After the study of beach damage, local communities decided to replant mangrove forests and clean out debris from coral reefs. These inexpensive actions will provide benefits not just for the villagers but also for sea creatures that use forest roots and coral for food, shelter, and nurseries.

In some areas, people have not been allowed to rebuild their homes along shorelines and must move inland. In crowded countries with little available land, this has not been easy. Fishermen suffered the most damage from the tsunami, and they prefer to live by the sea to watch their boats and nets. After the tsunami, some were sent to live in places so far from the sea that the transportation costs were more than their earnings as fishermen.

## Warnings

The 2004 tsunami revealed that the Indian Ocean was in desperate need of a tsunami warning system, and 25 seismic stations[10] relaying information to 26 information centers were installed. Signs were also put up to identify evacuation routes. Still, the system is not yet perfect. Another earthquake and tsunami struck Indonesia on July 17, 2006, but warnings were not passed along in time, and another 600 people died. Some suggest that the loudspeakers used by mosques to call Muslims to prayer would be effective for broadcasting tsunami warnings.

---

[10] **seismic stations** (sīz´mĭk stā´shənz): places that have sensors to detect ground motion, a clock, and a recorder for collecting data; must have several stations connected to a network to provide enough data to detect and locate earthquakes.

340    The 2004 event also revealed that the Pacific Ocean warning system, in use since the 1960s, had only three of its six seafloor pressure sensors in working order. Money for upkeep had been scarce, even though tsunamis are common in the Pacific Ocean. In 1946 a tsunami started by an Alaska quake killed 159 people in Hilo, Hawaii, 3,000 miles away. Another Alaska quake in 1964 was a 9.2 magnitude, the biggest ever recorded in North America. It killed 115 people in Alaska, and the tsunami that followed killed another 16 people in Oregon and California. After the 2004 tsunami scare, the

350    United States provided more funds to expand and update the warning system.

    Nature may provide advance warning signs of earthquakes if we learn to read them. In underwater studies along fault lines, for instance, interesting changes have been found in the populations of single-celled microorganisms called foraminifera. These tiny creatures, with shells the size of a grain of sand, are very particular about their environment. When the elevation of land changes, the organisms relocate. In underwater earthquake areas, they seem to move about 5

360    to 10 years before the great shaking caused by uplifting plates. Scientists hope to learn more about this because it is possible that the foraminifera can provide warnings for disasters of huge proportions.

## The "Orphan Tsunami"

It takes an underwater earthquake of **magnitude** 9.0 or above to generate big tsunami waves. Several events like this have already occurred on the West Coast of the United States, but few people have heard about them. The evidence has only recently been found, and much of it was not in places where scientists usually look. These mega events sometimes occurred

370    when people with a written language were not around to record them.

    The last event was over 300 years ago and has been called an "orphan tsunami" because some witnesses had no idea where it came from. The Samurai in Japan kept records of crop production for hundreds of years. On January 27, 1700, they recorded huge waves along 600 miles of coastline that caused flooded fields, ruined houses, fires, and shipwrecks. Since the Samurai were thousands of miles from the quake,

**magnitude**
(măg´nĭ-tōōd´) *n.*
*Magnitude* is a measure of the amount of energy released by an earthquake.

they did not feel the shaking. To them, the big waves were a
380 mysterious "high tide." Legends in Japan refer to this flooding
event also.

Where did this orphan tsunami come from? Thousands of
miles across the ocean, Native American myths in the Pacific
Northwest provide a possible answer. Tribes from California
and on up the coast to Vancouver Island have many stories that
refer to a day when the earth shook and the ocean crashed,
leaving villages wiped out and canoes stranded high in trees.
Often the event is described as a battle between a great whale
and a thunderbird. Makah elder Helma Ward said, "The tide
390 came in and never left. There was a whale in the river and
the people couldn't figure out how it got there." To pinpoint
the date, scientists have found evidence of a magnitude-9
earthquake off the Washington coast that warped the seafloor
on January 26, 1700. At the same time, a whole forest died just
before the growing season began, and soil samples reveal great
saltwater flooding in many coast areas.

 *There was a whale in the river and the people couldn't figure out how it got there.*

The epicenter of this earthquake was just off the coast of
Washington and Oregon, where the Juan de Fuca plate pushes
under the North American plate in the same manner as the
400 Burma and India plates. The next big earthquake here will
threaten 10 million people along 500 miles of coastline that
includes large cities like Seattle, Portland, San Francisco, and
Vancouver, B.C. A warning system has been added off the
West Coast and evacuation routes established. Scientists now
monitor 24 hours a day and must live within five minutes of
their work because some coastal areas could be swallowed up in
15 minutes, and every minute of advance warning will count.

The blend of myth and evidence found in the earth has
brought scientists and Native Americans to share a new way

410 of looking at the past called geomythology. Ancient stories tell us that events happened before and will happen again. Science studies the danger, while stories enrich the record and provide clues about frequency. Native Americans have developed a new interest too. Ron Brainard, chairman of the Coos Tribal Council in Coos Bay, Oregon, asked his mother to tell the stories again because before they didn't listen.

## Now You See It, Now You Don't

In the disaster of 2004, coral beds rose up to become land, and several islands sank. These events were recorded by eyewitnesses, cameras, satellites, and other measuring
420 devices. Sinking islands are more than myths. Six islands visited by early European explorers are now gone, some just under the waves.

In 1798, John Goldingham, a British astronomer and traveler to India, wrote down the details of a myth about the "Seven Pagodas," a group of temples from the seventh century that was swallowed up by the sea. The city was reported to be so beautiful that the gods sent a flood to engulf six of its seven temples.

That was the myth. Then came the 2004 tsunami, with
430 ferocious waves that shifted great volumes of beach sand. This scouring revealed handmade blocks and carvings of a lion, the head of an elephant, and a horse in flight, all at the mythical location of the Seven Pagodas. Did the tsunami uncover an ancient mythical place? Archaeologists have dated the carvings to the seventh century and are busy studying.

Myths from the South Pacific also tell of deities that "fish up" islands from the water and sometimes throw them back. Ancient tales around the world are providing clues about other prehistoric seismic events. When it's earth against earth,
440 nature keeps a record, and human survivors will always have a story to tell.

**COLLABORATIVE DISCUSSION** The last section of "Mammoth Shakes and Monster Waves" describes possible connections between myths and real-life events. With a partner, use evidence from the text to discuss whether you think legends can explain actual events in our earth's history.

# Analyze Structure: Cause and Effect

Writers often use patterns of organization to help explain particular ideas. One commonly used pattern is **cause-and-effect** organization, which shows the relationship between an event and its **cause** (an event or action that makes another event happen) or **effect** (the outcome of an event or action). For example, the author of "Mammoth Shakes and Monster Waves" explains that a huge underwater earthquake took place on December 26, 2004. The text then gives details about what happened after this event. The earthquake was the cause that resulted in multiple effects.

To analyze cause-and-effect relationships:

- Look for words and phrases, such as *because, cause, effect, led to,* and *since,* that help you identify specific relationships between events.
- Determine how the ideas or events are related. A single cause can have one or multiple effects. More than one cause can lead to one effect.

Often, a visual such as a diagram can also help you understand the relationship between events. A diagram is an illustration that shows how something works or the relationship between the parts of a whole. When you examine a diagram in a text, you integrate its information with that of the text. To **integrate,** or **synthesize,** means to take individual pieces of information and combine them in order to gain a better understanding of a subject.

# Determine Meanings of Words and Phrases

**Technical language** refers to a group of terms suited to a particular field of study or topic. The terms *epicenter, Richter scale,* and *seismic stations* in "Mammoth Shakes and Monster Waves" are all technical terms related to earthquakes. Often technical words are defined in the text or in footnotes. For example, the term *Richter scale* in line 8 is defined in a footnote. However, the word *plate* in line 3 is not. *Plate* in this instance does not mean "a dish." In this selection, it has a specific meaning related to earthquakes. As you analyze the selection, refer to a dictionary to help you determine how words are used in the text.

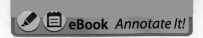
# Analyzing the Text

RI 1, RI 4, RI 5,
RI 7, RI 10,
SL 1a-d, SL 5

**Cite Text Evidence**   Support your responses with evidence from the text.

1. **Summarize**  Reread lines 1–18. Explain how the earthquake starts.

2. **Synthesize**  Review lines 30–75 and examine the diagram that follows this text. What information do you learn from the diagram and the caption that helps you understand what the author means by "flooded the Maldives and Seychelles"?

3. **Analyze**  Review lines 129–142. Then reread the footnote for *aboriginal*. What does the footnote explain that helps you understand the people's response to the tsunami?

4. **Cause/Effect**  Review lines 150–219. What cause-and-effect relationships can you identify in this section? Explain how the ideas and events are related.

5. **Interpret**  Reread lines 330–363. What kinds of warning systems have proved useful as a result of lessons learned from this tsunami?

## PERFORMANCE TASK

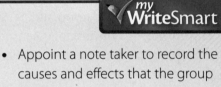

**Speaking Activity: Discussion**  With a small group, discuss the cause of the tsunami and its effects. Use details from "Mammoth Shakes and Monster Waves" in your discussion.

- Each member of the group should review the text and take notes on causes and effects.
- Appoint a member of the group to lead the discussion. The group leader should make sure that each group member has a chance to contribute his or her ideas to the discussion.

- Appoint a note taker to record the causes and effects that the group agrees on.
- Together, make a chart that shows these cause-and-effect relationships. Show how one event led to another and had multiple effects.
- Share your chart with the rest of the class.

# Critical Vocabulary

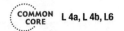 

| | | |
|---|---|---|
| rupture | gauge | traumatize |
| antibiotic | degradation | magnitude |

**Practice and Apply** For each vocabulary word, choose the sentence that best fits its meaning.

1. **rupture** After a freezing evening, my car's engine would not start.
   After I drove over broken glass, my car got a flat tire.

2. **gauge** We figured out that the storm left eight inches of snow.
   We were amazed by the beauty of the snowstorm.

3. **traumatize** Joan prefers cats to dogs because she thinks dogs are noisy.
   Joan fears dogs because she was bitten by one.

4. **antibiotic** The doctor gave me medicine for an ear infection.
   The doctor told me to get plenty of rest.

5. **degradation** The soil improved after compost was worked into it.
   The soil lacked nutrients after the drought.

6. **magnitude** The earthquake was measured to be quite small.
   The earthquake occurred at 5:50 in the evening.

# Vocabulary Strategy: Greek Affixes

An **affix** is a word part that can be added to the beginning or the end of a base word to form a new word. Many affixes come from ancient Greek. Knowing the meaning of Greek affixes can help you recognize and understand related words as well as build your vocabulary.

The Greek prefix *anti-* means "opposite" or "against." The word *antibiotics* refers to medicines that work against infections. Other words that share the Greek affix *anti-* include *antidote, antifreeze, antisocial,* and *anticrime.*

**Practice and Apply** Use a chart like the one shown to explore the meaning of more words with Greek affixes. List other words that share each affix. Be sure to use a dictionary to confirm the meanings of the other words.

| Greek Affix | Meaning | Example | Other Words |
|---|---|---|---|
| *auto-* | "self, same" | *autograph* | |
| *geo-* | "Earth" | *geography* | |
| *-phone* | "sound, voice" | *telephone* | |
| *-ism* | "an action or characteristic" | *criticism* | |

# Language Conventions: Shifts in Pronoun Person

A **pronoun** is a word that is used in place of a noun or another pronoun. The word that the pronoun refers to is its **antecedent.** Pronouns should always agree in number with their antecedents. Read this sentence from "Mammoth Shakes and Monster Waves":

> **As survivors returned to their villages, they often found that nothing remained—no familiar landmarks, no driveway, car, or motorbike.**

The pronouns *their* and *they* both agree with their third-person antecedent, *survivors.*

It is important to recognize and correct shifts in pronoun person. Read this sentence:

> **When people are terrified and anxious, we often don't make thoughtful decisions.**

The antecedent *people* is third person, but the pronoun *we* does not match because it is first person. This shift in person makes the sentence awkward and confusing. The correct pronoun to use is *they.*

Here's another example of a shift in pronoun person:

> **I heard wood splintering and glass breaking. Your heart started to beat like a drum.**

The antecedent *I* is first person, but the pronoun *Your* is second person. The correct pronoun to use is *My.*

**Practice and Apply**  Correct the shift in pronoun person in each sentence.

1. Megan was determined in her efforts to collect supplies to help the flood victims. By the end of the week, they had a truckload of goods to ship out.

2. Exhausted, we watched the sun set over the horizon. They were so tired, but still amazed at how beautiful it was.

3. I was inspired by the story about the people who helped transport its elderly neighbors from the storm site.

4. The captain shouted, "All of you need to move these vehicles. Our cars cannot block the street!"

5. Zoo visitors are enthusiastic when you see the big cats.

**Background** *On August 29, 2005, Hurricane Katrina ripped through the Gulf coast. It was one of the strongest storms to hit the United States in the last 100 years. With winds of more than 125 miles per hour, Katrina caused massive damage all along the coast. But no city was affected more than New Orleans. Almost 80 percent of the city was underwater; thousands of people were left homeless. Almost 2,000 people lost their lives, and hundreds more were missing. Years after the hurricane, parts of the city have still not been rebuilt.*

# from After the Hurricane

Poem by Rita Williams-Garcia

# Watcher
## After Katrina, 2005

Poem by Natasha D. Trethewey

**Rita Williams-Garcia** (b. 1957) *was writing stories and trying to get them published by the time she was twelve years old. Today, her writing draws on her experiences growing up in New York City and, more significantly, the issues faced by urban black teenagers in the modern world. For Williams-Garcia, writing for young people is her passion and her mission. She believes that teens hunger for stories that reflect their circumstances, and she hopes her writing strengthens their understanding of themselves and others.*

**Natasha D. Trethewey** (b. 1966) *has deep ties to the Gulf coast. She was born in Gulfport, Mississippi, and returned to the Gulf coast often as a child, spending her summers there with her mother's family and in New Orleans with her father. Her father, also a poet, encouraged her to write poems on long car trips to keep her from getting bored. Trethewey was named poet laureate of the United States in 2012. Her collection of poems* Native Guard *won the Pulitzer Prize in poetry in 2007.*

**SETTING A PURPOSE** As you read each poem, pay attention to the events that take place and how each speaker reacts to them.

# After the Hurricane
## Poem by Rita Williams-Garcia

If toilets flushed,
if babies slept,
if faucets ran,
old bodies didn't die in the sun,
5   if none of it were real,
if we weren't in it,
this could be a disaster movie with
helicopters whipping up sky overhead,
Special Effects brought in to create Lake George
10      and not the great Mississippi
        meeting Lake Pontchartrain.
Out-of-work waiters would pose as policemen,
locals as extras paid in box lunches.
For set design, dump raw sewage, trash everywhere,
15   news trucks, patrol cars, army tanks, Humvees.

If none of it were real,
if we weren't in it,
this could be a big-budget disaster flick
King, Jasper, and I'd rent
20   after band practice
like we did last Tuesday watching *Titanic* on Grandmama's
sofa.
That Jasper could *laaaugh* at all the actors drowning
while the band played—*glub, glub, glub*—to the death.

25   But this ain't that. We're waist high in it.
Camera crews bark, "Big Mike! Get this, over here!"
"Roll tape."
"Got that?"
"Good God!"
30   "Shut it down."

This ain't hardly no picture.
We're not on location.
We're herded. Domed in,
feels like for good
35  unless you caught a bus like Ma
or Jasper's family (save Jasper).
I still want to smash a camera,
break a lens, make them stop shooting.
But King says, "No, Freddie. Gotta show it.
40  Who'd believe it without film?"

Still no running water, no food, no power, no help.
The world is here but no one's coming.
The Guard[1] is here with rifles pointed.
The Red Cross got their tables set up.
45  Weathermen, anchors,[2] reporters, meteorologists,
a fleet of black Homeland SUVs.
The world is here
but where is the water? The food? The power?
The way to Ma or Jasper's people.
50  They just herd us, split us, film us, guard us.
No one said feed us. No one brought water.
The world is here but no one's coming.
Helicopters overhead beat up on our skies.

                    * * *

Miracle One.
55  King noses around the news guys,
runs back to Jasper and me.
"There's water trucks held up on the highway.
Gallons, girl! Water by the gallons.
Fresh drinking water.
60  Clean shower water.
See that, Freddie. The water company loves us.
Somebody thought to send us water."
Even with our trumpets drowned, King's chest swells.
He booms, "Brass Crew, are you with me?
65  Let's get outta here, bring back some water."

---

[1] **The Guard:** the National Guard of the United States, units of reserve soldiers that are controlled by each state of the United States. The National Guard responds to both the federal (national) and state governments for a variety of emergency needs, both in this country and abroad.

[2] **anchors** (ăng′kərs): people who organize and read the news on media newscasts (television, radio, online); they work with a team of reporters, camera operators, and so on to report the news.

How can I leave TK and Grandmama?
How can I leave, and be happy to leave?
Watch me. Just watch me
high step on outta here
70  for the water I say I'll bring back.
Honest to God, I heard "Brass Crew" and was gone.
I heard *Elbows up,*
*natural breath!*
That was enough.
75  How can I leave, and be happy to leave?
Easy. As needing to breathe new air.

King's got a First Trumpet stride. Jasper walks.
I lick the salt off my bare arms,
turn to look back at the people
80  held up by canes, hugging strollers, collapsible
black and newly colored people,
women with shirts for head wraps.
Salt dries my tongue.
I turn my eyes from them and walk.
85  I don't have to tell myself
it's not a school project for Ms. LeBlanc,
"The Colored Peoples of Freddie's Diorama."[3]

---

[3] **diorama** (dī′ə-răm′ə): a three-dimensional scene in which models of people, animals, or other objects are arranged in natural poses against a painted background.

Green pasted just so, around the huts just so.
The despair just right.
90  It's not my social studies diorama
depicting "Over There," across the Atlantic,
the Pacific. Bodies of water.
Way, way over there.
The refugees of the mudslides,
95  refugees of the tsunami,
refugees of Rwanda.
No. It is US. In state. In country.
Drowned but not separated by
bodies of water or by spoken language.
100  The despair is just right, no translation needed.
We are not the refugees in my social studies diorama.
We are 11th graders,
a broken brass line,
old homeowners, grandmamas, head chefs, street
105  performers, a saxophonist mourning the loss of his Selmer
horn of 43 years and wife of 38 years. We are aunties,
dry cleaners, cops' daughters, deacons, cement mixers,
auto mechanics, trombonists without trombones, quartets
scattered, communion servers, stranded freshmen, old
110  nuns, X-ray technicians, bread bakers, curators,[4] diabetics,
shrimpers,[5] dishwashers, seamstresses, brides-to-be, new
daddies, taxi drivers, principals, Cub Scouts crying, car
dealers, other dealers, hairstylists, too many babies, too
many of us to count.
115  Still wearing what we had on when it hit.
When we fled,
or were wheeled, piggybacked, airlifted, carried off.
Citizens herded.
We are Ms. LeBlanc, social studies teacher, a rag wrapped
120  around her head,
And Principal Canelle. He missed that last bus.

* * *

---

[4] **curators** (kyŏŏ-rāʹtərs):  people who manage and oversee; most often describes
those who manage a museum and its collection of art.
[5] **shrimpers** (shrĭmpʹərs):  people who catch shrimp—small edible sea animals
with a semi-hard outer shell.

Minor Miracle.
We walk past the Guard.
You'd think they'd see us
125 marching on outta here.
You'd think they'd stop us. Keep us domed.
But we're on the march, a broken brass line.
King, Jasper, and me, Fredericka.

King needs to lead; I need to leave.
130 Been following his lead since
band camp. Junior band. Senior band.
Box formations, flying diamonds, complicated transitions.
Jasper sticks close. A horn player, a laugher. Not a talker.
See anything to laugh about?
135 Jasper sticks close. Stays quiet. Maybe a nod.

Keeping step I would ask myself,
Aren't you ashamed? No.
Of band pride? No.
You band geek. So.
140 Aren't you ashamed? No.
You want to parade? So.
Raise your trumpet? So.
Aren't you ashamed? No.
To praise Saint Louis?
145 "Oh, when the saints go marching in?"
Aren't you ashamed? No.
Of strutting krewe⁶
On Mardi Gras? The Fourth of July?
These very streets
150 Purple and gold, bop
Stars and Stripes, bop
Aren't you ashamed?
To shake and boogie?
Aren't you ashamed?

---

⁶ **krewe** (kro͞o): any of several groups of people who organize and participate in
the annual Mardi Gras carnival in New Orleans.

155 To enjoy your march,
while Grandmama suffers
and no milk for TK?
Tell the truth. Aren't you ashamed?
No. I'm not ashamed.
160 I step high, elbows up.
Band pride.

King asks, "Freddie, what you thinking?"
I say, "I'm not thinking, King."
But I'm dried out on the inside.
165 Hungry talks LOUD, you know.
"Let's try the Beauxmart. The Food Circle. Something."

King knows better. He doesn't say.
Still, we go and find (no surprise)
the Beauxmart's been hit. Stripped. Smashed.
170 Forget about Food Circle and every corner grocery.
Nothing left but rotten milk,
glass shards.[7] Loose shopping carts.
Jasper sighs. Grabs a cart.

Stomach won't shut up.
175 Talking. Knotting. Cramping. I whine,
"Let's go to Doolie's."
Again, King knows better. Still, we go,
almost passed right by. Didn't see it until
Jasper points. King sighs.
180 Check out the D in Doolie's, blown clear off.
The outside boarded up, chained up, locked.
Black and red spray-painted:
LOOTERS WILL BE SHOT.

---

[7] **shards** (shärds):  small pieces of something that has been broken.

I can't believe it.
185 Doolie who buys block tickets to home games
Doolie who sponsors our team bus
Band instruments, uniforms (all underwater),
Chicken bucket championships. The band eats half-price.
My eyes say, *Freddie, believe the spray paint*:
190 *Big Sean Doolie will shoot the looters.*
Yeah. Big Sean Doolie.
Believe.

King (First Trumpet) was right,
he doesn't make me (Second) like I'm second.
195 A simple, "Come on, Brass. Let's get this water."
I follow King. Jasper pushes the cart.
First, Second, Third. No bop step,
high step, no feather head shake,
no shimmy[8] front, boogie back.
200 Just walk.

"Hear that?"
Another helicopter overhead.
Another chopper stirring up the Big Empty.
Wide blades good for nothing but whirling up
205 heavy heat, heavy stink on empty streets
full of ghosts and mosquitoes.
Swat all you want. Look around.
Nothing here but us in Big Empty.

---

[8] **shimmy** (shĭm´ē):  to do the shimmy, a dance involving rapid shaking of the body.

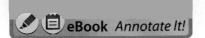 

# Analyze Structure

 COMMON CORE RL 5

A poem's **form** is the way its words and lines are arranged on a page. Some forms are also defined by poetic devices, such as rhyme and rhythm. A poem's form is closely linked to its meaning, which makes the poem's form important to its message.

**Free verse** is a form of poetry with no regular patterns of rhyme, rhythm, or line length. When poets write free verse, they can create rhythms that they think will best communicate their ideas.

"After the Hurricane" is written in free verse, which the poet can use to portray the sounds and rhythms of everyday speech. In lines 16–24, the poet uses both short and long line lengths to create rhythms that make the words sound like a person telling you a story. Line length can also be used to call attention to certain words and ideas.

To analyze free verse, ask questions such as the following:

- What ideas is the poet expressing? How does the use of free verse support those ideas?
- What rhythms are created by the line lengths in the poem? How do these poetic devices add to my understanding of the poem?

Notice where the poet ends each line as you analyze "After the Hurricane."

# Analyzing the Text

COMMON CORE RL 1, RL 2, RL 4, RL 5, RL 6

**Cite Text Evidence** Support your responses with evidence from the text.

1. **Summarize** Reread lines 1–30. How does the speaker describe what happens after the hurricane? What does the speaker compare the scene to?

2. **Analyze** Review lines 101–121 and examine how the poet arranges the words and lines. Describe the variations in line lengths. What circumstances is the poet trying to explain, and how does the form support those ideas?

3. **Compare** Review lines 129–161, in which the speaker tells about the friends' roles in the band. Compare these ideas with those in lines 184–200. How has the hurricane affected the friends' roles and changed the speaker's feelings? Explain which words show this.

# Watcher
## After Katrina, 2005
by Natasha D. Trethewey

At first, there was nothing to do but watch.
For days, before the trucks arrived, before the work
of cleanup, my brother sat on the stoop[1] and watched.

He watched the ambulances speed by, the police cars;
5   watched for the looters who'd come each day
to siphon[2] gas from the car, take away the generator,

the air conditioner, whatever there was to be had.
He watched his phone for a signal, watched the sky
for signs of a storm, for rain so he could wash.

10  At the church, handing out diapers and water,
he watched the people line up, watched their faces
as they watched his. And when at last there was work,

[1] **stoop** (sto͞op): a small porch or staircase that leads up to the door of a house or other building.

[2] **siphon** (sīˊfən): to move a liquid up and out of a container, over a barrier, and into a new container, using an inverted, U-shaped tube.

he got a job, on the beach, as a *watcher*.
Behind safety goggles, he watched the sand for bones,
15  searched for debris that clogged the great machines.

Riding the prow of the cleaners, or walking ahead,
he watched for carcasses[3]—chickens mostly, maybe
some cats or dogs. No one said *remains*.[4] No one

had to. It was a kind of faith, that watching:
20  my brother trained his eyes to bear
the sharp erasure[5] of sand and glass, prayed

there'd be nothing more to see.

**COLLABORATIVE DISCUSSION**  With a partner, use evidence from
the poems to discuss what happened during Hurricane Katrina
and how people who experienced it were affected.

---

[3] **carcasses:** (kär´kəs-əz):  dead bodies; usually referring to dead animals that
have been killed for food.

[4] **remains** (rĭ-mānz´):  all that is left after other parts have been taken away, used
up, or destroyed; here, refers to dead bodies of people.

[5] **erasure** (ĭ-rā´shər):  an act or instance of erasing—removing by rubbing, wiping,
or scraping; the state of being erased.

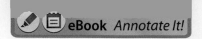 

# Analyze Structure

Many poems are written in traditional form. Poems in **traditional form** follow fixed rules, such as a certain number of lines, a rhyme scheme, and a definite structure.

A **line** of poetry is simply that: the text that appears on one line. The line is the core unit of a poem and can be a complete sentence, part of a sentence, or even a single word. Poets use **line breaks,** or the places where lines of poetry end, to add emphasis to certain words and phrases.

A **stanza** is a group of two or more lines that form a unit in a poem. A stanza is like a paragraph in prose. Depending on the form, the stanzas of a poem

- may or may not have the same number of lines
- will, most often, express a separate idea or emotion

In a traditional form, the stanzas are often a determined length.

When you analyze traditional forms of poetry, think about questions like the following:

- What specific idea does each stanza express?
- Why might the poet have chosen to use this form to structure the poem?
- Taken together, how do the stanzas help build the poem's meaning?

In the poem "Watcher," notice the number of lines in each stanza and how the ideas in the stanzas are connected through the use of the poem's form.

# Analyzing the Text

COMMON CORE RL 1, RL 2, RL 4, RL 5

 *Cite Text Evidence* Support your responses with evidence from the text.

1. **Interpret** Reread lines 1–3 of "Watcher." What do you notice about the length of each line? How does the shortest line contribute to the poem's meaning?

2. **Draw Conclusions** Reread lines 4–9 of "Watcher." What clues tell you that these stanzas work together as a complete idea? Do other stanzas in the poem work the same way? Why do you think the author chose to structure the poem this way?

# Determine Meanings of Words and Phrases

COMMON CORE RL 4

One of many poetic elements poets use is called alliteration. **Alliteration** is the repetition of consonant sounds at the beginning of words. This line from "After the Hurricane" includes two examples of alliteration:

**Out-of-work waiters would pose as policemen,**

The repeated *w* and *p* sounds add a bouncing rhythm to the line. The rhythm creates an almost lighthearted feeling for this part of the poem, where the poet shows how the speaker's situation could be a movie, except that it is actually happening.

By adding rhythm and repetition, alliteration can also affect meaning and tone. **Tone** refers to the poet's attitude and how he or she feels about a topic. The repeated *w* sound in lines 45–49 in "After the Hurricane" points out important words, such as *Weathermen, world, where, water,* and *way.* It helps create a tone that shows that the topic makes the poet feel a certain way about the incidents taking place in the aftermath of the storm.

Look for more examples of alliteration and its effect on tone as you analyze the two poems.

# Compare and Contrast Poetic Forms

COMMON CORE RL 9

To compare and contrast poetic forms, especially free verse and traditional forms, examine the following:

- the structure of the stanzas, including number of lines and line length
- emphasis created by line breaks
- the use of rhythm
- rhyme scheme or lack of rhyme
- imagery
- the use of alliteration

Notice how "After the Hurricane" and "Watcher" convey meaning through the use of their different forms.

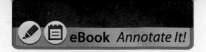
# Analyzing the Texts

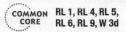

COMMON CORE   RL 1, RL 4, RL 5, RL 6, RL 9, W 3d

**Cite Text Evidence**  Support your responses with evidence from the text.

1. **Interpret**  Read aloud lines 201–208 of "After the Hurricane." What examples of alliteration do you hear? How does this sound connect with the topic and title, and what tone or feeling does this alliteration evoke?

2. **Identify**  Read aloud "Watcher" and identify the alliterative sound you hear most often. Which words are emphasized with this sound? How does it relate to the tone and meaning of the poem?

3. **Compare**  How is the tone in "Watcher" similar to or different from the tone in "After the Hurricane"? Tell why.

4. **Compare**  Review how "After the Hurricane" and "Watcher" are structured. How are their structures and general use of rhythm alike? How are they different?

5. **Analyze**  A poem's form can affect its meaning. How does each poem's form support the personality of the speaker that you hear in the poem's words and rhythms?

---

## PERFORMANCE TASK

**Writing Activity: Poem**  Write a poem about a disaster you have read about recently. Your poem can be written in free verse or in a structured form with stanzas.

- First, choose the event you will write about. Make sure you have enough information about what it was like.
- Decide on the main idea or message you want to convey. Do you want to create a vivid picture of the event or share a strong emotion?

- Think about your likely audience. Will they be familiar with the event?
- Decide who will be the speaker in your poem.
- Use imagery to bring the event to life.
- As you write your poem, be sure you choose a form that will best convey your ideas.

**James Berry** (b. 1924) *was raised in a tiny seaside village in Jamaica. At seventeen, he left home for the United States. Unhappy there, he returned to Jamaica four years later. Although Berry moved to England in 1948, much of his writing focuses on his early Caribbean home. He chooses to use the local language of his childhood in his writing because he wants to express the experience of living in his home village. Berry has won many literary awards for his poetry and stories.*

# THE BANANA TREE

## Short Story by James Berry

**SETTING A PURPOSE** As you read, pay attention to the clues that help you understand the relationship between the boy and his father. Write down any questions you have while reading.

In the hours the hurricane stayed, its presence made everybody older. It made Mr. Bass see that not only people and animals and certain valuables were of most importance to be saved.

From its very buildup the hurricane meant to show it was merciless, unstoppable, and, with its might, changed landscapes.

All day the Jamaican sun didn't come out. Then, ten minutes before, there was a swift shower of rain that raced by and was gone like some urgent messenger-rush of wind. And again everything went back to that quiet, that unnatural quiet. It was as if trees crouched quietly in fear. As if, too, birds knew they should shut up. A thick and low black cloud had covered the sky and shadowed everywhere, and made it seem like

10

night was coming on. And the cloud deepened. Its deepening spread more and more over the full stretch of the sea.

The doom-laden afternoon had the atmosphere of Judgment Day[1] for everybody in all the districts about. Everybody knew the hour of disaster was near. Warnings printed in bold lettering had been put up at post offices, police stations, and school-yard entrances and in clear view on shop walls in village squares.

Carrying children and belongings, people hurried in files and in scattered groups, headed for the big, strong, and safe community buildings. In Canerise Village, we headed for the schoolroom. Loaded with bags and cases, with bundles and lidded baskets, individuals carrying or leading an animal, parents shrieking for children to stay at their heels, we arrived there. And looking around, anyone would think the whole of Canerise was here in this vast superbarn of a noisy chattering schoolroom.

With violent gusts and squalls the storm broke. Great rushes, huge bulky rushes, of wind struck the building in heavy, repeated thuds, shaking it over and over and carrying on.

Families were huddled together on the floor. People sang, sitting on benches, desks, anywhere there was room. Some people knelt in loud prayer. Among the refugees' noises a goat bleated, a hen fluttered or cackled, a dog whined.

Mr. Jetro Bass was sitting on a soap box. His broad back leaned on the blackboard against the wall. Mrs. Imogene Bass, largely pregnant, looked a midget beside him. Their children were sitting on the floor. The eldest boy, Gustus, sat farthest from his father. Altogether, the children's heads made seven different levels of height around the parents. Mr. Bass forced a reassuring smile. His toothbrush mustache[2] moved about a little as he said, "The storm's bad, chil'run. Really bad. But it'll blow off. It'll spen' itself out. It'll kill itself."

Except for Gustus's, all the faces of the children turned up with subdued fear and looked at their father as he spoke.

---

[1] **Judgment Day:** a religious term for the end of the world.

[2] **toothbrush mustache** (mŭs´tăsh´): a small, rectangular unshaven area of hair on a man's upper lip.

"Das true wha' Pappy say," Mrs. Bass said. "The good Lord won' gi' we more than we can bear."

Mr. Bass looked at Gustus. He stretched fully through the sitting children and put a lumpy, blistery hand—though a huge hand—on the boy's head, almost covering it. The boy's clear brown eyes looked straight and unblinkingly into his father's face. "Wha's the matter, bwoy?" his dad asked.

He shook his head. "Nothin', Pappy."

"Wha' mek you say nothin'? I sure somet'ing bodder
60  you, Gustus. You not a bwoy who frighten easy. Is not the hurricane wha' bodder you? Tell Pappy."

"Is nothin'."

"You're a big bwoy now. Gustus—you nearly thirteen. You strong. You very useful fo' you age. You good as mi right han'. I depen' on you. But this afternoon—earlier—in the rush, when we so well push to move befo' storm broke, you couldn' rememba a t'ing! Not one t'ing! Why so? Wha' on you mind? You harborin' t'ings from me, Gustus?"

Gustus opened his mouth to speak but closed it again.
70  He knew his father was proud of how well he had grown. To strengthen him, he had always given him "last milk"³ straight from the cow in the mornings. He was thankful. But to him his strength was only proven in the number of innings he could pitch for his cricket team. The boy's lips trembled. What's the good of tellin' when Pappy don' like cricket. He only get vex⁴ an' say it's an evil game for idle hands! He twisted his head and looked away. "I'm harborin' nothin', Pappy."

"Gustus . . ."   — getting a hint smt will happen
80  At that moment a man called, "Mr. Bass!" He came up quickly. "Got a hymnbook, Mr. Bass? We want you to lead us singing."

The people were sitting with bowed heads, humming a song. As the **repressed** singing grew louder and louder, it sounded mournful in the room. Mr. Bass shuffled, looking around as if he wished to back out of the suggestion. But his rich voice and singing leadership were too famous. Mrs. Bass

**repress**
(rĭ-prĕs´) v. If you repress something, you hold it back or try to stop it from happening.

---

³ **last milk:** the last milk taken from milking a cow; this milk is usually the richest in nutrients and taste.
⁴ **vex:** dialect for *vexed*, meaning "annoyed."

already had the hymnbook in her hand, and she pushed it at her husband. He took it and began turning the leaves as he
90  moved toward the center of the room.

Immediately Mr. Bass was surrounded. He started with a resounding chant over the heads of everybody. "Abide wid me; fast fall the eventide . . . " He joined the singing but broke off to recite the next line. "The darkness deepen; Lord, wid me, abide . . . " Again, before the last long-drawn note faded from the deeply stirred voices, Mr. Bass intoned musically, "When odder helpers fail, and comfo'ts flee . . . "

In this manner he fired inspiration into the singing of hymn after hymn. The congregation swelled their throats,
100  and their mixed voices filled the room, pleading to heaven from the depths of their hearts. But the wind outside **mocked** viciously. It screamed. It whistled. It smashed everywhere up.

Mrs. Bass had tightly closed her eyes, singing and swaying in the center of the children who nestled around her. But Gustus was by himself. He had his elbows on his knees and his hands blocking his ears. He had his own worries.

**mock**
(mŏk)  *v.* To *mock* someone is to treat them with scorn or contempt.

© Shutterstock

What's the good of Pappy asking all those questions when he treat him so bad? He's the only one in the family without a pair of shoes! Because he's a big boy, he don't need anyt'ing an'
110 must do all the work. He can't stay at school in the evenings an' play cricket[5] because there's work to do at home. He can't have no outings with the other children because he has no shoes. An' now when he was to sell his bunch of bananas an' buy shoes so he can go out with his cricket team, the hurricane is going to blow it down.

It was true: the root of the banana was his "navel string."[6] After his birth the umbilical cord[7] was dressed with castor oil and sprinkled with nutmeg and buried, with the banana tree planted over it for him. When he was nine days old, the nana
120 midwife[8] had taken him out into the open for the first time. She had held the infant proudly and walked the twenty-five yards that separated the house from the kitchen, and at the back showed him his tree. "'Memba when you grow up," her toothless mouth had said, "it's you nable strings feedin' you tree, the same way it feed you from you mudder."

Refuse from the kitchen made the plant flourish out of all proportion. But the rich soil around it was loose. Each time the tree gave a shoot, the bunch would be too heavy for the soil to support; so it crashed to the ground, crushing the
130 tender fruit. This time, determined that his banana must reach the market, Gustus had supported his tree with eight props. And as he watched it night and morning, it had become very close to him. Often he had seriously thought of moving his bed to its root.

Muffled cries, and the sound of blowing noses, now mixed with the singing. Delayed impact of the disaster was happening. Sobbing was everywhere. Quickly the atmosphere became sodden with the wave of weeping outbursts.

---

[5] **cricket** (krĭk´ĭt): an English sport similar to baseball.

[6] **navel string:** a term for the umbilical cord.

[7] **umbilical cord** (ŭm-bĭl´ĭ-kəl kôrd): the cord through which an unborn baby (fetus) receives nourishment from its mother; a person's navel is the place where the cord was attached.

[8] **nana midwife:** a woman who helps other women give birth and cares for newborn children.

Mrs. Bass's pregnant belly heaved. Her younger children
140    were upset and cried, "Mammy, Mammy, Mammy . . . "

Realizing that his family, too, was overwhelmed by
the surrounding calamity, Mr. Bass bustled over to them.
Because their respect for him bordered on fear, his presence
quietened all immediately. He looked around. "Where's
Gustus! Imogene . . . where's Gustus!"

"He was 'ere, Pappy," she replied, drying her eyes. "I dohn
know when he get up."

Briskly Mr. Bass began combing the schoolroom to find
his boy. He asked; no one had seen Gustus. He called. There
150    was no answer. He tottered, lifting his heavy boots over heads,
fighting his way to the jalousie.[9] He opened it, and his eyes
gleamed up and down the road but saw nothing of the boy. In
despair Mr. Bass gave one last thunderous shout: "Gustus!"
Only the wind sneered.

By this time Gustus was halfway on the mile journey to
their house. The lone figure in the raging wind and shin-deep
road flood was tugging, snapping, and pitching branches out
of his path. His shirt was fluttering from his back like a boat
sail. And a leaf was fastened to his cheek. But the belligerent
160    wind was merciless. It bellowed into his ears and drummed a
deafening commotion. As he **grimaced** and covered his ears,
he was forcefully slapped against a coconut tree trunk that lay
across the road.

When his eyes opened, his round face was turned up to a
festered[10] sky. Above the tormented trees a zinc sheet writhed,
twisted, and somersaulted in the tempestuous flurry. Leaves
of all shapes and sizes were whirling and diving like attackers
around the zinc sheet. As Gustus turned to get up, a bullet
drop of rain struck his temple. He shook his head, held grimly
170    to the tree trunk, and struggled to his feet.

Where the road was clear, he edged along the bank. Once,
when the wind staggered him, he recovered with his legs wide
apart. Angrily he stretched out his hands with clenched fists
and shouted, "I almos' hol' you that time. . . . Come solid like
that again, an' we fight like man an' man!"

**grimace**
(grĭm´ĭs) *v.* If you
*grimace*, you twist
your face in an
unattractive way
because you are
unhappy, disgusted,
or in pain.

---

[9] **jalousie** (jăl´ə-sē): a window blind or shutter with adjustable thin slats.
[10] **festered** (fĕs´tərd): infected and irritated; diseased.

When Gustus approached the river he had to cross, it was flooded and blocked beyond recognition. Pressing his chest against the gritty road bank, the boy closed his weary eyes on the brink of the spating river. The wrecked footbridge had

180　become the harboring fort for all the debris, branches, and monstrous tree trunks which the river swept along its course. The river was still swelling. More accumulation arrived each moment, ramming and pressing the bridge. Under pressure it was cracking and shifting minutely toward a turbulent forty-foot fall.

Gustus had seen it! A feeling of dismay paralyzed him, reminding him of his foolish **venture**. He scraped his cheek on the bank looking back. But how can he go back? He has no strength to go back. His house is nearer than the school.

190　An' Pappy will only strap him for nothin' . . . for nothin' . . . no shoes, nothin', when the hurricane is gone.

With trembling fingers he tied up the remnants of his shirt. He made a bold step, and the wind half lifted him, ducking him in the muddy flood. He sank to his neck. Floating leaves, sticks, coconut husks, dead ratbats, and all manner of feathered creatures and refuse surrounded him. Forest vines under the water entangled him. But he struggled desperately until he clung to the laden bridge and climbed up among leafless branches.

200　His legs were bruised and **bore** deep scratches, but steadily he moved up on the slimy pile. He felt like a man at sea, in the heart of a storm, going up the mast of a ship. He rested his feet on a smooth log that stuck to the water-splashed heap like a black torso. As he strained up for another grip, the torso came to life and leaped from under his feet. Swiftly sliding down, he grimly clutched some brambles.

The urgency of getting across became more frightening, and he gritted his teeth and dug his toes into the debris, climbing with maddened determination. But a hard gust

210　of wind slammed the wreck, pinning him like a motionless lizard. For a minute the boy was stuck there, panting, swelling his naked ribs.

He stirred again and reached the top. He was sliding over a breadfruit limb when a flutter startled him. As he looked and saw the clean-head crow and glassy-eyed owl close together,

**venture**
(věn´chər) *n.*
A *venture* is a dangerous, daring, or poorly planned task or activity.

**bore**
(bôr) *v.* (past tense of *bear*) If you say a person *bore* something, you mean they carried it or had it on them; it is visible in some way.

there was a powerful jolt. Gustus flung himself into the air
and fell in the expanding water on the other side. When he
surfaced, the river had dumped the entire wreckage into the
gurgling gully. For once the wind helped. It blew him to land.

220    Gustus was in a daze when he reached his house. Mud
and rotten leaves covered his head and face, and blood caked
around a gash on his chin. He bent down, shielding himself
behind a tree stump whose white heart was a needly splinter,
murdered by the wind.

He could hardly recognize his yard. The terrorized trees
that stood were writhing in turmoil. Their thatched house had
collapsed like an open umbrella that was given a heavy blow.
He looked the other way and whispered, "Is still there! That's a
miracle. . . . That's a miracle."

230    Dodging the wind, he staggered from tree to tree until
he got to his own tormented banana tree. Gustus hugged the
tree. "My nable string!" he cried. "My nable string! I know you
would stan' up to it, I know you would."

The bones of the tree's stalky leaves were broken, and the wind lifted them and harassed them. And over Gustus's head the heavy fruit swayed and swayed. The props held the tree, but they were squeaking and slipping. And around the plant the roots stretched and trembled, gradually surfacing under loose earth.

240     With the rags of his wet shirt flying off his back, Gustus was down busily on his knees, bracing, pushing, tightening the props. One by one he was adjusting them until a heavy rush of wind knocked him to the ground. A prop fell on him, but he scrambled to his feet and looked up at the thirteen-hand bunch of bananas. "My good tree," he bawled, "hol' you fruit. . . . Keep it to you heart like a mudder savin' her baby! Don't let the wicked wind t'row you to the groun' . . . even if it t'row me to the groun'. I will not leave you."

    But several attempts to replace the prop were futile. The

250 force of the wind against his weight was too much for him. He thought of a rope to lash the tree to anything, but it was difficult to make his way into the kitchen, which, separate from the house, was still standing. The invisible hand of the wind tugged, pushed, and forcefully restrained him. He got down and crawled on his belly into the earth-floor kitchen. As he showed himself with the rope, the wind tossed him, like washing on the line, against his tree.

    The boy was hurt! He looked crucified against the tree. The spike of the wind was slightly withdrawn. He fell, folded

260 on the ground. He lay there unconscious. And the wind had no mercy for him. It shoved him, poked him, and molested his clothes like muddy newspaper against the tree.

    As darkness began to move in rapidly, the wind grew more vicious and surged a mighty gust that struck the resisting kitchen. It was heaved to the ground in a rubbled pile. The brave wooden hut had been shielding the banana tree but in its death fall missed it by inches. The wind charged again, and the soft tree gurgled—the fruit was torn from it and plunged to the ground.

270     The wind was less fierce when Mr. Bass and a searching party arrived with lanterns. Because the bridge was washed away, the hazardous roundabout journey had badly impeded them.

    Talks about safety were mockery to the anxious father. Relentlessly he searched. In the darkness his great voice echoed everywhere, calling for his boy. He was wrenching and ripping through the house wreckage when suddenly he vaguely remembered how the boy had been fussing with the banana tree. Desperate, the man struggled from the ruins, 280  flagging the lantern he carried.

The flickering light above his head showed Mr. Bass the forlorn and pitiful banana tree. There it stood, shivering and twitching like a propped-up man with lacerated throat and dismembered head. Half of the damaged fruit rested on Gustus. The father hesitated. But when he saw a feeble wink of the boy's eyelids, he flung himself to the ground. His bristly chin rubbed the child's face while his unsteady hand ran all over his body. "Mi bwoy!" he murmured. "Mi hurricane bwoy! The Good Lord save you. . . . Why you do this? Why 290  you do this?"

"I did want buy mi shoes, Pappy. I . . . I can't go anywhere 'cause I have no shoes. . . . I didn' go to school outing at the factory. I didn' go to Government House. I didn' go to Ol' Fort in town."

Mr. Bass sank into the dirt and stripped himself of his heavy boots. He was about to lace them to the boy's feet when the onlooking men prevented him. He tied the boots together and threw them over his shoulder.

Gustus's broken arm was strapped to his side as they 300  carried him away. Mr. Bass stroked his head and asked how he felt. Only then grief swelled inside him and he wept.

**COLLABORATIVE DISCUSSION** Think about what happens at the end of "The Banana Tree." With a partner, discuss how the storm may change the relationship between Gustus and his father. Use text evidence to support your ideas.

# Determine Meanings: Figurative Language

Great stories help readers feel as if they can see and hear the characters and action. **Imagery,** or rich sensory details, is one device authors use to help readers imagine a scene. Here is an example from "The Banana Tree":

> **Floating leaves, sticks, cocnut husks, dead ratbats, and all manner of feathered creatures and refuse surrounded him. Forest vines under the water entangled him.**

The details that appeal to your senses of sight and touch help you recognize that the author is using imagery.

**Figurative language** is language that uses words and expressions to express ideas that are different from their literal meanings. One type of figurative language, **personification** is when an animal, object, or phenomenon is described as behaving in a human way. The phrase "Only the wind sneered" is an example of personification from "The Banana Tree."

Identifying imagery and figurative language helps you determine the intended meaning of words and phrases and better understand what you read. To identify imagery, figurative language, and personification, ask:

- Do descriptions use rich sensory details? How is this imagery useful?
- Does the author use figurative language, such as personification, to make comparisons? How does it add to the story?

Look for additional imagery, figurative language, and personification as you analyze "The Banana Tree."

# Determine Meanings: Dialect

**Dialect** is a form of language that is spoken in a particular region by the people who live there. Writers use dialect to make dialogue sound authentic. In "The Banana Tree," the characters speak a Jamaican dialect in which English words are mixed with African words, pronunciations, and expressions:

> **"Wha' mek you say nothin'? I sure somet'ing bodder you, Gustus. You not a bwoy who frighten easy."**

One way to understand dialect is to read the text aloud to help you hear the sounds and rhythms of the language. Look for more examples of personification and dialect as you analyze "The Banana Tree."

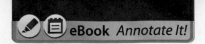
# Analyzing the Text

COMMON CORE  RL 1, RL 2, RL 4, RL 5, RL 10, W 3d

**Cite Text Evidence**  Support your responses with evidence from the text.

1. **Infer**  Review lines 32–39. What sensory details does the author use in these paragraphs? Explain why the author would use strong imagery near the beginning of the story.

2. **Draw Conclusions**  Reread lines 69–78. Toward the end of the paragraph, the writing shifts to dialect. Why is the author's choice to write Gustus's thoughts in dialect significant?

3. **Summarize**  Review lines 107–134. Explain why the banana tree is so important to Gustus.

4. **Interpret**  Read lines 171–175 aloud. In your own words, tell what Gustus is saying to the wind.

5. **Draw Conclusions**  Think about the danger and injuries Gustus faced because he would not let the hurricane constrain him. What conclusion can you draw about Gustus's character?

6. **Interpret**  Reread lines 230–235. What are two examples of personification the author uses? What impact does the personification have on the story?

7. **Evaluate**  How does the strong imagery in the story add to your understanding of the ideas the author wants to share?

## PERFORMANCE TASK

**Writing Activity: Description**  Write a description of a bad storm that you have experienced.

- First, write a summary of the event.
- Next, fill in sensory details. What did you see, feel, and hear?
- As you record your details, use specific nouns, verbs, and adjectives to create a clear picture of what you experienced.

- Use personification to make animals, buildings, or things in nature behave like humans.
- Review your writing to add or clarify details of the event.

# Critical Vocabulary

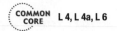 

repress        mock        grimace        venture        bore

**Practice and Apply**   Complete each sentence.

1. Jorge wished he could **repress** the loud noises because . . .

2. Hank didn't like it when Gail began to **mock** his singing because . . .

3. I had to **grimace** when I saw the menu choices because . . .

4. Mom said to think twice about taking a **venture** to the pond because . . .

5. The piano **bore** evidence of heavy use because . . .

# Vocabulary Strategy: Use Context Clues

**Context clues** are the words or phrases surrounding a word that provide hints about a word's meaning. Context clues can help you determine the correct meaning of **multiple-meaning words,** which are words that have more than one meaning.

In "The Banana Tree," Gustus's "legs were bruised and *bore* deep scratches." The word *bore* can have several meanings, including

- "to make a hole or drill into"
- "to make weary by being dull and tedious"
- "the past tense of *bear*," (as in "have as a visible characteristic")

The context clues help you figure out that in the example, *bore* means "the past tense of *bear*" as in "have as a visible characteristic."

Knowing whether a multiple-meaning word is being used as a noun, verb, modifier, or another part of a sentence can also help you determine its meaning. You can tell that *bore* is being used as a verb in the example.

**Practice and Apply**   Choose the correct meaning of each boldface word.

1. Drake's mother asked him to keep a close **watch** on his younger brother.
   **a.** the act of looking or observing attentively
   **b.** a small timepiece

2. Lena was surprised to see daffodils blooming so early in the **spring.**
   **a.** to leap or jump suddenly
   **b.** the season between winter and summer

3. Ms. Hamilton wondered why Nate wasn't **present.**
   **a.** gift
   **b.** in attendance

# Language Conventions: Capitalization

A **common noun** is a general name for a person, place, thing, or idea. Common nouns are not capitalized. A **proper noun** is one that names a specific or particular person, place, thing, or idea. Each word in a proper noun begins with a capital letter. Examples include the names of people, titles, countries, and religions. In the following example, notice how proper nouns are capitalized:

> **As the hurricane headed toward Jamaica, Gustus went with his parents, Mr. Jetro Bass and Mrs. Imogene Bass, to the strong and safe community buildings of Canerise Village.**

The chart gives some additional examples.

| Common Nouns | Proper Nouns |
| --- | --- |
| sheriff | Sheriff Ryan |
| museum | Heritage Museum |
| tropical storm | Tropical Storm Irene |

**Practice and Apply**   Correct each sentence so that all proper nouns are capitalized.

1. The red cross will arrive on Wednesday.

2. In 2005, the city of New orleans was devastated by hurricane Katrina.

3. Reporters gathered in the city square to hear what mayor Reynolds had to say.

4. Many nurses and physicians, including doctor Webb, helped hurricane victims in the emergency room at Mercy hospital.

5. Mr. and mrs. Carter spent several weeks at the Pleasant Valley shelter.

**Walter Lord** (1917–2002) *studied law at college, but he never practiced as a lawyer. After receiving his degree, he worked in a business information service in New York City. It was there that he got interested in writing. Lord's approach to writing changed the way many people read history. By mixing research and interviews, Lord connected readers to the immediacy of historical events. In particular, his account of the sinking of the* Titanic *is widely respected as an accurate, heartfelt account of a tragic disaster on the high seas.*

# from A Night to Remember

## History Writing by Walter Lord

**SETTING A PURPOSE** As you read, pay attention to the details that engage you in the circumstances of this historical event.

High in the crow's-nest of the new White Star Liner *Titanic*, Lookout Frederick Fleet peered into a dazzling night. It was calm, clear and bitterly cold. There was no moon, but the cloudless sky blazed with stars. The Atlantic was like polished plate glass; people later said they had never seen it so smooth.

This was the fifth night of the *Titanic*'s maiden voyage to New York, and it was already clear that she was not only the largest but also the most glamorous ship in the world.
10 Even the passengers' dogs were glamorous. John Jacob Astor had along his airedale Kitty. Henry Sleeper Harper, of the publishing family, had his prize Pekingese Sun Yatsen. Robert W. Daniel, the Philadelphia banker, was bringing back a champion French bulldog just purchased in Britain. Clarence Moore of Washington also had been dog-shopping,

but the 50 pairs of English foxhounds he bought for the Loudoun Hunt weren't making the trip.

That was all another world to Frederick Fleet. He was one of six lookouts carried by the *Titanic*, and the lookouts didn't worry about passenger problems. They were the "eyes of the ship," and on this particular night Fleet had been warned to watch especially for icebergs.

So far, so good. On duty at 10 o'clock . . . a few words about the ice problem with Lookout Reginald Lee, who shared the same watch . . . a few more words about the cold . . . but mostly just silence, as the two men stared into the darkness.

Now the watch was almost over, and still there was nothing unusual. Just the night, the stars, the biting cold, the wind that whistled through the rigging[1] as the *Titanic* raced across the calm, black sea at 22½ **knots**. It was almost 11:40 P.M. on Sunday, the 14th of April, 1912.

Suddenly Fleet saw something directly ahead, even darker than the darkness. At first it was small (about the size, he thought, of two tables put together), but every second it grew larger and closer. Quickly Fleet banged the crow's-nest bell three times, the warning of danger ahead. At the same time he lifted the phone and rang the bridge.

"What did you see?" asked a calm voice at the other end.

"Iceberg right ahead," replied Fleet.

"Thank you," acknowledged the voice with curiously detached courtesy. Nothing more was said.

For the next 37 seconds Fleet and Lee stood quietly side by side, watching the ice draw nearer. Now they were almost on top of it, and still the ship didn't turn. The berg towered wet and glistening far above the forecastle deck, and both men braced themselves for a crash. Then, miraculously, the bow began to swing to port.[2] At the last second the stem[3] shot into the clear, and the ice glided swiftly by along the starboard side. It looked to Fleet like a very close shave.

**knot**
(nŏt) *n.* a *knot* is a unit of speed used by ships. One knot is equal to one nautical mile, or about 1.85 kilometers per hour.

---

[1] **rigging** (rĭg´ĭng): the system of ropes, wires, pulleys, and hardware needed on the ship to hoist cargo, open hatches, or raise signal flags.

[2] **port:** the left-hand side of a ship facing forward.

[3] **stem:** the curved upright beam to which the hull timbers are joined to form the front of the ship.

50　　　At this moment Quartermaster George Thomas Rowe was standing watch on the after bridge. For him too, it had been an uneventful night—just the sea, the stars, the biting cold. As he paced the deck, he noticed what he and his mates called "Whiskers 'round the Light"—tiny splinters of ice in the air, fine as dust, that gave off myriads of bright colors whenever caught in the glow of the deck lights.

　　　Then suddenly he felt a curious motion break the steady rhythm of the engines. It was a little like coming alongside a dock wall rather heavily. He glanced forward—and stared

60　again. A windjammer, sails set, seemed to be passing along the starboard[4] side. Then he realized it was an iceberg, towering perhaps 100 feet above the water. The next instant it was gone, drifting astern[5] into the dark.

　　　Meanwhile, down below in the First Class dining saloon on D Deck, four other members of the *Titanic*'s crew were sitting around one of the tables. The last diner had long since departed, and now the big white Jacobean room was empty except for this single group. They were dining-saloon stewards, **indulging** in the time-honored pastime of all

70　stewards off duty—they were gossiping about their passengers.

　　　Then, as they sat there talking, a faint grinding jar seemed to come from somewhere deep inside the ship. It was not much, but enough to break the conversation and rattle the silver that was set for breakfast next morning.

　　　Steward James Johnson felt he knew just what it was. He recognized the kind of **shudder** a ship gives when she drops a propeller blade, and he knew this sort of mishap meant a trip back to the Harland & Wolff shipyard at Belfast— with plenty of free time to enjoy the hospitality of the port.

80　Somebody near him agreed and sang out cheerfully, "Another Belfast trip!"

　　　In the galley just to the stern, Chief Night Baker Walter Belford was making rolls for the following day. (The honor of baking fancy pastry was reserved for the day shift.) When the

**indulge**
(ĭn-dŭlj´) *v.* If you *indulge* in something, you allow yourself to do or have something you want.

**shudder**
(shŭd´ər) *n.* A *shudder* is a strong shiver or tremor.

---

[4] **starboard:** the right-hand side of a ship facing forward.
[5] **astern:** behind a ship.

jolt came, it impressed Belford more strongly than Steward
Johnson—perhaps because a pan of new rolls clattered off the
top of the oven and scattered about the floor.

The passengers in their cabins felt the **jar** too, and tried to
connect it with something familiar. Marguerite Frolicher, a
90 young Swiss girl accompanying her father on a business trip,
woke up with a start. Half-asleep, she could think only of the
little white lake ferries at Zurich making a sloppy landing.
Softly she said to herself, "Isn't it funny . . . we're landing!"

Major Arthur Godfrey Peuchen, starting to undress for
the night, thought it was like a heavy wave striking the ship.
Mrs. J. Stuart White was sitting on the edge of her bed, just
reaching to turn out the light, when the ship seemed to roll
over "a thousand marbles." To Lady Cosmo Duff Gordon,
waking up from the jolt, it seemed "as though somebody had
100 drawn a giant finger along the side of the ship." Mrs. John
Jacob Astor thought it was some mishap in the kitchen.

It seemed stronger to some than to others. Mrs. Albert
Caldwell pictured a large dog that had a baby kitten in its
mouth and was shaking it. Mrs. Walter B. Stephenson recalled
the first **ominous** jolt when she was in the San Francisco
earthquake—then decided this wasn't that bad. Mrs. E. D.

**jar**
(jär) *n.* A *jar* can be a
jolt or shock, as well
as a harsh, scraping
sound.

**ominous**
(ŏm´ə-nəs) *adj.*
Something that
is *ominous* is
frightening or
threatening.

Appleton felt hardly any shock at all, but she noticed an unpleasant ripping sound . . . like someone tearing a long, long strip of calico.

110     The jar meant more to J. Bruce Ismay, Managing Director of the White Star Line, who in a festive mood was going along for the ride on the *Titanic's* first trip. Ismay woke up with a start in his de-luxe suite on B Deck—he felt sure the ship had struck something, but he didn't know what.

    Some of the passengers already knew the answer. Mr. and Mrs. George A. Harder, a young honeymoon couple down in cabin E-50, were still awake when they heard a dull thump. Then they felt the ship quiver, and there was "a sort of rumbling, scraping noise" along the ship's side. Mr. Harder

120 hopped out of bed and ran to the porthole. As he looked through the glass, he saw a wall of ice glide by.

    The same thing happened to James B. McGough, a Gimbels buyer from Philadelphia, except his experience was somewhat more disturbing. His porthole was open, and as the berg brushed by, chunks of ice fell into the cabin.

    Like Mr. McGough, most of the *Titanic's* passengers were in bed when the jar came. On this quiet, cold Sunday night a snug bunk seemed about the best place to be. But a few shipboard die-hards were still up. As usual, most were in the

130 First Class smoking room on A Deck.

    And as usual, it was a very mixed group. Around one table sat Archie Butt, President Taft's military aide; Clarence Moore, the traveling Master of Hounds; Harry Widener, son of the Philadelphia streetcar magnate; and William Carter, another Main Liner. They were winding up a small dinner given by Widener's father in honor of Captain Edward J. Smith, the ship's commander. The Captain had left early, the ladies had been packed off to bed, and now the men were enjoying a final cigar before turning in too. The conversation

140 wandered from politics to Clarence Moore's adventures in West Virginia, the time he helped interview the old feuding mountaineer Anse Hatfield.

    Buried in a nearby leather armchair, Spencer V. Silverthorne, a young buyer for Nugent's department store in St. Louis, browsed through a new best seller, *The Virginian.* Not far off, Lucien P. Smith (still another Philadelphian)

struggled gamely through the linguistic[6] problems of a bridge game with three Frenchmen.

At another table the ship's young set was enjoying a somewhat noisier game of bridge. Normally the young set preferred the livelier Café Parisien, just below on B Deck, and at first tonight was no exception. But it grew so cold that around 11:30 the girls went off to bed, and the men strolled up to the smoking room.

Somebody produced a deck of cards, and as they sat playing and laughing, suddenly there came that grinding jar. Not much of a shock, but enough to give a man a start— Mr. Silverthorne still sits up with a jolt when he tells it. In an instant the smoking-room steward and Mr. Silverthorne were on their feet . . . through the aft door . . . past the Palm Court . . . and out onto the deck. They were just in time to see the iceberg scraping along the starboard side, a little higher than the Boat Deck. As it slid by, they watched chunks of ice breaking and tumbling off into the water. In another moment it faded into the darkness astern.

Others in the smoking room were pouring out now. As Hugh Woolner reached the deck, he heard a man call out, "We hit an iceberg—there it is!"

Woolner squinted into the night. About 150 yards astern he made out a mountain of ice standing black against the starlit sky. Then it vanished into the dark.

The excitement, too, soon disappeared. The *Titanic* seemed as solid as ever, and it was too bitterly cold to stay outside any longer. Slowly the group filed back, Woolner picked up his hand, and the bridge game went on. The last man inside thought, as he slammed the deck door, that the engines were stopping.

He was right. Up on the bridge First Officer William M. Murdoch had just pulled the engine-room telegraph handle all the way to "Stop." Murdoch was in charge of the bridge this watch, and it was his problem, once Fleet phoned the warning. A tense minute had passed since then—orders to Quartermaster Hitchens to turn the wheel hard-a-starboard[7] . . . a yank on the engine-room telegraph for "Full Speed Astern" . . . a hard push on the button closing the watertight doors . . . and finally those 37 seconds of breathless waiting.

---

[6] **linguistic** (lǐng-gwǐsˊtǐk): of or relating to language.

[7] **hard-a-starboard:** hard to the right.

Now the waiting was over, and it was all so clearly too late. As the grinding noise died away, Captain Smith rushed onto the bridge from his cabin next to the wheel-house.[8] There were
190 a few quick words:

"Mr. Murdoch, what was that?"

"An iceberg, sir. I hard-a-starboarded and reversed the engines, and I was going to hard-a-port[9] around it, but she was too close. I couldn't do any more."

"Close the emergency doors."

"The doors are already closed."

They were closed, all right. Down in boiler room No. 6, Fireman Fred Barrett had been talking to Assistant Second Engineer James Hesketh when the warning bell sounded and
200 the light flashed red above the watertight door leading to the stern. A quick shout of warning—an ear-splitting crash—and the whole starboard side of the ship seemed to give way. The sea cascaded in, swirling about the pipes and valves, and the two men leaped through the door as it slammed down behind them.

Barrett found things almost as bad where he was now, in boiler room No. 5. The gash ran into No. 5 about two feet beyond the closed compartment door, and a fat jet of sea water was spouting through the hole. Nearby, Trimmer George
210 Cavell was digging himself out of an avalanche of coal that had poured out of a bunker with the impact. Another stoker mournfully studied an overturned bowl of soup that had been warming on a piece of machinery.

It was dry in the other boiler rooms further aft, but the scene was pretty much the same—men picking themselves up, calling back and forth, asking what had happened. It was hard to figure out. Until now the *Titanic* had been a picnic. Being a new ship on her maiden voyage, everything was clean. She was, as Fireman George Kemish still recalls, "a good job . . . not
220 what we were accustomed to in old ships, slogging our guts out and nearly roasted by the heat."

All the firemen had to do was keep the furnaces full. No need to work the fires with slice bars, pricker bars, and rakes. So on this Sunday night the men were taking it easy—sitting

---

[8] **wheel-house** (hwēl´hous´): an enclosed area, usually on the bridge, from which the ship is controlled.

[9] **hard-a-port:** hard to the left.

around on buckets and the trimmers' iron wheel-barrows, shooting the breeze, waiting for the 12-to-4 watch to come on.

Then came that thud . . . the grinding, tearing sound . . . the telegraphs ringing wildly . . . the watertight doors crashing down. Most of the men couldn't imagine what it was—the
230 story spread that the *Titanic* had gone aground just off the Banks of Newfoundland. Many of them still thought so, even after a trimmer came running down from above shouting, "Blimey! We've struck an iceberg!"

About ten miles away Third Officer Charles Victor Groves stood on the bridge of the Leyland Liner *Californian*, bound from London to Boston. A plodding 6000-tonner, she had room for 47 passengers, but none were being carried just now. On this Sunday night she had been stopped since 10:30 P.M., completely blocked by drifting ice.
240 At about 11:10 Groves noticed the lights of another ship, racing up from the east on the starboard side. As the newcomer rapidly overhauled the motionless *Californian*, a blaze of deck lights showed she was a large passenger liner. Around 11:30 he knocked on the Venetian door of the chart room and told Captain Stanley Lord about it. Lord suggested contacting the new arrival by Morse lamp, and Groves prepared to do this.

Then, at about 11:40, he saw the big ship suddenly stop and put out most of her lights. This didn't surprise Groves very
250 much. He had spent some time in the Far East trade, where they usually put deck lights out at midnight to encourage the passengers to turn in. It never occurred to him that perhaps the lights were still on . . . that they only seemed to go out because she was no longer broadside but had veered sharply to port.

**COLLABORATIVE DISCUSSION** With a partner, review *A Night to Remember* and point out sections or passages that you especially enjoyed or found fascinating. Identify specific details and reasons why you found them engaging, useful, or memorable.

# Analyze Text: Narrative Nonfiction

**Narrative nonfiction** reads much like a fictional story, except that the characters, setting, and events are real rather than imaginary.

Using a real person's experiences and actual details of the events on the *Titanic* gives readers a full, clear picture of what the experience was like. As you analyze *A Night to Remember,* use these questions to identify elements of narrative nonfiction:

- What real-life details of setting and events are included? Why?
- Who are the real-life people, or characters, in the text?
- How is this text different from a newspaper article or a fictional story about the event?

# Analyze the Meanings of Words and Phrases

**Style** refers to a writer's unique way of communicating ideas. Many literary elements, including word choice, sentence structure, imagery, point of view, voice, and tone contribute to a writer's style.

**Tone** is the writer's attitude toward his or her subject. Adjectives are often used to describe the tone of a text, such as *serious, humorous, sarcastic,* and *respectful.*

The style and tone an author uses help readers understand ideas and makes the writing memorable. In *A Night to Remember*, the author describes the *Titanic* as "the most glamorous ship in the world," adding that "Even the passengers' dogs were glamorous." He supports that idea by describing a list of wealthy passengers—and their dogs. The careful details, precise choice of words, and slightly humorous tone help make up the author's style.

To analyze style and tone, think about these elements:

- **Word choice:** Does the author use powerful verbs, precise nouns, and vivid adjectives or adverbs? How does the author's word choice affect the tone of the text?
- **Sentence structure:** Are most sentences long or short? Does the author use a variety of sentence types?
- **Literary devices:** Does the author use strong imagery and sensory details, or devices such as repetition or exaggeration?

Look for more examples of Walter Lord's style and tone.

# Analyzing the Text

COMMON CORE  RI 1, RI 3, RI 4, RI 5, RI 10, W 7

**Cite Text Evidence**  Support your responses with evidence from the text.

1. **Predict**  Sometimes writers use **foreshadowing,** a hint that a future event will take place in the text.  Reread lines 18–26. What words, phrases, and sentences does the author use to hint at a future event?  What might you predict will happen?

2. **Interpret**  Reread lines 42–49. Describe the tone of this passage. Which words help convey the tone?

3. **Identify Patterns**  Reread lines 71–87.  How does the author describe the ship striking the iceberg? Explain the significance of the author's choice to present ideas this way.

4. **Analyze**  Reread lines 88–109.  What elements contribute to the author's style in these lines?  Describe the impact these elements have on the text.

5. **Compare**  Review lines 234–255. How do the events on the *Californian* compare with the events happening on the *Titanic*? How does this section contribute to the development of the events?

6. **Evaluate**  The author could have written the facts about the sinking as a piece of informational text. Instead, he wrote narrative nonfiction and included the words and experiences of people on the ship. Is Lord's telling of the events effective? Explain why.

---

## PERFORMANCE TASK

**Writing Activity: Research**  Conduct research to find out what happened to the *Titanic* after it struck the iceberg. Look for information that will help you form a full picture of the events.

- Use research sources—websites, encyclopedias, nonfiction books, and documentaries.
- Look for firsthand accounts from survivors.
- Take notes and record the sources of your information.

# Critical Vocabulary

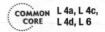

knot        indulge        shudder        jar        ominous

**Practice and Apply**  Answer each question.

1.  Who would be more likely to be discussing a **knot**? Why?
    the captain of an ocean liner        a racecar driver

2.  If you like chocolate, which of these might you **indulge** in? Why?
    a glass of lemonade        a hot fudge sundae        a pizza

3.  Which of the following might make you **shudder**? Why?
    sweeping the floor        remembering a bad dream        buying a gift

4.  Which of these would you describe as a **jar**? Why?
    closing a window        bumping into someone        taking a deep breath

5.  Which of these might be an **ominous** sound? Why?
    a door creaking open        a doorbell ringing        music

# Vocabulary Strategy: Specialized Vocabulary

The term **specialized vocabulary** refers to words and terms that are used in a particular occupation, activity, or field of study. Some specialized vocabulary, such as *starboard*, is used primarily by people when discussing sailing. Other terms, such as *knot,* may be familiar but have a special meaning in that field. Sometimes readers may be able to use context to determine the meaning of specialized vocabulary. In most cases, however, it is best to use a dictionary to find out or confirm a word's meaning.

**Practice and Apply**  Use a chart like the one here to explore the meaning of specialized vocabulary about ships and sailing. Use a dictionary as well as context to determine the precise meaning of each word.

| Term | Guessed Meaning | Dictionary Meaning |
| --- | --- | --- |
| *crow's nest* (line 1) | | |
| *bridge* (line 37) | | |
| *bow* (line 46) | | |
| *windjammer* (line 60) | | |

# Language Conventions: Consistency in Style and Tone

Good readers notice a change in style or tone. If a writer's style or tone changes abruptly, it can be jarring and cause the reader to lose focus or misunderstand ideas.

As a writer, you should work to maintain a consistent style and tone. Take a look at this excerpt from *A Night to Remember*:

> Meanwhile, down below in the First Class dining saloon on D Deck, four other members of the *Titanic*'s crew were sitting around one of the tables. The last diner had long since departed, and now the big white Jacobean room was empty except for this single group. They were dining-saloon stewards, indulging in the time-honored pastime of all stewards off duty—they were gossiping about their passengers.

Walter Lord uses a consistent style and tone in his writing. His sentences flow smoothly, and he uses precise word choices to describe people and their surroundings clearly and vividly. He creates a lightly humorous tone by using the formal-sounding phrase "indulging in the time-honored pastime" to describe the everyday activity of gossiping.

**Practice and Apply**  Edit the paragraphs to make them more consistent in style and tone.

"Just because I've never been fishing on a lake before doesn't mean I don't know what I'm doing," Jenn told Morgan. She reached in the bait bucket and fearlessly threaded an earthworm on the hook of her fishing pole. "See?" she smirked. "I can handle this!"

Morgan grinned. He said to be careful that she didn't rock the canoe.

Jenn laughed. "Check this out!" she chortled. Jenn stood up. She marched. She marched like she was in a parade. The canoe rocked from side to side. Talk about dangerous. Wasn't that a crazy thing to do?

**Background** *On April 14, 1912, at 11:40 P.M. ship's time, the great passenger ship RMS* Titanic *struck an iceberg in the North Atlantic Ocean. Hours later, in the early morning of April 15,* Titanic *plunged through the deep, frigid waters to the bottom of the sea.* Titanic *lay on the ocean floor undiscovered, until 1985, when it was finally found by ocean explorer Bob Ballard. In 2010, a group of the world's top underwater experts from the Woods Hole Oceanographic Institute took part in an expedition to the wreckage site to find out what might have caused the catastrophe.*

## MEDIA ANALYSIS

# *from* TITANIC at 100: Mystery Solved

**Documentary by James Cameron**

**SETTING A PURPOSE** Did *Titanic* have a fatal flaw? Was *Titanic* a weak ship? The research team in the documentary clip you are about to view believes they finally know the answers to these century-old questions. Using the team's images of the remains of the ship and interviews with experts, the documentary describes the dramatic circumstances of *Titanic*'s sinking.

As you view the documentary, pay attention to how scientists and other experts use the expedition's information to understand exactly how and why *Titanic* sank. Also pay attention to similarities and differences you notice between what the documentary reveals and what you learned in reading the narrative from *A Night to Remember*.

**Format:** Documentary
**Running Time:** 5:02

**AS YOU VIEW** As you view the clip from the documentary, consider how the information is presented and the impact it has on your understanding of the sinking of *Titanic*. Notice how the documentary explains the scientists' ideas, using different combinations of animation, interviews, film clips, narration, and sound, including music. Consider how each of these elements helps you understand the sequence of events and how scientists now interpret those events. As needed, pause the video and write notes about what impresses you and about ideas or questions you might want to talk about later. Replay or rewind the video so that you can clarify anything you do not understand.

**COLLABORATIVE DISCUSSION** With a small group, discuss how the discovery of new evidence has changed ideas about why the RMS *Titanic* sank. What techniques does the film clip use to convey these new ideas and evidence? Cite specific segments from the documentary to support your conclusions about what you learned.

# Interpret Diverse Media

A **documentary** is a nonfiction film that tells about important people, historic places, or major events. The purpose of a documentary may be to inform, to explain, or to persuade. Filmmakers gather information about a topic and present the material in an engaging way by using features such as these:

| Feature of a Documentary | How the Feature Might Be Used |
| --- | --- |
| **Voice-over narration:** the voice of an unseen speaker | • tells viewer what is most important<br>• summarizes key scenes or events |
| **Interviews:** question-and-answer conversations | • provide information from experts<br>• present another side to the story |
| **Animation:** the process of displaying images so they appear to move | • heightens interest<br>• provides visual support for complex ideas<br>• summarizes key ideas visually |
| **Footage:** recorded material such as reenactments, film clips, or news reports | • brings the topic to life<br>• provides details of a historical time<br>• reveals insights |
| **Primary sources:** material such as photos, diaries, or recordings from an event | • show real-life experiences<br>• provide details of a historical time<br>• provide reliable evidence |

To interpret the information presented in *Titanic at 100: Mystery Solved*, examine the film's features and learn what new evidence they contribute to the topic of why *Titanic* sank. As you review the documentary ask yourself:

- How is each feature used?
- What new information is presented?

# Integrate Information

To **integrate** information means to take individual pieces of information and synthesize, or combine, them in order to develop a coherent, or clearer, understanding of a topic. Think about new or important information presented in *Titanic at 100*. Then think about important information presented in *A Night to Remember*. To integrate information from both sources, ask yourself:

- What specific information does each source contribute?
- What features do the sources share? What features are unique to each source?

# Analyze Media

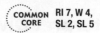
COMMON CORE   RI 7, W 4, SL 2, SL 5

**Cite Text Evidence**   Support your responses with evidence from the media.

1. **Infer**  What is the **central idea,** or most important idea about a topic, that the filmmaker wants to convey in *Titanic at 100: Mystery Solved*? Explain how this idea is supported in the documentary.

2. **Interpret**  What primary sources are included in the film clip? Explain how and why the filmmaker uses these materials.

3. **Analyze**  When does the filmmaker use voiceover narration? What information do you learn from the narration that images alone don't convey?

4. **Analyze**  Which features does the filmmaker use to help you understand the actual events that took place during the sinking of *Titanic* and how the passengers and crew reacted to these events?

5. **Evaluate**  Do you find the new evidence about *Titanic* convincing? Why or why not?

6. **Integrate**  Using information from *A Night to Remember* and from *Titanic at 100: Mystery Solved*, explain how effectively the two sources present events and bring them to life. What techniques unique to each source, print and media, help you understand the issues surrounding *Titanic*'s voyage?

---

# PERFORMANCE TASK

**Media Activity: Multimedia Presentation:**  Create a multimedia presentation or poster that describes how the excerpt from *A Night to Remember* and the film clip from *Titanic at 100: Mystery Solved* work together to give you a clearer understanding of what happened the night *Titanic* sank.

- Integrate information from the text with information from the documentary.

- Create an outline or detailed description of your presentation. Cite evidence for each piece of information. Include quotations.

- Gather visuals, such as graphics, photos, and illustrations that clarify your ideas.

- Decide how to organize and present your work. Share your poster display or computer presentation with the class.

COLLECTION **3**
# PERFORMANCE TASK A

*Interactive Lessons*
If you need help . . .
• **Conducting Research**
• **Giving a Presentation**
• **Using Media in a Presentation**

# Create a Multimedia Presentation

Millions of people around the world live in areas that are at risk for natural disasters, such as the tsunami you read about in this collection. Would you know what to do in the event of a natural disaster? In the following activity, you and a partner will create a multimedia presentation on how to prepare for a tsunami or other natural disaster, using "Mammoth Shakes and Monster Waves" and other selections from this collection.

**COMMON CORE**

**W 8** Gather relevant information.
**SL 4** Present claims, findings, and evidence.
**SL 5** Include multimedia components and visual displays.
**SL 6** Adapt speech to a variety of contexts and tasks.

## A successful multimedia presentation

- has a clear and consistent focus
- presents ideas clearly and logically
- includes graphics, text, music, and/or sound that effectively supports key points
- is organized in a way that is interesting and appropriate to purpose and audience
- includes information from texts read and outside research

**PLAN**

*my* **Notebook**

Use the annotation tools in your eBook to find evidence to support your ideas. Save each piece of information to your notebook.

**Gather Information** Review the events described in "Mammoth Shakes and Monster Waves." Look for information related to the tsunami survivors. What did they do? Why? What can you learn about preparedness from their stories?

**Do Further Research** Gain a better understanding of how to prepare for a tsunami or other natural disaster. Review at least two additional print and digital sources to find out what you can do.

- Consider research questions such as these: Can this disaster be detected? What are the warning signs? What can you do before, during, and after the disaster?
- Find facts, details, and examples to explain and support your points.
- Identify multimedia components—such as graphics, maps, videos, or sound—that emphasize your points.

**ACADEMIC VOCABULARY**

As you plan and deliver your presentation, be sure to use the academic vocabulary words.

*circumstance*
*constraint*
*impact*
*injure*
*significant*

- Use credible sources. Find books using keywords or searching by subject in the library. Use an Internet search engine to find other sources.

**Organize Your Ideas** Think about how you will organize your information. Create an outline that identifies each topic and subtopic in your presentation. Then map out your ideas in a graphic organizer, such as a storyboard, to help you present them clearly and logically.

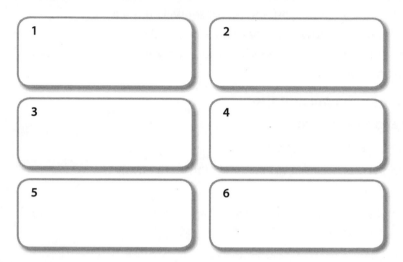

**Consider Your Purpose and Audience** Who will watch and listen to your presentation? What do you want your audience to know? Think about that audience as you prepare your presentation.

---

**PRODUCE**

**Design and Draft Your Presentation** Think about what you want your presentation to look like. Choose graphics that are appropriate for your purpose.

- Draft text that explains each topic and subtopic. Keep text brief and clear.

- Choose multimedia components that emphasize your most significant points. Make sure you have a clear purpose for each one.

- Check that all text and visuals are large and clear enough so that everyone in the audience can see them.

*my*WriteSmart

Produce a rough draft of your presentation using the authoring software of your choice. Then upload your draft to *my*WriteSmart for a peer and teacher review.

*my* **Write**Smart

Have a group of peers review your draft in *my*WriteSmart, along with your multimedia elements. Ask your reviewers to note any ideas or visuals that are unclear or not in a logical sequence.

**Evaluate Your Presentation**  Use the chart on the following page to evaluate your presentation. Work with your partner to determine whether your presentation has the intended impact. Consider the following:

- Check that your ideas are clearly and logically presented.
- Verify that your text includes specific and accurate information.
- Examine your visuals to make sure they are relevant and support key points.

**Practice Your Presentation**  Decide how you and your partner will present your information. Then take turns practicing it with your partner. You may want to make a recording of your presentation and watch it together.

- Use your voice effectively. Speak loudly enough to be heard, varying your pitch and tone.
- Maintain eye contact. Look directly at individuals in your audience.
- Use gestures and facial expressions to emphasize ideas and express emotion.

**Deliver Your Presentation**  Finalize your multimedia presentation and share it with your audience. Consider these options:

- Use your presentation to present a news report about emergency preparedness.
- Make a video recording of yourself or your partner and share it on your class or school website.
- Organize a group discussion to share your ideas about emergency preparedness where you live.

## MULTIMEDIA PRESENTATION

| | Ideas and Evidence | Organization | Language |
|---|---|---|---|
| **ADVANCED** | • The introduction clearly identifies the topic and its purpose and engages the audience.<br>• Important points and steps are supported with relevant facts and details.<br>• The conclusion effectively summarizes the topic and restates the purpose. | • The organization is effective; points and steps are arranged logically.<br>• Text, visuals, and sound are combined in a coherent manner.<br>• Transitions effectively link the steps and inform the reader. | • Oral and written language has a formal style.<br>• Language is precise; unfamiliar terms are explained.<br>• Sentences vary in pattern and structure.<br>• Spelling, capitalization, and punctuation are correct.<br>• Grammar and usage are correct. |
| **COMPETENT** | • The introduction clearly identifies the topic and its purpose but could be more engaging.<br>• Most important points and steps are supported with relevant facts and details.<br>• The conclusion partially summarizes the information and generally restates the purpose. | • The organization is generally effective, but one or two points or steps are out of sequence.<br>• Text, visuals, and sound are mostly combined in a coherent manner.<br>• A few more transitions are needed to link the steps and clarify the information. | • Oral and written language style is inconsistent in a few places.<br>• Most language and terms are precise and clear.<br>• Sentences vary somewhat in pattern and structure.<br>• Some spelling, capitalization, and punctuation mistakes occur.<br>• Some grammar and usage errors occur. |
| **LIMITED** | • The introduction is only partly informative; the topic and purpose are unclear.<br>• Most important points need more support from relevant facts and details.<br>• The conclusion summarizes some of the information but does not restate the purpose. | • The organization has gaps in logic and a confusing sequence.<br>• Text, visuals, and sound are combined in a disorganized way.<br>• More transitions are needed throughout to link important points. | • The language becomes informal in many places.<br>• Some language is precise; some unfamiliar terms are undefined.<br>• Sentence pattern and structure hardly vary; some fragments occur.<br>• Spelling, capitalization, and punctuation are often incorrect, but the ideas are still clear.<br>• Several grammar and usage errors occur. |
| **EMERGING** | • There is no introduction.<br>• Supporting facts and details are unreliable or missing.<br>• The conclusion is missing. | • The organization is not logical; the sequence of points and steps is disjointed.<br>• Visuals and sound are missing.<br>• No transitions are used, making the presentation difficult to understand. | • The style is inappropriate for the presentation.<br>• Language is repetitive and too general; unfamiliar terms are not defined.<br>• Repetitive, monotonous sentence structure and fragments make the presentation hard to follow.<br>• Spelling, capitalization, and punctuation are incorrect and distracting throughout.<br>• Grammar and usage errors interfere with meaning. |

COLLECTION **3**
# PERFORMANCE TASK B

*Interactive Lessons*
If you need help . . .
• **Writing a Narrative**
• **Writing as a Process**

# Write Narrative Nonfiction

In *A Night to Remember*, Walter Lord uses real people's experiences along with facts from reliable sources to give a moment-by-moment account of the events that happened the night the *Titanic* hit an iceberg. In the same style and tone, you will write a narrative nonfiction account of the events that happened after the ship hit the iceberg using *A Night to Remember* and other reference sources.

COMMON CORE

**W 3a–e** Write narratives.
**W 4** Produce clear and coherent writing.
**W 5** Develop and strengthen writing.
**W 6** Use technology to produce and publish writing.

## A successful narrative

- establishes a situation that introduces people, places, and events

- organizes an event sequence that unfolds naturally and logically

- uses dialogue, pacing, and relevant descriptive details to develop events

- uses precise words and sensory language to convey events and maintains a consistent style and tone

- provides a conclusion that follows from and reflects on the events

**PLAN**

*my* Notebook

**Establish the Situation** Narrative nonfiction is a retelling of a true story in which a series of events comes to life. After you read *A Night to Remember*, research the events that happened to the *Titanic* after it hit the iceberg. Then reread the firsthand accounts in *A Night to Remember*. Think about how they compare to the facts you found. Then consider the approach you will take in your story.

- Decide who the narrator will be. A narrator can be an observer or a person in the narrative.

- Think about what you want your readers to know. Identify the events and details that you think will have the greatest impact. Make sure the events are based on what really happened.

Use the annotation tools in your eBook to find facts about the events you will write about.

**ACADEMIC VOCABULARY**

As you plan, write, and review your narrative, be sure to use the academic vocabulary words.

*circumstance*
*constraint*
*impact*
*injure*
*significant*

- Keep in mind the style and tone of *A Night to Remember*. Consider how you will apply a similar style and tone in your narrative.

**Organize Your Information** In narrative nonfiction, the story is told in chronological order, or the order in which the events took place. A graphic organizer, such as a flow chart, can help you to describe events in a logical way.

**Brainstorm Images** Create mental images as you review the information you gathered. Consider which aspects of those images are most significant. Jot down words and phrases that describe sights, sounds, scents, tastes, or feelings.

**Consider Your Purpose and Audience** Think about who will read or listen to your narrative. Focus on the important details and circumstances that you want your audience to understand.

**PRODUCE**

*my*WriteSmart

Write your rough draft in *my*WriteSmart. Focus on getting your ideas down, rather than on perfecting your choice of language.

**Write Your Narrative** Review your notes and the information in your flow chart as you begin your draft.

- Create an introduction that will immediately engage the reader. Begin with action or dialogue that will catch the reader's interest.

- Use your graphic organizer to describe the sequence of events. Include descriptive details that will make your story come alive in the reader's mind.

- Pace your story appropriately. Use shorter sentences for fast-paced action. Use longer sentences to put more emphasis on a major event.

- Choose precise words and phrases that involve the senses and capture the action.

- Bring your narrative to a conclusion by telling how the events ended and giving the reader a new insight.

**Review Your Draft** Use the chart on the following page to evaluate your draft. Work with a partner to determine if you have effectively described the events after the *Titanic* hit the iceberg. Ask them to review the style and tone to make sure that it is similar to Walter Lord's in *A Night to Remember*. Consider the following:

Have a partner or a group of peers review your draft in *my*WriteSmart. Ask your reviewers to note any events that seem out of sequence or language that is unclear or confusing.

- Check that the narrative grabs the reader's attention. If necessary, add dialogue or sensory details that will make the reader want to keep reading.

- Make sure that the events are in the correct order. Delete any event that is not important, and add events that will help the reader understand the narrative or events that were significant as the event unfolded.

- Examine the pacing to make sure the action moves smoothly.

- Reread your conclusion. If necessary, add concluding dialogue or action that will make the events clearer.

- Make sure that you have used correct spelling, grammar, capitalization, and punctuation.

**PRESENT**

**Create a Finished Copy** Finalize your narrative and choose a way to share it with your audience. Consider these options:

- Present your narrative as an author's reading to the class.

- Post your narrative as a blog on a personal or school website.

- Dramatize your narrative in a one-person show.

| | Ideas and Evidence | Organization | Language |
|---|---|---|---|
| **ADVANCED** | • The introduction identifies the experience and setting and creates a strong impression.<br>• Background information helps to explain events.<br>• Dialogue, description, and reflection re-create the experience.<br>• The conclusion reflects on the significance of the experience and leaves readers with a new insight on the event. | • The organization is smooth, effective, and logical; events are organized chronologically.<br>• Pacing is clear and effective.<br>• Transitions logically connect events in sequence. | • Point of view, style, and tone are consistent and effective.<br>• Sensory language and vivid details creatively reveal people, places, and events.<br>• Sentences are varied and have a rhythmic flow.<br>• Spelling, grammar, usage, and mechanics are correct. |
| **COMPETENT** | • The introduction identifies the experience and setting but could be more compelling.<br>• More background is needed to explain one or two events.<br>• Dialogue and description generally re-create the experience.<br>• The conclusion reflects on the experience. | • The organization is generally logical; the sequence of events is confusing in a few places.<br>• Pacing is somewhat clear.<br>• More transitions would make the sequence of events clearer. | • Point of view, style, and tone are inconsistent in a few places.<br>• Some sensory language is used to reveal some people, places, and events.<br>• Sentences are somewhat varied.<br>• Some spelling, grammar, usage, or mechanics errors occur. |
| **LIMITED** | • The introduction briefly mentions the experience and only hints at the setting.<br>• More background is needed throughout.<br>• Dialogue and description are limited or missing entirely.<br>• The conclusion only hints at the significance of the experience. | • The organization is confusing; missing or extraneous events are distracting.<br>• Pacing is choppy and ineffective.<br>• Few transitions are used throughout. | • Point of view, style, and tone are inconsistent.<br>• Sensory language and details are mostly lacking.<br>• Sentences hardly vary; some fragments or run-on sentences are present.<br>• Multiple spelling, grammar, usage, or mechanics errors occur, but ideas are clear. |
| **EMERGING** | • The introduction does not present an identifiable experience.<br>• Necessary background is missing.<br>• Dialogue and description are unrelated or missing.<br>• There is no conclusion. | • There is no evident organization or sequence of events.<br>• There is no evident pacing of events.<br>• Transitions are not used, making the narrative difficult to understand. | • Point of view, style, and tone are never established.<br>• Sensory language is not used.<br>• Sentences do not vary; several fragments and run-on sentences are present.<br>• Significant spelling, grammar, usage, or mechanics errors create confusion and misunderstanding of ideas. |

# Making Your Voice Heard

**"**When people don't express themselves,
they die one piece at a time.**"**

—Laurie Halse Anderson

# Making Your Voice Heard

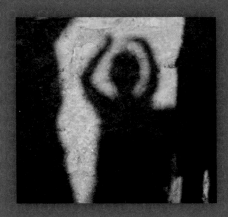

In this collection, you will explore the many ways people express their ideas—and themselves.

hmhfyi.com

COLLECTION

## PERFORMANCE TASK Preview

At the end of this collection, you will write a speech expressing your views about owning exotic animals, using selections from the collection to provide ideas, information, and support. Your challenge will be to justify your opinion with appropriate facts and examples and to convince others to share your opinion.

## ACADEMIC VOCABULARY

Study the words and their definitions in the chart below. You will use these words as you discuss and write about the texts in this collection.

| Word | Definition | Related Forms |
|------|-----------|---------------|
| **appropriate** (ə-prō′prē-ĭt) *adj.* | suitable or acceptable for a particular situation, person, place, or condition | appropriately, appropriateness |
| **authority** (ə-thôr′ĭ-tē) *n.* | an accepted source, such as a person or text, of expert information or advice | authoritative |
| **consequence** (kŏn′sĭ-kwĕns′) *n.* | something that logically or naturally follows from an action or condition | consequent, consequently, consequential |
| **justify** (jŭs′tə-fī′) *v.* | to demonstrate or prove to be just, right, reasonable, or valid | justifiably, justifiable, justification |
| **legal** (lē′gəl) *adj.* | permitted by law; of, related to, or concerned with law | legally, legalism, legality, legalize |

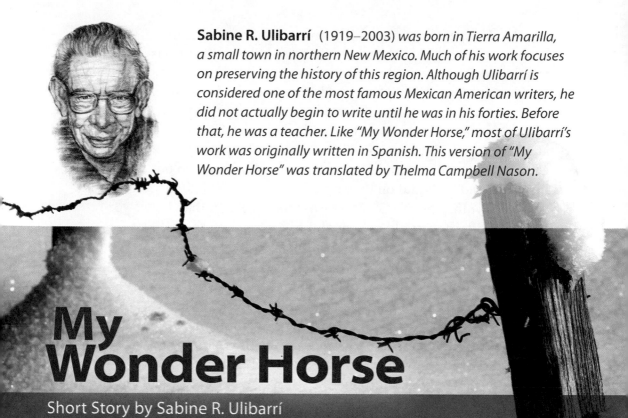

**Sabine R. Ulibarrí** (1919–2003) *was born in Tierra Amarilla, a small town in northern New Mexico. Much of his work focuses on preserving the history of this region. Although Ulibarrí is considered one of the most famous Mexican American writers, he did not actually begin to write until he was in his forties. Before that, he was a teacher. Like "My Wonder Horse," most of Ulibarrí's work was originally written in Spanish. This version of "My Wonder Horse" was translated by Thelma Campbell Nason.*

# My Wonder Horse

Short Story by Sabine R. Ulibarrí

**SETTING A PURPOSE** As you read, pay attention to why the narrator is fascinated by the Wonder Horse. Write down any questions you have while reading.

He was white. White as memories lost. He was free. Free as happiness is. He was fantasy, liberty, and excitement. He filled and dominated the mountain valleys and surrounding plains. He was a white horse that flooded my youth with dreams and poetry.

Around the campfires of the country and in the sunny patios of the town, the ranch hands talked about him with enthusiasm and admiration. But gradually their eyes would become hazy and blurred with dreaming. The lively talk
10 would die down. All thoughts fixed on the vision evoked by the horse. Myth of the animal kingdom. Poem of the world of men.

White and mysterious, he paraded his harem through the summer forests with lordly rejoicing. Winter sent him to the plains and sheltered hillsides for the protection of his females. He spent the summer like an Oriental potentate[1] in his woodland gardens. The winter he passed like an illustrious warrior celebrating a well-earned victory.

He was a legend. The stories told of the Wonder Horse were endless. Some true, others fabricated. So many traps, so many snares, so many searching parties, and all in vain. The horse always escaped, always mocked his pursuers, always rose above the control of man. Many a valiant cowboy swore to put his halter and his brand on the animal. But always he had to confess later that the mystic[2] horse was more of a man than he.

I was fifteen years old. Although I had never seen the Wonder Horse, he filled my imagination and fired my ambition. I used to listen open-mouthed as my father and the ranch hands talked about the phantom horse who turned into mist and air and nothingness when he was trapped. I joined in the universal obsession—like the hope of winning the lottery—of putting my lasso on him some day, of capturing him and showing him off on Sunday afternoons when the girls of the town strolled through the streets.

It was high summer. The forests were fresh, green, and gay. The cattle moved slowly, fat and sleek in the August sun and shadow. Listless and drowsy in the **lethargy** of late afternoon, I was dozing on my horse. It was time to round up the herd and go back to the good bread of the cowboy camp. Already my comrades would be sitting around the campfire, playing the guitar, telling stories of past or present, or surrendering to the languor of the late afternoon. The sun was setting behind me in a riot of streaks and colors. Deep, harmonious silence.

I sit drowsily still, forgetting the cattle in the glade. Suddenly the forest falls silent, a deafening quiet. The afternoon comes to a standstill. The breeze stops blowing, but it vibrates. The sun flares hotly. The planet, life, and time itself have stopped in an inexplicable way. For a moment, I don't understand what is happening.

Then my eyes focus. There he is! The Wonder Horse! At the end of the glade, on high ground surrounded by summer green. He is a statue. He is an engraving. Line and form and white stain on a green background. Pride, prestige, and art

**lethargy**
(lĕth´ər-jē) *n.* In a state of *lethargy*, a person experiences drowsiness, inactivity, and a lack of energy.

---

[1] **Oriental potentate** (pōt´n-tāt´): Asian king.
[2] **mystic** (mĭs´tĭk): inspiring a sense of mystery and wonder.

incarnate in animal flesh. A picture of burning beauty and virile[3] freedom. An ideal, pure and invincible, rising from the eternal dreams of humanity. Even today my being thrills when I remember him.

A sharp neigh. A far-reaching challenge that soars on high, ripping the virginal fabric of the rosy clouds. Ears at the point. Eyes flashing. Tail waving active defiance. Hoofs glossy and destructive. Arrogant ruler of the countryside.

The moment is never-ending, a momentary eternity. It no longer exists, but it will always live. . . . There must have been mares. I did not see them. The cattle went on their indifferent way. My horse followed them, and I came slowly back from the land of dreams to the world of toil. But life could no longer be what it was before.

That night under the stars I didn't sleep. I dreamed. How much I dreamed awake and how much I dreamed asleep, I do not know. I only know that a white horse occupied my dreams and filled them with vibrant sound, and light, and turmoil.

Summer passed and winter came. Green grass gave place to white snow. The herds descended from the mountains to the valleys and the hollows. And in the town they kept saying that the Wonder Horse was roaming through this or that secluded area. I inquired everywhere for his whereabouts. Every day he became for me more of an ideal, more of an idol, more of a mystery.

It was Sunday. The sun had barely risen above the snowy mountains. My breath was a white cloud. My horse was trembling with cold and fear like me. I left without going to mass. Without any breakfast. Without the usual bread and sardines in my saddlebags. I had slept badly but had kept the **vigil** well. I was going in search of the white light that galloped through my dreams.

On leaving the town for the open country, the roads disappear. There are no tracks, human or animal. Only a silence, deep, white, and sparkling. My horse breaks trail with his chest and leaves an unending wake, an open rift, in the white sea. My trained, concentrated gaze covers the landscape

**vigil**
(vĭj´əl) *n.* A *vigil* is an act or a time of watching, often during normal sleeping hours.

---

[3] **virile** (vîr´əl): having or showing male spirit, strength, vigor, or power.

from horizon to horizon, searching for the noble silhouette of the talismanic[4] horse.

It must have been midday. I don't know. Time had lost its meaning. I found him! On a slope stained with sunlight. We saw one another at the same time. Together, we turned to stone. Motionless, absorbed, and panting, I gazed at his beauty, his pride, his nobility. As still as sculptured marble, he allowed himself to be admired.

A sudden, violent scream breaks the silence. A glove 100 hurled into my face.[5] A challenge and a **mandate**. Then something surprising happens. The horse that in summer takes his stand between any threat and his herd, swinging

**mandate**
(măn´dāt´) *n.* A *mandate* is an authoritative command or instruction.

---

[4] **talismanic** (tăl´ĭs-măn´ĭk): possessing or believed to possess magical power.

[5] **A glove hurled into my face:** a defiant challenge. Historically, one man challenged another to a duel by throwing down a glove, or gauntlet.

back and forth from left to right, now plunges into the snow. Stronger than they, he is breaking trail for his mares. They follow him. His flight is slow in order to conserve his strength.

I follow. Slowly. Quivering. Thinking about his intelligence. Admiring his courage. Understanding his courtesy. The afternoon advances. My horse is taking it easy.

One by one the mares become weary. One by one, they drop out of the trail. Alone! He and I. My inner ferment[6] bubbles to my lips. I speak to him. He listens and is quiet.

He still opens the way, and I follow in the path he leaves me. Behind us a long, deep trench crosses the white plain. My horse, which has eaten grain and good hay, is still strong. Under-nourished as the Wonder Horse is, his strength is waning. But he keeps on because that is the way he is. He does not know how to surrender.

I now see black stains over his body. Sweat and the wet snow have revealed the black skin beneath the white hair. Snorting breath, turned to steam, tears the air. White spume above white snow. Sweat, spume,[7] and steam. Uneasiness.

I felt like an executioner. But there was no turning back. The distance between us was growing relentlessly shorter. God and Nature watched indifferently.

I feel sure of myself at last. I untie the rope. I open the lasso and pull the reins tight. Every nerve, every muscle is tense. My heart is in my mouth. Spurs pressed against trembling flanks. The horse leaps. I whirl the rope and throw the obedient lasso.

A frenzy of fury and rage. Whirlpools of light and fans of transparent snow. A rope that whistles and burns the saddletree. Smoking, fighting gloves. Eyes burning in their sockets. Mouth parched. Fevered forehead. The whole earth shakes and shudders. The long, white trench ends in a wide, white pool.

Deep, gasping quiet. The Wonder Horse is mine! Both still trembling, we look at one another squarely for a long time. Intelligent and realistic, he stops struggling and even takes a hesitant step toward me. I speak to him. As I talk, I approach him. At first, he flinches and **recoils**. Then he waits for me. The two horses greet one another in their own way. Finally,

**recoil**
(rĭ-koil´) v. To recoil from something is to shrink back, as if in fear.

---

[6] **ferment** (fûr´mĕnt´): agitation or excitement.
[7] **spume** (spyōom): foam or froth.

I succeed in stroking his mane. I tell him many things, and he seems to understand.

Ahead of me, along the trail already made, I drove him toward the town. Triumphant. Exultant. Childish laughter gathered in my throat. With my newfound manliness, I controlled it. I wanted to sing, but I fought down the desire. I wanted to shout, but I kept quiet. It was the ultimate[8] in happiness. It was the pride of the male adolescent. I felt myself a conqueror.

Occasionally the Wonder Horse made a try for his liberty, snatching me abruptly from my thoughts. For a few moments, the struggle was renewed. Then we went on.

It was necessary to go through the town. There was no other way. The sun was setting. Icy streets and people on the porches. The Wonder Horse full of terror and panic for the first time. He ran, and my well-shod horse stopped him. He slipped and fell on his side. I suffered for him. The **indignity**. The humiliation. Majesty degraded. I begged him not to struggle, to let himself be led. How it hurt me that other people should see him like that!

Finally we reached home.

"What shall I do with you, Mago?[9] If I put you into the stable or the corral, you are sure to hurt yourself. Besides, it would be an insult. You aren't a slave. You aren't a servant. You aren't even an animal."

I decided to turn him loose in the fenced pasture. There, little by little, Mago would become accustomed to my friendship and my company. No animal had ever escaped from that pasture.

My father saw me coming and waited for me without a word. A smile played over his face, and a spark danced in his eyes. He watched me take the rope from Mago, and the two of us thoughtfully observed him move away. My father clasped my hand a little more firmly than usual and said, "That was a man's job." That was all. Nothing more was needed. We understood one another very well. I was playing the role of a real man, but the childish laughter and shouting that bubbled up inside me almost destroyed the impression I wanted to create.

**indignity**
(ĭn-dĭg'nĭ-tē) *n.* An *indignity* is something that offends, insults, or injures one's pride or dignity.

---

[8] **ultimate** (ul'tə-mĭt): the greatest extreme; maximum.

[9] **Mago** (mä'gô): Spanish: magician, wizard.

That night I slept little, and when I slept, I did not know that I was asleep. For dreaming is the same when one really dreams, asleep or awake. I was up at dawn. I had to go to see my Wonder Horse. As soon as it was light, I went out into the cold to look for him.

The pasture was large. It contained a grove of trees and a small gully. The Wonder Horse was not visible anywhere, but I was not worried. I walked slowly, my head full of the events of yesterday and my plans for the futures. Suddenly
190  I realized that I had walked a long way. I quicken my steps. I look apprehensively around me. I begin to be afraid. Without knowing it, I begin to run. Faster and faster.

He is not there. The Wonder Horse has escaped. I search every corner where he could be hidden. I follow his tracks. I see that during the night he walked incessantly, sniffing, searching for a way out. He did not find one. He made one for himself.

I followed the track that led straight to the fence. And I saw that the trail did not stop but continued on the other side. It was a barbed-wire fence. There was white hair on the wire.
200  There was blood on the barbs. There were red stains on the snow and little red drops in the hoofprints on the other side of the fence.

I stopped there. I did not go any farther. The rays of the morning sun on my face. Eyes clouded and yet filled with light. Childish tears on the cheeks of a man. A cry stifled in my throat. Slow, silent sobs.

Standing there, I forgot myself and the world and time. I cannot explain it, but my sorrow was mixed with pleasure. I was weeping with happiness. No matter how much it hurt me,
210  I was rejoicing over the flight and the freedom of the Wonder Horse, the dimensions of his **indomitable** spirit. Now he would always be fantasy, freedom, and excitement. The Wonder Horse was transcendent. He had enriched my life forever.

My father found me there. He came close without a word and laid his arm across my shoulders. We stood looking at the white trench with its flecks of red that led into the rising sun.

**indomitable**
(ĭn-dŏm´ ĭ-tə-bəl)
*adj.* Something or someone that is *indomitable* is unable to be tamed or defeated.

**COLLABORATIVE DISCUSSION**  Think about what the narrator learns about the Wonder Horse. Does he have to capture the Wonder Horse to learn these things? Why or why not? With a partner, discuss your response. Point out text evidence that supports your ideas.

# Determine Theme

A **theme** is a story's message about life or human nature. The theme is different from the **topic,** which is simply the subject the author is writing about. A topic can be stated in a few words. However, it usually takes at least one full sentence to express the theme of a text. In addition, a text may have more than one theme.

A story's theme is not stated directly. Instead, readers need to figure it out using particular details in the text. To determine a story's theme, notice the following:

- the title of the story, which can suggest an important idea or symbol
- the main conflict faced by the main character and the lessons the character learns
- important statements that the narrator or main character make
- the setting, which can affect the characters and influence action
- **symbols,** which can be a person, place, or thing that stands for something beyond itself

As you analyze "My Wonder Horse," think about the important messages about life the author wants to share with readers. Use these ideas to determine the theme of the story.

# Describe Stories: Conflict

Every story centers on a conflict. A **conflict** is the problem or struggle that the main character faces.

- An **internal conflict** is a struggle that takes place within a character. An internal conflict is expressed through the character's thoughts and actions. The struggle often involves a decision the character must make.
- An **external conflict** is a struggle with a force outside of the character, such as another character, society, or nature.

To determine the conflicts in a story, ask yourself:

- What problems or struggles does the main character face?
- Is each struggle external or internal?

"My Wonder Horse" contains both external and internal conflicts. As you analyze "My Wonder Horse," notice the conflicts the main character faces.

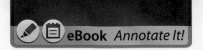
# Analyzing the Text

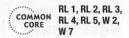

COMMON CORE

RL 1, RL 2, RL 3, RL 4, RL 5, W 2, W 7

**Cite Text Evidence** Support your responses with evidence from the text.

1. **Identify** Reread lines 6–25. What does the Wonder Horse do that makes him legendary? Tell what qualities and characteristics of the horse the men admire.

2. **Infer** Reread lines 26–34. What does the narrator tell about himself? Explain how this information helps you understand why he wants to capture the Wonder Horse.

3. **Analyze** Reread lines 50–57. Tell which words and phrases stand out in the description of the horse. What do these words suggest about the narrator's view of the horse?

4. **Interpret** What symbol is present in the story? What meaning does it have for the narrator?

5. **Cause/Effect** Reread lines 62–78. What is the internal conflict? How has this conflict developed and intensified?

6. **Analyze** Review lines 154–180. Describe an external conflict in the story.

7. **Connect** Think about conflicts in the story, and what the narrator learns from the Wonder Horse, its capture, and its escape. What are some important messages or themes the author shares?

# PERFORMANCE TASK

**Writing Activity: Essay** Find out more about wild mustangs or other wild animals of the West. Then write a one- or two-page informative essay.

- Use online and print resources to find information about your topic.

- Take notes about the animals' population, location, habits, and any threats to their existence.

- Share your essay with the class.

# Critical Vocabulary

COMMON CORE  L 4a, L 4d, L 5a, L 6

| | | |
|---|---|---|
| lethargy | vigil | mandate |
| recoil | indignity | indomitable |

**Practice and Apply** Answer each question and explain your answer.

1. Would you be more likely to experience **lethargy** after a good night's sleep or if you had very little sleep? Explain.

2. Would a bird enthusiast be more likely to hold an owl-watching **vigil** at night or during the day?

3. If a leader gives a clear **mandate,** are people more or less likely to listen to that person? Explain.

4. Would you be more likely to **recoil** from a snake or from an apple? Explain.

5. Which do you see as the greater **indignity**—tripping and falling in public or giving the wrong answer to a question in class?

6. If the opposing team is **indomitable,** is your team likely to win or lose?

## Vocabulary Strategy: Interpret Figures of Speech in Context

Writers often use **figures of speech,** or language that communicates meanings beyond the literal meaning of words to help them express ideas in imaginative ways. Here are three common figures of speech.

| A **simile** is a comparison between two unlike things that uses the words *like* or *as*. | A **metaphor** is a comparison of two unlike things that does *not* use the words *like* or *as*. | **Personification** is giving human qualities to an animal, thing, or idea. |
|---|---|---|

In "My Wonder Horse," there is "Only a silence, deep, white, and sparkling." This example of personification helps you see silence in a new and interesting way. The silence is compared to the snow and is personified as sparkling. The brightness of the snow helps you understand what *sparkling* means.

**Practice and Apply** Write a definition for each boldface word. Then use a dictionary to confirm your answers.

1. The **avaricious** sponge soaked up all the water on the counter.

2. Except for one sturdy bench, the stage props were as **flimsy** as a house made of paper.

# Language Conventions: Improving Expression

The author of "My Wonder Horse" chose **formal language,** or Standard English to describe the horse, the setting, and the narrator's thoughts. The author of "The Ravine" (Collection 1) included **informal language,** such as *shuddup,* to mimic how teenagers actually sound. Another author might use **slang,** or made-up words and ordinary words with new meanings, to create situations and characters that are authentic to a particular place and time.

Sometimes writers use a blend of informal and formal language to express certain ideas, or mix formal language with slang to create or highlight a contrast. Sometimes, however, a writer's methods of expression cause problems for the reader. Here are two strategies you should use to improve expression in writing:

- **Consider your audience.** Is your audience a group of students your own age, younger children, or professional adults? With students your own age, you can use more informal language, but slang might confuse younger students. You show respect for an older or professional audience by using a formal tone.
- **Use a consistent method of expression.** Knowing your audience will help you choose your tone. Your method of expression should be consistent. When a writer starts to stray from one method of expression to another, readers may be confused and wonder to whom the writer is speaking.

**Practice and Apply**   Edit and revise the dialogue to match the tone of the first paragraph.

As Karla passed the principal's office, she thought about how she admired that Ms. Hansen was quiet, but kind and direct. Karla's thoughts were interrupted when she heard Ms. Hansen's door open behind her.

"Hey," Karla heard Ms. Hansen say. "Where ya headed?"

"To get some grub," said Karla as she turned around.

"Whatcha been doing today?" asked Ms. Hansen.

"Been better," sighed Karla. "Epic fail."

**Background** *Wild animals are animals that live in nature. They can be as rare as a snow leopard or as common as a tree squirrel. Although many states have laws that prohibit owning a wild animal, thousands of people in the United States keep animals such as wolves, pythons, crocodiles, and bears as pets. Some people want to make it illegal to have these kinds of pets. They argue that these animals pose a safety and health risk to people and the environment. Others claim that with proper care, wild animals can safely live in captivity.*

# WILD ANIMALS AREN'T PETS

Editorial by USA TODAY

# LET PEOPLE OWN EXOTIC ANIMALS

Commentary by Zuzana Kukol

**SETTING A PURPOSE** As you read, focus on the facts and examples used to justify the points in the editorial by *USA TODAY* and the commentary by Zuzana Kukol, president and co-founder of Responsible Exotic Animal Ownership. Think about which points are convincing to you and which are not.

## Wild Animals Aren't Pets
### Editorial by USA TODAY

In many states, anyone with a few hundred dollars and a yen[1] for the unusual can own a python, a black bear or a big cat as a "pet." For $8,000 a baby white tiger can be yours. Sometimes, wild animals are even offered free: "Siberian tigers looking for a good home," read an ad in the *Animal Finder's Guide*.

Until recently, though, few people knew how easy it is to own a wild animal as a pet. Or how potentially tragic.

---

[1] **yen** (yĕn): a strong desire or inclination.

After Terry Thompson set his exotic animals free in Zanesville, Ohio, a sign on an expressway warned motorists that the animals were on the loose in the area.

But just as a 2007 raid on property owned by football star
10  Michael Vick laid bare the little known and cruel world of dogfighting, a story that unfolded in a small Ohio city recently opened the public's eyes to the little known, distressing world of "**exotic**" pets. We're not suggesting that people who own these animals are cruel. Many surely love them. But public safety, common sense and compassion for animals all **dictate** the same conclusion: Wild animals are not pets.

If that weren't already obvious, it became more so when collector Terry Thompson opened the cages on his Zanesville farm, springing dozens of lions, tigers, bears and other wild
20  creatures before killing himself. With animals running loose and darkness closing in, authorities arrived with no good choices to protect the public. They shot all but a handful of the animals as the nation watched, transfixed[2] and horrified.

Owners of "exotic" animals claim they rarely maim or kill. But is the death rate really the point?

**exotic**
(ĭg-zŏt´ĭk) *adj.*
Something that is *exotic* is from another part of the world.

**dictate**
(dĭk´tāt´) *v.* To *dictate* something is to require it to be done or decided.

---

[2] **transfixed** (trăns-fĭkst´): motionless, as with terror, amazement, or other strong emotion.

In 2009, a 2-year-old Florida girl was strangled by a 12-foot-long Burmese python, a family pet that had gotten out of its aquarium. That same year, a Connecticut woman was mauled and disfigured by a neighbor's pet chimp. Last year, a caretaker was mauled to death by a bear owned by a Cleveland collector. In Zanesville, it was the animals themselves, including 18 rare Bengal tigers, who became innocent victims.

Trade in these beautiful creatures thrives in the USA, where thousands are bred and sold through classified ads or at auctions centered in Indiana, Missouri and Tennessee. There's too little to stop it.

A 2003 federal law, which forbids the interstate transport of certain big cats, has stopped much of the trade on the Internet, according to the Humane Society of the U.S. But monkeys, baboons and other primates were left out, and measures to plug that hole have twice stalled in Congress.

Only collectors who exhibit animals need a federal license. Those, such as Thompson, who keep the animals as "pets" are left alone, unless states intervene.[3] And many do not. Eight—Alabama, Idaho, Ohio, Nevada, North Carolina, South Carolina, West Virginia and Wisconsin—have no rules, and in 13 others the laws are lax,[4] according to Born Free USA, which has lobbied for years for stronger laws.

After the Cleveland bear-mauling, then-Ohio Gov. Ted Strickland issued an emergency order to ban possession of wild animals. While it exempted[5] current owners, Thompson might have been forced to give up his **menagerie** because he had been cited for animal cruelty. We'll never know. Strickland's successor, John Kasich, let the order expire.

**menagerie**
(mə-năj´ə-rē) *n.*
A *menagerie* is a collection of live wild animals, often kept for showing to the public.

---

[3] **intervene** (ĭn´tər-vēn´): to come between so as to block or change an action.
[4] **lax** (lăks): not rigorous, strict, or firm.
[5] **exempted** (ĭg-zĕmpt´əd): freed or excused from following a law or duty which others must obey.

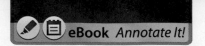
# Trace and Evaluate an Argument

The editorial you have just read is an **argument,** which is a carefully stated claim supported by reasons and evidence. An argument is made up of two parts. The **claim** is the writer's position on a problem or issue. The **support** is the reasons and evidence that help prove the claim. **Reasons** are statements made to explain a belief. **Evidence** is a specific reference, such as a fact, statistic, quotation, or opinion that is used to support a claim. Support in an argument is usually for or against an issue; it is used to justify a viewpoint.

To **trace,** or follow the reasoning, of an argument:

- Identify the claim, or the writer's position on the issue.
- Look for reasons and specific types of evidence (facts, statistics, quotations, or opinions) that support the claim.
- Identify **counterarguments,** which are statements that address opposing viewpoints.

To **evaluate** an argument, or decide whether it makes sense and is convincing:

- Determine whether the evidence supports the claim in a logical way.
- Make sure ideas are presented in a way that makes sense and is clear.
- Determine whether the counterarguments are adequately addressed.

As you analyze the editorial, look at how the author constructs and supports the argument.

# Analyzing the Text

**Cite Text Evidence**    Support your responses with evidence from the text.

1. **Identify**  What is the claim of the editorial? Where is it found?

2. **Summarize**  Reread lines 17–23. What specific evidence is used in this paragraph to support the editorial's claim?

3. **Interpret**  Reread lines 24–32. What counterargument does the author address?

4. **Summarize**  Reread lines 37–48. What legal issues make it possible for people to own exotic pets?

5. **Evaluate**  Do you think the writer's argument is convincing? Cite reasons and evidence from the text that you feel were the weakest or the strongest.

# Let People Own Exotic Animals
by Zuzana Kukol

The recent tragedy in Zanesville, Ohio brought back the question of whether private ownership of wild and exotic animals should be legal.

The simple answer is yes. Responsible private ownership of exotic animals should be legal if animal welfare is taken care of. Terry Thompson didn't represent the typical responsible owner. He had a criminal record and animal abuse charges. What Thompson did was selfish and insane; we cannot **regulate** insanity.

People keep exotic animals for commercial[1] reasons and as pets. Most exotic animals—such as big cats, bears or apes—are in commercial, federally inspected facilities. These animals are born in captivity, and not "stolen" from the wild. Captive breeding eliminates the pressure on wild populations, and also serves as a backup in case the animals go extinct.[2]

**regulate**
(rĕg′yə-lāt′) *v.* If you *regulate* something, you control or direct it according to a rule, principle, or law.

---

[1] **commercial** (kə-mûr′shəl): of or relating to commerce or trade.
[2] **extinct** (ĭk-stĭngkt′): no longer existing or living.

Dangers from exotic animals are low. On average in the United States, only 3.25 people per year are killed by captive big cats, snakes, elephants and bears. Most of these fatalities are owners, family members, friends and trainers voluntarily
20  on the property where the animals were kept. Meanwhile, traffic accidents kill about 125 people per day.

If we have the freedom to choose what car to buy, where to live, or what domestic animal to have, why shouldn't we have the same freedom to choose what species of wild or exotic animal to own and to love?

Would the Ohio situation be any different if the animals were owned by a government and their caretaker released them? Is this really about private ownership, or is it about certain people's personal issues with exotics in captivity?
30  If society overreacts and bans exotics because of actions of a few deranged[3] individuals, then we need to ban kids, as that is the only way to totally stop child abuse, and we need to ban humans, because that is the only way to stop murder. Silly, isn't it?

**COLLABORATIVE DISCUSSION** With a partner, discuss whether the editorial or the commentary most closely matches your point of view. Point out specific passages or ideas in each text with which you strongly agree or disagree.

---

[3] **deranged** (dĭ-rānj´d):  mentally unbalanced; insane.

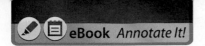

# Analyze the Meaning of Words and Phrases

COMMON CORE   RI 4

When a writer makes an argument for or against an issue, he or she will often use persuasive techniques to convince readers to see things their way. **Persuasive techniques** are methods used to influence others to adopt a certain opinion or belief or to act a certain way.

Persuasive techniques can make a strong argument even more powerful. They can also be used to disguise flaws in weak arguments. One persuasive technique that writers use is loaded language. **Loaded language** consists of words and phrases with strongly positive or negative connotations. (**Connotations** are meanings that are associated with a word *beyond* its dictionary meaning.)

To help you analyze loaded language:

- Look for words in the text that have strong impact. Think about how these words make you feel.
- Ask yourself if the argument is strong without the use of these words.

As you analyze "Let People Own Exotic Animals," look for examples of loaded language.

# Analyzing the Text

COMMON CORE   RI 1, RI 2, RI 3, RI 4

Cite Text Evidence   Support your responses with evidence from the text.

1. **Identify**  What is the claim of the commentary? Where is it found?

2. **Summarize**  Reread lines 10–15. According to the writer, where are most exotic animals kept and what is the benefit of breeding them?

3. **Analyze**  Reread lines 16–21. What specific evidence does the writer use to support the argument that people should be allowed to own exotic animals? Explain how the evidence is or is not directly related to the claim.

4. **Interpret**  Review lines 30–33. What examples of loaded language do you find? What are the positive or negative associations of these words?

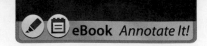

# Compare and Contrast: Arguments

 COMMON CORE  RI 8, RI 9

When you **compare and contrast** two arguments on the same issue, you analyze how each argument is presented. First, you trace and evaluate each argument: identify its claim, follow its support and reasoning, and decide whether it is convincing. Then you determine how each author's viewpoint or attitude toward the issue differs.

To compare and contrast persuasive writing texts:

- Look at the evidence each writer provide as support—facts, examples, statistics. Does the evidence support the claim in a logical way?
- Determine if the writers are trying to be persuasive by appealing to your emotions, to your logic, or to both. Look for words with strong positive or negative connotations.

# Analyzing the Text

COMMON CORE  RI 1, RI 2, RI 4, RI 6, RI 8, RI 9, W 1a-b, W 7

**Cite Text Evidence**   Support your responses with evidence from the texts.

1. **Compare**  Compare each writer's claim and the kinds of evidence that support it. Does each author include enough evidence to support the claim?

2. **Evaluate**  Examine each text and identify examples of loaded language. For each text, tell whether the author's word choices are effective and why.

3. **Identify**  Reread lines 4–9 of "Let People Own Exotic Animals." What counterargument does the author address?

4. **Critique**  Which argument do you think is more authoritative? Why?

# PERFORMANCE TASK

**Writing Activity: Essay**  Write an opinion essay telling whether or not you would own a particular exotic animal and why.

- First, conduct research on owning a specific exotic animal. Take notes on the care, safety, and feeding of this animal.

- Next, decide whether you would or would not own this animal as a pet.
- Then draft your essay, starting with a clearly stated claim.
- Use your research notes to provide evidence that supports your claim.

# Critical Vocabulary

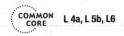 

exotic            dictate            menagerie            regulate

**Practice and Apply**  Answer each question, choosing one or more responses.

1. Which of the following could be described as **exotic**?
   a food from another country      a backpack      a rare type of orchid

2. Which of the following is something our government can **dictate**?
   how birthdays could be celebrated      taxes people have to pay

3. Which of these might you find in a **menagerie**?
   monkeys      a stuffed lion      stars

4. Which of the following are things we could **regulate**?
   laughter      dreams      how fast people should drive

## Vocabulary Strategy: Part-to-Whole Analogies

An **analogy** presents a relationship between pairs of words. Sometimes writers use analogies to explain unfamiliar ideas. A typical analogy begins with a pair of items that are related in some way. One of the most common analogies is part to whole. Here is an example, displayed first as a sentence and then with special symbols:

> *Baseball card* **is to** *collection* **as** *tiger* **is to** *menagerie.*
>
> baseball card : collection :: tiger : menagerie

Both versions express a part-to-whole relationship: *baseball card* and *tiger* are parts; *collection* and *menagerie* are wholes. In the second version, the single colon stands for "is to" and the double colon stands for "as." Examining the full analogy helps you understand how the word pairs are related.

**Practice and Apply**  Complete each part-to-whole analogy by choosing the letter of the best answer.

1. petal : _____ :: child : family
   **a.** flower
   **b.** stem

2. chapter : book :: _____ : army
   **a.** uniform
   **b.** soldier

3. Ohio : _____ :: lettuce : salad
   **a.** United States
   **b.** Zanesville

4. elbow : arm :: people : _____
   **a.** business
   **b.** population

# Language Conventions: Spell Words Correctly

The main reason for writing is to communicate ideas with others. That's why it is extremely important for writers to use and spell words correctly.

Many common words, such as *loose* and *lose,* are spelled differently and sound slightly different, but they are close enough to be easily confused or misused. Look at this example from "Wild Animals Aren't Pets":

> **With animals running loose and darkness closing in, authorities arrived with no good choices to protect the public.**

The word *loose* is commonly misspelled as *lose,* which is a different word with a different meaning. If the writer had misspelled *loose* as *lose,* readers would have been confused and distracted. The following words are often confused:

| |
|---|
| advice/advise |
| lie/lay |
| passed/past |
| than/then |
| two/too/to |
| their/there/they're |

**Practice and Apply** Choose the word from each commonly confused pair that correctly completes each sentence.

1. Gena would not (accept/except) Mindy's offer of a ride to school.

2. Do not discuss this any (farther/further) with the police until you have seen a lawyer.

3. The lawyer will (advice/advise) you of your rights.

4. The rusty fire escape did not look like it could (bare/bear) the weight of a small child.

5. Russell slammed his foot on the (brake/break) to avoid hitting the duck crossing the road in front of him.

6. The judge's ruling today will have a significant (affect/effect) on similar cases waiting to be heard.

7. Malia (passed/past) the library on her way to the store.

8. We would rather see a movie (than/then) go to the park.

**Sandra Cisneros** (b. 1954) *is one of seven children born to her Mexican father and Mexican American mother. When Cisneros was eleven, her family moved to a poor neighborhood in Chicago. Cisneros's first novel,* The House on Mango Street, *published in 1984, paints a picture of this neighborhood and the people who lived in it. It took Cisneros eight years to write the book. Cisneros has won many awards for her poems, short stories, and novels. She now lives in San Antonio, Texas.*

# Eleven

Short Story by Sandra Cisneros

**SETTING A PURPOSE** As you read, pay attention to how the narrator feels and the clues that help you understand why she feels the way she does.

What they don't understand about birthdays and what they never tell you is that when you're eleven, you're also ten, and nine, and eight, and seven, and six, and five, and four, and three, and two, and one. And when you wake up on your eleventh birthday you expect to feel eleven, but you don't. You open your eyes and everything's just like yesterday, only it's today. And you don't feel eleven at all. You feel like you're still ten. And you are—underneath the year that makes you eleven.

10   Like some days you might say something stupid, and that's the part of you that's still ten. Or maybe some days you might need to sit on your mama's lap because you're scared, and that's the part of you that's five. And maybe one day when you're all grown up maybe you will need to cry like if you're

three, and that's okay. That's what I tell Mama when she's sad and needs to cry. Maybe she's feeling three.

Because the way you grow old is kind of like an onion or like the rings inside a tree trunk or like my little wooden dolls that fit one inside the other, each year inside the next one.
20 That's how being eleven years old is.

You don't feel eleven. Not right away. It takes a few days, weeks even, sometimes even months before you say Eleven when they ask you. And you don't feel smart eleven, not until you're almost twelve. That's the way it is.

Only today I wish I didn't have only eleven years **rattling** inside me like pennies in a tin Band-Aid box. Today I wish I was one hundred and two instead of eleven because if I was one hundred and two I'd have known what to say when Mrs. Price put the red sweater on my desk. I would've known
30 how to tell her it wasn't mine instead of just sitting there with that look on my face and nothing coming out of my mouth.

"Whose is this?" Mrs. Price says, and she holds the red sweater up in the air for all the class to see. "Whose? It's been sitting in the coatroom for a month."

"Not mine," says everybody. "Not me."

"It has to belong to somebody," Mrs. Price keeps saying, but nobody can remember. It's an ugly sweater with red plastic buttons and a collar and sleeves all stretched out like you could use it for a jump rope. It's maybe a thousand years old
40 and even if it belonged to me I wouldn't say so.

Maybe because I'm skinny, maybe because she doesn't like me, that stupid Sylvia Saldívar says, "I think it belongs to Rachel." An ugly sweater like that, all **raggedy** and old, but Mrs. Price believes her. Mrs. Price takes the sweater and puts it right on my desk, but when I open my mouth nothing comes out.

"That's not, I don't, you're not . . . Not mine," I finally say in a little voice that was maybe me when I was four.

"Of course it's yours," Mrs. Price says. "I remember you
50 wearing it once." Because she's older and the teacher, she's right and I'm not.

Not mine, not mine, not mine, but Mrs. Price is already turning to page thirty-two, and math problem number four. I don't know why but all of a sudden I'm feeling sick inside, like the part of me that's three wants to come out of my eyes, only I squeeze them shut tight and bite down on my teeth real

**rattle**
(răt´l) v. If you hear something *rattle*, it is making a short, fast knocking sound as it moves.

**raggedy**
(răg´ĭ-dē) *adj.*
Something that is *raggedy* is worn out, torn, or frayed.

hard and try to remember today I am eleven, eleven. Mama is making a cake for me for tonight, and when Papa comes home everybody will sing Happy birthday, happy birthday to you.

60    But when the sick feeling goes away and I open my eyes, the red sweater's still sitting there like a big red mountain. I move the red sweater to the corner of my desk with my ruler. I move my pencil and books and eraser as far from it as possible. I even move my chair a little to the right. Not mine, not mine, not mine.

In my head I'm thinking how long till lunchtime, how long till I can take the red sweater and throw it over the schoolyard fence, or leave it hanging on a parking meter, or bunch it up into a little ball and toss it in the **alley**. Except when math
70   period ends Mrs. Price says loud and in front of everybody, "Now, Rachel, that's enough," because she sees I've shoved the red sweater to the tippy-tip corner of my desk and it's hanging all over the edge like a waterfall, but I don't care.

"Rachel," Mrs. Price says. She says it like she's getting mad. "You put that sweater on right now and no more nonsense."

"But it's not—"

"Now!" Mrs. Price says.

**alley**
(ăl´ē) *n.* An *alley* is a narrow street or passage behind or between city buildings.

## «You put that sweater on right now and no more nonsense.»

This is when I wish I wasn't eleven, because all the years inside of me—ten, nine, eight, seven, six, five, four, three,
80   two, and one—are pushing at the back of my eyes when I put one arm through one sleeve of the sweater that smells like cottage cheese, and then the other arm through the other and stand there with my arms apart like if the sweater hurts me and it does, all itchy and full of germs that aren't even mine.

That's when everything I've been holding in since this morning, since when Mrs. Price put the sweater on my desk, finally lets go, and all of a sudden I'm crying in front of everybody. I wish I was **invisible** but I'm not. I'm eleven and

**invisible**
(ĭn-vĭz´ə-bəl) *adj.* If something is *invisible*, you cannot see it.

it's my birthday today and I'm crying like I'm three in front
90   of everybody. I put my head down on the desk and bury my
face in my stupid clown-sweater arms. My face all hot and spit
coming out of my mouth because I can't stop the little animal
noises from coming out of me, until there aren't any more
tears left in my eyes, and it's just my body shaking like when
you have the hiccups, and my whole head hurts like when you
drink milk too fast.

     But the worst part is right before the bell rings for lunch.
That stupid Phyllis Lopez, who is even dumber than Sylvia
Saldívar, says she remembers the red sweater is hers! I take it
100  off right away and give it to her, only Mrs. Price pretends like
everything's okay.

     Today I'm eleven. There's a cake Mama's making
for tonight, and when Papa comes home from work we'll
eat it. There'll be candles and presents and everybody will
sing Happy birthday, happy birthday to you, Rachel, only it's
too late.

     I'm eleven today. I'm eleven, ten, nine, eight, seven, six,
five, four, three, two, and one, but I wish I was one hundred
and two. I wish I was anything but eleven, because I want
110  today to be far away already, far away like a runaway balloon,
like a tiny o in the sky, so tiny-tiny you have to close your eyes
to see it.

**COLLABORATIVE DISCUSSION**  With a partner, discuss how the
story events and other characters affect the narrator's feelings. Cite
specific passages to support your ideas.

# Analyze Word Choice and Tone

A piece of writing usually has a particular style. A **style** is a manner of writing; it involves *how* something is said rather than *what* is said. Style is shown through elements such as

- **word choice**—the way words and phrases are used to express ideas
- **sentence structure**—the types, patterns, and lengths of sentences used, including fragments (pieces of sentences)
- **dialogue**—realistic conversation between characters
- **tone**—the writer's attitude toward the subject, such as *serious, playful, mocking,* and *sympathetic*

The author's choice to tell "Eleven" from Rachel's point of view affects the style of the writing. For example, reread the first paragraph. Note that the writer uses a combination of long and short sentences and conversational words as if Rachel were talking directly to you. When Rachel describes how she feels about turning eleven, the tone might be described as *annoyed* or *grumpy*. These style elements draw us into Rachel's world and help us see the story from her perspective.

As you analyze "Eleven," find other examples of these techniques that reveal the writer's style and the tone of the story.

# Describe Characters' Responses

The way a writer develops characters is known as **characterization.** Writers develop their story characters through the characters' words, thoughts, and actions. They also use other methods, such as describing how a character looks, telling how other characters react to him or her, and by commenting directly on the character through the use of a narrator.

By noticing and analyzing these methods of characterization, readers can better understand what motivates the characters and makes them behave the way they do. As you analyze Rachel's character, ask yourself:

- What does she look like?
- What does she think about turning eleven?
- How does Mrs. Price treat her?
- How does Rachel respond to the conflict in the story?

As you analyze "Eleven," look for more examples of the author's characterization of Rachel as well as other characters in the story.

# Analyzing the Text

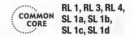

RL 1, RL 3, RL 4,
SL 1a, SL 1b,
SL 1c, SL 1d

**Cite Text Evidence** Support your responses with evidence from the text.

1. **Draw Conclusions** In "Eleven," Rachel says that when you're eleven, you're also ten, nine, eight, seven, six, five, four, three, two, and one. What does Rachel mean by this and why do you think the author chose these words to convey that meaning?

2. **Interpret** Reread lines 17–20. When Rachel says that growing old is "like an onion," she is using a **simile,** a comparison that uses the word *like* or *as*. What other similes does she use in lines 17–20, and what meaning do all the similes convey?

3. **Synthesize** Explain how Rachel's inability to speak up to Mrs. Price contributes to how she feels about turning eleven.

4. **Analyze** What are the consequences of Rachel's being unable to speak up to Mrs. Price? Explain why Rachel has such a negative reaction to wearing the sweater.

5. **Evaluate** Reread lines 97–101. What do Rachel's words about Phyllis and Sylvia reveal about her character? Are Rachel's comments justified? Why or why not?

6. **Analyze** How would you describe the tone at the end of the story? What techniques does the author use to convey this tone?

7. **Analyze** How would you describe the author's style? Describe some of the aspects that convey the author's style.

## PERFORMANCE TASK

**Speaking Activity: Discussion** In a small group, discuss the role of Mrs. Price as a minor character in "Eleven." Together, explain why Mrs. Price's actions are an important part of the story.

- Appoint one member of the group to take notes.
- List words that describe Mrs. Price.
- Describe Rachel's reactions to Mrs. Price as an authority figure.

- Discuss how the first-person point of view with Rachel as narrator affects how Mrs. Price is described and how the reader sees her.
- When the discussion is finished, review the key ideas expressed. Then share the group's ideas with the rest of the class. Be sure to point out examples in the story that support the group's ideas.

# Critical Vocabulary

COMMON CORE L 4c, L 5c, L 6

rattle          raggedy          alley          invisible

**Practice and Apply**  Use what you know about the Vocabulary words to answer the questions.

1. Which Vocabulary word goes with *narrow*? Why?

2. Which Vocabulary word goes with *noisy*? Why?

3. Which Vocabulary word goes with *shredded*? Why?

4. Which Vocabulary word goes with *hidden*? Why?

# Vocabulary Strategy: Denotations and Connotations

A word's **denotation** is its dictionary meaning. A word's **connotation** includes the feelings and ideas associated with it. For example, the dictionary definition of the word *frigid* is "extremely cold." The word *wintry* also means "cold," but the two words can have different connotations.

Writers use connotations of words to communicate positive or negative feelings. *Frigid* has the negative connotation of meaning the weather is so cold that you do not want to be outside in it. In contrast, *wintry* has a more positive connotation and may bring to mind crisp air or cheery snow flurries. Each word creates a different tone in the writing and elicits different feelings in the reader.

In "Eleven," Rachel describes the sweater as *raggedy,* which means "tattered, worn out." From this, you can tell that Rachel is angry partly because the sweater is in bad shape. Thinking about a word's connotation will help you to understand the writer's purpose in using that word.

**Practice and Apply**  Read the words in each group below. (The first word in each group is from "Eleven.") Look up any words you do not know in a dictionary. Then arrange each group of words in order from positive to negative connotation. Discuss your responses with a partner or small group.

1. *skinny, thin, gaunt, narrow, scrawny*

2. *raggedy, torn, ripped, frayed, shredded, tattered*

3. *hanging, dangling, drooping, falling, swinging*

4. *rattling, shaking, quivering, wobbling, jerking, jiggling*

5. *shoved, pushed, guided, propelled, crammed, forced*

6. *squeezed, jammed, crushed, stuffed, condensed, smashed, compressed*

# Language Conventions: Punctuating Dialogue

 COMMON CORE L 2

**Dialogue** is written conversation between two or more characters. In fiction, dialogue is usually set off with quotation marks. Keep the following rules in mind when you write dialogue:

- Put quotation marks before and after a speaker's exact words.
- Place punctuation marks, such as commas, question marks, and periods, inside the quotation mark.
- If a speaker tag, such as *she said,* comes before the quotation, set a comma after the speaker tag.
- If a speaker tag follows the exact words of the quotation, set a comma after the quotation but before the closing quotation mark.

Note how the following dialogue from "Eleven" follows the rules for punctuating dialogue:

> **"Whose is this?" Mrs. Price says, and she holds the red sweater up in the air for all the class to see. "Whose? It's been sitting in the coatroom for a month."**
>
> **"Not mine," says everybody. "Not me."**
>
> **"It has to belong to somebody," Mrs. Price keeps saying, but nobody can remember.**

**Practice and Apply**   Rewrite the incorrectly punctuated sentences, adding or correcting the punctuation as needed.

1. "Birthdays are not what you expect them to be" said Rachel.

2. Mrs. Price glared at me and said It is not appropriate to burst into tears in the middle of class.

3. "You think I'm skinny, don't you"? asked Rachel.

4. I don't," replied Sylvia.

5. "The sweater is mine, admitted Phyllis. I left it in the coatroom and forgot all about it."

**Background** *In the early 1900s, more than one million Mexicans immigrated to the United States. Many came to find jobs but found discrimination as well. During the same time period, the need for workers in Northern factories of the United States caused a mass migration of African Americans from the South. Many African Americans settled in Harlem, a neighborhood of New York City. There, writers, along with artists and musicians, worked to establish a proud cultural identity. This movement was called the Harlem Renaissance.*

# A VOICE
# Words Like FREEDOM

Poem by Pat Mora

Poem by Langston Hughes

**Pat Mora** (b. 1942) *was born in El Paso, Texas, to a Mexican American family that spoke both English and Spanish. Mora grew up speaking both languages, and today writes in English and in Spanish. When not writing, Mora spends much of her time encouraging children of all languages to read books. In 1996, she founded a holiday called "El día de los niños/El día de los libros." In English that means "Children's Day/Book Day."*

**Langston Hughes** (1902–1967) *began writing poetry as a child, but he didn't gain fame until he met a famous poet in a restaurant where Hughes was working. Hughes left several of his poems at the poet's table; the poet was impressed and helped introduce Hughes to a wider audience. Hughes became one of the most important voices in the Harlem Renaissance. Much of his work focuses on the experiences of his fellow African Americans who lived around him in Harlem.*

**SETTING A PURPOSE** As you read, focus on the challenges and feelings each poet expresses about being an American, paying close attention to how each poet's background affects his or her perspective.

# A VOICE
by Pat Mora

Even the lights on the stage unrelenting[1]
as the desert sun couldn't hide the other
students, their eyes also unrelenting,
students who spoke English every night

5   as they ate their meat, potatoes, gravy.
Not you. In your house that smelled like
rose powder, you spoke Spanish formal
as your father, the judge without a courtroom

in the country he floated to in the dark
10  on a flatbed truck. He walked slow
as a hot river down the narrow hall
of your house. You never dared to race past him,

to say, "Please move," in the language
you learned effortlessly, as you learned to run,
15  the language forbidden at home, though your mother
said you learned it to fight with the neighbors.

You liked winning with words. You liked
writing speeches about patriotism and democracy.
You liked all the faces looking at you, all those eyes.
20  "How did I do it?" you ask me now. "How did I do it

when my parents didn't understand?"
The family story says your voice is the voice
of an aunt in Mexico, spunky[2] as a peacock.
Family stories sing of what lives in the blood.

---

[1] **unrelenting** (ŭn´rĭ-lĕn´tĭng):  steady and persistent; continuing on without
   stopping.
[2] **spunky** (spŭng´kē):  spirited, plucky; having energy and courage.

25 You told me only once about the time you went
   to the state capitol, your family proud as if
   you'd been named governor. But when you looked
   around, the only Mexican in the auditorium,
   you wanted to hide from those strange faces.
30 Their eyes were pinpricks,[3] and you faked
   hoarseness. You, who are never at a loss
   for words, felt your breath stick in your throat

   like an ice-cube. "I can't," you whispered.
   "I can't." Yet you did. Not that day but years later.
35 You taught the four of us to speak up.
   This is America, Mom. The undo-able is done

   in the next generation.[4] Your breath moves
   through the family like the wind
   moves through the trees.

---

[3] **pinpricks** (pĭn′prĭks′): small wounds or punctures made by or as if by a pin.
[4] **generation** (jĕn′ə-rā′shən): all the people who are at the same stage of descent
   from a common ancestor; grandparents, parents, and children represent three
   different generations.

# WORDS LIKE FREEDOM
by Langston Hughes

There are words like *Freedom*
Sweet and wonderful to say.
On my heartstrings freedom sings
All day everyday.

5  There are words like *Liberty*
That almost make me cry.
If you had known what I know
You would know why.

**COLLABORATIVE DISCUSSION**  With a partner, discuss how "A Voice" and "Words Like Freedom" explore ideas such as freedom and equality. Use evidence from the texts in your discussion.

# Determine the Meaning of Figurative Language

COMMON CORE RL 4

Poets often use figurative language to express ideas. A **simile** is a comparison of two things that uses the words *like* or *as*. A **metaphor** is a comparison of two things that does not use *like* or *as*. Similes and metaphors help readers see ideas in an imaginative way. The poem "A Voice" opens with a simile:

> **Even the lights on the stage unrelenting as the**
> **desert sun couldn't hide the other students, . . .**

The simile emphasizes how unforgiving and severe the stage lights seem. This comparison helps readers understand how the speaker's mother felt.

To determine the meaning of a simile or metaphor, ask yourself:
- What two ideas is the poet comparing?
- What feelings and attitudes does the simile or metaphor help explain?

As you analyze "A Voice," look for other examples of figurative language.

# Analyze Tone

COMMON CORE RL 4, RL 6

Tone is another way a writer expresses ideas. A writer's **tone** is his or her attitude toward a subject. Tone is often described with a single adjective, such as *angry, playful,* or *mocking.* Writers establish tone through thoughts, actions, images, and word choices.

An **inference** is a logical guess. Readers can identify and put together clues, such as the poet's choice of words and images, to make inferences about a poem's tone.

In "A Voice," the simile "In your house that smelled like rose powder, you spoke Spanish formal . . ." provides a clue about the home of the speaker's mother. From this, readers can infer that the **speaker,** or the voice that "talks" to the reader, has a deep understanding of what her mother's home life was like. The speaker's tone can be described as *understanding*.

Use the following clues to make inferences about tone in the poems:
- Identify the topic.
- Pay attention to images and descriptions. Are they serious, silly, or frightening?
- Decide how the speaker feels about the subject. Does he or she feel happy, sad, or angry?

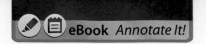
# Analyzing the Text

COMMON CORE RL 1, RL 2, RL 3, RL 4, RL 6, RL 9, W 3d

**Cite Text Evidence**   Support your responses with evidence from the text.

1. **Infer**  Review lines 6–14 of "A Voice," in which the speaker describes her grandfather. What is the simile in these lines? What inference can you make about the relationship between the speaker's mother and her father?

2. **Interpret**  Reread lines 17–23 of "A Voice." How does the speaker's mother feel about herself as a young girl? Explain how the simile in lines 22–23 shows the connection the mother has to her family.

3. **Interpret**   Reread lines 5–8 of "A Voice." Identify the metaphor in these lines. What does the metaphor tell you about the father?

4. **Connect**   Reread lines 34–35 of "A Voice." What lesson does the speaker say she learned from her mother, and how does the poet express this lesson now?

5. **Interpret**   Reread lines 37–39 of "A Voice." Describe the poet's tone. How does her tone help her convey the ideas she expresses?

6. **Analyze**  Think about the speaker's attitude in "Words Like Freedom." How would you describe the poet's tone?

7. **Compare**   Compare line 24 of "A Voice" with lines 3–4 of "Words Like Freedom." How are these metaphors similar in the experiences and ideas they address?

## PERFORMANCE TASK

**Writing Activity: Poem**  In "A Voice" and "Words Like Freedom," the poets express their opinions and make their voices heard. Write a poem in which you express your views about a freedom you enjoy, or about the freedom to have an opinion at all.

- Choose your topic. Be sure it is clear and specific.
- Choose a few adjectives that clearly tell how you feel about your topic. These words are the tone you want to create in your poem.

- Include at least one simile and one metaphor in your poem.
- Create comparisons that help express your ideas. Try a number of different ones until you find those that express your feelings in a vivid way.
- Review your word choices. Make sure they express your opinions precisely.
- Keep in mind the tone you chose as you review your work. Make adjustments as needed.

Interactive Lessons
If you need help . . .
• Writing an Argument
• Writing as a Process
• Using Textual Evidence

# Present an Argument in a Speech

COMMON CORE

W 1a–e Write arguments.
W 5 Develop and strengthen writing.
W 6 Use technology to produce and publish writing.
W 8 Gather relevant information from print and digital sources.
W 10 Write routinely.
SL 4 Present claims and findings.

A good argument can convince an audience to change their minds about a topic or to understand and accept an opposing position. In this activity, you will write and give an argument in a speech that justifies your views about whether people should own exotic animals. You will use evidence from "Wild Animals Aren't Pets," "Let People Own Exotic Animals," and other texts in the collection to support your position.

**A successful argument**

- contains an engaging introduction that clearly establishes the claim being made
- supports the claim with clear reasons and relevant evidence from a variety of credible sources
- establishes and maintains a formal style
- uses language that effectively conveys ideas and adds interest
- includes a conclusion that follows from the argument presented and leaves a lasting impression

**PLAN**

**Choose Your Position** Think about both sides of this argument: Should people own exotic animals? Then take the position you can argue most effectively.

**Gather Information** Review "Wild Animals Aren't Pets" and "Let People Own Exotic Animals."

- Focus on the reasons and evidence used in each argument to support the claim.
- Make a list of reasons you have taken the position you chose. Note evidence, such as facts, quotes, and examples, that will support your reasons.
- Review other texts in the collection. Look for additional evidence that will help support your claim.
- Understand counterclaims that might keep your audience from agreeing with you. Consider this information as it relates to your position.

*my*Notebook

Use the annotation tools in your eBook to find evidence that supports your claim. Save each piece of evidence to your notebook.

**ACADEMIC VOCABULARY**

As you plan and present your speech, be sure to use the academic vocabulary words.

√ appropriate
√ authority
√ consequence
√ justify
√ legal

**Organize Your Ideas** Think about how you will organize your speech. A graphic organizer, such as a hierarchy chart, can help you to present your ideas logically. To use it, place your claim in the top box, your reasons in the next row of boxes, and your evidence in the last row.

**Consider Your Purpose and Audience** Think about your audience as you write. Ask yourself: Who will listen to this speech? Which ideas will be most convincing to them? Your tone and word choice may be different for a group of classmates or friends than it would be for a group of adults.

PRODUCE

*my***WriteSmart**

Write your rough draft in *my*WriteSmart. Focus on getting your ideas down, rather than perfecting your choice of language.

**Draft Your Speech** As you draft your speech, keep the following in mind:

- Introduce the topic to your audience. Grab your listeners' attention with an interesting quote or surprising fact.

- State your position clearly. Use your notes and graphic organizer to create a logical sequence to your reasons and evidence. Include pertinent descriptions, facts, and details that support your claim.

- Acknowledge counterclaims and include credible responses.

- Maintain a formal writing style, and use transition words and phrases such as *because, therefore,* and *for that reason* to clarify relationships between ideas.

- Bring your speech to a conclusion. Restate your main points and remind your audience why you believe your position is the right one.

**Practice Your Speech** Read your speech aloud. Try speaking in front of a mirror, or make a recording of your speech and listen to it. Then practice your speech with a partner.

Have your partner or a group of peers review your draft in *my*WriteSmart. Ask your reviewers to note any reasons that do not support the claim or lack sufficient evidence.

- Use your voice effectively. Speak loudly, varying your pitch and tone.
- Maintain eye contact. Look directly at individuals in your audience.
- Use gestures and facial expressions that allow your audience to see how you feel.

**Evaluate Your Speech** Use the chart on the following page to evaluate the substance and style of your speech. Then make any necessary revisions. Consider the following:

- Check that your position is clear and that your claim is logically supported by reasons and evidence.
- Examine your evidence to make sure it is relevant and based on accurate, credible sources.
- Make sure your speech can keep your audience's attention and that it concludes with a statement that sums up your argument.

**Deliver Your Speech** Finalize your speech and share it with your audience. Consider these options:

- Present your speech as a webcast.
- Have a partner make a video recording of you presenting your speech and play it for your audience.

| | Ideas and Evidence | Organization | Language |
|---|---|---|---|
| **ADVANCED** | • The introduction grabs the audience's attention; the claim clearly states the speaker's position on an issue.<br>• Logical reasons and relevant evidence support the speaker's claim.<br>• Opposing claims are anticipated and effectively addressed.<br>• The concluding section effectively summarizes the claim. | • The reasons and evidence are organized logically throughout the speech.<br>• Transitions effectively connect reasons and evidence to the speaker's claim. | • The speech reflects a formal style.<br>• Sentence beginnings, lengths, and structures vary and have a rhythmic flow.<br>• Grammar, usage, and mechanics are correct. |
| **COMPETENT** | • The introduction could do more to grab the audience's attention; the speaker's claim states a position on an issue.<br>• Most reasons and evidence support the speaker's claim.<br>• Opposing claims are anticipated, but the responses need to be developed more.<br>• The concluding section restates the claim. | • The organization of reasons and evidence is logical in most places.<br>• A few more transitions are needed to connect reasons and evidence to the speaker's claim. | • The style becomes informal in a few places.<br>• Sentence beginnings, lengths, and structures vary somewhat.<br>• Some grammatical, usage, and mechanics errors are present. |
| **LIMITED** | • The introduction does not grab listeners' attention; the speaker's claim identifies an issue, but the position is not clearly stated.<br>• The reasons and evidence are not always logical or relevant.<br>• Opposing claims are anticipated but not addressed logically.<br>• The concluding section includes an incomplete summary of the claim. | • The organization of reasons and evidence is confusing in some places, and it often does not follow a pattern.<br>• Few transitions are used, but the speech is not difficult to understand. | • The style becomes informal in many places.<br>• Sentence structures rarely vary, and some fragments or run-on sentences are present.<br>• Grammar, usage, and mechanics are incorrect in many places, but the speaker's ideas are still clear. |
| **EMERGING** | • The introduction is confusing and does not state a claim.<br>• Supporting reasons and evidence are missing.<br>• Opposing claims are neither anticipated nor addressed.<br>• The concluding section is missing. | • A logical organization is not used; reasons and evidence are presented randomly.<br>• Transitions are not used, making the speech difficult to understand. | • The style is inappropriate for the speech.<br>• Repetitive sentence structure, fragments, and run-on sentences make the speech hard to follow.<br>• Many grammatical and usage errors change the meaning of ideas. |

# Decisions That Matter

"We must never forget that it is through our actions,
words, and thoughts that we have a choice."

—Sogyal Rinpoche

# Decisions That Matter

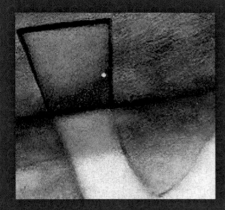

In this collection, you will explore how and why people make certain choices in their lives.

hmhfyi.com

COLLECTION

## PERFORMANCE TASK Preview

After reading this collection, you will have the opportunity to complete two performance tasks:

• In one, you will write a personal narrative about a key decision you had to make.

• In the second, you will write an opinion essay on how people's decisions shape their lives.

## ACADEMIC VOCABULARY

Study the words and their definitions in the chart below. You will use these words as you discuss and write about the texts in this collection.

| Word | Definition | Related Forms |
|---|---|---|
| **achieve** (ə-chēv´) *v.* | to perform or carry out with success; accomplish | achievement, achievable |
| **individual** (ĭn´də-vĭj´ oo-əl) *n.* | a single human being apart from a society or community | individuality, individualism, individually |
| **instance** (ĭn´stəns) *n.* | an example that is cited to prove or disprove a claim or illustrate a point | instances |
| **outcome** (out´kŭm´) *n.* | a natural result or consequence | outcomes |
| **principle** (prĭn´sə-pəl) *n.* | a rule or standard, especially of good behavior | principled, principles |

**Background** *Few American journeys are as varied or as respected as the journey of retired Army General Colin Powell. From his beginnings as a hard-working student, to his rescue of fellow soldiers from a burning helicopter in Vietnam, to his service in five different presidential administrations, Powell has lived his life leading by example. Many books have been written about Powell, among them one by author Warren Brown. Powell retired from public service in 2004 but continues to be vocal on political topics.*

## from It Worked for Me: In LIFE and LEADERSHIP

Memoir by Colin Powell

## from Colin Powell: MILITARY LEADER

Biography by Warren Brown

**SETTING A PURPOSE** As you read each text, pay attention to the examples that are used to portray Colin Powell's life. Write down any questions you have while reading.

# from It Worked for Me: In Life and Leadership
by Colin Powell

Back when I was a teenager in the Bronx, summer was a time for both fun and work. Starting at about age fourteen, I worked summers and Christmas holidays at a toy and baby furniture store in the Bronx. The owner, Jay Sickser, a Russian Jewish immigrant, hired me off the street as I walked past his store. "You want to make a few bucks unloading a truck in back?" he asked me. I said yes. The job took a couple of hours, and he paid me fifty cents an hour.

"You're a good worker," he told me when I'd finished. "Come back tomorrow."

That was the beginning of a close friendship with Jay and his family that continued through college and for the next fifty years, long after Jay had died. I worked part-time at the store a few hours a day during the summer and long hours during the Christmas season. I worked hard, a habit I got from my Jamaican immigrant parents. Every morning they left early for the garment district in Manhattan, and they came home late at night. All my relatives were hard workers. They came out of that common immigrant experience of arriving with nothing, expecting that the new life ahead of them would not be easy. Jamaicans had a joke: "That lazy brute, him only have two jobs."

After I'd worked at Sickser's for a couple of years, Jay grew concerned that I was getting too close to the store and the family. One day he took me aside. "Collie," he told me with a serious look, "I want you should get an education and do well. You're too good to just be a schlepper.[1] The store will go to the family. You don't have a future here." I never thought I did, but I always treasured him for caring enough about me to say so.

When I was eighteen I became eligible to get a union card, which meant I could get a full-time summer job with better pay (I continued to work at Sickser's during the Christmas season). I joined the International Brotherhood of Teamsters' Local 812, the Soft Drink Workers Union. Every morning I went downtown to the union hall to stand in line to get a day's work as a helper on a soft-drink truck. It was hard work, and I became an expert at tossing wooden twenty-four-bottle Coca-Cola cases by grabbing a corner bottle without breaking it.

After a few weeks, the foreman noticed my work and asked if I'd like to try driving a Coke truck. Since I was a teamster, I had a chauffeur's license and was authorized to drive a truck. The problem was that I had never driven a truck in my life. But, hey, why not? It paid better.

The next morning, I got behind the wheel of an ancient, stick shift, circa 1940 truck with a supervisor riding shotgun.[2]

---

[1] **schlepper** (shlĕp´ər): someone who carries things that are clumsy or difficult to move.

[2] **riding shotgun:** sitting in the front passenger seat of a vehicle, next to the driver; term comes from the early 1900s and refers to armed guards, often carrying shotguns, who would protect the cargo and the driver of a vehicle.

We carried three hundred cases, half on open racks on one side of the truck and half on the other. I asked the supervisor where we were going. "Wall Street," he said, and my heart skipped a beat as I imagined navigating the narrow streets and alleys of the oldest, most **claustrophobic**, and most mazelike part of New York City. I took off with all the energy and blind optimism of youth and managed to get through the day and somehow safely delivered the three hundred cases . . . in spite of my often overenthusiastic driving. My supervisor was white-knuckled with worry that I would deliver 150 cases onto the street as the old truck leaned **precariously** at corners I was taking much too fast. Though I delivered every case, my driving skills did not impress the supervisor, and my truck-driving career was over (they still kept me on as a helper). Nevertheless, I proudly took home a $20 salary that day to show my father.

The next summer, I wanted something better than standing in a crowd every morning hoping for a day's work. My opportunity came when the hiring boss announced one morning that the Pepsi plant in Long Island City was looking for porters to clean the floors, full-time for the summer. I raised my hand. I was the only one who did.

The porters at the Pepsi plant were all black. The workers on the bottling machines were all white. I didn't care. I just wanted work for the summer, and I worked hard, mopping up syrup and soda that had spilled from overturned pallets.

At summer's end, the boss told me he was pleased with my work and asked if I wanted to come back. "Yes," I answered, "but not as a porter." He agreed, and next summer I worked on the bottling machine and as a pallet stacker, a more **prestigious** and higher-paying job. It wasn't exactly the Selma March, but I integrated a bottling machine crew.

Very often my best didn't turn out that well. I was neither an athlete nor a standout student. I played baseball, football, stickball, and all the other Bronx sports, and I did my best, but I wasn't good at any. In school I was hardworking and dedicated, but never produced superior grades or matched the academic successes of my many high-achieving cousins. Yet my parents didn't pester me or put too much pressure on me. Their attitude was "Do your best—we'll accept your best, but nothing less."

**claustrophobic**
(klô´strə-fō´bĭk) *adj.*
A *claustrophobic* place feels uncomfortably closed or crowded.

**precarious**
(prĭ-kâr´ē-əs) *adj.*
If something is done in a *precarious* manner, it is done in a dangerously unstable or insecure way.

**prestigious**
(prĕ-stē´jəs) *adj.*
If something is *prestigious*, it has a greater level of people's respect or honor than others like it.

These experiences established a pattern for all the years
and careers that came afterward. Always do your best, no
matter how difficult the job, or how much you dislike it, your
90   bosses, the work environment, or your fellow workers. As the
old expression goes, if you take the king's coin, you give the
king his due.

I remember an old story told by the comedian Brother
Dave Gardner about two ditch diggers. One guy just loves
digging. He digs all day long and says nothing much. The
other guy digs a little, leans on his shovel a lot, and mouths off
constantly, "One of these days, I'm gonna own this company."

Time passes and guy number one gets a front-end trench
machine and just digs away, hundreds of feet a day, always
100  loving it. The other guy does the minimum, but never stops
mouthing off,[3] "One of these days, I'm gonna own this
company." No, guy number one doesn't end up owning the
company, but he does become a foreman working out of an
air-conditioned van. He often waves to his old friend leaning
on his shovel still insisting, "One of these days, I'm gonna own
this company." Ain't gonna happen.

In my military career I often got jobs I wasn't crazy about,
or I was put in situations that stretched me beyond my rank
and experience. Whether the going was rough or smooth, I
110  always tried to do my best and to be loyal to my superior and
the mission given to me.

---

[3] **mouthing off:** a slang term meaning to express opinions or complaints in a
loud, rude manner.

On my second tour in Vietnam, I was assigned as an infantry battalion executive officer, second in command, in the 23rd Infantry Division (Americal). I was very pleased with the assignment. As it happened, I had just graduated with honors from the Command and General Staff College at Fort Leavenworth, Kansas. Shortly after I arrived in Vietnam, a photo of the top five graduates appeared in *Army Times*. The division commanding general saw it, and I was pulled up to the division staff to serve as the operations officer, responsible for coordinating the combat operations of a twenty-thousand-man division. I was only a major and it was a lieutenant colonel's position. I would have preferred to stay with my battalion, but wasn't given that choice. It turned out to be very demanding and a stretch for me, but it marked a turning point in my career. Someone was watching.

Years later, as a brigadier general in an infantry division, I thought I was doing my best to train soldiers and serve my commander. He disagreed and rated me below standards. The report is still in my file. It could have ended my career, but more senior leaders saw other qualities and capabilities[4] in me and moved me up into more challenging positions, where I did well.

Doing your best for your boss doesn't mean you will always like or approve of what he wants you to do; there will be times when you will have very different **priorities** from his. In the military, your superiors may have very different ideas than you do about what should be your most important mission. In some of my units my superiors put an intense focus on reenlistment rates, AWOL rate, and saving bonds participation. Most of us down below would have preferred to keep our primary focus on training. Sure, those management priorities were important in principle, but they often seemed in practice to be distractions from our real work. I never tried to fight my superiors' priorities. Instead I worked hard to accomplish the tasks they set as quickly and decisively as I could. The sooner I could satisfy my superiors, the sooner they would stop bugging me about them, and the quicker I could move on to my own priorities. Always give the king his due first.

**priority**
(prī-ôr′ĭ-tē) *n.*
A *priority* is the thing that is most important to a person in a particular situation or relationship.

---

[4] **capabilities** (kā′pə-bĭl′ĭ-tēz): the things one is able to do or the talents one is able to develop.

By the end of my career in government, I had been appointed to the nation's most senior national security jobs, National Security Advisor, Chairman of the Joint Chiefs of Staff, and Secretary of State. I went about each job with the same attitude I'd had at Sickser's. . . .

In the years that have followed my government service, I have traveled around the country and shared my life's experience with many people in many different forums. At these events, I always emphasize, especially to youngsters, that 160 99 percent of work can be seen as noble.[5] There are few truly degrading[6] jobs. Every job is a learning experience, and we can develop and grow in every one.

If you take the pay, earn it. Always do your very best. Even when no one else is looking, you always are. Don't disappoint yourself.

---

[5] **noble** (nō´bəl): having or showing qualities of honor.
[6] **degrading** (dĭ-grā´dĭng): lowering or reducing in rank, dignity, respect, quality, or value.

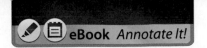 

## Analyze Text: Memoir

The text *It Worked for Me* is a **memoir,** a form of autobiographical writing in which a writer shares his or her personal experiences and observations of significant events. Memoirs are often written by people who have taken part in or observed important historical events. Elements of a memoir include the following:

- **first-person point of view,** meaning that it is told from the writer's own perspective. First-person pronouns, such as *I, me, my, our,* and *we,* are used throughout the text.
- descriptions of people and events that have influenced the writer
- personal thoughts and feelings

A memoir reflects how the writer remembers his or her own life and often only focuses on a specific aspect or period in the writer's life. A memoir is often written in an informal style. In *It Worked for Me,* Colin Powell recalls how he got a job driving a truck when he had never driven one before. He says, "But, hey, why not? It paid better."

As you analyze *It Worked for Me* and other memoirs, ask questions such as these:

- What does the author want to share? Why?
- Does the author communicate his or her ideas in an effective way?

## Analyzing the Text

Cite Text Evidence   Support your responses with evidence from the text.

1. **Summarize** Review lines 62–77. What specific incident in his life is Powell writing about? Why might this incident be important for Powell to include in his memoir?

2. **Interpret** Review lines 87–92. What do you think is the meaning of the expression "If you take the king's coin, you give the king his due"? Why do you think Powell shares this message?

3. **Evaluate** One important element of a memoir is the inclusion of people and events that influenced the writer. Review the selection. Which person or event do you think was most influential in his life? Why do you think so?

# *from* Colin Powell: Military Leader

by Warren Brown

Colin Luther Powell was born on April 5, 1937, in New York City's Harlem district. Formerly an area of open farmland and country estates, Harlem became a residential neighborhood in the late 19th century, when a mixture of wealthy and working-class whites moved there to escape Manhattan's congested[1] downtown area. To keep pace with the growing demand for housing, real estate developers constructed magnificent town houses and apartment buildings in this uptown section. By 1900, Harlem had
10  emerged as one of the most desirable places to live in the city.

These developers overestimated the demand for housing, however, and by the early 1900s many apartments in Harlem were empty because not enough people could afford to live in such a high-rent district. Desperate to fill the vacant apartments, Harlem landlords drastically lowered their rents. The sudden availability of quality housing attracted large numbers of blacks seeking to escape the racial violence and poor living conditions in
20  the city's congested West Side ghetto, and they moved to Harlem in droves. By the beginning of World War I, 50,000 blacks resided in Harlem and formed a vibrant community with a middle-class standard of living.

Colin's parents, Luther Theopolis Powell and the former Maud Ariel McKoy, arrived in Harlem during the early 1920s, when the community was at its most prosperous.[2] Both parents were from the island of Jamaica and had left their Caribbean homeland in the hope of finding their fortune in the United States. Like so many
30  other immigrants drawn by the booming American economy during the 1920s, they settled in New York City, the thriving metropolis at the mouth of the Hudson River; with its bustling port and enormous wealth, the

---

[1] **congested** (kən-jĕst´əd):  overcrowded.
[2] **prosperous** (prŏs´pər-əs):  successful; well-to-do.

city seemed to offer limitless opportunity to anyone who sought a better life.

Neither Luther Powell nor Maud McKoy had finished high school, and so they had little choice but to join the large pool of working-class immigrants that served as the backbone of the city's labor force. Luther, a husky young man with a pleasant, round face, found work as a shipping clerk in a garment factory. At a picnic one day in the Bronx, New York City's only mainland borough, he met Maud McKoy. Shortly afterward, the pair married and made their home in Harlem.

Meanwhile, Harlem had begun to take on a special **allure**. As it became one of the few areas in the country where blacks could enjoy an unusually high quality of life, its writers, musicians, and actors celebrated their racial heritage and promoted their own culture. This awakening of black artistic and intellectual achievement came to be known as the Harlem Renaissance.

Yet underneath the surface of this growing, closely knit community lay the symptoms of decline. By 1930, 200,000 of New York City's 327,000 blacks lived in Harlem, and they were all crowded together in an area that had housed only a quarter of that number 15 years earlier. When the Great Depression began to ravage[3] the nation in the 1930s, Harlem was especially hard hit. Long lines of unemployed people in search of food and clothing stretched in front of the local churches and charity organizations. Families evicted from their apartments because they could not pay the rent crowded into the homes of relatives or lived on the street. What had previously been one of New York City's most beautiful areas began to deteriorate[4] rapidly.

It was into this black community, in desperate decline but still treasuring proud memories, that Colin Powell was born. He lived in Harlem until he was three years old; then his parents decided it was time to relocate. In 1940, Luther and Maud Powell packed their belongings; and with Colin and his sister, Marylin, who was five and a half years older than him, in tow, they followed the city's ever expanding elevated railway line northeast, across the Harlem River to the Bronx.

The Powells settled in Hunts Point, a working-class neighborhood in the southeastern section of the borough.

**allure**
(ə-lŏŏr′) *n.* An *allure* is a power of attraction, an ability to interest or entice others.

---

[3] **ravage** (răv′ĭj): destroy in a severe, drastic way.
[4] **deteriorate** (dĭ-tîr′ē-ə-rāt′): to fall apart; to break down in quality or value.

The family made its home in a walk-up apartment building on Kelly Street. In time, the area would reach the extreme levels of urban decay and devastation that have come to characterize Harlem. But in the 1940s, residents called the borough "the beautiful Bronx," and Harlemites who moved into Hunts Point's blue-collar neighborhood felt that they had moved up in the world.

Although the local population was <u>mainly Jewish</u>, Hunts Point contained a mixture of New York City's various immigrant groups. Jews mixed freely with blacks, Irish, Italians, Poles, and Puerto Ricans, and their children mingled unselfconsciously in play. As a result, young Colin never paid much attention to the color of his skin. "I grew up in a neighborhood where everybody was a minority," he recalled. "I never thought there was something wrong with me because I was black."

The fact that his parents came from Jamaica also contributed to Colin's lack of self-consciousness about his race. Even though blacks in Jamaica were British subjects, they rarely experienced the sort of racial oppression that many black Americans, particularly those in the southern states, endured. When Powell's parents arrived in the United States, they did not view themselves as second-class citizens, and they never allowed their children to think that way either.

Instead, Luther and Maud Powell instilled[5] in their son and daughter a strong faith in the Anglican church and a healthy respect for formal education. They wanted Colin and Marylin to do well in life and insisted that getting ahead in America depended on learning as much as possible. As a result, the Powell children often received lectures from their parents to "strive for a good education. Make something of your life."

Luther and Maud Powell also told their children that only hard work and **perseverance** could lead to success. Colin recalled later, "There was something of a tradition of hard work being the way to succeed, and there was simply an expectation that existed in the family—you were supposed to do better. And it was a bloody disappointment to the family if you didn't."

**perseverance**
(pûr´sə-vîr´əns) *n.* To have *perseverance* is to stay focused on a plan, a belief, or a purpose.

---

[5] **instilled** (ĭn-stĭld´): introduced slowly and with consistent, constant effort.

Colin's parents certainly led by example. Each morning, Luther Powell left home at an early hour to catch the elevated train to his job in New York City's Garment District, and he remained there all day, never returning home from work until at least 7:00 or 8:00 in the evening. Maud Powell found a job as a seamstress, and she too spent many long hours doing her work. "It wasn't a matter of spending a great deal of time with my parents discussing things," Colin remembered. "We didn't sit down at night . . . and review the work of the day. It was just the way they lived their lives."

 **I never thought there was something wrong with me because I was black.**

Even though both his parents worked, young Colin never went unsupervised during the day. Maud's mother, who was known to everyone as Miss Alice, and other relatives stayed with him and his sister to enforce discipline. In addition, nearby families made a habit of watching one another's children. Marylin recalled years later that "when you walked down the street, you had all these eyes watching you."

In spite of this upbringing, Colin showed few signs during his childhood of responding to his parents' desire that he apply himself in school. Early on in elementary school, when he was about eight years old, he attempted to play hooky. The young truant estimated the time wrong, however, and arrived home too early. A family friend caught him, and a family discussion ensued. In the days that followed, an adult was always present to take Colin by the hand and lead him to the classroom door.

Colin, however, did not change his ways. As a fifth grader at Public School 39, he was such a lackluster[6] student that he landed in the slow class. At both Intermediate School 52 and Morris High School, he continued to apply himself indifferently.[7] In his own words, he "horsed around a lot" and managed to keep his grades only barely above passing. His unspectacular marks kept him from realizing an ambition to

---

[6] **lackluster** (lăk´lŭs´tər): lacking brightness and energy; dull.

[7] **indifferently** (ĭn-dĭf´ər-ənt-lē): without interest or feeling, either for or against.

attend the Bronx High School of Science, one of the nation's finest schools.

By this time, Colin had developed into a tall, strong teenager with a natural flair for leadership. At Morris High
150 School, he was elected class representative, served as treasurer of the Service League, whose members helped out around the school, and lettered in track. Neighborhood youths learned not to push him around. He moved freely among Hunts Point's various racial groups and even managed to learn some Yiddish while working after school at Sickser's, a store that sold baby furniture. In his free time, Colin and his best friend, Gene Norman, raced bicycles along the sweeping curve of Kelly Street or played games of stickball.

When Colin graduated from Morris High School in early
160 1954, he said that he wanted to become an engineer; but in reality, he had very little idea of what he wanted to do with his life. His parents, insisting that he lift himself out of Hunts Point's "$40-a-week, lower blue-collar environment," made it clear that they expected him to go to college. Colin had no particular urge to get a higher education, but he had a deeply ingrained sense of obedience to his mother and father. If they expected him to attend college, he would go.

Colin applied to New York University and to the City College of New York. Despite his low grades, both institutions
170 accepted him. Tuition costs helped Colin narrow down his choice. New York University charged students $750 per year to attend. The City College of New York, situated on 138th Street in upper Manhattan, enrolled any graduate from a New York City high school for only a token $10 fee. Accordingly, on a cold winter day in February 1954, Colin took a bus to Manhattan and began his life as a City College student.

Colin enrolled in City College's engineering program, and he did moderately well at first, ending his initial semester with a B average. But during the summer of 1954,
180 he took a mechanical drawing course, and it proved to be the most miserable summer of his life. When, on a boiling hot afternoon, his instructor asked him to imagine a cone intersecting a plane in space, Colin decided that he had had enough of engineering and dropped out of the program.

Colin decided to change his major to geology, not because of any strong interest in the subject but because he thought it would be easy. He did not push himself very hard and saw his average creep down to a C.

Nevertheless, Colin was about to display his first real enthusiasm for a school-related activity. During his first spring at City College, he had noticed uniformed members of the Army Reserve Officers' Training Corps walking around the campus. The ROTC offered students military training that could lead to a commission[8] as an officer in the U.S. Army. Colin decided that he liked the serious look of the members of the Pershing Rifles, the ROTC drill team, who wore small whipped cords on their uniform shoulders.

Colin already possessed a mild interest in the military. In high school, he had closely followed the unfolding of the Korean War. His interest aroused, Colin signed up for the ROTC for the fall semester of 1954 and pledged himself to the Pershing Rifles.

At that point, Colin had no intention of making the army a career. He wanted only to find a way to escape from New York City for a while and, in his own words, "have some excitement." Besides, joining the ROTC would help him find work. He expected to serve no more than two years in the army after graduating from college "and then come home and get a real job." But as it turned out, he had stumbled onto his life's calling.

**COLLABORATIVE DISCUSSION** With a partner, discuss which parts of Colin Powell's life you found most interesting. Point out examples in both texts that support your ideas, and tell what they indicate about Powell as an individual.

---

[8] **commission** (kə-mĭsh´ən): the act of granting an individual certain powers or authority to carry out a particular duty; also, an official document from a government granting a particular rank in the armed forces.

# Analyze Text: Biography

The text you have just read is from a biography of Colin Powell. A **biography** is a true account of a person's life, written by another person. Elements of a biography include the following:

- **third-person point of view,** meaning that it is told by an outside narrator who is not connected to or involved in the events
- descriptions of events, people, and experiences that have shaped the subject's life
- **quotations,** or exact words, from the subject as well as from people who know or knew the subject

A writer of a biography researches many sources in order to present accurate information on an individual. The events in a biography are often presented in **chronological order,** or the order in which they occurred. Dates and words and phrases such as *by 1900, during the early 1920s, meanwhile, when Colin graduated, later,* and *during* may be used to point out the **sequence,** or order of events. For example, *Colin Powell: Military Leader* begins with "Colin Powell was born on April 5, 1937 . . . "

As you analyze the text from *Colin Powell: Military Leader* or other biographies, ask yourself questions such as the following:

- What is the author's purpose for writing the biography?
- Does the author's research include quotations from the subject or from people who knew the subject? What do the quotations tell me?
- Does the biography seem accurate? How can I tell?

# Analyzing the Text

COMMON CORE   RI 1, RI 3, RI 5, RI 6

> *Cite Text Evidence*   Support your responses with evidence from the text.

1. **Infer**  Review lines 24–35. How can you tell that the text is from a biography?

2. **Interpret**  Review lines 72–89. What information does the author provide about Hunts Point? What do you think is the author's reason for including this information?

3. **Analyze**  Review the text to determine over what period of time the events in *Colin Powell: Military Leader* take place. Then make a timeline that shows when the most important events occur.

4. **Synthesize**  What purposes do you think the author had for writing *Colin Powell: Military Leader*?

# Analyze Texts: Sources

Research sources can be grouped based on how closely those who created them are or were to the events being described. **Primary sources** are materials created by people who witnessed or took part in a particular event. **Secondary sources** are records of events that were created some time after the events occurred. Unlike primary sources, secondary sources are made by people who were not directly involved in an event or present when it occurred. This chart shows examples of primary and secondary sources:

| Primary Sources | Secondary Sources |
| --- | --- |
| letters | encyclopedias |
| diaries | textbooks |
| autobiographies | biographies |
| eyewitness accounts | news articles |

A person writing his or her memoir likely uses a number of primary sources while writing. The memoir itself is also a primary source. Someone writing a biography might use some primary sources, but the majority of the research will come from secondary sources. A biography is considered a secondary source.

# Compare and Contrast: Memoir and Biography

When you compare and contrast a memoir and a biography, you analyze the way each writer presents the subject and the events and influences in the subject's life.

Here are some questions you can ask to compare and contrast a memoir and a biography:

- What is each author's purpose for writing? Do the authors share the same purpose, or are their purposes different?
- How are the authors' presentations of events alike and different?
- How is the impression you get of the person alike and different in each text? Does the author of the memoir sound very different from the person written about in the biography? Does one text seem more accurate or reliable?

Use these questions to help you analyze *It Worked for Me* and *Colin Powell: Military Leader* and to understand a more complete picture of the subject.

# Analyzing the Texts

COMMON CORE RI 3, RI 6, RI 7, RI 9, W 9b, SL 4, SL 6

**Cite Text Evidence**    Support your responses with evidence from the texts.

1. **Infer**  What is Powell's purpose for writing his memoir? Explain how it is similar to or different from Warren Brown's purpose for writing the biography.

2. **Compare**  Review lines 1–15 in *It Worked for Me* and lines 148–158 in *Colin Powell: Military Leader*. How does the portrayal of Powell's after-school job differ in each text? Explain why each author treated this event differently.

3. **Compare**  Compare lines 78–86 of Powell's memoir with lines 139–147 in the biography. How are the two descriptions of Powell alike and different? Tell whether you think one is more accurate than the other and if so, why.

4. **Draw Conclusions**  Review *Colin Powell: Military Leader*. What primary and secondary sources do you think the author might have used?

5. **Evaluate**  Review each text. Which one do you think paints a more accurate portrayal of Colin Powell? Why?

# PERFORMANCE TASK

**Speaking Activity: Speech**  Colin Powell's advice to readers is "Always do your very best." Present a speech that explains how this principle helped shape Powell's life and career.

- As you write your speech, include information from the texts that indicates how experiences, people, and events influenced Powell.
- Be sure to present your ideas in a logical order. Include details that support each idea.

- Practice delivering your speech in a formal way, using appropriate eye contact, correct volume, and clear pronunciation.
- Check that you have not used any vague pronouns that might confuse listeners.
- When you present your speech, remember Powell's principle and do your very best!

# Critical Vocabulary

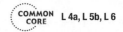 

claustrophobic          precarious          prestigious
priority                allure              perseverance

**Practice and Apply**  Answer each question. Explain your response.

1. If you feel a room is **claustrophobic,** would you enjoy being in it? Why?

2. If a stack of dishes is balanced in a **precarious** way, will you add more to the pile or rearrange them in shorter stacks? Why?

3. Which is more **prestigious** to a marathon runner, competing in a race with friends or being invited to run in an event in another country? Why?

4. If your **priority** is to go to college and start your own company, would you work to excel in school or do just enough work to get by? Why?

5. Which job has more **allure** to a student who wants to be a journalist— delivering newspapers or writing for the school newspaper? Why?

6. If a worker wants to show her boss that she has **perseverance,** would she volunteer to complete a difficult task or take a vacation? Why?

## Vocabulary Strategy: Analogies

An **analogy** presents a relationship between pairs of words. Sometimes writers use analogies to explain unfamiliar ideas. A typical analogy begins with a pair of items that are related in some way. One common word relationship is item-to-category. Here is an example, displayed first as a sentence and then using special symbols:

> *Claustrophic is to fear as newspaper is to periodicals.*
>
> **claustrophobic : fear :: newspaper : periodicals**

An **item-to-category analogy** relates an individual item (claustrophobic; newspaper) to its category (fear; periodicals). In the second version of each analogy, the single colon stands for "is to" and the double colon stands for "as." Examining each full analogy helps you understand how the word pairs are related.

**Practice and Apply**  Complete each analogy by choosing the best answer.

1. horse : animal :: _____ : plant
   **a.** tomato    **b.** leaf

2. kitchen : room :: _____ : record
   **a.** property    **b.** diary

3. fingerprint : _____ :: oil : painting
   **a.** smudge    **b.** identification

4. jewels : sparkling :: _____ : prestigious
   **a.** awards    **b.** socks

# Language Conventions: Correct Vague Pronouns

**Pronouns** are words used in place of a noun or another pronoun, such as *he, she,* or *it.* The word that the pronoun refers to is its **antecedent.** Sometimes errors in writing occur when pronouns do not clearly refer to an antecedent. Here's an example:

> **In the new movie about aliens, they have some great computer-generated imagery.**

The pronoun *they* is vague because the antecedent is unclear; does it refer to the aliens or to the people who made the movie? To get rid of the vague pronoun, the sentence could be rewritten like this:

> **The new movie about aliens has some great computer-generated imagery.**

Sometimes a vague pronoun tries to refer to a general idea rather than a specific event. For example, *It Worked for Me* begins with a recollection of an event that led to Colin Powell's first job (lines 1–10). Line 11 begins "That was the beginning of a close friendship . . ." The pronoun *That* is vague because it does not refer directly to any particular event.

Sometimes a pronoun is vague when it could refer to more than one antecedent, like this: *When Julian and his father played chess, he often won.* The vague pronoun *he* makes it hard to tell who won. The word *he* needs to be replaced with the name of the person who won: *When Julian and his father played chess, Julian often won.*

Always review your writing to check for and correct vague pronouns.

**Practice and Apply** Rewrite the sentences to correct the vague pronoun.

1. James was tired and wanted to stay at home. That was the reason he missed the concert.

2. In the military, you have more soldiers than leaders.

3. Kelly frowned at Ms. Patterson's remarks. They made her sound like she was complaining.

4. Gloria was late for school, and she forgot her homework. This got her in trouble with Mr. Goodson.

5. Martina gathered her courage, took a deep breath, and called Jana. She thought her voice sounded strange.

6. According to the government report, they say that more families are applying for help.

**Background** *In 1954, the United States Supreme Court ruled that segregation in public schools (the practice of having "separate but equal" schools for whites and blacks) was unconstitutional. This decision meant that schools had to begin integrating students at all levels. Schoolchildren, particularly in the southern United States, prepared to face the anger, hatred, and often violence of those who opposed this policy. In 1958, in the midst of this difficult time,* **R. V. Cassill** *(1919–2002) wrote this story.*

# The First Day of School

Short Story by R. V. Cassill

**SETTING A PURPOSE** As you read, pay close attention to the interactions of the Hawkins family and the clues that indicate what is significant about this first day of school.

Thirteen bubbles floated in the milk. Their pearl transparent hemispheres[1] gleamed like souvenirs of the summer days just past, rich with blue reflections of the sky and of shadowy greens. John Hawkins jabbed the bubble closest to him with his spoon, and it disappeared without a ripple. On the white surface there was no mark of where it had been.

"Stop tooling[2] that oatmeal and eat it," his mother said. She glanced meaningfully at the clock on the varnished cupboard. She nodded a heavy, emphatic affirmation[3] that now the clock was boss. Summer was over, when the gracious

---

[1] **hemispheres** (hĕm´ĭ-sfîrz´): half of a sphere, which is a three-dimensional circular, or ball, shape.

[2] **tooling** (tōō´lĭng): working with something, as with a tool such as a spoon.

[3] **affirmation** (ăf´ər-mā´shən): positive, strong support of the truth of something.

oncoming of morning light and the stir of early breezes promised that time was a luxury.

"Audrey's not even down yet," he said.

"Audrey'll be down."

"You think she's taking longer to dress because she wants to look nice today?"

"She likes to look *neat*."

"What I was thinking," he said slowly, "was that maybe she didn't feel like going today. Didn't feel *exactly* like it."

"Of course she'll go."

"I meant she might not want to go until tomorrow, maybe. Until we see what happens."

"Nothing's going to happen," his mother said.

"I know there isn't. But what if it did?" Again John swirled the tip of his spoon in the milk. It was like writing on a surface that would keep no mark.

"Eat and be quiet. Audrey's coming, so let's stop this here kind of talk."

He heard the tap of heels on the stairs, and his sister came down into the kitchen. She looked fresh and cool in her white dress. Her lids looked heavy. She must have slept all right—and for this John felt both envy and a faint **resentment**. He had not really slept since midnight. The heavy traffic in town, the long wail of horns as somebody raced in on the U.S. highway holding the horn button down, and the restless murmur, like the sound of a celebration down in the courthouse square, had kept him awake after that. Each time a car had passed their house his breath had gone tight and sluggish. It was better to stay awake and ready, he had told himself, than to be caught asleep.

"Daddy gone?" Audrey asked softly as she took her place across the table from her brother.

"He's been gone an hour," their mother answered. "*You* know what time he has to be at the mine."

"She means, did he go to work today?" John said. His voice had risen impatiently. He met his mother's stout[4] gaze in a staring contest, trying to make her admit by at least some flicker of expression that today was different from any other day. "I thought he might be down at Reverend Specker's," John

**resentment**
(rĭ-zĕnt´mənt) *n.* If you feel *resentment*, you feel anger or irritation.

---

4 **stout** (stout): bold, brave, determined.

said. "Cal's father and Vonnie's and some of the others are going to be there to wait and see."

Maybe his mother smiled then. If so, the smile was so faint that he could not be sure. "You know your father isn't much of a hand for waiting," she said. "Eat. It's a quarter past eight."

As he spooned the warm oatmeal into his mouth he heard the rain crow calling again from the trees beyond the railroad embankment. He had heard it since the first light came before dawn, and he had thought, Maybe the bird knows it's going to rain, after all. He hoped it would. *They won't come out in the rain,* he had thought. Not so many of them, at least. He could wear a raincoat. A raincoat might help him feel more protected on the walk to school. It would be a sort of disguise, at least.

But since dawn the sun had lain across the green Kentucky trees and the roofs of town like a clean, hard fire. The sky was as clear as fresh-washed window glass. The rain crow was wrong about the weather. And still, John thought, its **lamenting**, repeated call must mean something.

His mother and Audrey were talking about the groceries she was to bring when she came home from school at lunch time. A five-pound bag of sugar, a fresh pineapple, a pound of butter . . .

"Listen!" John said. Downtown the sound of a siren had begun. A volley of automobile horns broke around it as if they meant to drown it out. "*Listen* to them."

"It's only the National Guard, I expect," his mother said calmly. "They came in early this morning before light. And it may be some foolish kids honking at them, the way they would. Audrey, if Henry doesn't have a good-looking roast, why then let it go, and I'll walk out to Weaver's this afternoon and get one there. I wanted to have something a little bit special for our dinner tonight."

So . . . John thought . . . she wasn't asleep last night either. Someone had come **stealthily** to the house to bring his parents word about the National Guard. That meant they knew about the others who had come into town, too. Maybe all through the night there had been a swift passage of messengers through the neighborhood and a whispering of information that his mother meant to keep from him. Your folks told you, he reflected bitterly, that nothing is better than knowing. Knowing whatever there is in this world to be known. That

**lament**
(lə-měnt´) *v.* If you *lament*, you are wailing or crying as a way of expressing grief.

**stealthily**
(stĕl´thə-lē) *adv.* To do something *stealthily* means doing it quietly and secretly so no one notices.

was why you had to be one of the half dozen kids out of some nine hundred colored of school age who were going today to start classes at Joseph P. Gilmore High instead of Webster. Knowing and learning the truth were worth so much they said—and then left it to the hooting rain crow to tell you that things were worse than everybody had hoped.

Something had gone wrong, bad enough wrong so the
100    National Guard had to be called out.

"It's eight twenty-five," his mother said. "Did you get that snap sewed on right, Audrey?" As her experienced fingers examined the shoulder of Audrey's dress they **lingered** a moment in an involuntary, sheltering caress. "It's all arranged," she told her children, "how you'll walk down to the Baptist Church and meet the others there. You know there'll be Reverend Chader, Reverend Smith, and Mr. Hall to go with you. It may be that the white ministers will go with you, or they may be waiting at school. We don't know. But now you
110    be sure, don't you go farther than the Baptist Church alone." Carefully she lifted her hand clear of Audrey's shoulder. John thought, Why doesn't she hug her if that's what she wants to do?

**linger**
(lĭng´gər)  v. To *linger* means to leave slowly and reluctantly, not wanting to go.

> ❝ Something had gone wrong, bad enough wrong so the National Guard had to be called out. ❞

He pushed away from the table and went out on the front porch. The dazzling sunlight lay shadowless on the street that swept down toward the Baptist Church at the edge of the colored section. The street seemed awfully long this morning, the way it had looked when he was little. A chicken was clucking contentedly behind their neighbor's house, feeling
120    the warmth, settling itself into the sun-warmed dust. Lucky chicken.

He blinked at the sun's glare on the concrete steps leading down from the porch. He remembered something else from the time he was little. Once he had kicked Audrey's doll buggy down these same steps. He had done it out of meanness—for some silly reason he had been mad at her. But as soon as the buggy had started to bump down, he had understood how terrible it was not to be able to run after it and stop it. It had

gathered speed at each step and when it hit the sidewalk it had
spilled over. Audrey's doll had smashed into sharp little pieces
on the sidewalk below. His mother had come out of the house
to find him crying harder than Audrey. "Now you know that
when something gets out of your hands it is in the Devil's
hands," his mother had explained to him. Did she expect him
to forget—now—that that was always the way things went to
smash when they got out of hand? Again he heard the siren
and the hooting, mocking horns from the center of town.
Didn't his mother think *they* could get out of hand?

He closed his eyes and seemed to see something like a doll
buggy bump down long steps like those at Joseph P. Gilmore
High, and it seemed to him that it was not a doll that was
riding down to be smashed.

He made up his mind then. He would go today, because
he had said he would. Therefore he had to. But he wouldn't
go unless Audrey stayed home. That was going to be his
condition. His bargaining looked perfect. He would trade
them one for one.

His mother and Audrey came together onto the porch. His
mother said, "My stars, I forgot to give you the money for the
groceries." She let the screen door bang as she went swiftly
back into the house.

As soon as they were alone, he took Audrey's bare arm
in his hand and pinched hard. "You gotta stay home," he
whispered. "Don't you know there's thousands of people down
there? Didn't you hear them coming in all night long? You
slept, didn't you? All right. You can hear them now. Tell her
you're sick. She won't expect you to go if you're sick. I'll knock
you down, I'll smash you if you don't tell her that." He bared
his teeth and twisted his nails into the skin of her arm. "Hear
them horns," he hissed.

He forced her halfway to her knees with the strength of
his fear and rage. They swayed there, locked for a minute. Her
knee dropped to the porch floor. She lowered her eyes. He
thought he had won.

But she was saying something and in spite of himself he
listened to her almost whispered refusal. "Don't you know
anything? Don't you know it's harder for them than us? Don't
you know Daddy didn't go to the mine this morning? They
laid him off on account of us. They told him not to come if
we went to school."

Uncertainly he relaxed his grip. "How do you know all that?"

"I listen," she said. Her eyes lit with a sudden spark that seemed to come from their absolute brown depths. "But I don't let on all I know the way you do. I'm not a . . ." Her last word sunk so low that he could not exactly hear it. But if his ear missed it, his understanding caught it. He knew she had said "coward."

He let her get up then. She was standing beside him, 180 **serene** and prim when their mother came out on the porch again.

"Here, child," their mother said to Audrey, counting the dollar bills into her hand. "There's six, and I guess it will be all right if you have some left if you and Brother get yourselves a cone to lick on the way home."

John was not looking at his sister then. He was already turning to face the shadowless street, but he heard the unmistakable **poised** amusement of her voice when she said, "Ma, don't you know we're a little too old for that?"

190 "Yes, you are," their mother said. "Seems I had forgotten that."

They were too old to take each other's hand, either, as they went down the steps of their home and into the street. As they turned to the right, facing the sun, they heard the chattering of a tank's tread on the pavement by the school. A voice too distant to be understood bawled a military command. There were horns again and a crescendo[5] of boos.

Behind them they heard their mother call something. It was lost in the general racket.

200 "What?" John called back to her. "What?"

She had followed them out as far as the sidewalk, but not past the gate. As they hesitated to listen, she put her hands to either side of her mouth and called to them the words she had so often used when she let them go away from home.

"Behave yourselves," she said.

**serene**
(sə-rēn´) *adj.* If you are *serene*, you are calm and unflustered.

**poised**
(poizd) *adj.* To be *poised* means to be calm and assured, showing balanced feeling and action.

**COLLABORATIVE DISCUSSION** With a small group, discuss how John, Audrey, and their parents react to and feel about the first day of school, citing text evidence to support your ideas.

---

[5] **crescendo** (krə-shĕn´dō): a slow, gradual increase in volume, intensity, or force.

# Determine Meanings of Words and Phrases

COMMON CORE RL 4

The **mood** of a story is the overall atmosphere or feeling that a writer creates for the reader. Mood can be described as cheerful, romantic, somber, peaceful, eerie, and so on. Writers create mood by

- carefully choosing words to describe the setting, characters, and plot
- using imagery that appeals to the five senses to help readers imagine how things look, feel, smell, taste, and sound
- showing what the characters think and how they talk

Using your understanding of these techniques can help you determine the meanings of words and phrases that contribute to the mood of a story. For example, John's mother says, "Eat and be quiet. Audrey's coming, so let's stop this here kind of talk." This dialogue helps the reader identify the mood as somber.

As you analyze "The First Day of School," identify the mood of different scenes, noting the techniques the writer uses to achieve that mood.

# Describe Stories: Flashback

COMMON CORE RL 3, RL 5

Events in a story are often presented in the order in which they occur. However, sometimes an author will use a **flashback,** which is an interruption of the current action to present events that took place at an earlier time. A flashback provides information that can help readers better understand a character's current situation and experience.

To identify and understand a flashback, ask yourself:

- What words indicate that this event takes place earlier in time?
- What sets the flashback in motion?
- How is the flashback connected to the current situation in the story?
- What have I learned about a character or event from the flashback?

Look for flashbacks as you analyze "The First Day of School."

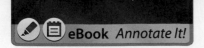
# Analyzing the Text

COMMON CORE RL 1, RL 3, RL 4, RL 5, W 2a–b, W 2e–f, W 9a, W 10

**Cite Text Evidence**   Support your responses with evidence from the text.

1. **Compare**   Reread lines 1–7. Compare the effect of the author's word choice in the description of the bubbles and then in the description of John's actions. What is the mood in each of these scenes? How does the mood change?

2. **Infer**   Reread lines 114–121. Why does John envy the chicken?

3. **Analyze**   Review lines 122–147. What is the connection between what John remembers and what is happening in the story now? Describe what you learn about John and how the flashback moves the plot of the story forward.

4. **Draw Conclusions**   Reread lines 192–197. How would you describe the mood in this scene? What words does the author use that help you identify the mood?

5. **Evaluate**   John's mother will not acknowledge that the day is different from any other day. How does her attitude affect her children? Do you think she is portrayed realistically? Tell why or why not.

6. **Interpret**   How would you describe the mood at the end of the story? How is the mood conveyed?

## PERFORMANCE TASK

**Writing Activity: Essay**   How does John feel about his first day at this new school? Why does he resolve to go only if Audrey stays home?

- Write a one-page essay that explains John's feelings and actions about his first day at school.
- Include your ideas about why he resolves to go to school only if his sister stays home.

- Support your explanation by telling how John responds to events in his past as well as in the present.
- Cite specific examples from the text that help explain your ideas.
- Provide a concluding statement that supports your explanation of John's feelings and tells why his actions are significant.

# Critical Vocabulary

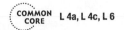 

| | | |
|---|---|---|
| resentment | lament | stealthily |
| linger | serene | poised |

**Practice and Apply** Answer these questions.

1. Why might you feel **resentment** toward a sibling who easily masters a sport you struggle to play well?

2. Would you congratulate or comfort a teammate who **laments** a game's outcome? Why?

3. If you moved **stealthily,** how would you describe your behavior?

4. Would you be more likely to **linger** at the end of a dentist appointment or at a school dance? Why?

5. Does a **serene** sky indicate stormy or sunny weather? Why?

6. If someone looked **poised** at a job interview, would that person be feeling calm or nervous? Explain.

## Vocabulary Strategy: Using a Thesaurus

To express an idea clearly when you write, you need to use precise words. A thesaurus is one type of reference tool that can help. A **thesaurus** is a reference book of synonyms—words that have nearly the same meaning.

A thesaurus works like a dictionary; you simply look up the word you are interested in. You will find a list of synonyms for the word, and often a list of antonyms, or words with opposite meanings, as well. Many word-processing programs contain an electronic thesaurus tool, and there are thesauruses on the Internet as well. To use an online thesaurus:

- Look for a search box and type your word in it.
- Click on the appropriate onscreen icon (for example, a magnifying glass) and the thesaurus will display the word's definition and any number of synonyms. Antonyms may appear as well.
- You may also be able to click an icon to hear a pronunciation.

**Practice and Apply** Use a thesaurus to select a synonym for each of the vocabulary words on this page. Then use each synonym in a sentence that shows its meaning, as in this example for *resentment*.

| Word | Synonym | Sentence |
|---|---|---|
| *resentment* | *animosity* | I could feel my opponent's *animosity* after I won our match. |

# Language Conventions: Varying Sentence Patterns

Authors use a variety of sentence patterns to make their writing smooth, clear, and interesting to read. A **sentence pattern** refers to how a sentence is structured. Review the sentence patterns and examples shown in the chart.

| Sentence Pattern | Description and Example |
|---|---|
| **Simple** | one independent clause<br>**She looked fresh and cool in her white dress.** |
| **Compound** | two or more independent clauses joined with commas and coordinating conjunctions such as *and, or, but, nor, yet, so*<br>**He heard the tap of heels on the stairs, and his sister came down into the kitchen.** |
| **Complex** | one independent clause and one or more subordinate clauses that can be used as nouns or modifiers<br>**He wouldn't go unless Audrey stayed home.** |
| **Compound-Complex** | two or more independent clauses and one or more subordinate clauses<br>**As John ate his oatmeal, he heard a crow calling and he heard the sound of trucks.** |

Writers pay attention to sentence patterns because the right combination of short and long sentences creates rhythm. In the opening paragraph of "The First Day of School," the author uses a combination of simple, compound, and compound-complex sentences. A rhythm of action and reflection is established, and the reader is immediately engaged.

Reread lines 30–45. Notice the contrast of long and short sections. The longer section engages you with its imagery and provides background and insight into John's character. The short segments of dialogue keep the pace of the story moving swiftly.

**Practice and Apply**  Change the sentence pattern of each sentence or group of sentences. First, identify the original pattern used in each sentence. Then revise, using a different sentence pattern for each item.

1.  John hadn't slept very well the night before because the sounds of car horns and loud voices kept waking him up.

2.  Audrey came down the stairs. She acted prim. The dress she had chosen looked fresh and cool.

3.  Their mother came onto the porch. She called to them. She followed them down the street.

**Robert Frost** (1874–1963) *is considered one of the outstanding American poets of the twentieth century. Born in San Francisco, California, he moved with his family to New England when he was eleven. His first poem was published in 1894. Frost drew inspiration for much of his poetry from New England life and the countryside where he grew up and lived for most of his adult life. He was honored with many awards throughout his life, including four Pulitzer Prizes.*

# The Road Not Taken

Poem by Robert Frost

**SETTING A PURPOSE** As you read the poem, pay attention to the thoughts and feelings the speaker has about making a choice.

Two roads diverged[1] in a yellow wood,
And sorry I could not travel both
And be one traveler, long I stood
And looked down one as far as I could
5  To where it bent in the undergrowth;

Then took the other, as just as fair,
And having perhaps the better claim,
Because it was grassy and wanted wear;
Though as for that the passing there
10  Had worn them really about the same,

---

[1] **diverged** (dĭ-vûrjd´): branched out; went in different directions.

And both that morning equally lay
In leaves no step had trodden[2] black.
Oh, I kept the first for another day!
Yet knowing how way leads on to way,
15 I doubted if I should ever come back.

I shall be telling this with a sigh
Somewhere ages and ages hence:
Two roads diverged in a wood, and I—
I took the one less traveled by,
20 And that has made all the difference.

**COLLABORATIVE DISCUSSION** At the end of the poem, the speaker says that choosing the road "less traveled" has "made all the difference." However, the poem is titled "The Road Not Taken." With a partner, discuss why the poet might have titled the poem this way. Support your ideas with evidence from the poem.

---
[2] **trodden** (trŏd´n): walked on or trampled.

# Determine Theme

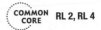 

In a story or poem, the **theme** is the message about life or human nature that the author wants to share. Using a symbol is one way to share a theme. A **symbol** is a person, a place, an object, or an activity that stands for something beyond itself. To identify a poem's theme, keep the following clues in mind:

- The poem's title may suggest what the poem will focus on.
- A poet's use of images often helps to convey a poem's theme.
- Repeated words and phrases tell you how the **speaker,** or voice of the poem, feels.

To determine symbols and their relationship to a theme, look for:

- things, places, or people that the author emphasizes or that seem to have importance
- how the symbols are related to the theme

Look for symbols and how they add to the poet's theme as you analyze "The Road Not Taken."

# Analyze Structure

**Rhyme** is the repetition of sounds at the ends of words. A pattern of rhymes developed throughout a poem is called a **rhyme scheme.** A rhyme scheme is noted by assigning a letter of the alphabet, beginning with *a*, to each line. Lines that rhyme are given the same letter. The first stanza of "The Road Not Taken" has a rhyme scheme of *abaab*.

Poems often have a regular rhythm, or meter. In poetry, **meter** is the regular pattern of stressed (´) and unstressed (˘) syllables in a line. Take a look at the meter in these lines from "The Road Not Taken":

˘ ´ ˘ ´ ˘ ´ ˘ ˘ ´
**And both that morning equally lay**

˘ ´ ˘ ´ ˘ ´ ˘ ´
**In leaves no step had trodden black.**

If you tap your foot while you read the lines aloud, you will hear the regular meter of stressed and unstressed syllables. To analyze rhyme and meter in "The Road Not Taken" and other poems, follow these steps:

- Look for patterns to help you identify the rhyme scheme and meter.
- Consider how the rhymes and meter relate to important ideas in the poem. Do rhymes point out key words? Does the meter create a familiar rhythm?

# Analyzing the Text

COMMON CORE
RL 1, RL 2, RL 4,
RL 5, RL 10,
SL 1a–b, SL 1d

**Cite Text Evidence**   Support your responses with evidence from the text.

1. **Infer** In line 1, the speaker describes an instance where "Two roads diverged in a yellow wood." What might "yellow wood" describe in nature, and what might the phrase be a symbol for?

2. **Interpret** Review the title of the poem and lines 1–10. What does the word "Road" symbolize in the title? What do the woods symbolize? Explain what helped you determine what the symbols mean.

3. **Analyze** Read aloud lines 11–15, tapping your foot with each stressed syllable. What physical activity does the meter remind you of? What words emphasized by stressed syllables express important ideas?

4. **Draw Conclusions** Review lines 16–20. The poet rhymes *sigh* with *I* and *less travelled by*. What conclusions can you draw about the speaker's attitude or feelings from the use of these rhyming words?

5. **Analyze** What themes do you find in the poem? Explain which theme you think is most important.

---

## PERFORMANCE TASK

**Speaking Activity: Discussion** With a small group, compare and contrast the poet's choice in "The Road Not Taken" with Audrey's choice in "The First Day of School."

- Discuss what each decision tells about the speaker in the poem and the character in the story. Think about instances in each text that support the choices they make.
- Explain how the characters' decisions contribute to the theme of each selection.
- Make sure that everyone in the group knows to be prepared for the discussion and when it will take place.

- On your own, review the texts and take notes to prepare thoughts and ideas you will bring to the discussion.
- Be sure your ideas are focused on the topic and are supported by evidence from the texts.
- During the discussion, work as a group to share your ideas and build on those of others in a collaborative way.
- Ask one person to record the group's ideas. Work together to create a summary of the discussion to share with others.

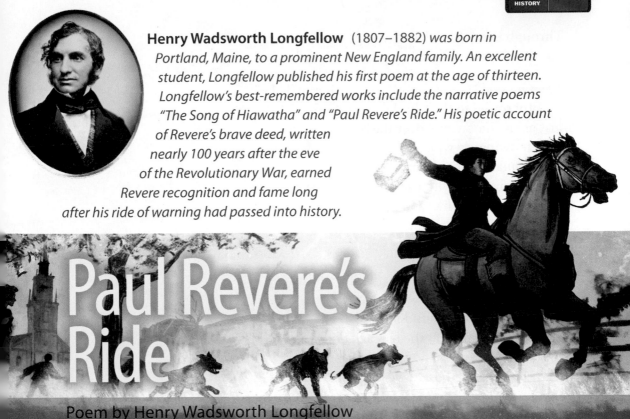

**Henry Wadsworth Longfellow** (1807–1882) *was born in Portland, Maine, to a prominent New England family. An excellent student, Longfellow published his first poem at the age of thirteen. Longfellow's best-remembered works include the narrative poems "The Song of Hiawatha" and "Paul Revere's Ride." His poetic account of Revere's brave deed, written nearly 100 years after the eve of the Revolutionary War, earned Revere recognition and fame long after his ride of warning had passed into history.*

# Paul Revere's Ride

Poem by Henry Wadsworth Longfellow

**SETTING A PURPOSE** As you read, pay attention to how Longfellow honors Paul Revere in his description of the midnight ride.

Listen, my children, and you shall hear
Of the midnight ride of Paul Revere,
On the eighteenth of April, in Seventy-five;
Hardly a man is now alive
5  Who remembers that famous day and year.

He said to his friend, "If the British march
By land or sea from the town to-night,
Hang a lantern aloft in the belfry arch
Of the North Church tower as a signal light,—
10  One if by land, and two if by sea;
And I on the opposite shore will be,
Ready to ride and spread the alarm

Through every Middlesex[1] village and farm,
For the country folk to be up and to arm."

15 Then he said "Good-night!" and with muffled oar
Silently rowed to the Charlestown shore,
Just as the moon rose over the bay,
Where swinging wide at her moorings[2] lay
The *Somerset*, British man-of-war;[3]
20 A phantom ship, with each mast and spar[4]
Across the moon like a prison bar,
And a huge black hulk, that was magnified
By its own reflection in the tide.

Meanwhile, his friend through alley and street
25 Wanders and watches, with eager ears,
Till in the silence around him he hears
The muster of men at the barrack door,
The sound of arms, and the tramp of feet,
And the measured tread of the grenadiers,[5]
30 Marching down to their boats on the shore.
Then he climbed the tower of the Old North Church,
By the wooden stairs, with stealthy tread,[6]
To the belfry chamber overhead,
And startled the pigeons from their perch
35 On the somber[7] rafters, that round him made
Masses and moving shapes of shade,—
By the trembling ladder, steep and tall,
To the highest window in the wall,
Where he paused to listen and look down
40 A moment on the roofs of the town
And the moonlight flowing over all.

---

[1] **Middlesex:** a county in eastern Massachusetts—the setting of the first battle of the Revolutionary War on April 19, 1775.

[2] **moorings** (mŏŏr´ĭngs): the place where a ship is docked and secured by lines, cables, or anchors.

[3] **man-of-war:** a warship, often a large sailing ship, bearing cannons and other guns.

[4] **spar:** a pole used to support a ship's sails or rigging.

[5] **grenadiers** (grĕn´ə-dîrz´): British foot soldiers of the first regiment of the royal household.

[6] **stealthy tread** (stĕl´thē trĕd): quiet, sneaky footsteps.

[7] **somber** (sŏm´bər): gloomy, dark.

Beneath, in the churchyard, lay the dead,
In their night encampment on the hill,
Wrapped in silence so deep and still
45　That he could hear, like a sentinel's[8] tread,
The watchful night-wind, as it went
Creeping along from tent to tent,
And seeming to whisper, "All is well!"
A moment only he feels the spell
50　Of the place and the hour, and the secret dread
Of the lonely belfry and the dead;
For suddenly all his thoughts are bent
On a shadowy something far away,
Where the river widens to meet the bay,—
55　A line of black that bends and floats
On the rising tide like a bridge of boats.

Meanwhile, impatient to mount and ride,
Booted and spurred, with a heavy stride
On the opposite shore walked Paul Revere.
60　Now he patted his horse's side,
Now he gazed at the landscape far and near,
Then, impetuous,[9] stamped the earth,
And turned and tightened his saddle girth;[10]
But mostly he watched with eager search
65　The belfry tower of the Old North Church,
As it rose above the graves on the hill,
Lonely and spectral[11] and somber and still.
And lo! as he looks, on the belfry's height
A glimmer, and then a gleam of light!
70　He springs to the saddle, the bridle he turns,
But lingers and gazes, till full on his sight
A second lamp in the belfry burns.

A hurry of hoofs in a village street,
A shape in the moonlight, a bulk in the dark,
75　And beneath, from the pebbles, in passing, a spark
Struck out by a steed flying fearless and fleet;
That was all! And yet, through the gloom and the light,

---

[8] **sentinel** (sĕn´tə-nəl): a guard or sentry.
[9] **impetuous** (ĭm-pĕch´o͞o-əs): acting suddenly, on impulse.
[10] **saddle girth:** the strap attaching a saddle to a horse's body.
[11] **spectral** (spĕk´trəl): ghostly.

The fate of a nation was riding that night;
And the spark struck out by that steed, in his flight,
80 Kindled the land into flame with its heat.
He has left the village and mounted the steep,
And beneath him, tranquil and broad and deep,
Is the Mystic,[12] meeting the ocean tides;
And under the alders[13] that skirt its edge,
85 Now soft on the sand, now loud on the ledge,
Is heard the tramp of his steed as he rides.

It was twelve by the village clock,
When he crossed the bridge into Medford town.
He heard the crowing of the cock,
90 And the barking of the farmer's dog,
And felt the damp of the river fog,
That rises after the sun goes down.

It was one by the village clock,
When he galloped into Lexington.
95 He saw the gilded weathercock
Swim in the moonlight as he passed,
And the meeting-house windows, black and bare,
Gaze at him with a spectral glare,
As if they already stood aghast[14]
100 At the bloody work they would look upon.

It was two by the village clock,
When he came to the bridge in Concord town.
He heard the bleating of the flock,
And the twitter of birds among the trees,
105 And felt the breath of the morning breeze
Blowing over the meadow brown.
And one was safe and asleep in his bed
Who at the bridge would be first to fall,
Who that day would be lying dead,
110 Pierced by a British musket ball.

---

[12]**Mystic:** a short river flowing into Boston Harbor.
[13]**alder** (ôl´dər):  tree of the birch family.
[14]**aghast** (ə-găst´):  terrified, shocked.

You know the rest. In the books you have read
How the British Regulars fired and fled,—
How the farmers gave them ball for ball,
From behind each fence and farmyard wall,
115  Chasing the redcoats down the lane,
Then crossing the fields to emerge again
Under the trees at the turn of the road,
And only pausing to fire and load.

So through the night rode Paul Revere;
120  And so through the night went his cry of alarm
To every Middlesex village and farm,—
A cry of defiance, and not of fear,
A voice in the darkness, a knock at the door,
And a word that shall echo for evermore!
125  For, borne on the night-wind of the Past,
Through all our history, to the last,
In the hour of darkness and peril and need,
The people will waken and listen to hear
The hurrying hoof-beats of that steed,
130  And the midnight message of Paul Revere.

**COLLABORATIVE DISCUSSION**  Review the poem's final stanza.
With a partner, discuss how Longfellow appeals to American
ideals and virtues. Identify words and phrases from the stanza that
support your ideas.

# Analyze Structure

Poetry that tells a story is called **narrative poetry.** Like a short story, a narrative poem has the following elements:

- one or more **characters** or individuals who take part in the action
- a **setting**—the time and place where the story occurs
- a **plot,** or series of events that center on a conflict faced by a main character or individual

Use the chart that follows to help you analyze narrative poetry elements.

| Element | Questions to Ask and Answer |
|---|---|
| **Characters or Individuals** | Who takes part in the action? Who is the main character? |
| | What is the main character like? How would you describe his or her traits? How does he or she respond or change as the story moves on? |
| **Setting** | What information or clues tell you where and when the story takes place? |
| | How is the setting important to the story? What impact, if any, does it have upon the outcome? |
| **Plot** | What central conflict or struggle does the main character face? |
| | What important events shape the story's action? |
| | How is the conflict resolved? |

For example, in "Paul Revere's Ride," lines 1–23 tell you about the setting:

- The action takes place on April 18, 1775.
- The description "Just as the moon rose over the bay" shows that the action takes place at night.

Sometimes narrative poetry may contain a **refrain,** the same word, phrase, or line repeated several times. Poets often use refrains to emphasize a particular word or idea or to establish a mood. A refrain can also help develop a poem's **rhythm,** or beat.

Identify the elements of narrative poetry as you analyze "Paul Revere's Ride."

# Analyzing the Text

COMMON CORE  RL 1, RL 2, RL 3, RL 4, RL 5, RL 7, W 2a–f, W 4, W 9a, W 10, SL 1

**Cite Text Evidence**   Support your responses with evidence from the text.

1. **Summarize**  Reread lines 6–14. What is the plan that Paul Revere discusses with his friend? What is the purpose of the plan?

2. **Analyze**  Review lines 24–56. Tell what events these lines describe. What are some sensory details that help you imagine the events and settings?

3. **Analyze**  Review lines 57–72. What words does the poet use to help you understand Paul Revere's character and how he behaves while he waits for a signal?

4. **Interpret**  Read lines 73–86 aloud. Is the rhythm in these lines slow and leisurely, or quick and insistent? How does the rhythm contribute to the action?

5. **Identify Patterns**  Review lines 87–110. How does the poet use a refrain to develop plot events? Why do you think he includes the information in lines 97–100 and 107–110?

## Speaking and Listening

Listen to an audio version of "Paul Revere's Ride." How is hearing the speech different than reading it? With a partner or small group, choose a section of the poem. Discuss how the audio version compares to reading the poem on your own.

## PERFORMANCE TASK

**Writing Activity: Analysis**  "Paul Revere's Ride" retells an event in American history. Write an essay that analyzes how the individual stanzas fit into the poem's overall structure.

- Choose three or four stanzas.
- Decide how each stanza helps develop the plot. Note the ideas you want to include.
- Take notes about details and information you will include to support your ideas.

- Plan and organize your essay. Draft the ideas you will discuss and details to support them.
- Use a formal writing style.
- Include linking and transition words to show how your ideas are related.
- Use clear, precise language.
- Be sure your introduction and conclusion help readers understand your topic.

**Background** *On September 11, 2001, four United States passenger jets were hijacked by terrorists. Two jets were flown into the World Trade Center in New York City; one jet attacked the Pentagon in Washington, D.C. The fourth hijacked jet, United Flight 93, widely believed to be headed toward the United States Capitol, was still flying as the news of the other jet crashes broke. To prevent yet another disaster, the passengers of Flight 93 banded together to end their flight, sacrificing their own lives. The passengers' valiant choice destroyed the terrorists' plans and saved the lives of countless others on that tragic day.*

# MEDIA ANALYSIS

# COVERING NEWS EVENTS

## On Doomed Flight, Passengers Vowed to Perish Fighting
**News Article by Jodi Wilgoren and Edward Wong**

## Memorial Is Unveiled for Heroes of Flight 93
**TV Newscast by CBS News**

**SETTING A PURPOSE** In this lesson, you'll analyze a news article that tells the story of United Flight 93. You will also view a television newscast that describes a memorial event held in 2011 that honored those who died on Flight 93. As you read and view each media selection, pay attention to how information is given and to the facts and details that reporters choose to use as they describe each event.

# On Doomed Flight, Passengers Vowed to Perish Fighting

**Jodi Wilgoren and Edward Wong**
**New York Times,** Sep. 13, 2001

They told the people they loved that they would die fighting.

In a series of cellular telephone calls to their wives, two passengers aboard the plane that crashed into a Pennsylvania field instead of possibly toppling a national landmark learned about the horror of the World Trade Center. From 35,000 feet, they relayed harrowing[1] details about the hijacking in progress to the police. And they vowed to try to thwart the enemy, to prevent others from dying even if they could not save themselves.

Lyzbeth Glick, 31, of Hewitt, N.J., said her husband, Jeremy, told her that three or four 6-foot-plus passengers aboard United Airlines Flight 93 from Newark bound for San Francisco planned to take a vote about how to proceed, and joked about taking on the hijackers with the butter knives from the in-flight breakfast. In a telephone interview last night, Ms. Glick said her husband told her "three Arab-looking men with red headbands," carrying a knife and talking about a bomb, took control of the aircraft.

"He was a man who would not let things happen," she said of her high school sweetheart and husband of five years, the father of a 12-week-old daughter, Emerson. "He was a hero for what he did, but he was a hero for me because he told me not to be sad and to take care of our daughter and he said whatever happened he would be O.K. with any choices I make.

"He said, 'I love you, stay on the line,' but I couldn't," added Ms. Glick, 31, a teacher at Berkeley College. "I gave the phone to my dad. I don't want to know what happened."

Another passenger, Thomas E. Burnett Jr., an executive at a San Francisco-area medical device company, told his wife, Deena, that one passenger had already been stabbed to death but that a group was "getting ready to do something."

---

[1] **harrowing** (hărˊō ĭng): extremely distressing.

"I pleaded with him to please sit down and not draw attention to himself," Ms. Burnett, the mother of three young daughters, told a San Francisco television station. "And he said: 'No, no. If they're going to run this into the ground we're going to have to do something.' And he hung up and he never called back."

The accounts revealed a spirit of defiance amid the
40 desperation. Relatives and friends and a congressman who represents the area around the crash site in Pennsylvania hailed the fallen passengers as patriots.

"Apparently they made enough of a difference that the plane did not complete its mission," said Lyzbeth Glick's uncle, Tom Crowley, of Atlanta. In an e-mail message forwarded far and wide, Mr. Crowley urged: "May we remember Jeremy and the other brave souls as heroes, soldiers and Americans on United Flight 93 who so gallantly gave their lives to save many others."

50 Like others on the doomed plane, Mr. Glick, 31, and Mr. Burnett, 38, had not originally planned to be aboard the 8 a.m. flight. Mr. Glick, who worked for an Internet company called Vividence, was heading to the West Coast on business, and Mr. Burnett, chief operating officer for Thorntec Corporation, was returning home from a visit to the company's Edison, N.J., office.

Lauren Grandcolas of San Rafael, Calif., left an early-morning message on her husband's answering machine saying she would be home earlier than expected from her
60 grandmother's funeral. Mark Bingham, 31, who ran a public relations firm, had felt too sick to fly on Monday, but was racing to make an afternoon meeting with a client in San Francisco.

The plane was airborne by 8:44 a.m., according to radar logs, and headed west, flying apparently without incident until it reached Cleveland about 50 minutes later. At 9:37, it turned south and headed back the way it came. Mr. Bingham, a 6-foot-5 former rugby player who this summer ran with the bulls in Pamplona, Spain, called his mother, Alice
70 Hoglan. "He said, 'Three guys have taken over the plane and they say they have a bomb,'" said Ms. Hoglan, a United flight attendant.

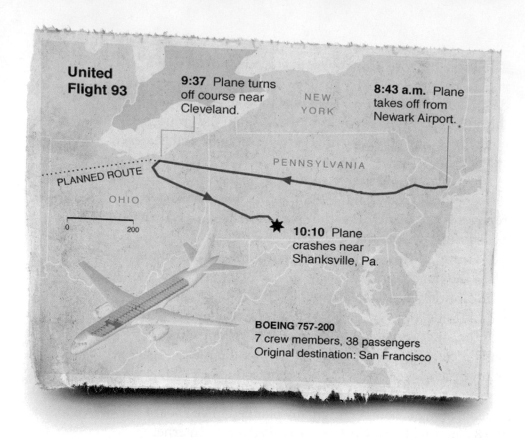

Map showing planned route and actual route of United Flight 93.

CNN reported last night that it had obtained a partial transcript[2] of cockpit chatter, and that a source who had listened to the air-traffic control tape said a man with an Arabic accent had said in broken English: "This is the captain speaking. Remain in your seat. There is a bomb on board. Stay quiet. We are meeting with their demands. We are returning to the airport."

80     Another passenger on the sparsely populated plane barricaded himself in the bathroom and dialed 911. Ms. Grandcolas tried to wake her husband, Jack, but got the answering machine. "We're having problems," she said, according to her neighbor, Dave Shapiro, who listened to the message. "But I'm comfortable," she said, and then, after a pause, added, "for now."

---

[2] **transcript:** a written or printed copy.

(bg) ©Shutterstock; (fg) From The New York Times, September 13, 2001 © 2001 The New York Times

Mr. Glick, a muscular 6-foot-4 water sportsman, and Mr. Burnett, a 6-1 former high school football player, called their wives over and over, from about 9:30 a.m. until the crash at about 10:10 a.m., chronicling[3] what was happening, urging them to call the authorities, vowing to fight, saying goodbye.

"He sounded sad and scared, but calm at the same time," Ms. Glick said. "He said people weren't too panicked. They had moved everybody to the back of the plane. The three men were in the cockpit, but he didn't see the pilots and they made no contact with the passengers, so my feeling is they must have killed them."

In a radio interview with KCBS in San Francisco, Ms. Burnett said her husband of nine years called four times—first just reporting the hijacking, later asking her for information about the World Trade Center disaster, eventually suggesting the passengers were formulating a plan to respond.

"I could tell that he was alarmed and trying to piece together the puzzle, trying to figure out what was going on and what he could do about the situation," Ms. Burnett said. "He was not giving up. His adrenaline was going. And you could just tell that he had every intention of solving the problem and coming on home."

Ms. Glick said that at one point, she managed to create a conference call between her husband and 911 dispatchers. "Jeremy tracked the second-by-second details and relayed them to the police by phone," Mr. Crowley wrote in his e-mail account of the calls. "After several minutes describing the scene, Jeremy and several other passengers decided there was nothing to lose by rushing the hijackers."

At the crash site near Shanksville, Pa., a local politician and law enforcement officials said the wives' accounts made sense.

"I would conclude there was a struggle, and a heroic individual decided they were going to die anyway and, 'Let's bring the plane down here,'" said Representative John P. Murtha, a Democrat who represents the area and serves on the Defense Appropriations Committee.

An F.B.I. official said of Mr. Murtha's theory, "It's reasonable what he said, but how could you know?"

---

[3] **chronicling** (krŏn´ĭ-klĭng): providing a detailed record or report.

While the women cherished their final words and their husbands' seeming heroism, other people's relatives and friends struggled to reconstruct their last conversations with their lost loved ones.

130    Between sobs, Doris Gronlund recalled how her daughter, Linda, an environmental lawyer from Long Island who was headed for a vacation in wine country with her boyfriend, Joseph DeLuca, called on Monday to relay her flight numbers, just in case anything happened.

David Markmann last saw his upstairs neighbor, Honor Elizabeth Wainio, on Sunday night, standing on her balcony in Plainfield, N.J. Ms. Wainio, 28, was a regional manager of the Discovery Channel's retail stores.

When the Newark flight crashed, "things started clicking
140    in my mind," Mr. Markmann said. He dialed Ms. Wainio's home number— no answer. The cell phone rang four times and went to voice mail. He called again, and again and again and again, 15 times or more, until 2 P.M. yesterday, when he saw the list of Flight 93's passengers on the United Airlines Web site.

"I wasn't getting a phone call back," he said, "so I kind of had a feeling."

**COLLABORATIVE DISCUSSION**  If there were no survivors on Flight 93, how do we know what actually happened on the flight? With a partner, discuss the information presented by family members of the passengers. Do you think that the information provides a full account of the events? Cite evidence from the text to support your ideas.

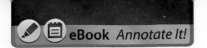
# Analyze Structure

COMMON CORE   RI 2, RI 3, RI 5, RI 7

News is information on events, people, and places in your community, the nation, and the world. News reports can be found in television newscasts, online wire services, magazines, documentaries, and newspaper articles, such as the article about United Flight 93 that you just read.

In order to give a complete account of an event, newspaper articles should answer six basic questions—**who, what, when, where, why,** and **how.** Reporters often use the 5 *W*s and *H* questions as an outline for writing reports. The best news reports answer these questions and include additional information.

Newspaper articles may also use graphics. **Graphics** are visual elements whose purpose is to provide additional information about events. Graphics may be charts, maps, diagrams, timelines, or other visuals.

Look for answers to the six basic news questions and think about the purpose of the graphic as you analyze the newspaper article.

# Analyzing the Media

COMMON CORE   RI 2, RI 3, RI 5, RI 7

*Cite Text Evidence*  Support your responses with evidence from the text.

1. **Summarize**  Review the news story and fill out the following chart to record the story's 5 *W*s and *H*.

| 5 *W*s and *H* Questions | |
| --- | --- |
| *Who* is the report about? | |
| *What* happened to this person or persons? | |
| *When* did it happen? | |
| *Where* did it happen? | |
| *Why* did it happen? | |
| *How* did it happen? | |

2. **Interpret**  The writer includes information about the passengers by recounting phone calls they made to family members on the ground. What is the impact of this information?

3. **Analyze and Evaluate**  What additional information does the graphic provide about United Flight 93? Explain whether this information is helpful or not, and why.

# Memorial Is Unveiled for Heroes of Flight 93

**Format:** TV newscast
**Running Time:** 2:22 minutes

**AS YOU VIEW** As you view the newscast, consider the 5 *Ws* and *H* of news reports and how this newscast presents the answers to those questions. Notice how the newscast explains the event using a combination of interviews, film clips, narration, and quotations from different people. Consider how each of these elements helps you understand the outcome of United Flight 93, what the individuals on the plane achieved, and what the event meant to their families and to the nation.

Pause the video to write notes about ideas or questions you might want to talk about later. Note any facts or details that support your ideas. Replay or rewind the video as needed.

**COLLABORATIVE DISCUSSION** With a partner or small group, discuss the purpose of each news report and what you learned from it. What is the same and different about the information in each report? Tell whether you find one of the reports more compelling, and if so, why. Cite specific evidence or techniques from the reports to support your ideas.

©BBC Motion Gallery

# Interpret Information

The makers of news reports use different sources to provide people with information. A **source** is someone or something that provides information. News reports and newscasts use a variety of sources, including the following:

- **Experts** are people who are knowledgeable in a field or a subject area.
- **Witnesses** are people who are present at an event and can give a first-hand account of something seen, heard, or experienced.
- **Footage** is recorded material that gives information about a subject or event. Footage can include film clips, photographs, and interviews.

  **Interviews,** which are question-and-answer conversations between two or more people, are often included in news reports. Interviews are a direct way to find out information from experts, witnesses, and others, such as family members in the newscast you just viewed, who might have information to share about an event or topic. Often, a reporter will include **quotations** from interviews, as well as other sources, as part of a news report, article, or newscast. In newscasts, like the one you just viewed, these quotations are called **sound bites.**

  As you analyze the newscast "Memorial Is Unveiled for Heroes of Flight 93," consider how these elements are used and how effective each one is in conveying different types of information.

## Analyzing the Media

**Cite Text Evidence**   Support your responses with evidence from the media.

1. **Identify and Infer**  Fill out a chart like this and give one example of each type of source from the newscast.

| Experts | |
|---|---|
| Witnesses | |
| Footage | |

2. **Analyze**  What do the interviews with family members help you to understand about their feelings and reactions?

3. **Interpret and Evaluate**  How does the footage that shows the World Trade Center and the Pentagon affect your understanding and opinions about the events of September 11, 2001? Describe how viewing the footage of the memorial event affects your response to the actions of the passengers on United Flight 93.

# Integrate Information

 COMMON CORE   RI 7, SL 2

To integrate information means to take individual pieces of information and synthesize, or combine, them in order to develop a coherent, or clearer, understanding of a topic. Think about the information you read in the news article "On Doomed Flight, Passengers Vowed to Perish Fighting." Then think about the newscast from ten years later, "Memorial Is Unveiled for Heroes of Flight 93." You can use the information from both reports to better understand what happened on September 11, 2001. To integrate information from these reports, ask yourself:

- What is the purpose of each news report? What specific information does each report contribute?
- What features do the reports share? What features are unique to each?

# Analyzing the Media

 COMMON CORE   RI 7, W 6, W 8, SL 1, SL 2 SL 4, SL 5

**Cite Text Evidence**   Support your responses with evidence from the media.

1. **Interpret** Use a chart like this to list the types of sources used in each news report.

| News Report | Sources Used |
|---|---|
| **"On Doomed Flight..."** | |
| **"Memorial Is Unveiled..."** | |

2. **Integrate** Explain how the passage of ten years affects the perspective presented in the newscast in comparison with the perspective presented in the news article. How have people's views and reactions changed or remained the same over ten years?

3. **Analyze and Integrate** How do the specific details and elements presented in each news report work together to help you understand the significance of the events surrounding United Flight 93?

## PERFORMANCE TASK

**Media Activity: Commentary** Work in a small group to create an audio recording for a commentary, or an opinion piece about a local or school news issue related to the Collection 5 topic "Decisions That Matter."

- With your group, brainstorm the local or school issue to report on.
- Conduct research and gather information about the issue.
- As a group, record opinions and have members provide comments.

*Interactive Lessons*
If you need help . . .
• **Writing Narratives**
• **Writing as a Process**
• **Producing and Publishing with Technology**

# Write a Personal Narrative

In this collection, Colin Powell and other individuals are faced with important decisions that have significant outcomes. Like Colin Powell's memoir, *It Worked for Me*, a personal narrative reflects the writer's experiences, feelings, and personality. A personal narrative, however, is much shorter than a memoir and usually deals with a single subject or event. In this activity, you will write a personal narrative about a decision you made or will make that will have an impact on your immediate future.

**A successful personal narrative**

- provides a captivating introduction that clearly establishes the situation

- organizes events in a sequence that unfolds naturally and logically

- uses descriptive details that offer insight on significant experiences and feelings

- uses words and phrases that create vivid images

- provides a conclusion that follows from the narrated experiences and events

COMMON
CORE

**W 3a–e** Write narratives.
**W 4** Produce clear and coherent writing.
**W 5** Develop and strengthen writing as needed.
**W 10** Write routinely.

---

**PLAN**

*my* **Notebook**

**Establish the Situation**  A personal narrative is a text that describes a memorable experience or time period in a person's life. Making an important decision is often the subject of a personal narrative. Consider an important decision in Colin Powell's life, such as his first job or joining the military. How did this decision affect his future? Then think about important decisions you have made or might have to make that will impact your future.

- Consider how the decision or experience is important to you. Is it important now, or was it important in the past?

- Determine whether you have a story to tell about your decision and experience.

- Identify the feelings you have about the decision or experience.

Use the annotation tools in your eBook to find examples of decisions Colin Powell made that made a significant impact on his life.

**ACADEMIC VOCABULARY**

As you plan and present your personal narrative, be sure to use the academic vocabulary words.

*achieve*

*individual*

*instance*

*outcome*

*principle*

- Think about how your decision changed your feelings or ideas.
- Specify the most important thing you want the reader to know about your decision.

**Organize Your Ideas** In a personal narrative, you are the narrator, or the person telling the story. A graphic organizer can help you organize your ideas and describe the events in a logical way.

> Setting:

> Events:

> Details:

> Feelings:

> Conclusion:

**Brainstorm Details** Think about how you picture your experience in your mind. Which aspects of those images are most significant for you? Describe these images using words and phrases that provide specific sensory details and achieve the sense of importance you want your reader to feel about your decision.

**Consider Your Purpose and Audience** Who will read your personal narrative? What do you want them to understand about your experience? Think about your audience as you prepare to write. Your wording and tone may be different for a group of classmates or friends than it would be for a group of adults.

**PRODUCE**

*my*WriteSmart

**Draft Your Personal Narrative** Review the information in your graphic organizer as you begin your draft.

Write your rough draft in *my*WriteSmart. Focus on getting your ideas down, rather than perfecting your choice of language.

- Begin with an introduction that clearly establishes your purpose and grabs the attention of your audience.
- Use the first-person point of view. Write details that clearly convey what you feel about your decision.
- Refer to your graphic organizer to help you present events in a clear and logical sequence.

- Elaborate on your ideas and include descriptive details to capture your experience for readers.

- Conclude your personal narrative by telling what impact your decision has had or will have on your life. Reflect on what made the experience significant for you by explaining what you learned or how the outcome changed some aspect of your life.

## REVISE

**Review Your Draft**  Use the chart on the following page to evaluate your draft. Work with a partner to determine if you have described your experience clearly and have included details that will interest readers. Then revise as necessary. Be sure to consider these points in each other's drafts:

- Examine the sequence of events. Delete any event that is not important to describing your experience. If necessary, add events that will help readers understand the experience. Check that the order of events is clear and that you have included transition words such as *next, finally,* or *a day later.*

- Make sure that you have described your experience in a way that creates a vivid image for readers. Check that your descriptions include details that make your feelings clear.

- Decide if dialogue would add interest or reveal the decision you faced in a more interesting way.

- Check that you have clearly explained why the decision you made is significant for you. If necessary, add a sentence or two to better show your thoughts and feelings about the experience.

*my* **WriteSmart**

Have your partner or a group of peers review your draft in *my*WriteSmart. Ask your reviewers to note any parts of your narrative that do not follow a logical sequence.

## PRESENT

**Create a Finished Copy**  Finalize your personal narrative and choose a way to share it with your audience. Consider these options:

- Present your personal narrative orally to your class.

- Post your personal narrative as a blog entry on a personal or school website.

- Dramatize your personal narrative in a one-person theater performance.

| | Ideas and Evidence | Organization | Language |
|---|---|---|---|
| **ADVANCED** | • The introduction is engaging and clearly establishes the writer's subject and situation.<br>• Descriptive details, strong feelings, and reflection effectively re-create the experience and offer insight.<br>• The conclusion effectively summarizes the experience and reflects on the writer's decision. | • The organization is effective; ideas are arranged logically and unfold naturally.<br>• Details successfully clarify the relationships between the experience and decision the writer makes. | • The writing maintains a first-person point of view and reflects the personality of the writer.<br>• Sentence beginnings, lengths, and structures vary and have a rhythmic flow.<br>• Spelling, capitalization, and punctuation are correct.<br>• Grammar and usage are correct. |
| **COMPETENT** | • The introduction could do more to grab the audience's attention; the writer states the subject and situation.<br>• Most details are strong and vivid, but a few could be more relevant to the experience.<br>• The conclusion summarizes the experience but could do more to reflect on the writer's decision. | • The organization of ideas could be clearer in a few places but is generally logical and natural.<br>• A few more details are needed to clarify the relationships between ideas. | • The writing mostly maintains a first-person point of view but is inconsistent in some places.<br>• Sentence beginnings, lengths, and structures vary somewhat.<br>• Some spelling, capitalization and punctuation mistakes occur.<br>• Some grammatical and usage errors are repeated in the narrative. |
| **LIMITED** | • The introduction does not engage the reader; the writer does not clearly state the subject and/or situation.<br>• The details are not always strong or relevant.<br>• The conclusion does not adequately summarize the experience and does little to reflect on the writer's decision. | • The organization of ideas is logical in some places, but it often doesn't follow a natural or stable pattern.<br>• Many more details are needed to clarify the relationships between ideas. | • The writer's point of view is inconsistent throughout.<br>• Sentence structures barely vary, and some fragments or run-on sentences are present.<br>• Several spelling and capitalization mistakes occur, and punctuation is inconsistent.<br>• Grammar and usage are incorrect in many places. |
| **EMERGING** | • The introduction is confusing.<br>• Details are missing.<br>• The conclusion is missing or does not summarize the experience and decision. | • The organization is not logical or natural; details are presented randomly.<br>• The relationships between ideas and details are not made clear. | • The writer's point of view is inconsistent and inappropriate.<br>• Repetitive sentence structure, fragments, and run-on sentences make the writing monotonous and hard to follow.<br>• Spelling and capitalization are often incorrect, and punctuation is missing in several places.<br>• Many grammatical and usage errors change the meaning of the writer's ideas. |

# PERFORMANCE TASK B

Interactive Lessons

If you need help . . .
• Writing Arguments
• Writing as a Process
• Evaluating Sources
• Using Textual Evidence

# Write an Opinion Essay

In "Paul Revere's Ride," Longfellow memorializes Revere's brave ride on the eve of the Revolutionary War and what this ride meant for the freedom of the American colonies. In this activity, you will draw from this poem and other texts in the collection to write an opinion essay. You will give your views on how people's decisions, no matter how big or small, can have consequences that shape not only the individuals themselves but entire communities as well.

**COMMON CORE**

**W 1a–e** Write arguments.
**W 4** Produce clear and coherent writing.
**W 5** Develop and strengthen writing.
**W 9b** Draw evidence from literary or informational texts.
**W 10** Write routinely.

## A successful opinion essay

- contains an engaging introduction that clearly states the opinion, or claim
- supports the claim with logical reasons and relevant evidence
- establishes and maintains a formal style
- uses language that clarifies the relationships among claims and reasons
- concludes by providing a section that follows from the opinion presented

**PLAN**

*my* **Notebook**

Use the annotation tools in your eBook to find evidence that supports your claim. Save each piece of evidence to your notebook.

**Clarify Understanding** Reread "Paul Revere's Ride." Think about the decisions that Paul Revere made before and during his ride. Then think about the poet's decision to write about Paul Revere. Decide whether you think the decisions each person made had a significant effect on his life. Then review other texts in the collection.

- Identify the outcome of the decisions each individual made.
- Think about how their decisions affected others.
- Determine whether their decisions helped them achieve their goals.

**Form an Opinion** Think about how things might have been different if the people you read about had made different choices. Then form an opinion on how people's decisions can shape their lives.

**ACADEMIC VOCABULARY**

As you write your opinion essay, be sure to use the academic vocabulary words.

*achieve*
*individual*
*instance*
*outcome*
*principle*

- Make a list of the reasons why you have the opinion that you do.
- Jot down evidence in the texts that supports your reasons. Look for facts, quotes, and examples.
- Think about what you want your audience to understand about your views.

**Organize Your Ideas** Think about how you will organize your essay. A graphic organizer, such as a hierarchy chart, can help you to present your ideas logically.

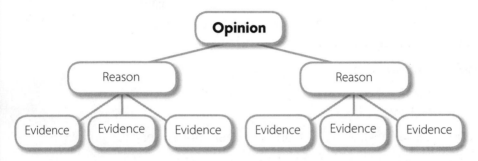

**Consider Your Purpose and Audience** Think about who will read or listen to your essay, and what you want them to understand. Your tone and word choice should be appealing and targeted toward them. Keep this in mind as you prepare to write.

PRODUCE

**Draft Your Essay** Review the information in your graphic organizer as you begin your draft.

- Begin by introducing the topic and stating your opinion. Include an attention-grabbing lead, such as a quote, a story, or an interesting example from the texts. Be sure to use a formal tone.
- Write your claim and support it with reasons and evidence from the texts. Use the information in your graphic organizer to help you organize your reasons and evidence logically.
- Include transition words and phrases such as *because, therefore,* and *for that reason* that will link your claims and reasons and make your opinion clearer and more coherent.

*my*WriteSmart

Write your rough draft in *my*WriteSmart. Focus on getting your ideas down, rather than perfecting your choice of language.

- Write a conclusion that summarizes your claim, restating the most important reasons and evidence, to leave your audience with a lasting impression.

## REVISE

**Evaluate Your Essay**  Use the chart on the following page to evaluate the substance and style of your essay. Then make any needed revisions. Consider the following:

- Check that your opinion is clear and logically supported with a number of reasons and evidence.
- Examine your evidence to make sure it is relevant. Look back at the selections to make sure you've accurately used text evidence to support your reasons.
- Make sure your essay keeps your audience's attention and concludes with a section that sums up your opinion.

**my WriteSmart**

Have a partner or a group of peers review your draft in myWriteSmart. Ask your reviewers to note any reasons that do not support your opinion or lack sufficient evidence.

## PRESENT

**Create a Finished Copy**  Finalize your essay and choose a way to share it with your audience. Consider these options:

- Present your essay as an oral report.
- Post your essay as a blog on a personal or school website.
- Present your ideas in a debate with someone who has an opposing opinion.

| | Ideas and Evidence | Organization | Language |
|---|---|---|---|
| **ADVANCED** | • The introduction skillfully pulls the reader in; the writer clearly states an opinion on a topic.<br>• Logical reasons and relevant evidence convincingly support the writer's opinion.<br>• The concluding section effectively summarizes the opinion and leaves a lasting impression. | • The reasons and evidence are organized logically and consistently to persuasive effect.<br>• Transitions successfully clarify the relationships between the opinion and reasons. | • The writing maintains a formal style.<br>• Sentence beginnings, lengths, and structures vary and have a rhythmic flow.<br>• Spelling, capitalization, and punctuation are correct.<br>• Grammar and usage are correct. |
| **COMPETENT** | • The introduction could do more to grab the audience's attention; the writer states an opinion on a topic.<br>• Most reasons and evidence support the writer's opinion, but they could be more convincing.<br>• The concluding section restates the opinion and leaves a lasting impression. | • The organization of reasons and evidence is confusing in a few places.<br>• A few more transitions are needed to connect the reasons to the opinion. | • The style is informal in a few places.<br>• Sentence beginnings, lengths, and structures vary somewhat.<br>• Some spelling, capitalization and punctuation mistakes occur.<br>• Some grammatical and usage errors are repeated in the essay. |
| **LIMITED** | • The introduction is incomplete; the writer identifies a topic, but the opinion is not clearly stated.<br>• The reasons and evidence are not always logical or relevant.<br>• The concluding section includes an incomplete summary of the opinion and does not leave a lasting impression. | • The organization of reasons and evidence is logical in some places, but it often doesn't follow a pattern.<br>• Transitions are not adequately used to connect the reasons to the opinion. | • The style becomes informal in many places.<br>• Sentence structures barely vary, and some fragments or run-on sentences are present.<br>• Several spelling and capitalization mistakes occur, and punctuation is inconsistent.<br>• Grammar and usage are incorrect in many places. |
| **EMERGING** | • The introduction is confusing.<br>• Supporting reasons and evidence are missing.<br>• The concluding section is missing. | • A logical organization is not used; reasons and evidence are presented randomly.<br>• Transitions are not used, making the essay difficult to understand. | • The style is inappropriate for the essay.<br>• Repetitive sentence structure, fragments, and run-on sentences make the writing monotonous and hard to follow.<br>• Spelling and capitalization are often incorrect, and punctuation is missing in most places.<br>• Many grammatical and usage errors change the meaning of ideas. |

# What Tales Tell

❝ The destiny of the world is determined less by the battles that are lost and won than by the stories it loves and believes in. ❞

—Harold Goddard

# What Tales Tell

In this collection, you will explore how traditional stories reveal the values of a culture.

hmhfyi.com

©Robert Llewellyn/Corbis

---

COLLECTION

## PERFORMANCE TASK Preview

After reading this collection, you will have the opportunity to complete two performance tasks:

• In one, you will write a literary analysis about the values and qualities of a culture discussed in one selection.

• In the second, you will rewrite one of the selections in the collection as a play.

---

## ACADEMIC VOCABULARY

Study the words and their definitions in the chart below. You will use these words as you discuss and write about the texts in this collection.

| Word | Definition | Related Forms |
|---|---|---|
| **emphasize** (ĕm′fə-sīz′) *v.* | to give something special importance or attention | emphasis, emphatic, emphatically |
| **occur** (ə-kûr′) *v.* | to take place; happen | occurrence |
| **period** (pîr′ē-əd) *n.* | a particular length of time, often referring to a specific time in history or in a culture | periodic, periodically |
| **relevant** (rĕl′ə-vənt) *adj.* | important to, connected to, or significant to an issue, event, or person in some way | relevance, irrelevant, irrelevance |
| **tradition** (trə-dĭsh′ən) *n.* | the passing down of various elements of a culture from generation to generation; a custom | traditional, traditionally, traditionalist |

**Rosemary Sutcliff** (1920–1992) *was a well-known British children's author and reteller of myths and legends. She spent her childhood in Malta and on other naval bases where her father was a naval officer. Sutcliff was chronically ill from a very young age and confined to a wheelchair for most of her life. Her mother, a great oral storyteller, told Rosemary many legends and myths of their native Britain. Sutcliff wrote her first novel in 1950 and never stopped; she was still writing on the morning of her death.*

# from BLACK SHIPS BEFORE TROY
## The Story of THE ILIAD

Greek Myth by Rosemary Sutcliff

**SETTING A PURPOSE** As you read, pay attention to how the quarrels of the gods and goddesses are relevant to the lives of the humans and the problems that occur because of their quarrels. Write down any questions you have while reading.

## THE GOLDEN APPLE

I N THE HIGH and far-off days when men were heroes and walked with the gods, Peleus, king of the Myrmidons, took for his wife a sea nymph called Thetis, Thetis of the Silver Feet. Many guests came to their wedding feast, and among the mortal guests came all the gods of high Olympus.

But as they sat feasting, one who had not been invited was suddenly in their midst: Eris, the goddess of discord,[1] had been left out because wherever she went she took trouble with

---

[1] **discord** (dĭs′kôrd′): disagreement; tension or strife.

her; yet here she was, all the same, and in her blackest mood,
10 to avenge the insult.

All she did—it seemed a small thing—was to toss down on the table a golden apple. Then she breathed upon the guests once, and vanished.

The apple lay gleaming among the piled fruits and the brimming wine cups; and bending close to look at it, everyone could see the words "To the fairest" traced on its side.

Then the three greatest of the goddesses each claimed that it was hers. Hera claimed it as wife to Zeus, the All-father, and queen of all the gods. Athene claimed that she had the better
20 right, for the beauty of wisdom such as hers surpassed all else. Aphrodite only smiled, and asked who had a better claim to beauty's prize than the goddess of beauty herself.

They fell to arguing among themselves; the argument became a quarrel, and the quarrel grew more and more bitter, and each called upon the assembled guests to judge between them. But the other guests refused, for they knew well enough that, whichever goddess they chose to receive the golden apple, they would make enemies of the other two.

In the end, the three took the quarrel home with them to
30 Olympus. The other gods took sides, some with one and some with another, and the ill will between them dragged on for a long while. More than long enough in the world of men for a child born when the quarrel first began, to grow to manhood and become a warrior or a herdsman. But the immortal gods do not know time as mortals know it.

Now on the northeast coast of the Aegean Sea, there was a city of men. Troy was its name, a great city surrounded by strong walls, and standing on a hill hard by the shore. It had grown rich on the tolls that its kings demanded from
40 merchant ships passing up the nearby straits[2] to the Black Sea cornlands and down again. Priam, who was now king, was lord of wide realms and long-maned horses, and he had many sons about his hearth. And when the quarrel about the golden apple was still raw and new, a last son was born to him and his wife Queen Hecuba, and they called him Paris.

There should have been great rejoicing, but while Hecuba still carried the babe within her, the soothsayers[3] had foretold

---

[2] **strait** (strāt): a narrow channel of water that joins two larger bodies of water.

[3] **soothsayer** (sooth´sā´ər): someone who claims to be able to predict the future.

that she would give birth to a firebrand[4] that should burn down Troy. And so, when he was born and named, the king bade a servant carry him out into the wilderness and leave him to die. The servant did as he was bid; but a herdsman searching for a missing calf found the babe and brought him up as his own.

The boy grew tall and strong and beautiful, the swiftest runner and the best archer in all the country around. So his boyhood passed among the oak woods and the high hill-pastures that rose toward Mount Ida. And there he met and fell in love with a wood nymph called Oenone, who loved him in return. She had the gift of being able to heal the wounds of mortal men, no matter how sorely they were hurt.

Among the oak woods they lived together and were happy—until one day the three jealous goddesses, still quarreling about the golden apple, chanced to look down from Olympus, and saw the beautiful young man herding his cattle on the slopes of Mount Ida. They knew, for the gods know all things, that he was the son of Priam, king of Troy, though he himself did not know it yet; but the thought came to them that he would not know who they were, and therefore he would not be afraid to judge between them. They were growing somewhat **weary** of the argument by then.

So they tossed the apple down to him, and Paris put up his hands and caught it. After it the three came down, landing before him so lightly that their feet did not bend the mountain grasses, and bade him choose between them, which was the fairest and had best right to the prize he held in his hand.

First Athene, in her gleaming armor, fixed him with sword-gray eyes and promised him supreme wisdom if he would name her.

Then Hera, in her royal robes as queen of heaven, promised him vast wealth and power and honor if he awarded her the prize.

Lastly, Aphrodite drew near, her eyes as blue as deep-sea water, her hair like spun gold wreathed around her head, and, smiling honey-sweet, whispered that she would give him a wife as fair as herself if he tossed the apple to her.

**weary**
(wîr´ē) *adj.* If you are growing *weary*, you are getting tired of something, either physically or mentally.

---

[4] **firebrand** (fīr´brănd´): a person who creates trouble or leads a revolt.

And Paris forgot the other two with their offers of wisdom and power, forgot also, for that moment, dark-haired Oenone in the shadowed oak woods; and he gave the golden apple to Aphrodite.

90 Then Athene and Hera were angry with him for refusing them the prize, just as the wedding guests had known that they would be; and both of them were angry with Aphrodite. But Aphrodite was well content, and set about keeping her promise to the herdsman who was a king's son.

She put a certain thought into the heads of some of King Priam's men, so that they came cattle-raiding at the full of the moon and drove off Paris' big beautiful herd-bull, who was lord of all his cattle. Then Paris left the hills and came down into Troy, seeking his bull. And there Hecuba, his mother,

100  chanced to see him, and knew by his likeness to his brothers and by something in her own heart that he was the son she had thought dead and lost to her in his babyhood. She wept for joy and brought him before the king; and seeing him living and so good to look upon, all men forgot the prophecy, and Priam welcomed him into the family and gave him a house of his own, like each of the other Trojan princes.

There he lived whenever he would, but at other times he would be away back to the oak woods of Mount Ida, to his love Oenone.

110  And so things went on happily enough for a while.

But meantime, across the Aegean Sea, another wedding had taken place, the marriage of King Menelaus of Sparta to the Princess Helen, whom men called Helen of the Fair Cheeks, the most beautiful of all mortal women. Her beauty was famous throughout the kingdoms of Greece, and many kings and princes had wished to marry her, among them Odysseus, whose kingdom was the rocky island of Ithaca.

Her father would have none of them, but gave her to Menelaus. Yet, because he feared trouble between her suitors

120  at a later time, he caused them all to swear that they would stand with her husband for her sake, if ever he had need of them. And between Helen and Odysseus, who married her cousin Penelope and loved her well, there was a lasting friendship that stood her in good stead when she had sore need of a friend, years afterward.

Even beyond the farthest bounds of Greece, the fame of Helen's beauty traveled, until it came at last to Troy, as Aphrodite had known that it would. And Paris no sooner heard of her than he determined to go and see for himself if

130  she was indeed as fair as men said. Oenone wept and begged him to stay with her; but he paid no heed, and his feet came no more up the track to her woodland cave. If Paris wanted a thing, then he must have it; so he begged a ship from his father, and he and his companions set out.

All the length of the Aegean Sea was before them, and the winds blew them often from their true course. But they came at last to their landfall, and ran the ship up the beach and climbed the long hill tracks that brought them to the fortress-palace of King Menelaus.

140    Slaves met them, as they met all strangers, in the outer court, and led them in to wash off the salt and the dust of the long journey. And presently, clad in fresh clothes, they were standing before the king in his great hall, where the fire burned on the raised hearth in the center and the king's favorite hounds lay sprawled about his feet.

"Welcome to you, strangers," said Menelaus. "Tell me now who you are and where you come from, and what brings you to my hall."

"I am a king's son, Paris by name, from Troy, far across the
150  sea," Paris told him. "And I come because the wish is on me to see distant places, and the fame of Menelaus has reached our shores, as a great king and a generous host to strangers."

"Sit then, and eat, for you must be way-weary with such far traveling," said the king.

And when they were seated, meat and fruit, and wine in golden cups were brought in and set before them. And while they ate and talked with their host, telling the adventures of their journey, Helen the queen came in from the women's quarters, two of her maidens following, one carrying her baby
160  daughter, one carrying her ivory spindle and distaff[5] laden with wool of the deepest violet color. And she sat down on the far side of the fire, the women's side, and began to spin. And as she spun, she listened to the stranger's tales of his journeying.

And in little snatched glances their eyes went to each other through the fronding[6] hearth-smoke. And Paris saw that Menelaus' queen was fairer even than the stories told, golden as a corn-stalk and sweet as wild honey. And Helen saw, above all things, that the stranger prince was young. Menelaus had been her father's choice, not hers, and though their marriage
170  was happy enough, he was much older than she was, with the first gray hairs already in his beard. There was no gray in the gold of Paris' beard, and his eyes were bright and there was laughter at the corners of his mouth. Her heart quickened as she looked at him, and once, still spinning, she snapped the violet thread.

---

[5] **distaff** (dĭs´tăf´): a staff that holds the unspun flax or wool from which the spinner draws thread when spinning by hand.

[6] **fronding** (frŏnd´ĭng): getting wispy; starting to look like the leaf of a fern, which is called a frond.

For many days Paris and his companions remained the guests of King Menelaus, and soon it was not enough for Paris to look at the queen. Poor Oenone was quite forgotten, and he did not know how to go away leaving Helen of the Fair
180 Cheeks behind.

So the days went by, and the prince and the queen walked together through the cool olive gardens and under the white-flowered almond trees of the palace; and he sat at her feet while she spun her violet wool, and sang her the songs of his own people.

And then one day the king rode out hunting. Paris made an excuse not to ride with him, and he and his companions remained behind. And when they were alone together, walking in the silvery shade of the olives while his
190 companions and her maidens amused themselves at a little distance, Paris told the queen that it was for sight of her that he had come so far, and that now he had seen her, he loved her to his heart's core and could not live without her.

"You should not have told me this," said Helen. "For I am another man's wife. And because you have told me it will be the worse for me when you go away and must leave me behind."

"Honey-sweet," said Paris, "my ship is in the bay; come with me now, while the king, your husband, is away from
200 home. For we belong together, you and I, like two slips of a vine sprung from the same stock."

And they talked together, on and on through the hot noontide with the crickets churring, he urging and she holding back. But he was Paris, who always got the things he wanted; and deep within her, her heart wanted the same thing.

And in the end she left her lord and her babe and her honor; and followed by his companions, with the maidens wailing and pleading behind them, he led her down the
210 mountain paths and through the passes to his ship waiting on the seashore.

So Paris had the bride that Aphrodite had promised him, and from that came all the sorrows that followed.

# SHIP-GATHERING

W HEN MENELAUS returned from hunting and found his queen fled with the Trojan prince, the black grief and the red rage came upon him, and he sent word of the wrong done to him and a furious call for aid to his brother, black-bearded Agamemnon, who was High King over all the other kings of Greece.

220     And from golden Mycenae of the Lion Gate where Agamemnon sat in his great hall, the call went out for men and ships. To ancient Nestor of Pylos, to Thisbe, where the wild doves croon, to rocky Pytho, to Ajax the mighty, Lord of Salamis, and Diomedes of the Loud War Cry whose land was Argos of the many horses, to the cunning Odysseus among the harsh hills of Ithaca, even far south to Idomeneus of Crete, and many more.

        And from Crete and Argos and Ithaca, from the mainland and the islands, the black ships put to sea, as the kings
230     gathered their men from the fields and the fishing and took up bows and spears for the keeping of their oath, to fetch back Helen of the Fair Cheeks and take vengeance upon Troy, whose prince had carried her away.

        Agamemnon waited for them with his own ships in the harbor of Aulis; and when they had gathered to him there, the great fleet sailed for Troy.

        But one of the war-leaders who should have been with them was lacking, and this was the way of it. Before ever Paris was born, Thetis of the Silver Feet had given a son to King
240     Peleus, and they called him Achilles. The gods had promised that if she dipped the babe in the Styx, which is one of the rivers of the underworld, the sacred water would proof him against death in battle. So, gladly she did as she was bidden, but dipping him headfirst in the dark and bitter flood, she held on to him by one foot. Thus her fingers, pressed about his heel, kept the waters from reaching that one spot. By the time she understood what she had done it was too late, for the thing could not be done again; so ever after she was afraid for her son, always afraid.

250     When he was old enough, his father sent him to Thessaly, with an older boy, Patroclus, for his companion, to Chiron, the wisest of all the Centaurs. And with the other boy, Chiron taught him to ride (on his own back) and trained him in all

the warrior skills of sword and spear and bow, and in making the music of the lyre, until the time came for him to return to his father's court.

But when the High King's **summons** went out and the black ships were launched for war, his mother sent him secretly to the Isle of Scyros, begging King Lycomedes to have him dressed as a maiden and hidden among his own daughters, so that he might be safe.

How it came about that Achilles agreed to this, no one knows. Maybe she cast some kind of spell on him, for love's sake. But there he remained among the princesses, while the ships gathered in the world outside.

But Thetis' loving plan failed after all, for, following the seaways eastward, part of the fleet put in to take on fresh water at Scyros, where the whisper was abroad that Prince Achilles was **concealed**.

King Lycomedes welcomed the warriors but denied all knowledge of the young prince. The leaders were desperate to find him, for Calchas, chief among the soothsayers who sailed with them, had said that they would not take Troy without him. Then Odysseus, who was not called the Resourceful for nothing, blackened his beard and eyebrows and put on the dress of a trader, turning his hair up under a seaman's red cap, and with a staff in one hand and a huge pack on his back went up to the palace.

When the girls heard that there was a trader in the palace forecourt, out from the women's quarters they all came running, Achilles among them, veiled like the rest, to

**summons**
(sŭm´ənz) *n.* A *summons* is a call or a notice by an authority to appear somewhere or to do something.

**conceal**
(kən-sēl´) *v.* If you *conceal* something, you hide it and keep it from being found or seen.

see him undo his pack. And when he had done so, each of them chose what she liked best: a wreath of gold, a necklace of amber, a pair of turquoise earrings blue as the sky, a skirt of embroidered scarlet silk, until they came to the bottom of the pack. And at the bottom of the pack lay a great sword of bronze, the hilt studded with golden nails. Then the last of the girls, still closely veiled, who had held back as though waiting all the while, swooped forward and caught it up, as
290 one well used to the handling of such weapons. And at the familiar feel of it, the spell that his mother had set upon him dissolved away.

"This for me!" said Prince Achilles, pulling off his veil.

Then the kings and chieftains of the fleet greeted and rejoiced over him. They stripped off his girl's garments and dressed him in kilt and cloak as befitted a warrior, with his new sword slung at his side; and they sent him back to his father's court to claim the ships and the fighting men that were his by right, that he might add them to the fleet.

300 His mother wept over him, saying, "I had hoped to keep you safe for the love I bear you. But now it must be for you to choose. If you bide here with me, you shall live long and happy. If you go forth now with the fighting men, you will make for yourself a name that shall last while men tell stories round the fire, even to the ending of the world. But you will not live to see the first gray hair in your beard, and you will come home no more to your father's hall."

"Short life and long fame for me," said Achilles, fingering his sword.

310 So his father gave him fifty ships, fully manned, and Patroclus to go with him for his friend and sword-companion. And his mother, weeping still, armed him in his father's armor; glorious war gear that Hephaestus, the smith of the gods, had made for him.

And he sailed to join the black ships on their way to Troy.

## QUARREL WITH THE HIGH KING

THE GREEKS did not have smooth sailing. Storms beat them this way and that, and more than once they met with enemy fleets and had to fight them off. But at last they came in sight of the coast below Troy city.

320      Then they made a race of it, the rowers quickening the oar beat, thrusting their ships through the water, each eager to come first to land. The race was won by the ship of Prince Protesilaus, but as the prince sprang ashore, an arrow from among the defenders took him in the throat and he dropped just above the tide line, the first of the Greeks to come ashore, the first man to die in the long war for Troy.

     The rest followed him and quickly drove back the Trojan warriors, who were ill prepared for so great an enemy war-host. And when that day's sun went down, they were
330 masters of the coastwise dunes and reedbeds and rough grass that fringed the great plain of Troy.

     They beached their ships, and built halls and huts in front of them to live in, so that in a while there was something like a seaport town. And in that town of turf and timber they lived while year after year of war went by.

     Nine times the wild almonds flowered and fruited on the rocky slopes below the city. Nine times summer dried out the tamarisk scrub among the grave mounds of long-dead kings. The ships' timbers rotted, and the high fierce hopes that the
340 Greeks had brought with them grew weary and dull-edged.

     They knew little of siege warfare. They did not seek to dig trenches round the city, nor to keep watch on the roads by which supplies and fighting men of allied countries might come in; nor did they try to break down the gates or scale the high walls. And the Trojans, ruled by an old king and a council of old men, remained for the most part within their city walls, or came out to skirmish[7] only a little way outside them, though Hector, their war-leader and foremost among the king's sons, would have attacked and stormed the Greek
350 camp if he had had his will.

     But there were other, lesser cities along the coast that were easier prey; and the men of the black ships raided these and drove off their cattle for food and their horses for the chariots that they had built, and the fairest of their women for slaves.

     On one of these raids far down the coast, when the almond trees were coming into flower for the tenth time, they captured and brought back two beautiful maidens, Chryseis and Briseis, among the spoils[8] of war. Chryseis was given to

---

[7] **skirmish** (skûr´mĭsh):  to engage in a minor battle in war.
[8] **spoils** (spoilz):  property taken from the losers by the winners of a battle or conflict.

Agamemnon, who as High King always received the richest of
the plunder, while Briseis was awarded to Achilles, who had
led the raid.

Chryseis' father, who was a priest of Apollo, the Sun
God, followed and came to the Greek camp, begging for his
daughter back again, and offering much gold for her ransom.
But Agamemnon refused, and bade the old man be gone, with
cruel insults. And there it seemed that the thing was ended.

But soon after, fever came upon the Greek camp. Many
died, and the smoke of the death-fires hung day and night
along the shore, and in **despair** the Greeks begged the
soothsayer Calchas to tell them the cause of the evil. And
Calchas watched the flight of birds and made patterns in the
sand, and told them that Apollo, angry on behalf of his priest,
was shooting arrows of **pestilence** into the camp from his
silver bow; and that his anger would not be cooled until the
maiden Chryseis was returned to her father.

On hearing this, Agamemnon fell into a great rage, and
though the other leaders urged him to release the girl, he
swore that if he did so, then he would have Briseis out from
Achilles' hall in her place.

Then Achilles, who had grown to care for Briseis, would
have drawn his sword to fight for her. But gray-eyed Athene,
who was for the Greeks because Aphrodite was for Paris and
the Trojans, put it into his mind that no man might fight the
High King, and that all manner of evils, from defeat in battle
to bad harvests, would come of it if he did. Even so, a bitter
quarrel flared between them, though wise old Nestor tried to
make peace.

Achilles, who despite his youth was the proudest and
hottest-hearted of all the Greek leaders, called Agamemnon a
greedy coward with the face of a dog and the heart of a deer.
"It is small part you play in the fighting, but you take other
men's prizes from them when the fighting is over, robbing
them of the reward and the honor that is rightfully theirs—
for this one reason, that you have the power to do it, because
you are the High King!"

"I am the High King!" agreed Agamemnon, his face
blackening as though a storm cloud gathered over it. "I have
the power, even as you say, and let you not forget it! Also, as
High King I have the right, and let you not forget that either,
you who are no more than a prince among other princes!"

**despair**
(dĭ-spâr´) *n.* A
complete loss of
hope is called *despair.*

**pestilence**
(pĕs´tə-ləns) *n.* A
*pestilence* is often
a fatal illness or
evil influence that
spreads quickly to
many people.

The quarrel roared on, despite all that the other leaders could do to stop it. And in the end it was Achilles who had the final word.

"Lord Agamemnon, you have dishonored me; and therefore now I swear on all the gods that I will fight for you no more! Nor will I take any part in this struggle against Troy until my honor is made good to me again!" And he strode out from the council gathering and went back to his own part of the camp, his own hall and his own black ships; and all the men of his own country with him.

410

# "I am the High King!"

Then Agamemnon, in a black and silent rage, caused Chryseis to be put into one of his ships, and cattle with her for a sacrifice to Apollo, and ordered Odysseus to take command of the ship and return the girl to her father. And as soon as the ship had sailed, he sent his heralds[9] to fetch Briseis from Achilles' hall and bring her to his own.

Achilles made no more attempt to resist, and stood by as though turned to stone while the girl was led weeping away. But when she was gone he went down to the cold seashore and flung himself down upon the tide line and wept his heart away.

420

And his mother, Thetis of the Silver Feet, heard the voice of his furious grief from her home in the crystal palaces of

---

[9] **heralds** (hĕr′əldz): those who announce important news; messengers.

the sea, and she came up through the waters like a sea mist rising, no one seeing her except her son. And she sat down beside him and stroked his hair and his bowed shoulders and said, "What bitter grief is this? Tell me the darkness that is in your heart."

So, chokingly, Achilles told her what she asked; and in his grief and bitter fury, he demanded that she go to Zeus the Thunderer, chief of all the gods, and pray him for a Trojan victory that should make the High King feel the loss of his greatest captain and do him honor and beg for his return.

Thetis promised that she would do as he asked. But it could not be done at once, for the father of the gods was absent about some matter in the far-most part of his world, and it must wait for his return to Olympus.

So for twelve days Achilles remained by his ships, waiting and **brooding** on his wrongs. And Odysseus, having returned Chryseis to her father with the proper sacrifices and prayers and purification, came again to the ship-strand, with the promise that Apollo was no longer set against them, and had lifted the plague-curse away.

But still Briseis wept in the hall of the High King, and Achilles sat among his ships, nursing his anger as though it were a red rose in his breast.

**brood**
(bro͞od) *v.* If you *brood*, you are deep in thought, maybe worrying or feeling depressed about something.

**COLLABORATIVE DISCUSSION** Gods and goddesses in Greek mythology often create or add to problems for mortals. With a partner, review the myth and discuss how gods and goddesses become involved in the lives of humans. Do they solve problems, or make them worse?

# Describe Stories: Myth

A **myth** is a traditional story told long ago in a particular culture. Myths were created as attempts to explain occurrences in nature, describe historical events, or act as a guide to social customs and human nature. Like fictional stories, myths have elements such as setting, characters, plot, conflict, and resolution. In addition, specific elements of myth often include:

- events in nature, such as the origin of the world and the seasons
- heroes, such as warriors or leaders who have admirable qualities
- gods and goddesses, who are immortal and have superhuman abilities but possess human emotions and shortcomings

Arguments or conflicts between two or more gods occur frequently in myths. Other characteristics might include a journey, quest, or battle, or a mortal's good or bad interaction with a god or goddess.

To analyze myths, ask questions such as the following:

- What is the conflict in the myth? Is it resolved? How?
- Who are the main characters? How do these characters change or respond as the plot moves toward resolution?
- Why was this myth important to the culture that created it?

# Determine Theme

A **theme** is a message or lesson about life or human nature from a story or myth. To determine and analyze a myth's theme, ask yourself these questions: *What is the important lesson the myth teaches? How is this message conveyed?*

Summarizing key events may also help you determine a myth's theme. To **summarize** plot, make a list of the important events. Here is a list of events from *Black Ships Before Troy*:

- A last son, Paris, is born to King Priam and Queen Hecuba.
- However, soothsayers have foretold that this son will burn down Troy.
- The king orders a servant to leave the baby in the wilderness.
- A herdsman finds the baby and raises Paris.

These events explain how the king thought he could avoid what had been foretold by leaving his son to die in the wilderness. His error points out this theme or message: *You can't change one's fate or destiny*.

As you analyze *Black Ships Before Troy*, look for elements of myth and use them to help you determine the theme or message.

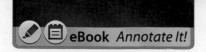
# Analyzing the Text

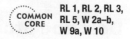

COMMON CORE

RL 1, RL 2, RL 3, RL 5, W 2a–b, W 9a, W 10

**Cite Text Evidence** Support your responses with evidence from the text.

1. **Summarize** Review lines 1–35. What events create the central conflict of the myth? Tell why this myth might have been created.

2. **Identify** Review lines 54–70. What elements of myth do you find?

3. **Infer** Reread lines 86–89 and lines 126–134. What words would you use to describe Paris' character? Tell whether you think these traits are strengths or weaknesses and why.

4. **Cause/Effect** Review lines 202–236. What happens to set a great battle in motion? Explain the connection between this event and the fortune told to Paris' parents.

5. **Interpret** Reread the story of Achilles in lines 237–249. What theme does it share about mothers? Tell what life lesson you feel it teaches about strength and weakness.

6. **Analyze** Review lines 355–375. Explain how this conflict might have taught an important lesson in the culture of the ancient Greeks.

7. **Predict** Review lines 411–446. Has the conflict Achilles faces been resolved? Tell how this might affect what happens in events to come.

## PERFORMANCE TASK

**Writing Activity: Analysis** Several major events occur in *Black Ships Before Troy*. Choose one event to analyze, explaining how the plot unfolds and how the characters respond or change. Be sure to cite evidence from the text.

- First, summarize the key event and the conflict that takes place.

- Take notes on what the main characters are like and what they think and do.

- Use your summary and notes as you write your essay. Include evidence from the text to support your ideas.

# Critical Vocabulary

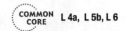

| weary | summons | conceal |
|-------|---------|---------|
| despair | pestilence | brood |

**Practice and Apply** Choose the correct response to answer each question.

1. Which of these would a group of **weary** toddlers be likely to do—play a wild game of tag or take a nap? Why?

2. Would a messenger be likely to **conceal** a **summons** from his king? Why or why not?

3. If a hiker experienced **despair** because she lost her supplies, would she rest and **brood** over her situation? Why or why not?

4. Would you go to a place where **pestilence** had spread? Why or why not?

# Vocabulary Strategy: Cause-to-Effect Analogies

An **analogy** presents a relationship between pairs of words. Sometimes writers use analogies to explain unfamiliar ideas. A typical analogy begins with a pair of items that are related in some way. One common word relationship is cause to effect. **Cause-to-effect analogies** show a **cause,** something that happens, and the **effect,** something that happens as a result. Here is an example, displayed first as a sentence and then with special symbols:

> *Weary* is to *sleep* as *virus* is to *pestilence.*
>
> weary : sleep :: virus : pestilence

Both versions express a cause-to-effect analogy: *weary* and *virus* are the causes; *sleep* and *pestilence* are the effects. In the second version, the single colons stand for "is to" and the double colon stands for "as." Examining the full analogy helps you understand how the word pairs are related.

**Practice and Apply** Complete each cause-to-effect analogy by choosing the best answer.

1. drought : famine :: _____ : despair
   **a.** tragedy
   **b.** friendship

2. recklessness : _____ :: pain : discomfort
   **a.** safety
   **b.** accident

3. crime : imprisonment :: _____ : accomplishment
   **a.** completion
   **b.** perseverance

4. quarrel : discord :: _____ : merriment
   **a.** joking
   **b.** talking

# Language Conventions: Spell Words Correctly

Spelling words correctly is important if you want to communicate your ideas well. Misspelled words can confuse readers and weaken the ideas you're trying to express.

Some words change spelling when suffixes are added while other words do not. Here are some examples:

**argue + -ing = arguing    surround + -ed = surrounded**

It can be difficult to remember which words have spelling changes and which ones do not. Here are two rules that will help you when you add suffixes to words.

---

Before adding a suffix beginning with a vowel or **y** to a word ending in silent **e,** drop the **e.**

**amuse + -ing = amusing    love + -able = lovable**

In most words ending with a consonant, simply add the suffix without changing the spelling of the base word.

**demand + -ed = demanded    strong + -er = stronger**

---

As a writer, you don't want a misspelled word to interrupt or confuse your readers, so spelling words correctly is important!

**Practice and Apply**  Complete each sentence by forming a new word from the base word and suffix in parentheses.

1. The golden apple was _____ to three goddesses. (desire + -able)

2. Paris _____ to give Athene or Hera the apple. (refuse + -ed)

3. Helen and Odysseus had a _____ friendship. (last + -ing)

4. King Priam is _____ Paris into his family. (welcome + -ing)

5. Achilles _____ to join the black ships on their way to Troy. (sail + -ed)

6. Thetis was _____ about Achilles going into battle. (nerve + -ous)

7. The Trojan warriors were not _____ for the Greeks. (prepare + -ed)

**Kate Hovey** *first read the stories of Greek mythology in third grade and has been reading them ever since. Her interest in gods and goddesses grew during her childhood visits to the Getty Villa, a museum in Malibu, California, that was built to imitate an ancient Roman villa. The museum's collection of marble statues from the Greco-Roman period helped her imagine the ancient voices of the gods and goddesses that inspire her. Hovey is a metalsmith and mask-maker as well, using her arts of poetry, storytelling, and drama to bring the world of Greek mythology to life.*

# The Apple of Discord I

Poem by Kate Hovey

**SETTING A PURPOSE** As you read, focus on how Eris compares herself to the other gods and goddesses.

Eris (Goddess of Discord) Speaks

Lofty[1] Olympians
   like to exclude
lesser immortals
   who aren't imbued[2]
5  with the kind of power
   they so admire.
Still, I'm a goddess,
   and I require
certain courtesies,
10    a little care and concern,

---

[1] **lofty** (lôf´tē):  very tall; having high qualities of character; arrogant or pompous.
[2] **imbued** (ĭm-byo͞od´):  permeated; spreading or flowing throughout.

but the gods are hardheaded;
   they never learn.
So I came, uninvited,
   to the sea queen's wedding
15 and threw a gold apple
   far out on the spreading,
goddess-strewn lawn.
   Inscribed, "for the fairest,"
it caused a commotion—
20    weren't they embarrassed
to squabble that way?
   Hera, Athena,
and vain Aphrodite,
   tugging and pulling—
25 what high and mighty
   hypocrites![3] They claim
*I'm* the foul one!
They think they can blame
   my wedding surprise
30 for the horrors at Troy,
   when *they* are the guilty ones—
they who destroy,
   who sacrifice heroes,
Earth's glorious sons,
35    like bulls on an altar—
brave, innocent ones.
   To their lasting shame,
they let Troy burn.
   The gods are hardheaded;
40    they never learn.

**COLLABORATIVE DISCUSSION** How does Eris, the Goddess
of Discord, see herself in relation to other gods and goddesses?
Discuss your ideas with a partner, using evidence from the poem.

---

[3] **hypocrites** (hĭp´ə-krĭts´): people who pretend to have beliefs, feelings, or virtues
  that they actually do not have; falseness.

# Determine Meanings of Words and Phrases

If a writer wants to make fun of a well-known story, he or she writes a parody of it. A **parody** is a humorous imitation of another writer's work. Usually a parody will:

- follow the form of the original text or story, but also might put a twist on the story and use a different form
- tell the story from a different character's point of view

Writers of parodies often add humor through exaggerated descriptions and double meanings of words and phrases. For example, in "The Apple of Discord I," when Eris describes the three goddesses as "high and mighty hypocrites," (lines 25–26) she is using figurative language that means the goddesses are arrogant and bossy. However, she also emphasizes the literal meanings of the words—the powerful goddesses live high atop Mount Olympus and they are, indeed, mighty.

As you analyze elements of parody in "The Apple of Discord I," think about these questions:

- How does the writer add a twist to or change the original story as told in *Black Ships Before Troy: The Story of The Iliad*? How does this add humor to the parody?
- How does the writer use language in a humorous way?

# Compare and Contrast Genres

When you compare and contrast a myth and a parody of the same myth, you analyze the characteristics of each text, how the events in each version are presented, and the techniques each author uses to achieve his or her purpose.

Ask these questions to compare and contrast a myth and a parody of the same myth:

- What is each author's purpose for writing?
- What elements of myth are found in each text?
- How is each author's presentation of events alike and different?
- How are characters portayed in each text? How are they alike and different?
- The author of the parody makes fun of the original work. What techniques does he or she use to accomplish this goal?

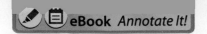 

# Analyzing the Text

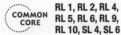 COMMON CORE  RL 1, RL 2, RL 4, RL 5, RL 6, RL 9, RL 10, SL 4, SL 6

**Cite Text Evidence**   Support your responses with evidence from the text.

1. **Infer**  Reread lines 1–7. Eris describes herself as one of the "lesser immortals." What phrase does she use to describe the three goddesses? Tell why this description is humorous.

2. **Interpret**  Reread lines 19–26. What words and phrases does Eris use to describe the three goddesses and their behavior? Explain what these word choices tell you about what she thinks of them, and how she sees herself.

3. **Analyze**  Compare Eris' word choices in lines 1–27 with those in lines 28–40. As the poem progresses, how does Eris' tone change? Tell what language choices contribute to the change in tone.

4. **Infer**  Review lines 1–40 of "The Apple of Discord I." What is the **theme,** or message about life, of the poem? What repeated statements help you infer the theme?

5. **Compare**  A **symbol** is a person, place, or thing that stands for something else. In this poem and in *Black Ships Before Troy,* what is the symbol and what does it stand for? Do you think that the symbolic meaning is the same or different in the two texts? Cite evidence from both texts to support your ideas.

6. **Compare and Contrast**  Review lines 1–94 of *Black Ships Before Troy.* Compare how the events in the myth are described with Eris' description of the events in "The Apple of Discord I." How are the descriptions alike? How are they different?

---

# PERFORMANCE TASK

**Speaking Activity: Speech**  "The Apple of Discord I" is told from the point of view of Eris, the Goddess of Discord. Do you agree with her that Hera, Aphrodite, and Athene are the ones responsible for the "horrors at Troy"? Give a speech that presents your opinion. Use facts and details from the poem to support it.

- Review the poem. Determine whether or not you agree with Eris.

- Write a statement that clearly presents your claim.
- Draft your speech, using evidence from the poem to support your claim.
- Practice your speech, using appropriate eye contact, adequate volume, and clear pronunciation.
- Present your ideas in a logical, organized way that helps listeners understand them.

**Ai-Ling Louie** (b. 1949) *grew up in the suburbs of New York City hearing stories from her parents and their friends. While working as a teacher and a children's librarian, Louie wrote her first book,* Yeh-Shen: A Cinderella Story from China, *a traditional folk tale passed down from her grandmother. The original story is one of the oldest written Cinderella stories in the world (A.D. 618–907), written several centuries before the first European Cinderella story (A.D. 1634, Italy). Now, Louie devotes her time to writing, family, and visiting schools to share stories, just as her family did for her.*

# Yeh-Shen

## A CINDERELLA STORY FROM CHINA

Chinese Folk Tale by Ai-Ling Louie

**SETTING A PURPOSE** As you read, pay attention to how the story of Yeh-Shen is similar to and different from familiar Cinderella stories that you know.

In the dim past, even before the Ch'in and the Han dynasties,[1] there lived a cave chief of southern China by the name of Wu. As was the custom in those days, Chief Wu had taken two wives. Each wife in their turn had presented Wu with a baby daughter. But one of the wives sickened and died, and not too many days after that Chief Wu took to his bed and died too.

Yeh-Shen, the little orphan, grew to girlhood in her stepmother's home. She was a bright child and lovely too, with skin as smooth as ivory and dark pools for eyes. Her stepmother was jealous of all this beauty and goodness, for her

10

---

[1] **Ch'in** (chǐn) **and the Han** (hän) **dynasties** (dī´nə-stēz): groups that held power in China. The Ch'in dynasty ruled from 221 to 206 B.C., and the Han dynasty ruled from 206 B.C. to A.D. 220.

own daughter was not pretty at all. So in her displeasure, she gave poor Yeh-Shen the heaviest and most unpleasant chores.

The only friend that Yeh-Shen had to her name was a fish she had caught and raised. It was a beautiful fish with golden eyes, and every day it would come out of the water and rest its head on the bank of the pond, waiting for Yeh-Shen to feed it. Stepmother gave Yeh-Shen little enough food for herself, but the orphan child always found something to share with her
20  fish, which grew to enormous size.

Somehow the stepmother heard of this. She was terribly angry to discover that Yeh-Shen had kept a secret from her. She hurried down to the pond, but she was unable to see the fish, for Yeh-Shen's pet wisely hid itself. The stepmother, however, was a crafty woman, and she soon thought of a plan. She walked home and called out, "Yeh-Shen, go and collect some firewood. But wait! The neighbors might see you. Leave your filthy coat here!" The minute the girl was out of sight, her stepmother slipped on the coat herself and went down again
30  to the pond. This time the big fish saw Yeh-Shen's familiar jacket and heaved itself onto the bank, expecting to be fed. But the stepmother, having hidden a dagger in her sleeve, stabbed the fish, wrapped it in her garments, and took it home to cook for dinner.

When Yeh-Shen came to the pond that evening, she found her pet had disappeared. Overcome with grief, the girl **collapsed** on the ground and dropped her tears into the still waters of the pond.

"Ah, poor child!" a voice said.

40  Yeh-Shen sat up to find a very old man looking down at her. He wore the coarsest of clothes, and his hair flowed down over his shoulders.

"Kind uncle, who may you be?" Yeh-Shen asked.

"That is not important, my child. All you must know is that I have been sent to tell you of the wondrous powers of your fish."

"My fish, but sir . . ." The girl's eyes filled with tears, and she could not go on.

The old man sighed and said, "Yes, my child, your fish
50  is no longer alive, and I must tell you that your stepmother is once more the cause of your sorrow." Yeh-Shen gasped in horror, but the old man went on. "Let us not dwell on things that are past," he said, "for I have come bringing you a gift.

**collapse**
(kə-lăps´) *v.* If you *collapse*, you fall down suddenly.

Now you must listen carefully to this: The bones of your fish are filled with a powerful spirit. Whenever you are in serious need, you must kneel before them and let them know your heart's desire. But do not waste their gifts."

Yeh-Shen wanted to ask the old sage[2] many more questions, but he rose to the sky before she could utter another word. With heavy heart, Yeh-Shen made her way to the dung heap to gather the remains of her friend.

Time went by, and Yeh-Shen, who was often left alone, took comfort in speaking to the bones of her fish. When she was hungry, which happened quite often, Yeh-Shen asked the bones for food. In this way, Yeh-Shen managed to live from day to day, but she lived in dread that her stepmother would discover her secret and take even that away from her.

So the time passed and spring came. Festival time was approaching: It was the busiest time of the year. Such cooking and cleaning and sewing there was to be done! Yeh-Shen had hardly a moment's rest. At the spring festival young men and young women from the village hoped to meet and to choose whom they would marry. How Yeh-Shen longed to go! But her stepmother had other plans. She hoped to find a husband for her own daughter and did not want any man to see the beauteous Yeh-Shen first. When finally the holiday arrived, the stepmother and her daughter dressed themselves in their finery and filled their baskets with sweetmeats.[3] "You must remain at home now, and watch to see that no one steals fruit from our trees," her stepmother told Yeh-Shen, and then she departed for the **banquet** with her own daughter.

As soon as she was alone, Yeh-Shen went to speak to the bones of her fish. "Oh, dear friend," she said, kneeling before the precious bones, "I long to go to the festival, but I cannot show myself in these rags. Is there somewhere I could borrow clothes fit to wear to the feast?" At once she found herself dressed in a gown of azure blue,[4] with a cloak of kingfisher feathers draped around her shoulders. Best of all, on her tiny feet were the most beautiful slippers she had ever seen. They were woven of golden threads, in a pattern like the scales of a fish, and the **glistening** soles were made of solid gold. There

**banquet**
(băng´kwĭt) *n.* A *banquet* is a huge, elaborate feast with many kinds of food and drink.

**glisten**
(glĭs´ən) *v.* An object that *glistens* is sparkly and shiny.

---

[2] **sage** (sāj): a person respected for his or her wisdom, judgment, and experience.
[3] **sweetmeats** (swēt´mēts´): any kind of sweet food or delicacy.
[4] **azure blue** (ăzh´ər bloo): a light purplish blue.

was magic in the shoes, for they should have been quite heavy, yet when Yeh-Shen walked, her feet felt as light as air.

"Be sure you do not lose your golden shoes," said the spirit of the bones. Yeh-Shen promised to be careful. Delighted with her transformation[5], she bid a fond farewell to the bones of her fish as she slipped off to join in the merrymaking.

That day Yeh-Shen turned many a head as she appeared at the feast. All around her people whispered, "Look at that beautiful girl! Who can she be?"

But above this, Stepsister was heard to say, "Mother, does she not resemble our Yeh-Shen?"

Upon hearing this, Yeh-Shen jumped up and ran off before her stepsister could look closely at her. She raced down the mountainside, and in doing so, she lost one of her golden slippers. No sooner had the shoe fallen from her foot than all her fine clothes turned back to rags. Only one thing remained—a tiny golden shoe. Yeh-Shen hurried to the bones of her fish and returned the slipper, promising to find its mate. But now the bones were silent. Sadly Yeh-Shen realized that she had lost her only friend. She hid the little shoe in her bedstraw, and went outside to cry. Leaning against a fruit tree, she sobbed and sobbed until she fell asleep.

The stepmother left the gathering to check on Yeh-Shen, but when she returned home she found the girl sound asleep, with her arms wrapped around a fruit tree. So thinking no more of her, the stepmother rejoined the party. Meantime, a villager had found the shoe. Recognizing its worth, he sold it to a merchant, who presented it in turn to the king of the island kingdom of T'o Han.

The king was more than happy to accept the slipper as a gift. He was **entranced** by the tiny thing, which was shaped of the most precious of metals, yet which made no sound when touched to stone. The more he marveled at its beauty, the more determined he became to find the woman to whom the shoe belonged. A search was begun among the ladies of his own kingdom, but all who tried on the sandal found it impossibly small. **Undaunted**, the king ordered the search widened to include the cave women from the countryside where the slipper had been found. Since he realized it would take many years for every woman to come to his island and test her

**entrance**
(ĕn-trăns´) v. To *entrance* is to fill with delight or wonder.

**undaunted**
(ŭn-dôn´tĭd) adj. An *undaunted* person is someone who is strongly courageous, not discouraged or disheartened.

---

[5] **transformation** (trăns´fər-mā´shən): a significant change in appearance or form, usually for the better.

foot in the slipper, the king thought of a way to get the right woman to come forward. He ordered the sandal placed in a pavilion[6] by the side of the road near where it had been found, and his herald announced that the shoe was to be returned to its original owner. Then from a nearby hiding place, the king and his men settled down to watch and wait for a woman with tiny feet to come and claim her slipper.

140   All that day the pavilion was crowded with cave women who had come to test a foot in the shoe. Yeh-Shen's stepmother and stepsister were among them, but not Yeh-Shen—they had told her to stay home. By day's end, although many women had eagerly tried to put on the slipper, it still had not been worn. Wearily, the king continued his vigil[7] into the night.

> ## All that day the pavilion was crowded with cave women who had come to test a foot in the shoe.

It wasn't until the blackest part of night, while the moon hid behind a cloud, that Yeh-Shen dared to show her face at the pavilion, and even then she tiptoed **timidly** across the wide floor. Sinking down to her knees, the girl in rags 150   examined the tiny shoe. Only when she was sure that this was the missing mate to her own golden slipper did she dare pick it up. At last she could return both little shoes to the fish bones. Surely then her beloved spirit would speak to her again.

Now the king's first thought, on seeing Yeh-Shen take the precious slipper, was to throw the girl into prison as a thief. But when she turned to leave, he caught a glimpse of her face.

**timid**
(tĭmʹĭd) *adj.* To act in a *timid* manner is to act shyly, fearfully, or hesitantly.

---

[6] **pavilion** (pə-vilʹyən): a decorated tent.

[7] **vigil** (vĭjʹəl): a time of watching, often during normal sleeping hours.

At once the king was struck by the sweet harmony of her features, which seemed so out of keeping with the rags she wore. It was then that he took a closer look and noticed that she walked upon the tiniest feet he had ever seen.

160

With a wave of his hand, the king signaled that this tattered creature was to be allowed to depart with the golden slipper. Quietly, the king's men slipped off and followed her home.

All this time, Yeh-Shen was unaware of the excitement she had caused. She had made her way home and was about to hide both sandals in her bedding when there was a pounding at the door. Yeh-Shen went to see who it was—and found a king at her doorstep. She was very frightened at first, but

170

the king spoke to her in a kind voice and asked her to try the golden slippers on her feet. The maiden did as she was told, and as she stood in her golden shoes, her rags were transformed once more into the feathered cloak and beautiful azure gown.

Her loveliness made her seem a heavenly being, and the king suddenly knew in his heart that he had found his true love.

Not long after this, Yeh-Shen was married to the king. But fate was not so gentle with her stepmother and stepsister.

180

Since they had been unkind to his beloved, the king would not permit Yeh-Shen to bring them to his palace. They remained in their cave home, where one day, it is said, they were crushed to death in a shower of flying stones.

**COLLABORATIVE DISCUSSION**  With a small group, discuss how story elements, such as characters, setting, and plot events, in the story of Yeh-Shen and other Cinderella stories are alike and different.

# Describe Stories: Folk Tales

A **folk tale** is a story that has been passed down from generation to generation by being told aloud. No matter what culture they come from, folk tales are alike in a number of ways.

- They are often set in the distant past.
- They may include humans and animals as characters, as well as superhuman beings that behave in ways that humans cannot.
- Story events may involve fantastic or supernatural occurrences that could not take place in the real world.
- A wise lesson or message about life is often presented.

Like other types of stories, folk tales have story elements such as setting, characters, plot, conflict, and resolution. As you analyze *Yeh-Shen*, ask:

- Who are the main characters? How does the central character change or respond as the story progresses?
- How would you summarize the conflict and main plot events? How is the conflict resolved?
- What important lesson or message does this folk tale share?

# Describe Stories: Foreshadowing

Stories that are suspenseful are exciting to read. Foreshadowing is one way writers add suspense to a story. **Foreshadowing** is a hint that a writer provides to suggest that future events will take place in a story. It makes readers eager to find out what happens, creating suspense as the story unfolds.

When Yeh-Shen first meets a mysterious old man, he tells her how the spirit of a fish can provide help when she needs it. Then he warns her not to waste its gifts. This foreshadowing suggests to readers that a time may come when Yeh-Shen will not be able to turn to the fish's spirit for assistance.

As you analyze *Yeh-Shen*, look for examples of foreshadowing.

- Pay attention to warnings that characters share, references to danger, or unpleasant outcomes. Also note how the setting impacts the story.
- Use foreshadowing to make predictions about what might happen later on in the story.
- Follow the events as the story's plot unfolds to find out whether your predictions were accurate.

# Analyzing the Text

COMMON CORE · RL 1, RL 2, RL 3, RL 5, RL 9, W 3a–e

**Cite Text Evidence**   Support your responses with evidence from the text.

1. **Identify**  Review lines 1–20. What elements of folk tales can you identify in these lines?

2. **Cause/Effect**  Reread lines 21–34. Describe what happens to the fish and explain why it happens.

3. **Compare**  Review lines 39–61. A magic helper, like the old man, is sometimes found in folk tales. How is this magic helper similar to and different from magic helpers in other stories you know?

4. **Predict**  Reread lines 82–97. What warning does Yeh-Shen receive from the spirit of the fish? Using this foreshadowing, what might you predict will happen?

5. **Summarize**  Summarize the events that unfold in lines 139–183. How do they lead to the resolution of the story's conflict?

6. **Infer**  What is the **theme,** or message about life, of *Yeh-Shen: A Cinderella Story from China*? Explain how the events in the story contribute to the theme.

## PERFORMANCE TASK

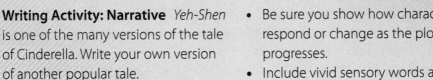

**Writing Activity: Narrative** *Yeh-Shen* is one of the many versions of the tale of Cinderella. Write your own version of another popular tale.

- First, decide how your tale will be similar to and different from the original version.
- Use narrative techniques, such as dialogue and description, to present and develop plot events.

- Be sure you show how characters respond or change as the plot progresses.
- Include vivid sensory words and phrases to help readers "see" characters and events.
- End your story with a strong resolution to the plot and its conflict.

# Critical Vocabulary

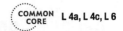 

| collapse | banquet | glisten |
|----------|---------|---------|
| entrance | undaunted | timid |

**Practice and Apply**  Answer each question.

1. When have you been so tired you could have **collapsed**? Why?

2. When have you been to a **banquet**? What was it like?

3. When have you seen something **glisten**? Tell about it.

4. When have you been **entranced** by something? Tell about it.

5. When were you **undaunted** by a difficult task? What did you do?

6. Have you ever seen someone who was **timid**? Tell about it.

# Vocabulary Strategy: Using a Glossary

A **glossary** is a list of specialized terms and their definitions. As with a dictionary, terms are arranged in alphabetical order. Sometimes a glossary includes pronunciation and syllabication for terms. A glossary is usually located at the back of a book. Most often, if a word is in boldface type in the text, you will find the term in the glossary. Glossaries can be useful when:

| you want to find more information about a term that is not defined |
|---|
| you want to check the meaning of a word you infer from context |
| you are studying for a test and want to review the meaning of key terms |
| you do not have a dictionary available |

Many textbooks include glossaries. Some, like this one, have more than one glossary. Each glossary includes terms in a particular category. In this textbook, for example, you will find glossaries for Academic Vocabulary, Critical Vocabulary, and Literary and Informational Terms.

**Practice and Apply**  Use the glossaries at the end of this book to answer the questions.

1. Is *foreshadowing* the same thing as *suspense*? Explain your answer.

2. What words or phrases mean about the same thing as *undaunted*?

3. How are the syllables in *technician* divided?

4. How is *generalization* different from *conclusion*?

# Language Conventions:
# Spell Words Correctly

Spelling words correctly is important if you want to communicate your ideas well. Misspelled words can confuse readers and weaken the ideas you're trying to express.

You know that when you want to show that something is happening now or has happened in the past, you add *-ed* or *-ing* to the verb. Keep in mind, though, that for one-syllable words with a short vowel that end in a consonant, you double the consonant when you add *-ed* or *-ing*. Here are some examples:

**wrap   wrapped**      **hit   hitting**      **drag   dragging**

If you don't double the consonant when you add *-ed* or *-ing*, the word you form will have a long vowel sound and may be confusing to readers, especially if it is not a recognizable word.

> **The storm drains were *cloged* with leaves and branches.**

Sometimes the misspelling will confuse a reader because it is a recognizable word, but it doesn't make sense in the sentence.

> **Megan froze as the *taping* at her window grew louder and more insistent.**

As a writer, you don't want a misspelled word to interrupt or confuse your readers, so spelling words correctly is important!

**Practice and Apply**  Write the past or present form of each verb in parentheses to complete each sentence.

1. At the airport, Meesha greeted her aunt and _____ her. (hug)

2. We were _____ to stop by the art museum if we had time. (plan)

3. Kevin sliced the tomatoes, and Gordon _____ the celery. (chop)

4. The student group was _____ with ideas for a holiday fair. (brim)

5. First, Ms. Chester _____ the old varnish from the bookshelves. (strip)

6. Clark waited in his room, idly _____ his guitar. (strum)

# The Prince and the Pauper

Novel by Mark Twain Dramatized by Joellen Bland

**Background**  *The historical novel* The Prince and the Pauper *was written by* **Mark Twain** *in 1882; it was his first attempt at historical fiction. The tale takes place in England in 1547, the year that Prince Edward, the nine-year-old son of King Henry VIII, was crowned King Edward VI.*

*The novel has been adapted into stage, film, and even comic book versions. The adaptation you are about to read was written by* **Joellen Bland**, *who has been writing scripted versions of classic stories for more than 30 years. This one-act play continues the tradition of this famous novel and its travels through American culture.*

**Mark Twain**  *(1835–1910) is one of America's greatest and most beloved writers. His real name was Samuel Clemens, but he changed it when he began his writing career. Twain was born in Florida, Missouri. When he was four years old, he moved with his family to Hannibal, Missouri, a bustling town along the Mississippi River, where he lived until he was seventeen. Hannibal and the Mississippi River inspired many of Twain's most famous novels, including* The Adventures of Tom Sawyer (1876) *and* The Adventures of Huckleberry Finn (1885). *Twain wrote 28 books and many short stories, letters, and comic sketches, all for the enjoyment of readers for many decades to come.*

**SETTING A PURPOSE**  As you read, pay attention to how the details of the setting, characters' actions, feelings, and events build and support the themes of the play.

## CHARACTERS

Edward, Prince of Wales
Tom Canty, the Pauper
Lord Hertford
Lord St. John
King Henry VIII
Herald
Miles Hendon
John Canty, Tom's father
Hugo, a young thief
Two Women

Justice
Constable
Jailer
Sir Hugh Hendon
Two Prisoners
Two Guards
Three Pages
Lords and Ladies
Villagers

## Scene 1

**Time:** *1547.*

**Setting:** *Westminster Palace, England. Gates leading to courtyard are at right. Slightly to the left, off courtyard and inside gates, interior of palace anteroom¹ is visible. There is a couch with a rich robe draped on it, screen at rear, bellcord, mirror, chairs, and a table with*
10  *bowl of nuts, and a large golden seal on it. Piece of armor hangs on one wall. Exits are rear and downstage.*

**At Curtain Rise:** *Two Guards— one at right, one at left—stand in front of gates, and several* Villagers *hover nearby, straining to see into courtyard where* Prince *may be seen through fence, playing. Two Women enter right.*

20  **1st Woman.** I have walked all morning just to have a glimpse of Westminster Palace.

**2nd Woman.** Maybe if we can get near enough to the gates, we can have a glimpse of the young Prince. (Tom Canty, *dirty and ragged, comes out of crowd and steps close to gates.*)

**Tom.** I have always dreamed of
30  seeing a real Prince! (*Excited, he presses his nose against gates.*)

**1st Guard.** Mind your manners, you young beggar! (*Seizes* Tom *by collar and sends him sprawling into crowd.* Villagers *laugh, as* Tom *slowly gets to his feet.*)

**Prince** (*rushing to gates*). How dare you treat a poor subject of the King in such a manner! Open the gates
40  and let him in! (*As* Villagers *see* Prince, *they take off their hats and bow low.*)

---

¹ **anteroom** (ăn´tē-rōōm´): an outer room that leads to another room and is often used as a waiting room.

©Shutterstock

**Villagers** (*shouting together*). Long live the Prince of Wales! (Guards *open gates and* Tom *slowly passes through, as if in a dream.*)

**Prince** (*to* Tom). You look tired, and you have been treated cruelly. I am Edward, Prince of Wales.
50 What is your name?

**Tom** (*looking around in awe*). Tom Canty, Your Highness.

**Prince.** Come into the palace with me, Tom. (Prince *leads* Tom *into anteroom.* Villagers *pantomime conversation, and all but a few exit.*) Where do you live, Tom?

**Tom.** In the city, Your Highness, in Offal Court.

60 **Prince.** Offal Court? That is an odd name. Do you have parents?

**Tom.** Yes, Your Highness.

**Prince.** How does your father treat you?

**Tom.** If it please you, Your Highness, when I am not able to beg a penny for our supper, he treats me to beatings.

**Prince** (*shocked*). What! Beatings?
70 My father is not a calm man, but he does not beat me. (*looks at* Tom *thoughtfully*) You speak well and have an easy grace. Have you been schooled?

**Tom.** Very little, Your Highness. A good priest who shares our house in Offal Court has taught me from his books.

**Prince.** Do you have a pleasant life
80 in Offal Court?

**Tom.** Pleasant enough, Your Highness, save when I am hungry. We have Punch and Judy shows, and sometimes we lads have fights in the street.

**Prince** (*eagerly*). I should like that. Tell me more.

**Tom.** In summer, we run races and swim in the river, and we love to
90 wallow in the mud.

**Prince** (*sighing, wistfully*). If I could wear your clothes and play in the mud just once, with no one to forbid me, I think I could give up the crown!

**Tom** (*shaking his head*). And if I could wear your fine clothes just once, Your Highness . . .

**Prince.** Would you like that?
100 Come, then. We shall change places. You can take off your rags and put on my clothes—and I will put on yours. (*He leads* Tom *behind screen, and they return shortly, each wearing the other's clothes.*) Let's look at ourselves in this mirror. (*leads* Tom *to mirror*)

**Tom.** Oh, Your Highness, it is not proper for me to wear such clothes.

110 **Prince** (*excitedly, as he looks in mirror*). Heavens, do you not see it? We look like brothers! We have the same features and bearing.[2] If we went about together, dressed alike, there is no one who could say which is the Prince of Wales and which is Tom Canty!

---

[2] **features and bearing:** parts of the face and ways of standing or walking.

**Tom** (*drawing back and rubbing his hand*). Your Highness, I am
120 frightened. . . .

**Prince.** Do not worry. (*seeing* Tom *rub his hand*) Is that a bruise on your hand?

**Tom.** Yes, but it is a slight thing, Your Highness.

**Prince** (*angrily*). It was shameful and cruel of that guard to strike you. Do not stir a step until I come back. I command you! (*He picks
130 up golden Seal of England[3] and carefully puts it into piece of armor. He then dashes out to gates.*) Open! Unbar the gates at once! (2nd Guard *opens gates, and as* Prince *runs out, in rags,* 1st Guard *seizes him, boxes him on the ear, and knocks him to the ground.*)

**1st Guard.** Take that, you little beggar, for the trouble you have
140 made for me with the Prince. (Villagers *roar with laughter.*)

**Prince** (*picking himself up, turning on* Guard *furiously*). I am Prince of Wales! You shall hang for laying your hand on me!

**1st Guard** (*presenting arms; mockingly*). I salute Your Gracious Highness! (*Then, angrily,* 1st Guard *shoves* Prince *roughly aside.*) Be
150 off, you mad bag of rags! (Prince *is surrounded by* Villagers, *who hustle him off.*)

**Villagers** (*ad lib,[4] as they exit, shouting*). Make way for His Royal Highness! Make way for the Prince of Wales! Hail to the Prince! (*etc.*)

**Tom** (*admiring himself in mirror*). If only the boys in Offal Court could see me! They will not believe me
160 when I tell them about this. (*looks around anxiously*) But where is the Prince? (*Looks cautiously into courtyard.* Two Guards *immediately snap to attention and salute. He quickly ducks back into anteroom as* Lords Hertford *and* St. John *enter at rear.*)

**Hertford** (*going toward* Tom, *then stopping and bowing low*). My
170 Lord, you look distressed. What is wrong?

**Tom** (*trembling*). Oh, I beg of you, be merciful. I am no Prince, but poor Tom Canty of Offal Court. Please let me see the Prince, and he will give my rags back to me and let me go unhurt. (*kneeling*) Please, be merciful and spare me!

**Hertford** (*puzzled and disturbed*).
180 Your Highness, on your knees? To me? (*bows quickly, then, aside to* St. John) The Prince has gone mad! We must inform the King. (*to* Tom) A moment, your Highness. (Hertford *and* St. John *exit rear.*)

**Tom.** Oh, there is no hope for me now. They will hang me for certain! (Hertford *and* St. John *re-enter, supporting* King. Tom *watches*

---

[3] **Seal of England:** a device used to stamp a special design, usually a picture of the ruler, onto a document, thus indicating that it has royal approval.

[4] **ad lib:** talk together about what is going on, but without an actual script.

190 *in awe as they help him to couch,*
*where he sinks down wearily.*)

**King** (*beckoning* Tom *close to him*).
Now, my son, Edward, my prince.
What is this? Do you mean to
deceive me, the King, your father,
who loves you and treats you
so kindly?

**Tom** (*dropping to his knees*). You
are the King? Then I have no hope!

200 **King** (*stunned*). My child, you are
not well. Do not break your father's
old heart. Say you know me.

**Tom.** Yes, you are my lord the
King, whom God preserve.

**King.** True, that is right. Now, you
will not deny that you are Prince
of Wales, as they say you did just a
while ago?

**Tom.** I beg you, Your Grace,
210 believe me. I am the lowest of your
subjects, being born a pauper, and
it is by a great mistake that I am
here. I am too young to die. Oh,
please, spare me, sire!

**King** (*amazed*). Die? Do not talk
so, my child. You shall not die.

**Tom** (*gratefully*). God save you, my
king! And now, may I go?

**King.** Go? Where would you go?

220 **Tom.** Back to the alley where I was
born and bred to misery.

**King.** My poor child, rest your
head here. (*He holds* Tom's *head
and pats his shoulder, then turns to*
Hertford *and* St. John.) Alas, I am
old and ill, and my son is mad. But
this shall pass. Mad or sane, he is
my heir and shall rule England.
Tomorrow he shall be installed and
230 confirmed in his princely dignity!
Bring the Great Seal!

**Hertford** (*bowing low*). Please, Your Majesty, you took the Great Seal from the Chancellor two days ago to give to His Highness the Prince.

**King.** So I did. (*to* Tom) My child, tell me, where is the Great Seal?

**Tom** (*trembling*). Indeed, my lord, I do not know.

240

**King.** Ah, your affliction hangs heavily upon you. 'Tis no matter. You will remember later. Listen, carefully! (*gently, but firmly*) I command you to hide your affliction in all ways that be within your power. You shall deny to no one that you are the true prince, and if your memory should fail you upon any occasion of state, you shall be advised by your uncle, the Lord Hertford.

250

**Tom** (*resigned*). The King has spoken. The King shall be obeyed.

**King.** And now, my child, I go to rest. (*He stands weakly, and* Hertford *leads him off, rear.*)

**Tom** (*wearily, to* St. John). May it please your lordship to let me rest now?

260

**St. John.** So it please Your Highness, it is for you to command and us to obey. But it is wise that you rest, for this evening you must attend the Lord Mayor's banquet in your honor. (*He pulls bellcord, and* Three Pages *enter and kneel before* Tom.)

**Tom.** Banquet? (*Terrified, he sits on couch and reaches for cup of water,*

270

but 1st Page *instantly seizes cup, drops on one knee, and serves it to him.* Tom *starts to take off his boots, but* 2nd Page *stops him and does it for him. He tries to remove his cape and gloves, and* 3rd Page *does it for him.*) I wonder that you do not try to breathe for me also! (*Lies down cautiously.* Pages *cover him with robe, then back away and exit.*)

280

**St. John** (*to* Hertford, *as he enters*). Plainly, what do you think?

**Hertford.** Plainly, this. The King is near death, my nephew the Prince of Wales is clearly mad and will mount the throne mad. God protect England, for she will need it!

**St. John.** Does it not seem strange that madness could so change his manner from what it used to be? It troubles me, his saying he is not the Prince.

290

**Hertford.** Peace, my lord! If he were an impostor and called himself Prince, that would be natural. But was there ever an impostor, who being called Prince by the King and court, denied it? Never! This is the true Prince gone mad. And tonight all London shall honor him. (Hertford *and* St. John *exit.* Tom *sits up, looks around helplessly, then gets up.*)

300

**Tom.** I should have thought to order something to eat. (*sees bowl of nuts on table*) Ah! Here are some nuts! (*looks around, sees Great Seal in armor, takes it out, looks at it curiously*) This will make a good

310

nutcracker. (*He takes bowl of nuts, sits on couch and begins to crack nuts with Great Seal and eat them, as curtain falls.*)

## Scene 2

**Time:** *Later that night.*

**Setting:** *A street in London, near Offal Court. Played before the curtain.*

**At Curtain Rise:** Prince *limps in,* 320 *dirty and tousled. He looks around wearily. Several* Villagers *pass by, pushing against him.*

**Prince.** I have never seen this poor section of London. I must be near Offal Court. If I can only find it before I drop! (John Canty *steps out of crowd, seizes* Prince *roughly.*)

**Canty.** Out at this time of night, and I warrant you haven't brought 330 a farthing⁵ home! If that is the case and I do not break all the bones in your miserable body, then I am not John Canty!

**Prince** (*eagerly*). Oh, are you his father?

**Canty.** *His* father? I am *your* father, and—

**Prince.** Take me to the palace at once, and your son will be 340 returned to you. The King, my father, will make you rich beyond your wildest dreams. Oh, save me, for I am indeed the Prince of Wales.

---
⁵ **farthing** (fär´thǐng): a former British coin worth one-fourth of a British penny.

**Canty** (*staring in amazement*). Gone stark mad! But mad or not, I'll soon find where the soft places lie in your bones. Come home! (*starts to drag* Prince *off*)

350 **Prince** (*struggling*). Let me go! I am the Prince of Wales, and the King shall have your life for this!

**Canty** (*angrily*). I'll take no more of your madness! (*raises stick to strike, but* Prince *struggles free and runs off, and* Canty *runs after him*)

## Scene 3

**Setting:** *Same as Scene 1, with addition of dining table, set with dishes and goblets, on raised* 360 *platform. Throne-like chair is at head of table.*

**At Curtain Rise:** *A banquet is in progress.* Tom, *in royal robes, sits at head of table, with* Hertford *at his right and* St. John *at his left. Lords and* Ladies *sit around table eating and talking softly.*

**Tom** (*to* Hertford). What is this, my Lord? (*holds up a plate*)

370 **Hertford.** Lettuce and turnips, Your Highness.

**Tom.** Lettuce and turnips? I have never seen them before. Am I to eat them?

**Hertford** (*discreetly*). Yes, Your Highness, if you so desire. (Tom *begins to eat food with his fingers. Fanfare of trumpets is heard, and* Herald *enters, carrying scroll. All* 380 *turn to look.*)

**Herald** (*reading from scroll*). His Majesty, King Henry VIII, is dead! The King is dead! (*All rise and turn to* Tom, *who sits, stunned.*)

**All** (*together*). The King is dead. Long live the King! Long live Edward, King of England! (*All bow to* Tom. Herald *bows and exits.*)

**Hertford** (*to* Tom). Your Majesty, 390 we must call the council. Come, St. John. (Hertford *and* St. John *lead* Tom *off at rear.* Lords *and* Ladies *follow, talking among themselves. At gates, down right,* Villagers *enter and mill about.* Prince *enters right, pounds on gates and shouts.*)

**Prince.** Open the gates! I am the Prince of Wales! Open, I say! And though I am friendless with no 400 one to help me, I will not be driven from my ground.

**Miles Hendon** (*entering through crowd*). Though you be Prince or not, you are indeed a gallant lad and not friendless. Here I stand to prove it, and you might have a worse friend than Miles Hendon.

**1st Villager.** Tis another prince in disguise. Take the lad and dunk 410 him in the pond! (*He seizes* Prince, *but* Miles *strikes him with flat of his sword. Crowd, now angry, presses forward threateningly, when fanfare of trumpets is heard offstage.* Herald, *carrying scroll, enters up left at gates.*)

**Herald.** Make way for the King's messenger! (*reading from scroll*) His Majesty, King Henry VIII, 420 is dead! The King is dead! (*He exits right, repeating message, and* Villagers *stand in stunned silence.*)

(bg) ©Shutterstock; (fg) Frank Riccio

**Prince** (*stunned*). The King is dead!

**1st Villager** (*shouting*). Long live Edward, King of England!

**Villagers** (*together*). Long live the King! (*shouting, ad lib*) Long live King Edward! Heaven protect
430 Edward, King of England! (*etc.*)

**Miles** (*taking* Prince *by the arm*). Come, lad, before the crowd remembers us. I have a room at the inn, and you can stay there. (*He hurries off with stunned Prince.* Tom, *led by* Hertford, *enters courtyard up rear.* Villagers *see them.*)

**Villagers** (*together*). Long live the
440 King! (*They fall to their knees as curtains close.*)

## Scene 4

**Setting:** Miles' *room at the inn. At right is table set with dishes and bowls of food, a chair at each side. At left is bed, with table and chair next to it, and a window. Candle is on table.*

**At Curtain Rise:** Miles *and* Prince *approach table.*

450 **Miles.** I have had a hot supper prepared. I'll bet you're hungry, lad.

**Prince.** Yes, I am. It's kind of you to let me stay with you, Miles. I am truly Edward, King of England, and you shall not go unrewarded. (*sits at table*)

**Miles** (*to himself*). First he called himself Prince, and now he is

460 King. Well, I will humor him. (*starts to sit*)

**Prince** (*angrily*). Stop! Would you sit in the presence of the King?

**Miles** (*surprised, standing up quickly*). I beg your pardon, Your Majesty. I was not thinking. (*Stares uncertainly at* Prince, *who sits at table, expectantly.* Miles *starts to uncover dishes of food, serves* Prince
470 *and fills glasses.*)

**Prince.** Miles, you have a gallant way about you. Are you nobly born?

**Miles.** My father is a baronet,[6] Your Majesty.

**Prince.** Then you must also be a baronet.

**Miles** (*shaking his head*). My father banished me from home
480 seven years ago, so I fought in the wars. I was taken prisoner, and I have spent the past seven years in prison. Now I am free, and I am returning home.

**Prince.** You have been shamefully wronged! But I will make things right for you. You have saved me from injury and possible death. Name your reward and if it be
490 within the compass of my royal power, it is yours.

**Miles** (*pausing briefly, then dropping to his knee*). Since Your Majesty is pleased to hold my simple duty worthy of reward,

---

[6] **baronet** (băr´ə-nĭt): a rank of honor in Britain, below a baron and above a knight.

I ask that I and my successors[7] may hold the privilege of sitting in the presence of the King.

**Prince** (*taking* Miles' *sword, tapping him lightly on each shoulder*). Rise and seat yourself. (*returns sword to* Miles, *then rises and goes over to bed*)

**Miles** (*rising*). He should have been born a king. He plays the part to a marvel! If I had not thought of this favor, I might have had to stand for weeks. (*sits down and begins to eat*)

**Prince.** Sir Miles, you will stand guard while I sleep? (*lies down and instantly falls asleep*)

**Miles.** Yes, Your Majesty. (*With a rueful look at his uneaten supper, he stands up.*) Poor little chap. I suppose his mind has been disordered with ill usage. (*covers* Prince *with his cape*) Well, I will be his friend and watch over him. (*Blows out candle, then yawns, sits on chair next to bed, and falls asleep. John Canty and* Hugo *appear at window, peer around room, then enter cautiously through window. They lift the sleeping* Prince, *staring nervously at* Miles.)

**Canty** (*in loud whisper*). I swore the day he was born he would be a thief and a beggar, and I won't lose him now. Lead the way to the camp Hugo! (Canty *and* Hugo *carry* Prince *off right, as* Miles *sleeps on and curtain falls.*)

---

[7] **successors** (sək-sĕs′ərs): those, in sequence or line of succession, who have a right to property, to hold title or rank, or to hold the throne one after the other.

**Time:** *Two weeks later.*

**Setting:** *Country village street.*

**Before Curtain Rise:** Villagers *walk about.* Canty, Hugo, *and* Prince *enter.*

**Canty.** I will go in this direction. Hugo, keep my mad son with you, and see that he doesn't escape again! (*exits*)

**Hugo** (*seizing* Prince *by the arm*). He won't escape! I'll see that he earns his bread today, or else!

**Prince** (*pulling away*). I will not beg with you, and I will not steal! I have suffered enough in this miserable company of thieves!

**Hugo.** You shall suffer more if you do not do as I tell you! (*raises clenched fist at* Prince) Refuse if you dare! (Woman *enters, carrying wrapped bundle in a basket on her arm.*) Wait here until I come back. (Hugo *sneaks along after* Woman, *then snatches her bundle, runs back to* Prince, *and thrusts it into his arms.*) Run after me and call, "Stop, thief!" But be sure you lead her astray! (*Runs off.* Prince *throws down bundle in disgust.*)

**Woman.** Help! Thief! Stop, thief! (*rushes at* Prince *and seizes him, just as several* Villagers *enter*) You little thief! What do you mean by robbing a poor woman? Somebody bring the constable! (Miles *enters and watches.*)

**1st Villager** (*grabbing* Prince). I'll teach him a lesson, the little villain!

**Prince** (*struggling*). Take your hands off me! I did not rob this woman!

**Miles** (*stepping out of crowd and pushing man back with the flat of his sword*). Let us proceed gently, my friends. This is a matter for the law.

**Prince** (*springing to* Miles' *side*). You have come just in time, Sir Miles. Carve this rabble to rags!

**Miles.** Speak softly. Trust in me and all shall go well.

**Constable** (*entering and reaching for* Prince). Come along, young rascal!

**Miles.** Gently, good friend. He shall go peaceably to the Justice.

**Prince.** I will not go before a Justice! I did not do this thing!

**Miles** (*taking him aside*). Sire, will you reject the laws of the realm, yet demand that your subjects respect them?

**Prince** (*calmer*). You are right, Sir Miles. Whatever the King requires a subject to suffer under the law, he will suffer himself while he holds the station of a subject. (Constable *leads them off right.* Villagers *follow. Curtain.*)

## Scene 6

**Setting:** *Office of the Justice. A high bench is at center.*

**At Curtain Rise:** Justice *sits behind bench.* Constable *enters with* Miles *and* Prince, *followed by* Villagers. Woman *carries wrapped bundle.*

**Constable** (*to* Justice). A young thief, your worship, is accused of stealing a dressed pig from this poor woman.

**Justice** (*looking down at* Prince, *then* Woman). My good woman, are you absolutely certain this lad stole your pig?

**Woman.** It was none other than he, your worship.

**Justice.** Are there no witnesses to the contrary? (*All shake their heads.*) Then the lad stands convicted. (*to* Woman) What do you hold this property to be worth?

**Woman.** Three shillings and eight pence, your worship.

**Justice** (*leaning down to* Woman). Good woman, do you know that when one steals a thing above the value of thirteen pence, the law says he shall hang for it?

**Woman** (*upset*). Oh, what have I done? I would not hang the poor boy for the whole world! Save me from this, your worship. What can I do?

**Justice** (*gravely*). You may revise the value, since it is not yet written in the record.

**Woman.** Then call the pig eight pence, your worship.

640 **Justice.** So be it. You may take your property and go. (Woman *starts off, and is followed by* Constable. Miles *follows them cautiously down right.*)

**Constable** (*stopping* Woman). Good woman, I will buy your pig from you. (*takes coins from pocket*) Here is eight pence.

**Woman.** Eight pence! It cost me three shillings and eight pence!

650 **Constable.** Indeed! Then come back before his worship and answer for this. The lad must hang!

**Woman.** No! No! Say no more. Give me the eight pence and hold your peace. (Constable *hands her coins and takes pig.* Woman *exits, angrily.* Miles *returns to bench.*)

**Justice.** The boy is sentenced to a fortnight[8] in the common jail. Take
660 him away, Constable! (Justice *exits.* Prince *gives* Miles *a nervous glance.*)

**Miles** (*following* Constable). Good sir, turn your back a moment and let the poor lad escape. He is innocent.

**Constable** (*outraged*). What? You say this to me? Sir, I arrest you in—

**Miles.** Do not be so hasty! (*slyly*) The pig you have purchased for
670 eight pence may cost you your neck, man.

**Constable** (*laughing nervously*). Ah, but I was merely jesting with the woman, sir.

**Miles.** Would the Justice think it a jest?

**Constable.** Good sir! The Justice has no more sympathy with a jest than a dead corpse! (*perplexed*)
680 Very well, I will turn my back and see nothing! But go quickly! (*exits*)

**Miles** (*to* Prince). Come, my liege.[9] We are free to go. And that band of thieves shall not set hands on you again, I swear it!

**Prince** (*wearily*). Can you believe, Sir Miles, that in the last fortnight, I, the King of England, have escaped from thieves and begged for food
690 on the road? I have slept in a barn with a calf! I have washed dishes in a peasant's kitchen, and narrowly escaped death. And not once in all my wanderings did I see a courier[10] searching for me! Is it no matter for commotion and distress that the head of state is gone?

**Miles** (*sadly, aside*). Still busy with his pathetic dream. (*to* Prince) It
700 is strange indeed, my liege. But come, I will take you to my father's home in Kent. We are not far away. There you may rest in a house with seventy rooms! Come, I am all impatience to be home again! (*They exit,* Miles *in cheerful spirits,* Prince *looking puzzled, as curtains close.*)

---

8 **fortnight:** 14 days; two weeks.

9 **my liege** (lēj): my lord.
10 **courier** (ko͝or´ē-ər): messenger.

## Scene 7

**Setting:** *Village jail. Bare stage, with barred window on one wall.*

710 **At Curtain Rise:** Two Prisoners, *in chains, are onstage.* Jailer *shoves* Miles *and* Prince, *in chains, onstage. They struggle and protest.*

**Miles.** But I tell you, I am Miles Hendon! My brother, Sir Hugh, has stolen my bride and my estate!

**Jailer.** Be silent! Impostor! Sir Hugh will see that you pay well for claiming to be his dead brother
720 and for assaulting him in his own house! (*exits*)

**Miles** (*sitting, with head in hands*). Oh, my dear Edith . . . now wife to my brother Hugh, against her will, and my poor father . . . dead!

**1st Prisoner.** At least you have your life, sir. I am sentenced to be hanged for killing a deer in the King's park.

730 **2nd Prisoner.** And I must hang for stealing a yard of cloth to dress my children.

**Prince** (*moved; to* Prisoners). When I mount my throne, you shall all be free. And the laws that have dishonored you shall be swept from the books. (*turning away*) Kings should go to school to learn their own laws and be merciful.

740 **1st Prisoner.** What does the lad mean? I have heard that the King is mad, but merciful.

**2nd Prisoner.** He is to be crowned at Westminster tomorrow.

**Prince** (*violently*). King? What King, good sir?

**1st Prisoner.** Why, we have only one, his most sacred majesty, King Edward the Sixth.

**2nd Prisoner.** And whether he be mad or not, his praises are on all men's lips. He has saved many innocent lives, and now he means to destroy the cruelest laws that oppress the people.

**Prince** (*turning away, shaking his head*). How can this be? Surely it is not that little beggar boy! (*Sir Hugh enters with* Jailer.)

**Sir Hugh.** Seize the impostor!

**Miles** (*as* Jailer *pulls him to his feet*). Hugh, this has gone far enough!

**Sir Hugh.** You will sit in the public stocks for two hours, and the boy would join you if he were not so young. See to it, jailer, and after two hours, you may release them. Meanwhile, I ride to London for the coronation![11] (*Sir Hugh exits and* Miles *is hustled out by* Jailer.)

**Prince.** Coronation! What does he mean? There can be no coronation without me! (*curtain falls*)

## Scene 8

**Time:** *Coronation Day.*

**Setting:** *Outside gates of Westminster Abbey, played before curtain. Painted screen or flat at rear represents Abbey. Throne is in center. Bench is near it.*

**At Curtain Rise:** Lords *and* Ladies *crowd Abbey. Outside gates,* Guards *drive back cheering* Villagers, *among them* Miles.

**Miles** (*distraught*). I've lost him! Poor little chap! He has been swallowed up in the crowd! (*Fanfare of trumpets is heard, then silence.* Hertford, St. John, Lords *and* Ladies *enter slowly, in a procession, followed by* Pages, *one of whom carries crown on a small cushion.* Tom *follows procession, looking about nervously. Suddenly,* Prince, *in rags, steps out from crowd, his hand raised.*)

**Prince.** I forbid you to set the crown of England upon that head. I am the King!

**Hertford.** Seize the little vagabond!

**Tom.** I forbid it! He is the King! (*kneels before* Prince) Oh, my lord the King, let poor Tom Canty be the first to say, "Put on your crown and enter into your own right again." (Hertford *and several* Lords *look closely at both boys.*)

**Hertford.** This is strange indeed. (*to* Tom) By your favor, sir, I wish to ask certain questions of this lad.

**Prince.** I will answer truly whatever you may ask, my lord.

**Hertford.** But if you have been well trained, you may answer my questions as well as our lord the King. I need a definite proof. (*thinks a moment*) Ah! Where lies

---

[11] **coronation** (kôr´ə-nā´shən): the act of crowning someone king or queen. In England, coronations usually take place at a large church in London called Westminster Abbey.

the Great Seal of England? It has been missing for weeks, and only the true Prince of Wales can say where it lies.

**Tom.** Wait! Was the seal round and thick, with letters engraved on it? (Hertford *nods.*) I know where it is, but it was not I who put it there. The rightful King shall tell you. (*to* Prince) Think, my King, it was the very last thing you did that day before you rushed out of the palace wearing my rags.

**Prince** (*pausing*). I recall how we exchanged clothes, but have no recollection[12] of hiding the Great Seal.

**Tom** (*eagerly*). Remember when you saw the bruise on my hand, you ran to the door, but first you hid this thing you call the Seal.

**Prince** (*suddenly*). Ah! I remember! (*to* St. John) Go, my good St. John, and you shall find the Great Seal in the armor that hangs on the wall in my chamber. (St. John *hesitates, but at a nod from* Tom, *hurries off.*)

**Tom** (*pleased*). Right, my King! Now the scepter[13] of England is yours again. (St. John *returns in a moment with Great Seal.*)

**All** (*shouting*). Long live Edward, King of England! (Tom *takes off his cape and throws it over* Prince's *rags. Trumpet fanfare is heard.*

St. John *takes crown and places it on* Prince. *All kneel.*)

**Hertford.** Let the small impostor be flung into the Tower!

**Prince** (*firmly*). I will not have it so. But for him, I would not have my crown. (*to* Tom) My poor boy, how was it that you could remember where I hid the Seal, when I could not?

**Tom** (*embarrassed*). I did not know what it was, my King, and I used it to . . . to crack nuts. (*All laugh, and* Tom *steps back.* Miles *steps forward, staring in amazement.*)

**Miles.** Is he really the King? Is he indeed the sovereign of England, and not the poor and friendless Tom o' Bedlam[14] I thought he was? (*He sinks down on bench.*) I wish I had a bag to hide my head in!

**1st Guard** (*rushing up to him*). Stand up, you mannerless clown! How dare you sit in the presence of the King!

**Prince.** Do not touch him! He is my trusty servant, Miles Hendon, who saved me from shame and possible death. For his service, he owns the right to sit in my presence.

**Miles** (*bowing, then kneeling*). Your Majesty!

**Prince.** Rise, Sir Miles. I command that Sir Hugh Hendon, who sits within this hall, be seized and put

---

[12]**recollection** (rĕk´ə-lĕk´shən): a memory or recalling to mind of something that happened before.

[13]**scepter** (sĕp´tər): a staff held by a king or queen as an emblem of authority.

[14]**Tom o' Bedlam:** an insane person, such as someone hospitalized at St. Mary of Bethlehem Hospital, or Bedlam Hospital, in London.

under lock and key until I have
need of him. (*beckons to* Tom)

890  From what I have heard, Tom
Canty, you have governed the
realm with royal gentleness and
mercy in my absence. Henceforth,
you shall hold the honorable title
of King's Ward! (Tom *kneels and
kisses* Prince's *hand.*) And because
I have suffered with the poorest of
my subjects and felt the cruel force
of unjust laws, I pledge myself to a
900  reign of mercy for all! (*All bow low,
then rise.*)

**All** (*shouting*). Long live the
King! Long live Edward, King of
England! (*curtain*)

**COLLABORATIVE DISCUSSION**  With a small group, identify
themes you can take away from the play. Explain how different
elements of the play support your ideas.

# Describe Drama

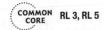 

A **drama,** or play, is a form of literature that is meant to be performed by actors in front of an audience. The author of a play is called a playwright or dramatist. In some ways, a drama is similar to a story.

A play is structured in the following way:

- A play is divided into **acts,** which are like chapters in a book. Each act can be divided into smaller sections, called scenes.
- A **scene** presents an episode of the plot and usually occurs at a single place and time. A play's plot unfolds in a series of episodes as it moves toward a resolution, similar to a story.

A short drama, like "The Prince and the Pauper," may be presented as a **one-act play,** in which each episode of the plot is presented as one scene.

The written format of a play consists of these elements:

- A drama is written in the form of a **script**. A script usually includes a cast of characters, dialogue, and stage directions.
- A **cast of characters** is a list of all the characters in the play, often in order of appearance. This list is usually found at the beginning of the play and sometimes includes descriptions of the characters.
- In drama, **dialogue** (written conversation between two or more characters) and actions tell the story. Characters' dialogue reveals their thoughts, feelings, and traits as the plot moves forward.
- **Stage directions** are instructions in the text about how to perform the drama. Some stage directions tell about the scenery and setting. Other stage directions appear within the dialogue to explain to actors how to say or emphasize a line or speech, or to describe a physical action the character should perform.

Although a drama is similar to a story, one important difference is that a play is meant to be performed. Watching a play and reading a play are two different experiences. Think about this as you analyze "The Prince and the Pauper" or other dramas, using questions such as the following:

- How is the play structured? Is it divided into acts, or is it just one act? Why might the playwright have chosen this structure?
- What is the play's main conflict? How does the plot unfold, and how is the conflict resolved?
- Who are the main characters? How do I learn about what they are like and how they respond to events?
- How is the experience of reading a drama different from watching a live performance of it? In what ways does the script help me?

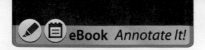
# Analyzing the Text

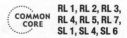

COMMON CORE — RL 1, RL 2, RL 3, RL 4, RL 5, RL 7, SL 1, SL 4, SL 6

**Cite Text Evidence**   Support your responses with evidence from the text.

1. **Summarize** Review lines 29–137. Who are the two main characters? How would you describe the main conflict introduced in this scene?

2. **Compare** Compare how Tom responds to his new situation in Scene One, lines 157–280, with how the Prince behaves in Scene Two, lines 323–352. Do the boys react in similar or different ways? What do their words and behavior tell you about what they are like?

3. **Analyze** Review Scene Four, lines 442–532, in which Miles serves the Prince a meal. How are the stage directions helpful to readers?

4. **Analyze** Review lines 710–732 in Scene Seven. How does the dialogue help you understand what has happened to Miles?

5. **Draw Conclusions** Review lines 774–904 in Scene Eight. How is the play's conflict resolved? Think about the two main characters. Have either of them undergone any great changes? Why or why not?

6. **Synthesize** The play is based on a novel by Mark Twain. Think about the plot and characters. What aspects of the story make it well suited to a dramatic performance?

# PERFORMANCE TASK

**Speaking Activity: Dramatic Reading** With a small group, rehearse and then perform a portion of the play. Then watch another group perform a portion of the play.

- Use the stage directions and what you know about the character to help you deliver your lines in a convincing way.

- When you rehearse and perform, work to use appropriate eye contact,

speak at an adequate volume, and pronounce words clearly.

- When you watch the performance, contrast it with what you "see" and "hear" when you read the text on your own.

- Share your ideas with your group, using examples from the text or the performance to support those ideas. Write a brief summary of your discussion.

**Simone Payment** *has college degrees in both psychology and education. She has taught elementary school, worked in book publishing, and worked for a health care company. Payment is the author of dozens of books for children and young adults. She has written biographies of both historical and contemporary characters. She has also written nonfiction books about a wide variety of subjects, including Greek mythology, the pony express, famous movie monsters, and robotics.*

# The Role of Myths in Ancient Greece
## *from* Greek Mythology

Essay by Simone Payment

**SETTING A PURPOSE** As you read, focus on the origin of myths and on understanding the relevance of myths in ancient Greek culture.

Many cultures have stories that have been passed down through the ages. These stories—called myths—are tales of gods and goddesses, monsters, and adventure. The myths from ancient Greece may be the best known of all cultures' mythologies, and perhaps the most exciting. The myths of the Greeks, which have been told for thousands of years, are still enjoyed today.

What we call classical Greece (from the sixth to the fourth centuries BC) gave future civilizations more than just stories. The ancient Greeks made huge contributions to modern culture in Greece and elsewhere. In fact, ancient Greece is often called the cradle of Western civilization. This is because so much of modern life is based on contributions from the Greeks. The United States current system of government, democracy, came from Greek civilization. The Olympics

10

began in ancient Greece. Great Greek thinkers made **revolutionary** discoveries in astronomy, biology, and medicine. Ancient Greeks also wrote stories and plays that are still read and performed today. Their art and architecture also
20 live on in modern times.

Ancient Greece was not in the exact location where Greece is today. It included parts of what are now Turkey and Italy. There were dense forests and steep, rocky cliffs along the coast. Inland, there were snow-covered mountains. Many islands dotted the Aegean Sea off the eastern coast of Greece.

In the earliest days of Greece, the country was divided into small, individually governed areas called city-states. City-states were often separated by forests or mountains and were far apart, and the **dialects** spoken in each city-state
30 varied. Because of these barriers, people did not travel much, so city-states did not frequently interact. If you were born in a particular city-state, you would usually live there your whole life. As a result, each city-state had its own myths that most residents knew and told over and over again.

Starting in the fourth century BC, Alexander the Great (the king of Macedon, a part of Greece) began invading other countries. His successes brought Greeks together politically. Some city-states began to work together, sometimes against a common enemy. By that time, they also shared a
40 common language. People began to travel and move to other city-states. They also began to travel outside of Greece. This travel helped spread Greek myths around the country and to other countries.

Everyday life was not always easy in ancient Greece. People did not live as long as they do now. Life was more difficult, with no modern conveniences such as heat or running water. People had to kill animals and farm for food. The hardships in their daily lives led the ancient Greeks to look to their gods and goddesses for help. They believed that the **immortal**
50 gods and goddesses had a great deal of power. The gods and goddesses could be helpful to humans if the humans showed them the proper respect. To show respect to the gods and goddesses, Greeks worshipped at their local temples. They wanted to stay in good favor with the higher powers for fear that they might be punished. They also believed that the gods and goddesses might punish not just them but their whole community.

**revolutionary**
(rĕv´ə-lōo´shə-nĕr´ē) *adj.* Something that is *revolutionary* causes important and sometimes sudden changes in a situation.

**dialect**
(dī´ə-lĕkt´) *n.* A *dialect* is a regional language variation, characterized by differences in pronunciation, grammar, or vocabulary.

**immortal**
(ĭ-môr´tl) *adj.* If someone or something is *immortal*, it will never die.

In addition to regular visits to local temples, Greeks also held special festivals to honor specific gods or goddesses. Each god and goddess worshipped by the Greeks played a specific role in life.

The word "myth" comes from the Greek word *mythos*, which literally means "story." However myths were much more than simple stories to the Greeks. They were an important part of Greek life. They were passed from person to person and from generation to generation.

Myths tell several types of stories. Some are tales of adventure based on actual events. For example, Homer's *The Iliad* is based on the Trojan War, a ten-year war between the Greeks and the people of the Turkish city of Troy.

Myths were more than just accounts of exciting occurrences. They also told stories about such **monumental** events as the creation of human beings. In ancient Greece, there was no one text, such as the Bible or the Koran, to explain everything about a particular religion's view of the world. Instead, myths served the purpose of providing answers.

Myths also taught important lessons. For example, they might have warned against being too proud. One version of the Greek myth of Arachne tells how Arachne was turned into a spider for bragging about her weaving skills.

The ancient Greeks also created myths to help them make sense of natural phenomena[1] that they could explain in no other way. For example, the Greeks did not understand why earthquakes occurred. A story about the god Poseidon punishing his enemies by shaking the ground underneath them offered Greeks an answer. Poseidon was also believed to control the sea. His changing moods could explain why the sea was calm one day and stormy the next.

**monumental**
(mŏn′yə-mĕn′tl) *adj.*
A *monumental* event is one that is of outstanding significance.

## Different Cultures, Similar Myths

If you study ancient cultures, you can see that many of them have myths. Myths are often similar from culture to culture. This is most likely because there are certain qualities of life that are important or meaningful to people everywhere.

---

[1] **phenomena** (fĭ-nŏm′ə-nə): occurrences, circumstances, or facts that can be perceived by the senses.

Mount Olympus is the highest mountain in Greece. It is regarded as the home of gods and goddesses in Greek mythology. The gods and goddesses were known as Olympians who, according to myth, claimed the mountain after winning a war. As a result, Mount Olympus became a symbol of ancient cultural development in Greece.

Each culture creates myths that reflect its beliefs, which are often a result of its circumstances. For example, myths may be influenced by the geography of the country in which a civilization lives. Mount Olympus, a towering, snow-covered mountain in Greece, became known as the home of the gods in Greek mythology. The top of the mountain was so high and so unreachable to the Greeks that they said the gods and goddesses must live there. Myths are also personalized by what is important to a particular country or culture.

100

# How Myths Spread

Many of the Greek myths were based on people and events from even earlier times. In the very early days of Greece (about 2000 BC), Greeks had huge fleets of ships and attacked neighboring countries. About 1,000 years later, Greece had entered a less heroic era. People were poor and life was hard, so they told stories of a more exciting time. Men called bards (poets or story-tellers) would memorize the stories and then
110 travel around the countryside, telling these tales. During the time when each city-state was **isolated** from the others, stories varied. Bards might change the story slightly, adding their own exciting details.

Eventually, myths were written down in a format similar to a poem. Some of the myths, when written down, were up to 1,000 lines long. Homer (circa[2] eighth or ninth century BC) was one of the most famous bards. He wrote two landmark works, *The Iliad* and *The Odyssey*. *The Iliad* tells the story of the Trojan War. *The Odyssey* tells the many adventures of
120 the Greek hero Odysseus. Two other famous written myths are *Theogony* and *Works and Days* by Hesiod (circa 800 BC). *Theogony* is the story of the creation of the gods. *Works and Days* offers advice on how to farm or on which days to do certain things, like cut your fingernails. Also included in *Works and Days* are myths, such as the story of Pandora.

Greeks heard myths at an early age. Elders[3] would tell the stories to young children. Sometimes the stories were used as warnings to get children to behave. Young children also learned about myths at school, although in most places in
130 ancient Greece, only boys went to school.

Adults heard myths at social gatherings and informal meetings. Myths were also recited as a part of rituals at religious temples. In addition, bards might tell myths—or even sing them—for wealthy people or kings. The theater was an important part of Greek life, and sometimes choirs would perform myths as plays.

**isolate**
(ī´sə-lāt´) *v.* To *isolate* something is to set it apart or separate it from others.

---

[2] **circa** (sûr´kə): in approximately; about or around the specified time.
[3] **elders** (ĕl´dərz): older, influential members of a family, tribe, or community.

# How Do We Know About Greek Myths?

Greek myths have been passed down for thousands of years. There are several ways we have learned about them. One is through written works, such as books or plays, that were created by later cultures based on stories from ancient Greece. These works have survived and are still enjoyed today. We have also learned about ancient Greek myths through artwork such as sculptures and paintings. The Greeks sometimes told their myths in the form of art, for example creating a sculpture of Zeus or a painting of Aphrodite. Sometimes they made mosaics[4] depicting important myths. They also decorated vases and other containers with stories of their heroes, heroines, gods, and goddesses. Even Greek coins were often decorated with images from myths. Many Greek sculptures still exist today in museums. We can even see some floor mosaics in their original locations. Hopefully, these relics[5] will be preserved for years to come.

**COLLABORATIVE DISCUSSION**  With a partner, discuss ways myths were important to the ancient Greeks and why myths are still relevant today. Cite evidence from the text to support your ideas.

---

[4] **mosaics** (mō-zā´ĭks):  pictures or decorative designs made of small colored pieces of tile or stone, set into a surface.

[5] **relics** (rĕl´ĭks):  things that have lasted over time, especially those objects or customs whose original culture has disappeared.

# Analyze Structure

COMMON CORE RI 5

A **pattern of organization** is the way ideas and information are arranged in a nonfiction text. One common pattern of organization authors use is **central (main) idea and supporting details**. The **central,** or most important, **idea** is supported by **details,** words, phrases, or sentences that tell more about the central idea.

If you look at lines 94–102 in "The Role of Myths," you can tell that the first sentence of the paragraph expresses the central idea that each culture creates myths that reflect its beliefs. The sentences that follow give details about how the geography of ancient Greece helped shape these beliefs.

Questions such as the following will help you analyze the central idea and supporting details as a pattern of organization:

- For an individual paragraph: What is the central idea? How are the details arranged to tell more about the central idea?
- For sections under headings: What central idea does the author discuss in this section? How do details add more information?
- How does a section or paragraph fit into the overall structure of the text? How does it help develop the writer's ideas?

# Cite Evidence

COMMON CORE RI 1

When you analyze a text, you examine it carefully for a reason, such as to figure out its structure, to determine an author's point of view, or to see how well a writer presents and supports a claim.

To support your analysis of a text, you need to **cite textual evidence**. This means that you have to identify specific pieces of relevant information from the text to support your ideas. When you cite evidence, you show that your analysis connects to the text in a logical way. Keep in mind these points:

- The evidence needs to clearly support your analysis or idea. For example, if you are analyzing how geography helped form Greek mythology in "The Role of Myths," you might cite evidence that includes information from lines 26–34.
- Whether you are presenting your analysis orally or in written form, it is a good idea to use linking words and phrases, such as *for example, because,* or *this shows.* Linking words and phrases help emphasize to readers or listeners how your idea is connected to the text.
- If in your writing you quote directly from the text to cite evidence for your ideas, set off the quoted material with quotation marks.

# Analyzing the Text

COMMON CORE  RI 1, RI 2, RI 3, RI 5, SL 1a–d

**Cite Text Evidence**  Support your responses with evidence from the text.

1. **Identify**  Review lines 8–20. Identify the central idea in this paragraph. What details support the central idea?

2. **Identify Patterns**  Reread lines 26–57. What is the central idea of the first paragraph, and what details tell more about it? Tell whether the next two paragraphs follow a similar pattern of organization.

3. **Draw Conclusions**  Reread lines 82–89. Based on what you learn in this paragraph, how would you describe the character or personality of the god Poseidon?

4. **Cite Evidence**  Review lines 103–136 in the section "How Myths Spread." Identify evidence that supports the conclusion that myths were intertwined with every part of the lives of the ancient Greeks.

5. **Cite Evidence**  Review lines 114–152. Cite evidence to support the conclusion that myths helped to preserve Greek culture.

6. **Evaluate**  How does the author's use of **subheadings,** or titles that indicate the beginning of a new topic, contribute to the pattern of organization used in "The Role of Myths in Ancient Greece"? Tell whether you think this pattern of organization is effective and why.

## PERFORMANCE TASK

**Speaking Activity: Discussion**  With a small group, have a discussion about the purpose of myths and how they influenced ancient Greek culture.

- As a group, decide on questions your group will attempt to answer.
- Pick group moderators who will keep track of the questions and make sure that all members have opportunities to share ideas.

- Have group members review the text and prepare ideas and details to answer the questions.
- During the discussion, listen to ideas closely and respectfully. Find opportunities to share additional information or perspectives.
- Review key ideas together and demonstrate understanding through shared reflection and paraphrasing.

# Critical Vocabulary

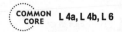 

| | | |
|---|---|---|
| **revolutionary** | **dialect** | **immortal** |
| **monumental** | **isolate** | |

**Practice and Apply**  Answer each question.

1. Which vocabulary word goes with *speak*? Why?

2. Which vocabulary word goes with *task* or *significant*? Why?

3. Which vocabulary word goes with *change* and *radical*? Why?

4. Which vocabulary word goes with *alone*? Why?

5. Which vocabulary word goes with *live forever*? Why?

## Vocabulary Strategy: Latin Roots

Sometimes you can figure out the meaning of an unfamiliar word by examining its root. A **root** is a word part that contains the core meaning of the word. For example, *volut-* comes from a Latin root that can mean "turn" or "roll." You can find this root in the vocabulary word *revolutionary* and use the meaning of the root to figure out that *revolutionary* describes a major change, or turn, in thinking.

Another way to use Latin roots to help you determine the meaning of an unfamiliar word is to think of other words that include the same root and create a word family. Then you can think over the related meanings of the words in that family to help you arrive at a meaning for the unfamiliar word.

**Practice and Apply**  Complete a word web like the one shown with other words that share the roots *volut-* and *volv-*. Tell how the meanings of the words are related.

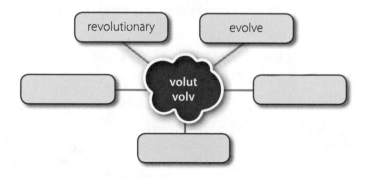

# Language Conventions: Parentheses

**Parentheses** are punctuation marks that are used to set off useful but less important information in a sentence. Here's an example from "The Role of Myths in Ancient Greece":

> **What we call classical Greece (from the sixth to the fourth centuries BC) gave future civilizations more than just stories.**

The information within the parentheses clarifies what the author calls "classical Greece," but it is of less importance than the rest of the information in the sentence.

Here are some reasons you might use parentheses:

> To enclose information that is related but not of primary importance:
> *The movie (we all loved it) runs about ninety minutes.*
>
> To enclose directions or other information that explains something:
> *Sam's Shoe Store (at the Cherry Mall) is having a storewide sale.*
>
> To repeat numbers or figures to ensure accuracy:
> *The cost of the service will be three hundred dollars ($300) a month.*

Use parentheses so that information you want to include but that is not of great importance doesn't interrupt the flow of a sentence.

**Practice and Apply**  For each sentence, write the word or words that should be in parentheses.

1. Gloria introduced us to Lily I think her last name is Nicholls at the party this weekend.

2. Paris often called the City of Lights is one of the world's most popular tourist destinations.

3. The reception will be held at the Hubbard Hotel west of Marlborough Avenue on Saturday from one to five o'clock.

4. Mr. Martinez Gina's uncle will be picking us up at the airport.

5. Players must hold a minimum of three 3 cards at all times.

6. Available to all residents of Pine Grove, the library open every day except Monday offers a wealth of reading materials in all formats.

Interactive Lessons

If you need help...
- **Writing Informative Texts**
- **Writing as a Process**
- **Using Textual Evidence**

# Write a Literary Analysis

Myths and tales often teach readers what values and qualities are most important to a culture. In this activity, you will write a literary analysis in which you analyze the values and qualities you learned about in *Black Ships Before Troy*. You will draw on ideas and examples from selections in this collection to help you write your analysis.

COMMON
CORE

**RL 1** Cite textual evidence.
**W 2a–f** Write informative/explanatory texts.
**W 4** Produce clear and coherent writing.
**W 5** Develop and strengthen writing.
**W 9a** Draw evidence from literary texts.
**W 10** Write routinely over extended and shorter time frames.

## A successful literary analysis

- cites evidence from the text that strongly supports the presented ideas and analysis

- is organized in a way that is appropriate for the purpose and audience

- establishes and maintains a formal writing style

- conveys ideas through the selection, organization, and analysis of relevant content

## PLAN

**Analyze the Story** Reread the excerpt from *Black Ships Before Troy*. Take notes related to the theme and the values and qualities of the culture that are revealed through the theme.

- Identify the events leading up to the Trojan War. What was its main cause?

- Think about the characters' personalities. How are the characters described? What do they say and do? What effect do they have on others?

- Consider the setting. How does the time period and place reflect the values and qualities of the culture?

- Identify symbols or repeated ideas, such as the importance of gold or the idea of honor. What insights do they give into the values and qualities of the culture?

*my*Notebook

Use the annotation tools in your eBook to find evidence to support your analysis. Save each piece of evidence to your notebook.

ACADEMIC
VOCABULARY

As you write your analysis, be sure to use the academic vocabulary words.

*emphasize*

*occur*

*period*

*relevant*

*tradition*

**Develop a Controlling Idea** Use your notes and examples from other selections in the collection to plan your analysis.

- Draft your controlling idea. This is the main point you want to emphasize in your analysis. You can modify or refine this statement as needed when you write.
- Decide what values and qualities you will discuss and identify story evidence that reveals them.
- Create a graphic organizer like this one to organize your ideas.

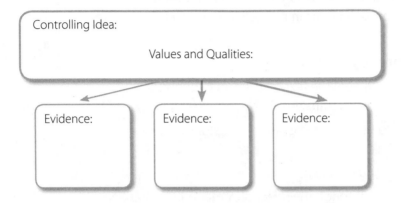

Controlling Idea:

Values and Qualities:

Evidence:

Evidence:

Evidence:

**Consider Audience and Purpose** Think about the audience as you prepare to write. It may include classmates who have read the story, as well as others who haven't read the story. How will you support your ideas to appeal to readers who might have different views? What will people who haven't read the story need to know to understand and appreciate your analysis?

**PRODUCE**

**Draft Your Literary Analysis** Use your notes and your graphic organizer to draft your literary analysis.

- Start with an attention-grabbing question or comment, and state your controlling idea to introduce your topic.
- Organize your ideas in a logical way. You may wish to discuss the values and qualities along with the related story evidence, or you may wish to organize your analysis around the major events in the story, explaining how each one helps to reveal the values and qualities of the culture.
- Include a brief summary of the story.

**my WriteSmart**

Write your rough draft in myWriteSmart. Focus on getting your ideas down, rather than perfecting your choice of language.

- Be sure to develop your topic with concrete details, quotations, or other relevant examples to support your ideas.
- Conclude your analysis with a summary of your main points and your own insights.

**Evaluate Your Draft** Use the chart on the following page to evaluate the substance and style of your analysis. Then make any necessary revisions. Consider the following:

- Examine your controlling idea to decide if it clearly represents the focus you have chosen.
- Make sure that the flow of ideas in your analysis is clear and that the organization is logical.
- Check whether you have included sufficient supporting evidence from the story.
- Evaluate whether your conclusion restates your main points and clearly offers a new insight to your readers.

*my* **WriteSmart**

Have your partner or a group of peers review your draft in *my*WriteSmart. Ask your reviewers to note any ideas that seem unsupported or any details that are irrelevant to your controlling idea.

**Create a Finished Copy** Finalize your literary analysis. Then choose a way to share it with your audience. Consider these options:

- Present your literary analysis in a speech to your classmates.
- Post your analysis as a blog on a personal or school website.
- Send your analysis to a magazine or newspaper that publishes literary reviews.

| | Ideas and Evidence | Organization | Language |
|---|---|---|---|
| **ADVANCED** | • The introduction clearly identifies the topic and engages the reader.<br>• The controlling idea presents a specific idea about the theme and its relevance.<br>• Specific, relevant details support the key points.<br>• The concluding section summarizes the analysis and offers an insight. | • Key points and supporting details are organized effectively and logically throughout the literary analysis.<br>• Transitions successfully show the relationships among ideas and concepts. | • The writing style is appropriately formal.<br>• Language is precise and captures the writer's thoughts with originality.<br>• Sentences vary in pattern and structure.<br>• Grammar, usage, and mechanics are correct. |
| **COMPETENT** | • The introduction identifies the topic but could be more engaging.<br>• The controlling idea makes a point about the relevance of the theme.<br>• Some key points need more support.<br>• The concluding section summarizes most of the analysis but doesn't offer an insight. | • The organization of key points and supporting details is confusing in a few places.<br>• A few more transitions are needed to clarify the relationships among ideas and concepts. | • The writing style is inconsistent in a few places.<br>• Most language is precise and captures the writer's thoughts.<br>• Sentences vary somewhat in pattern and structure.<br>• Some errors in grammar, usage, and mechanics occur. |
| **LIMITED** | • The introduction is only partly informative. The topic is unclear.<br>• The controlling idea only hints at a main point.<br>• Details support some key points but are often too general.<br>• The concluding section gives an incomplete summary without insight. | • Some key points are organized logically, but many supporting details are out of place.<br>• More transitions are needed throughout the literary analysis to connect ideas. | • The writing style becomes informal in several places.<br>• Language is repetitive or too general in places.<br>• Sentence pattern and structure hardly vary; some fragments occur.<br>• Many errors in grammar, usage, and mechanics occur, but the writer's ideas are still clear. |
| **EMERGING** | • There is no introduction.<br>• The controlling idea is unclear.<br>• Details are irrelevant or missing.<br>• The literary analysis lacks a concluding section. | • A logical organization is not apparent.<br>• Transitions are not used. | • The writing style is inappropriate.<br>• Language is inaccurate, repetitive, and too general throughout.<br>• Repetitive sentence structure and fragments make the literary analysis hard to follow.<br>• Errors in grammar, usage, and mechanics change the meaning of the writer's ideas. |

COLLECTION 6
# PERFORMANCE TASK B

Interactive Lessons
• **Writing a Narrative**
• **Writing as a Process**
• **Giving a Presentation**

# Write a Play

In this collection you read classic stories that teach important lessons or attempt to explain different types of phenomena in the world. One of these, a play based on the novel *The Prince and the Pauper,* brings a classic story to life through dialogue and action. In this activity, you will adapt another selection (or part of a selection) in this collection as a play. Then you will perform the play for an audience.

**A successful play**

- establishes a situation with an attention-grabbing introduction by a narrator or character
- develops a plot that has a clear beginning, middle, and end
- uses dialogue, pacing, and action to develop events and characters
- is structured in acts and scenes
- includes stage directions and a cast of characters
- provides a conclusion that resolves the problem with a memorable ending

**COMMON CORE**

**RL 7** Compare and contrast the experience of reading to listening or viewing.
**W 3a–e** Write narratives.
**W 4** Produce clear and coherent writing.
**W 5** Develop and strengthen writing.
**SL 6** Adapt speech to a variety of contexts and tasks.

---

**PLAN**

**Choose a Selection** Review the selections in the collection. Choose a story or a part of a story you think could be rewritten into an entertaining play.

**Understand the Story** In order to write a good play, you must have a good understanding of the story. Reread the story you have chosen. Be sure you know every detail and that you understand the plot and the characters. Then think about how you want to present the story. You may want to write the play just as the story is written, or you may want to change certain elements.

**Organize Your Ideas** Identify important elements in the story, such as setting, events, and dialogue that are vital to the plot. A graphic organizer, such as a story map, can help you to organize your ideas in a logical way.

**my Notebook**

Use the annotation tools in your eBook to mark up key details that you might want to include. Save each detail to your notebook.

**ACADEMIC VOCABULARY**

As you write your play, be sure to use the academic vocabulary words.

*emphasize*

*occur*

*period*

*relevant*

*tradition*

| Setting: |
| --- |

▼

| Characters: |
| --- |

▼

| Plot Events: |
| --- |

▼

| Outcome: |
| --- |

**Consider Your Purpose and Audience** Who will watch your play? Why would they be interested in the story? Think about your audience as you prepare to write.

PRODUCE

**Draft Your Script** Review your notes and your graphic organizer. Use "The Prince and the Pauper" as a guide as you write your script.

**myWriteSmart**

Write your rough draft in *my*WriteSmart. Focus on getting your ideas down, rather than perfecting your choice of language.

- Examine the story. A script needs action and dialogue. Which pieces of information in the story could be left out without changing it?

- Think about the setting. How will you describe to your audience the time period and place?

- Consider whether your script needs a narrator. Do certain points need to be explained to move the story forward?

- Write in the present tense. Keep in mind that the events are happening "now," or as the play is being performed.

- Add stage directions and sound effects. These help the actors better understand the action in the play.

**Stage the Play** Staging a play is the process of choosing and designing the space for the play. Think about the space you will use to perform your play. Use your script as a guide to create your stage plan.

- Think about where the action takes place. What props and scenery will you need?

- Determine the blocking, or how the actors move on the stage. Will they need to come in and out of the stage through a door? Do they need a large open space to move around in?
- Think about the costumes you will need. Good costumes help tell about the time and place in which the story happens.

*my*WriteSmart

Have a partner or a group of peers review your draft in *my*WriteSmart. Ask your reviewers to note any confusing areas in the plot, difficulties understanding which character is speaking, or any elements that are missing in the play.

**Evaluate Your Play** Use the chart on the following page to evaluate your play. Consider the following:

- Examine the organization of the script. Check that all elements of the story are included and creatively developed.
- Make sure that the dialogue and the narrator effectively move the story forward.
- Check that stage directions are clear and brief.
- Be sure your conclusion is effective and believable.

**Rehearse Your Play** Choose actors for your play and spend time rehearsing the play. Create a schedule to be sure you are ready for the date of the performance.

- Read aloud the script with the other cast members. Answer any questions they have.
- Practice how the actors will move on the stage, and coordinate lines with physical actions.
- Focus one rehearsal on technical aspects, such as lighting, sounds, and any changes needed to the set.
- Conduct a dress rehearsal with actors in full costume.

**Perform Your Play** Finalize your script, and perform your play for the class. Consider these options:

- Record your play and post it on a personal or school website.
- Present your script to a local theater group.
- Submit your script to a play-writing contest.

After you watch the play, compare and contrast the experience of reading the original story with viewing the play.

| | Ideas and Evidence | Organization | Language |
|---|---|---|---|
| **ADVANCED** | • The play has a clear beginning, middle, and end.<br>• The play's setting is clearly described.<br>• Scene changes occur smoothly and at the right time.<br>• Descriptive dialogue and details help develop the events, characters, and setting.<br>• The problem is solved in a natural or realistic way that leaves the audience with a lasting impression. | • The script is organized into acts and scenes effectively; the sequence of events is clear.<br>• Pacing keeps the reader curious.<br>• Stage directions concisely connect acts and scenes. | • The point of view is effective and consistent throughout the play.<br>• Vivid sensory details reveal the setting, characters, and action.<br>• Dialogue is sharp, clear, and actively moves the plot forward.<br>• Stage directions are clear and direct.<br>• Spelling, capitalization, and punctuation are correct.<br>• Grammar and usage are correct. |
| **COMPETENT** | • The play contains a clear beginning, middle, or ending, but not all three.<br>• The play has a specific location, but it is not clearly defined.<br>• Most, but not all scene changes occur smoothly and at the right time.<br>• Descriptive dialogue and details help tell the story, but main events could be more vividly portrayed.<br>• The problem is solved, but the resolution seems somewhat contrived. | • The script is organized into acts and scenes, but the sequence of events is confusing at times.<br>• Pacing could move along more quickly.<br>• Stage directions mostly connect acts and scenes. | • The point of view shifts at times.<br>• More sensory details are needed to keep the action moving.<br>• Dialogue is unclear in parts but moves the plot forward.<br>• Stage directions are sometimes unclear.<br>• Some spelling, capitalization, and punctuation mistakes occur.<br>• Some grammar and usage errors, but the writer's ideas are still clear. |
| **LIMITED** | • The beginning is a little unclear and is not always focused on the main character or conflict.<br>• The setting is described, but details are not relevant.<br>• Scene changes are rough or not timed well.<br>• Descriptive dialogue and details are missing; main events are inadequately portrayed.<br>• The conclusion leaves some questions unanswered. | • The script generally lacks act and/or scene organization; too many or too few events confuse the plot.<br>• Pacing is choppy or distracting.<br>• Stage directions are distracting. | • The point of view is inconsistent.<br>• Sensory details do not advance the plot.<br>• Dialogue is mostly unclear, random, or missing.<br>• Stage directions are generally unclear.<br>• Several spelling and capitalization mistakes occur, and punctuation is inconsistent.<br>• Grammar and usage are incorrect in many places. |
| **EMERGING** | • The beginning does not establish the subject of the story.<br>• The play's setting is not described.<br>• Scene changes do not occur at the right time.<br>• Descriptive details and dialogue are unrelated or missing.<br>• The conclusion does not include a resolution to the problem. | • The script lacks acts and/or scenes; a sequence of events is missing.<br>• Pacing is ineffective.<br>• Stage directions are missing. | • The play lacks a clear point of view.<br>• Sensory details are rarely or never used.<br>• Dialogue is unclear or missing.<br>• Stage directions are missing.<br>• Spelling, capitalization, and punctuation are incorrect throughout.<br>• Grammar and usage errors change the meaning of the writer's ideas. |

# Writing an Argument

COMMON CORE W 1a-e, W 4

Many of the Performance Tasks in this book ask you to craft an argument in which you support your ideas with text evidence. Any argument you write should include the following sections and characteristics.

## Introduction

Clearly state your **claim**—the point your argument makes. As needed, provide context or background information to help readers understand your position. Note the most common opposing views as a way to distinguish and clarify your ideas. From the very beginning, make it clear for readers why your claim is strong; consider providing an overview of your reasons or a quotation that emphasizes your view in your introduction.

*EXAMPLES*

| | |
|---|---|
| **vague claim:** We need more bike lanes. | **precise claim:** The city should provide more bike lanes. Several of the city's thorough-fares are dangerous for cyclists because the roadways don't provide designated safe areas for bikers to ride in. |
| **not distinguished from opposing view:** Many people think riding a bike is unsafe. | **distinguished from opposing view:** While some people consider bike lanes a distraction for car drivers, cyclists have never caused an auto accident when they were in their own lane. |
| **confusing relation-ship of ideas:** People love to bike. Fewer cars on the road is better. | **clear relationship of ideas:** By providing cyclists with dedi-cated space on roads, the city is ensuring that riders can travel safely. |

## Development of Claims

The body of your argument must provide strong, logical reasons for your claim and must support those reasons with relevant evidence. A **reason** tells why your claim is valid; **evidence** provides specific examples that illustrate a reason. In the process of developing your claim you should also refute **counterclaims,** or opposing views, with equally strong reasons and evidence. To demonstrate that you have thoroughly considered your view, look at both the strengths and limitations of your claim and opposing claims. The goal is not to undercut your argument, but rather to answer your readers' potential objections to it. Be sure, too, to consider how much your audience may already know about your topic in order to avoid boring or confusing readers.

*EXAMPLES*

| | |
|---|---|
| **claim lacking reasons:** Bike lanes are important because people would use them and they would help the environment. | **claim developed by reasons:** By providing bike lanes, more cyclists will feel comfortable riding on city streets and will opt to ride their bikes rather than drive their cars. With fewer cars on the roads, the city's pollution will improve as less green-house gases will be omitted. |
| **omission of limita-tions:** People who oppose this idea and who hate to exercise admit there is no downside to adding bike lanes to city streets. | **fair discussion of limitations:** We should not forget to include safety precautions. All bike lanes should be clearly marked, and it should be mandatory that all cyclists wear helmets when riding on city streets. |

continued

| inattention to audience's knowledge: Bikes made with cromoly or aluminum frames are safe to ride on porous asphalt pavements. | awareness of audience's knowledge: Those unfamiliar with biking should know that most bike accidents in urban environments happen in cities that don't have dedicated bike lanes. |
|---|---|

## Links Among Ideas

Even the strongest reasons and evidence will fail to sway readers if it is unclear how the reasons and evidence relate to the central claim of an argument. Make the connections clear for your readers, using transitional words and phrases as a bridge between ideas.

### EXAMPLES

**transitional word linking claim and reason:** All residents will benefit from more bike lanes on city streets. First, with fewer cars on the road, the city's traffic conditions will improve, as will its air pollution.

**transitional phrase linking reason and evidence:** Biking on city streets in dedicated bike lanes would reduce rush hour traffic. In fact, several cities with bike lanes on every street report that with more people biking to work and less of them driving, rush hour traffic is a thing of the past.

## Appropriate Style and Tone

An effective argument is most often written in a direct and formal style. The style and tone you choose in an argument should not be an afterthought—the way you express your argument can either drive home your ideas or detract from them. Even as you argue in favor of your viewpoint, take care to remain objective in tone.

### EXAMPLES

| informal style: Because bike lanes on city streets benefit all residents, even those who don't own a bike, the city should pay for the lanes' construction with tax dollars. | formal style: Because bike lanes help all residents by reducing the chances of bike and auto accidents and reducing traffic and air pollution, the city should provide funding for the project. |
|---|---|
| biased tone: There is no logical reason to oppose more bike lanes on city streets. | objective tone: Arguments against this plan have not been as compelling as the statistics and evidence provided by cities that have bike lanes. |

## Conclusion

Your conclusion may range from a sentence to a full paragraph, but it must wrap up your argument in a satisfying way; a conclusion that sounds tacked-on helps your argument no more than providing no conclusion at all. A strong conclusion is a logical extension of the argument you have presented. It carries forth your ideas through an inference, question, quotation, or challenge.

### EXAMPLES

**inference:** Support for a safe and healthy city comes from our government leaders.

**question:** Don't all residents want to live in a city that promotes health and wellness and is committed to lessening pollution?

**quotation:** After Chicago installed its first two-way bike route with dedicated traffic signals, Mayor Rahm Emauel said ". . . having bike lanes is important to the quality of life in Chicago."

**challenge:** Having dedicated bike lanes on city roads demonstrates the city's commitment to the health and safety of its residents and sets it apart from other towns that lack such facilities.

# Writing an Informative Essay

COMMON CORE W 2a-f, W 4

Most of the Performance Tasks in this book ask you to write informational or explanatory texts in which you present a topic and examine it thoughtfully through a well-organized analysis of relevant content. Any informative or explanatory text that you create should include the following parts and features.

## Introduction

Develop a strong **thesis statement**. That is, clearly state your **topic** and the **organizational framework** through which you will connect or **distinguish** elements of your topic. For example, you might state that your text will compare ideas, examine causes and effects, or explore a problem and its solutions.

*EXAMPLES*

| Topic: animal adoptions |
| --- |
| **Sample Thesis Statements** |
| **Compare-contrast:** When deciding whether to adopt an animal from a shelter or buy one from a breeder, consider the satisfaction of rescuing a dog in addition to the differences in cost. |
| **Cause-effect:** Because of these tough economic times, many dog owners can't afford their pets and are having to surrender their dogs to shelters, which are experiencing a worsening canine overpopulation problem. |
| **Problem-solution:** If more people would adopt from shelters instead of purchasing from breeders, space in shelters could be freed up to save the 5 million dogs in the United States currently in need of good homes. |

Clarifying the organizational framework up front will help you organize the body of your text, come up with **headings** you can use to guide your readers, and identify **graphics** that you may need to clarify information. For example, if you compare and contrast the procedures and costs when adopting a pet from a shelter versus buying one from a breeder, you might create a chart like the one shown to guide your writing. You could include the same chart in your paper as a graphic for readers. The row or column headings serve as natural paragraph headings.

|  | Shelter Adoptions | Breeder Adoptions |
| --- | --- | --- |
| **Procedures** | Extensive background checks required of potential owners; spaying/neutering animal required within 30 days of adoption | No necessary verification of name and address or criminal background; spaying/neutering animal not mandatory |
| **Costs** | Typically between $50–$100, which may include the animal's spaying/neutering | Usually $3,000 or more for a specific breed; spaying/neutering costs extra, typically $150 or more |

## Development of the Topic

In the body of your text, flesh out the organizational framework you established in your introduction with strong supporting paragraphs. Include only support directly relevant to your topic. Don't rely on a single source, and make sure the sources you do use are reputable and current. The table that follows illustrates types of support you might use to develop aspects of your topic. It also shows how transitions link text sections, create cohesion, and clarify the relationships among ideas.

| Types of Support in Explanatory/ Informative Texts | Uses of Transitions in Explanatory/ Informative Texts |
|---|---|
| **Facts and examples:** One cause of overcrowding in animal shelters is economic hardship; *for example, when home foreclosures increase, the populations of animal shelters also rise.* | *One cause* signals the shift from the introduction to the body text in a cause-and-effect essay. *For example* introduces the support for the cause being cited. |
| **Concrete details:** On the other hand, while it is sad for dogs to be surrendered to a shelter, *it is better than letting the dog loose on the streets or chaining the dog outside with no food.* | *On the other hand* transitions the reader from one point of comparison to another in a compare-contrast essay. |
| **Statistics:** *Turn to the Humane Society of the United States if you doubt the scope of the problem.* Each year more than 5 million dogs are abandoned on the streets or given up by owners to shelters. | The entire transitional sentence introduces the part of a problem-solution essay that demonstrates the existence of a problem. |

## Style and Tone

Use formal English to establish your credibility as a source of information. To project authority, use the language of the domain, or field, that you are writing about. However, be sure to define unfamiliar terms to avoid using jargon your audience may not know. Provide extended definitions when your audience is likely to have limited knowledge of the topic.

Using quotations from reputable sources can also give your text authority; be sure to credit the source of quoted material. In general, keep the tone objective, avoiding slang or biased expressions.

**Informal, jargon-filled, biased language:** Backyard breeders only care about themselves and value money over life. They have no regard for an animal's welfare, and they reuse these dogs over and over again for breeding purposes until the dog dies. The puppies are treated even worse, raised in deplorable conditions, malnourished, and given no medical attention.

**Extended definition in formal style and objective tone:** Of the more than 50 million dogs in the United States, more than two-thirds come from "backyard breeders." A backyard breeder, as defined by the Humane Society of the United States, "breeds dogs for quick sales, with or without adequate care for the dogs' or puppies' health and seldom requires pre-sale testing for diseases and/or genetic abnormalities in the dogs and puppies."

## Conclusion

Wrap up your essay with a concluding statement or section that sums up or extends the information in your essay.

### EXAMPLES

**Articulate implications:** If people continue to support backyard breeders, this country's homeless dog problem will never be remedied. People need to support shelters so that owners can be found for all of the 5 million dogs in need of new homes. Otherwise, this dog overpopulation crisis will continue.

**Emphasize significance:** The number of dogs waiting to die in shelters will only keep increasing if people do not start adopting dogs from shelters. By adopting from a shelter and not buying from a breeder, you help free up space in the shelter so another homeless dog can be rescued.

# Writing a Narrative

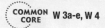 

When you are writing a fictional tale, an autobiographical incident, or a firsthand biography, you write in the narrative mode. That means telling a story with a beginning, a climax, and a conclusion. Though there are important differences between fictional and nonfiction narratives, you use similar processes to develop them.

## Identify a Problem, Situation, or Observation

For a nonfiction narrative, think about a problem you have dealt with or an observation you've made about your life. For fiction, try to invent a problem or situation that can unfold in interesting ways.

*EXAMPLES*

| Problem (nonfiction) | As a vegetarian, I find it almost impossible to find healthy foods to eat when traveling. |
|---|---|
| Situation (fiction) | Tommy, the new kid at school, has been experiencing bullying by several of his classmates, who mock his Texas accent. |

## Establish a Point of View

Decide who will tell your story. If you are writing a reflective essay about an important experience or person in your own life, you will be the narrator of the events you relate. If you are writing a work of fiction, you can choose to create a first-person narrator or tell the story from the third-person point of view. In that case, the narrator can focus on one character or reveal the thoughts and feelings of all the characters. The examples show the differences between first- and third-person narrator.

| First-person narrator (nonfiction) | At the airport, at gas stations, and at most hotels, I have had a hard time finding foods that are not made with animal products. It seems that most items are loaded with meats, cheeses, and oils. |
|---|---|

| Third-person narrator (fiction) | Tommy's first day at his new school was brutal. The kids made fun of the way he talked, imitating him mercilessly. At lunch, a group of boys taunted Tommy by calling him names, and one boy even threw food at him. |
|---|---|

## Gather Details

To make real or imaginary experiences come alive on the page, you will need to use narrative techniques like description and dialogue. The questions in the left column in the chart that follows can help you search your memory or imagination for the details that will form the basis of your narrative. You don't have to respond in full sentences, but try to capture the sights, sounds, and feelings that will bring your narrative to life.

| Who, What, When, Where? | Narrative Techniques |
|---|---|
| **People:** Who are the people or characters involved in the experience? What did they look like? What did they do? What did they say? | **Description:** Tommy moved from Texas to New York, and he loves wearing cowboy boots and flannel shirts to school. Jason, who sits behind Tommy in English class, is always laughing at Tommy's clothes and Texas accent. Jason said loudly, "Doesn't that guy look like he should be at a rodeo?" Tommy turned around and said, "Why thank you. I take that as a compliment because rodeos are really cool!" |

| Experience: What led up to or caused the event? What is the main event in the experience? What happened as a result of the event? | Description: After my dad's heart attack, he needed to change the way he ate and eliminate animal products and fats from his diet. My dad began to eat a diet of vegetables, fruits, and whole grains. To show our support, my mom and I also adopted a vegetarian diet. |
|---|---|
| Places: When and where did the events take place? What were the sights, sounds, and smells of this place? | Description: I was sitting by my dad's hospital bed. The room was dark except for the glow of street lights that flickered through the window blinds. The only sound was the rattling hum of my dad's respirator. |

## Sequence Events

Before you begin writing, list the key events of the experience or story in chronological, or time, order. Place a star next to the point of highest tension—for example, the point at which a key decision determines the outcome of events. In fiction, this point is called the climax, but a gripping nonfiction narrative will also have a climactic event.

To build suspense—the uncertainty a reader feels about what will happen next—you'll want to think about the pacing or rhythm of your narrative. Consider disrupting the chronological order of events by beginning at the end, then starting over. Or interrupt the forward flow of events with a flashback, which takes the reader to an earlier point in the narrative.

Another way to build suspense is with multiple plot lines. For example, the personal narrative about the father who has a heart attack involves a second plot line in which the father and his family eat better in an effort to avoid health complications like heart disease. Both plot lines intersect when the father gets out of the hospital and makes a commitment to be healthier, enlisting his family's support.

## Use Vivid Language

As you revise, make an effort to use vivid language. Use precise words and phrases to describe feelings and action. Use telling details to show, rather than directly state, what a character is like. Use sensory language that lets readers see, feel, hear, smell, and taste what you or your characters experienced.

| First Draft | Revision |
|---|---|
| My dad's newfound appreciation for life was contagious, inspiring me to do things I had never done before. | Walking outside for the first time since his heart attack, my dad breathed in, exhaling to say, "I will make healthier choices for myself and inspire my family to eat well." |
| As I walked around the airport food court, I looked through each restaurant's menu and could not find one healthy entree. | Hamburgers, French fries, sodas—nothing on the restaurants' menus was healthy; everything was ladened with animal fat. |
| As Tommy walked along the hallway, he could see something dripping down the front of his locker. | Tommy could feel his face get hotter, anger boiling up as he approached his locker. It was covered with garbage. |

## Conclusion

At the conclusion of the narrative, you or your narrator will reflect on the meaning of the events. The conclusion should follow logically from the climactic moment of the narrative. The narrator of a personal narrative usually reflects on the significance of the experience —the lessons learned or the legacy left.

### EXAMPLES

As my dad rounds the corner, I see him approaching the marathon's finish line. I raise a sign that says, "Dad! We Are Proud of You!" and yell out his name. He waves and glides by, crossing the finish line. After losing over 60 pounds, my dad is not the same as he was in that hospital bed a year ago. He is a new man.

# Conducting Research

COMMON CORE W 7, W 8

The Performance Tasks in this book will require you to complete research projects related to the texts you've read in the collections. Whether the topic is stated in a Performance Task or is one you generate, the following information will guide you through your research project.

## Focus Your Research and Formulate a Question

Some topics for a research project can be effectively covered in three pages; others require an entire book for a thorough treatment. Begin by developing a topic that is neither too narrow nor too broad for the time frame of the assignment. Also check your school and local libraries and databases to help you determine how to choose your topic. If there's too little information, you'll need to broaden your focus; if there's too much, you'll need to limit it.

With a topic in hand, formulate a research question; it will keep you on track as you conduct your research. A good research question cannot be answered in a single word. It should be open-ended. It should require investigation. You can also develop related research questions to explore your topic in more depth.

### EXAMPLES

| Possible topics for *Titanic* | The ship *Titanic*—too broad *Titanic's* captain Edward Smith—too narrow Settings and events—fact or fiction? |
|---|---|
| Possible research question | To what extent are the circumstances involving *Titanic's* sinking based on fact? |
| Related questions | Is it true that *Titanic* sank because its captain ignored warnings of icebergs and forged ahead instead of taking a different route? Was it because the Irish did not properly build the ship to withstand the impact from an ice field? Were the testimonies from employees at Harland & Wolfe, the architecture firm that constructed the ship, more credible than accounts from ship captains who confirmed they had sent messages to *Titanic* about seeing masses of ice in the Atlantic? |

## Locate and Evaluate Sources

To find answers to your research question, you'll need to investigate primary and secondary sources, whether in print or digital formats. **Primary sources** contain original, firsthand information, such as diaries, autobiographies, interviews, speeches, and eyewitness accounts. **Secondary sources** provide other people's versions of primary sources in encyclopedias, newspaper and magazine articles, biographies, and documentaries.

Your search for sources begins at the library and on the World Wide Web. Use **advanced search features** to help you find things quickly. Add a minus sign (–) before a word that should not appear in your results. Use an asterisk (*) in place of unknown words. List the name and location of each possible source, adding comments about its potential usefulness. Assessing, or evaluating, your sources is an important step in the research process. Your goal is to use sources that are credible, or reliable and trustworthy.

| Criteria for Assessing Sources | |
|---|---|
| **Relevance:** It covers the target aspect of my topic. | • How will the source be useful in answering my research question? |
| **Accuracy:** It includes information that can be verified by more than one authoritative source. | • Is the information up-to-date? Are the facts accurate? How can I verify them?<br>• What qualifies the author to write about this topic? Is he or she an authority? |
| **Objectivity:** It presents multiple viewpoints on the topic. | • What, if any, biases can I detect? Does the writer favor one view of the topic? |

## Incorporate and Cite Source Material

When you draft your research project, you'll need to include material from your sources. This material can be **direct quotations, summaries,** or **paraphrases** of the original source material. Two well-known **style manuals** provide information on how to cite a range of print and digital sources: the *MLA Handbook for Writers of Research Papers* (published by the Modern Language Association) and Kate L. Turabian's *A Manual for Writers* (published by The University of Chicago Press). Both style manuals provide a wealth of information about conducting, formatting, drafting, and presenting your research, including guidelines for citing sources within the text (called parenthetical citations) and preparing the list of Works Cited, as well as correct use of the mechanics of writing. Your teacher will indicate which style manual you should use. The following examples use the format in the *MLA Handbook.*

Any material from sources must be completely documented, or you will commit **plagiarism,** the unauthorized use of someone else's words or ideas. Plagiarism is not honest. As you take notes for your research project, be sure to keep complete information about your sources so that you can cite them correctly in the body of your paper. This applies to all sources, whether print or digital. Having complete information

will also enable you to prepare the list of Works Cited. The list of Works Cited, which concludes your research project, provides author, title, and publication information for both print and digital sources. The following pages show the *MLA Handbook's* Works Cited citation formats for a variety of sources.

### EXAMPLES

| | |
|---|---|
| **Direct quotation**<br>[The writer] is citing a quote from the British Broadcasting Corporation (BBC) on *Titanic's* sinking.] | In a BBC news report, "*Titanic:* Sinking the Myths," journalist Paul Louden-Brown reports that ". . . little thought was given to how a ship, 852 feet in length, might . . . avoid collision with an iceberg." |
| **Summary**<br>[The writer is summarizing the BBC news report's conclusion on the sinking of *Titanic.*] | *Titanic's* captain failed the ship's crew and passengers by not heeding iceberg warnings and not slowing down *Titanic* when ice was reported to be in the ship's path. The captain also allowed lifeboats to leave the ship partially full, causing hundreds more passengers to die. |
| **Paraphrase**<br>[The writer is paraphrasing, in his own words, facts asserted in the BBC report, as well as transcripts from the 1912 U.S. Senate hearings on the *Titanic's* sinking.] | The *Titanic* disaster is a reminder of how weak mankind is compared to the forces of nature, and how the mistakes of those in charge, *Titanic's* captain in this instance, can put people in grave danger and cause them to die. The first lifeboat to leave the ship's side had a capacity of 40 but only carried 12 people. |

# MLA Citation Guidelines

Today, you can find free websites that generate ready-made citations for research papers, using the information you provide. Such sites have some time-saving advantages when you're developing a Works Cited list. However, you should always check your citations carefully before you turn in your final paper. If you are following MLA style, use these guidelines to evaluate and finalize your work.

## Books

### One author

Lastname, Firstname. *Title of Book*. City of Publication: Publisher, Year of Publication. Medium of Publication.

### Two authors or editors

Lastname, Firstname, and Firstname Lastname. *Title of Book*. City of Publication: Publisher, Year of Publication. Medium of Publication.

### Three authors

Lastname, Firstname, Firstname Lastname, and Firstname Lastname. *Title of Book*. City of Publication: Publisher, Year of Publication. Medium of Publication.

### Four or more authors

The abbreviation *et al.* means "and others." Use *et al.* instead of listing all the authors.

Lastname, Firstname, et al. *Title of Book*. City of Publication: Publisher, Year of Publication. Medium of Publication.

### No author given

*Title of Book*. City of Publication: Publisher, Year of Publication. Medium of Publication.

### An author and a translator

Lastname, Firstname. *Title of Book*. Trans. Firstname Lastname. City of Publication: Publisher, Year of Publication. Medium of Publication.

### An author, a translator, and an editor

Lastname, Firstname. *Title of Book*. Trans. Firstname Lastname. Ed. Firstname Lastname. City of Publication: Publisher, Year of Publication. Medium of Publication.

## Parts of Books

### An introduction, a preface, a foreword, or an afterword written by someone other than the author(s) of a work

Lastname, Firstname. Part of Book. *Title of Book*. By Author of book's Firstname Lastname. City of Publication: Publisher, Year of Publication. Page span. Medium of Publication.

**A poem, a short story, an essay, or a chapter in a collection of works by one author**

Lastname, Firstname. "Title of Piece." *Title of Book*. Ed. Firstname Lastname. City of Publication: Publisher, Year of Publication. Page span. Medium of Publication.

**A poem, a short story, an essay, or a chapter in an anthology of works by several authors**

Lastname, Firstname. "Title of Piece." *Title of Book*. Ed. Firstname Lastname. City of Publication: Publisher, Year of Publication. Page range. Medium of Publication.

## Magazines, Newspapers, and Encyclopedias

### An article in a newspaper

Lastname, Firstname. "Title of Article." *Title of Book Periodical* Day Month Year: pages. Medium of Publication.

### An article in a magazine

Lastname, Firstname. "Title of Article." *Title of Book Periodical* Day Month Year: pages. Medium of Publication.

### An article in an encyclopedia

"Title of Article." *Title of Encyclopedia*. Year ed. Medium of Publication.

## Miscellaneous Nonprint Sources

### An interview

Lastname, Firstname. Personal interview. Day Month Year.

### A video recording

*Title of Recording*. Producer, Year. Medium of Publication.

## Electronic Publications

### A CD-ROM

"Title of Piece." *Title of CD*. Year ed. City of Publication: Publisher, Year of Publication. CD-ROM.

### A document from an Internet site

Entries for online sources should contain as much information as available.

Lastname, Firstname. "*Title of Piece*." Information on what the site is. Year. Web. Day Month Year (when accessed).

# Participating in a Collaborative Discussion

COMMON CORE SL 1a–d

Often, class activities, including the Performance Tasks in this book, will require you to work collaboratively with classmates. Whether your group will analyze a work of literature or try to solve a community problem, use the following guidelines to ensure a productive discussion.

## Prepare for the Discussion

A productive discussion is one in which all the participants bring useful information and ideas to share. If your group will discuss a short story the class read, first re-read and annotate a copy of the story. Your annotations will help you quickly locate evidence to support your points. Participants in a discussion about an important issue should first research the issue and bring notes or information sources that will help guide the group. If you disagree with a point made by another group member, your case will be stronger if you back it up with specific evidence from your sources.

### EXAMPLES

**disagreeing without evidence:** I don't think Mark Twain is relevant today because people would rather learn about current events through social media.

**providing evidence for disagreement:** I disagree that author Mark Twain, who addresses important cultural topics through works of fiction, is relevant today. With so much information about current events readily available on the Internet and on social media sites, kids don't want to take the time to read a book to learn about social issues. They would rather get their news and commentary immediately from the Web and read a story's comments section to see how others feel about the topic. Plus, Twain's humor is more satirical than kids today are used to. Kids prefer humor that is more blunt.

## Set Ground Rules

The rules your group needs will depend on what your group is expected to accomplish. A discussion of themes in a poem will be unlikely to produce a simple consensus; however, a discussion aimed at developing a solution to a problem should result in one strong proposal that all group members can support. Answer the following questions to set ground rules that fit your group's purpose:

- What will this group produce? A range of ideas, a single decision, a plan of action, or something else?
- How much time is available? How much of that time should be allotted to each part of the discussion (presenting ideas, summarizing or voting on final ideas, creating a product such as a written analysis or speech)?
- What roles need to be assigned within the group? Do we need a leader, a note-taker, a timekeeper, or other specific roles?
- What is the best way to synthesize our group's ideas? Should we take a vote, list group members as "for" or "against" in a chart, or use some other method to reach a consensus or sum up the results of the discussion?

## Move the Discussion Forward

Everyone in the group should be actively involved in synthesizing ideas. To make sure this happens, ask questions that draw out ideas, especially from less-talkative members of the group. If an idea or statement is confusing, try to paraphrase it, or ask the speaker to explain more about it. If you disagree with a statement, say so politely and explain in detail why you disagree.

*SAMPLE DISCUSSION*

| | |
|---|---|
| **HEIDI:** David, how do you feel about Mark Twain's relevance today? We would love to hear your thoughts. | *Question draws out quiet member* |
| **DAVID:** On one hand, I think Twain's stories are inspirational and students should read them to learn about issues of the past. But who wants to take time to read a book when you can use the Internet and get the information immediately? | *Response relates discussion to larger ideas* |
| **KIM:** I think students should be required to spend time reading a book and cultivating their own opinions rather than being persuaded by radical discussions on the Internet. | *Question challenges David's conclusion* |
| **MATT:** Yes, students should form their own opinions, but we are in an age when speed is king. People want to know about the news almost before it happens, and they want to discuss social issues without having to read a long book. | *Response elaborates on ideas* |
| **MOLLY:** Evidence has shown that when students rely on the Internet to get information instead of reading and thinking about ideas first, they don't learn how to think on their own or how to organize their ideas into cohesive arguments. The Internet seems to take away their ability to think critically and independently. | *Paraphrases idea and challenges it further based on evidence* |

## Respond to Ideas

In a diverse group, everyone may have a different perspective on the topic under discussion, and that's a good thing. Consider what everyone has to say, and don't resist changing your view if other group members provide convincing evidence for theirs. If, instead, you feel more strongly than ever about your view, don't hesitate to say so and provide

reasons related to what those with opposing views have said. Before wrapping up the discussion, try to sum up the points on which your group agrees and disagrees.

*SAMPLE DISCUSSION*

| | |
|---|---|
| **MOLLY:** We have a little time before class ends. Can we come to an agreement? <br><br> **HEIDI:** I think the main points to vote on are: Is the Internet the best source for commentary or does reading books by authors like Twain help cultivate students' own ideas about social issues? What do you guys think? | *Molly and Heidi try to summarize points of agreement* |
| **MATT:** I still think today's students want quick answers about social issues. They want to use the Internet for research. Reading long books is something my parents would do. We are different; we were raised on the Internet. | *Matt maintains his position* |
| **HEIDI:** I am leaning toward thinking that books and the Internet can work together. You can read a book and form your own opinions. Then you can go on the Internet and see what others are saying about similar topics. <br><br> **DAVID:** I agree with Heidi. Why can't books and the Internet both be useful but for different reasons? Books allow you to dig deep into a topic, whereas the Internet gives you an instant outlet to see what others think. | *Heidi and David qualify their views based on what they have heard* |
| **KIM:** I'm with David and Heidi. I think students should read a book first and then investigate what others are saying on the Internet. | *Kim supports her position by making a new connection* |

# Debating an Issue

COMMON CORE SL 3, SL 4

The selection and collection Performance Tasks in this text will direct you to engage in debates about issues relating to the selections you are reading. Use the guidelines that follow to have a productive and balanced argument about both sides of an issue.

## The Structure of a Formal Debate

In a debate, two teams compete to win the support of the audience about an issue. In a **formal debate,** two teams, each with two members, present their arguments on a given proposition or policy statement. One team argues for the proposition or statement and the other team argues against it. Each debater must consider the proposition closely and must research both sides of it. To argue convincingly either for or against a proposition, a debater must be familiar with both sides of the issue.

## Plan the Debate

The purpose of a debate is to allow participants and audience members to consider both sides of an issue. Use these planning suggestions to hold a balanced and productive debate.

- **Identify Debate Teams** Form groups of six members based on the issues that the Performance Tasks include. Three members of the team will argue for the affirmative side of the issue—that is, they support the issue. The other three members will argue for the negative side of the issue—that is, they do not support the issue.
- **Appoint a Moderator** The moderator will present the topic and goals of the debate, keep track of the time, and introduce and thank the participants.
- **Research and Prepare Notes** Search the texts you've read as well as print and online sources for valid reasons and evidence to support your team's claim. As with argument, be sure to anticipate possible opposing claims and compile evidence to counter those claims. You will use notes from your research during the debate.
- **Assign Debate Roles** One team member will introduce the team's claim and supporting evidence. Another team member will respond to questions and opposing

claims in an exchange with a member of the opposing team. The last member will present a strong closing argument.

## Hold the Debate

A formal debate is not a shouting match—rather, a well-run debate is an excellent forum for participants to express their viewpoints, build on others' ideas, and have a thoughtful, well-reasoned exchange of ideas. The moderator will begin by stating the topic or issue and introducing the participants. Participants should follow the moderator's instructions concerning whose turn it is to speak and how much time each speaker has.

| Speaker | Role | Time |
|---|---|---|
| **Affirmative Speaker 1** | Present the claim and supporting evidence for the affirmative ("pro") side of the argument. | 5 minutes |
| **Negative Speaker 1** | Ask probing questions that will prompt the other team to address flaws in the argument. | 3 minutes |
| **Affirmative Speaker 2** | Respond to the questions posed by the opposing team and counter any concerns. | 3 minutes |
| **Negative Speaker 2** | Present the claim and supporting evidence for the negative ("con") side of the argument. | 5 minutes |

*continued*

| Speaker | Role | Time |
|---|---|---|
| **Affirmative Speaker 3** | Summarize the claim and evidence for the affirmative side and explain why your reasoning is more valid. | 3 minutes |
| **Negative Speaker 3** | Summarize the claim and evidence for the negative side and explain why your reasoning is more valid. | 3 minutes |

*FORMAL DEBATE FORMAT*

## Evaluate the Debate

Use the following guidelines to evaluate a team in a debate.

- Did the team prove that the issue is significant? How thorough was the analysis?
- How well did the team effectively argue that you should support its affirmative or negative side of the proposition or issue?
- How effectively did the team present reasons and evidence, including evidence from the texts, to support the proposition?
- How effectively did the team rebut, or respond to, arguments made by the opposing team?
- Did the speakers maintain eye contact and speak at an appropriate rate and volume?
- Did the speakers observe proper debate etiquette—that is, did they follow the moderator's instructions, stay within their allotted time limits, and treat their opponents respectfully?

# Reading Informational Texts: Patterns of Organization

Reading any type of writing is easier once you recognize how it is organized. Writers usually arrange ideas and information in ways that best show how they are related. There are several common patterns of organization:

- main idea and supporting details
- chronological order
- cause-effect organization
- compare-and-contrast organization
- problem-solution order

Writers try to present their arguments in ways that will help readers follow their reasoning and accept their viewpoints.

## 1. Main Idea and Supporting Details

**Main idea and supporting details** is a basic pattern of organization in which a central idea about a topic is supported by details. The **main idea** is the most important idea about a topic that a particular text or paragraph conveys. **Supporting details** are words, phrases, or sentences that tell more about the main idea. The main idea may be directly stated at the beginning and then followed by supporting details, or it may merely be implied by the supporting details. It may also be stated after it has been implied by supporting details.

### Strategies for Reading

- To find a stated main idea in a paragraph, identify the paragraph's topic. The topic is what the paragraph is about and can usually be summed up in one or two words. The word, or synonyms of it, will usually appear throughout the paragraph. Headings and subheadings are also clues to the topics of paragraphs.
- Ask: What is the topic sentence? The topic sentence states the most important idea, message, or information the paragraph conveys about this topic. It is often the first sentence in a paragraph; however, it may appear at the end.
- To find an implied main idea, ask yourself: Whom or what did I just read about? What do the details suggest about the topic?

- Formulate a sentence stating this idea and add it to the paragraph. Does your sentence express the main idea?

Notice how the main idea is expressed in each of the following models.

> **Model:**
> **Main idea as the first sentence**
>
> Technology consists of all the ways in which people apply knowledge, tools, and inventions to meet their needs. Technology dates back to early humans. At least 2 million years ago, people made stone tools for cutting. Around 1,500 BC, early humans also made carrying bags, stone hand axes, awls (tools for piercing holes in leather or wood), and drills.

*Main idea* — Technology consists of all the ways in which people apply knowledge, tools, and inventions to meet their needs.

*Supporting details* — Technology dates back to early humans... and drills.

> **Model:**
> **Main idea as the last sentence**
>
> In time, humans developed more complex tools, such as hunting bows made of wood. They learned to make flint spearheads and metal tools. Early humans used tools to hunt and butcher animals and to construct simple forms of shelter. Technology—these new tools—gave humans more control over their environment and set the stage for a more settled way of life.

*Supporting details* — In time, humans developed more complex tools... simple forms of shelter.

*Main idea* — Technology—these new tools—gave humans more control over their environment and set the stage for a more settled way of life.

## Model:
## Implied main idea

Prehistoric art exists in Africa, Asia, Europe, Australia, and the Americas. Cave paintings thousands of years old show lively images of bulls, stallions, and bison. Prehistoric jewelry and figurines also have been found. Early humans may have worn these items. Other items may have had religious meaning.

> **Implied main idea:** Early humans created art and art objects for many purposes.

### Practice and Apply

Read each paragraph, and then do the following:

1. Identify the main idea in the paragraph, using one of the strategies discussed on the previous page.
2. Identify whether the main idea is stated or implied in the paragraph.

Yellow is the best color to paint a room with few windows, or with windows that admit little sunlight. Yellow is a light color, so it will make the room seem larger and will relieve the darkness. Yellow paint will also make it seem as if the sun is always shining, even on a rainy day. Finally, yellow will add warmth to the room.

The trombone is the only instrument with a long slide that the player moves back and forth to play different pitches. Flutes and piccolos have perfectly straight tubes; all other wind instruments have tubes that taper and end in bell shapes. The French horn is distinctive for its curved, curled shape and its bell that points backward.

## 2. Chronological Order

**Chronological order** is the arrangement of events in the order in which they happen. This type of organization is used in short stories and novels, historical writing, biographies, and autobiographies. To show the order of events, writers use order words, such as *before, after, next,* and *later,* and time words and phrases that identify specific times of day, days of the week, and dates, such as *the next morning, Friday,* and *on June 6, 2009.*

### Strategies for Reading

- Look in the text for headings and subheadings that may indicate a chronological pattern of organization, such as *Early Life* or *The Later Years.*
- Look for words and phrases that identify times, such as *in a year, three weeks later, in AD 79,* and *the next day.*
- Look for words that signal order, such as *first, afterward, then, during,* and *finally,* to see how events or steps are related.
- Note that a paragraph or passage in which ideas and information are arranged chronologically will have several words or phrases that indicate time order, not just one.
- Ask yourself: Are the events in the paragraph or passage presented in time order?

Notice the words and phrases that signal time in the first two paragraphs of the following model.

> The great Chinese teacher Confucius was born in 551 BC. His father died when he was three years old. Although Confucius came from a very poor family, he studied hard and became well-educated.
>
> By the time he was 15, in 536 BC, Confucius's heart was set on learning. In his 30s, Confucius started his teaching career. He later became one of the most important teachers in history. One of his teachings was that people should treat each other the way they would like to be treated. His teachings still seem wise after 2,500 years.
>
> When Confucius died in 479 BC, he had many followers. About 100 years later, one of his followers, Mencius, began spreading Confucius's ideas. Mencius extended these ideas and added some of his own. He taught that people are basically good and that everyone has equal value. For that reason, he believed that rulers are no better than their subjects. A good king, he said, must treat his people well.

**Events**

**Time phrase**

After Mencius died in 289 BC, Hsun-tzu carried on Confucius' teachings. Hsun-tzu lived from about 300 to 230 BC. He did not agree with Mencius that people were basically good. Instead, he taught that human nature was evil. He did believe that education and strong laws and governments could help people become good. Some people say that Hsun-tzu's teachings about strong government later helped the dictator Shih Huang Ti to conquer China and set up the Ch'in Dynasty in 221 BC.

**Order word**

---

### Practice and Apply

Reread the preceding model and then do the following:

1. List at least four words or phrases in the last three paragraphs that indicate time or order.
2. List all the events in Confucius's life that are mentioned in the model.
3. Create a timeline, beginning with Confucius's birth and ending in 479 BC, that shows all the events you listed for step 2.

## 3. Cause-Effect Organization

**Cause-effect organization** is a pattern of organization that shows the relationships between events, ideas, and trends. Cause-effect relationships may be directly stated or merely implied by the order in which the information is presented. Writers often use the cause-effect pattern in historical and scientific writing. Cause-effect relationships may have several forms.

One cause with one effect

| Cause | Effect |
| --- | --- |

One cause with multiple effects

| Cause | Effect |
| --- | --- |
|  | Effect |

Multiple causes with a single effect

| Cause |  |
| --- | --- |
| Cause | Effect |

A chain of causes and effects

| Effect | Effect | Cause | ▶ | Effect |
| --- | --- | --- | --- | --- |

### *Strategies for Reading*

- Look for headings and subheadings that indicate a cause-effect pattern of organization, such as "Effects of Hurricanes."
- To find the effect or effects, read to answer the question "What happened?"
- To find the cause or causes, read to answer the question "Why did it happen?"
- Look for words and phrases that help you identify specific relationships between events, such as *because, since, had the effect of, led to, as a result, resulted in, for that reason, due to, therefore, if . . . then,* and *consequently.*
- Look closely at each cause-effect relationship. Do not assume that because one event happened before another, the first event caused the second event.
- Use graphic organizers like the diagrams shown to record cause-effect relationships as you read.

Notice the words that signal causes and effects in the following model.

### Model:
### Watch Out for Mosquitoes

If you spend any time outdoors in the summer, at some point you will probably find yourself covered with mosquito bites. Mosquitoes can transmit serious diseases such as yellow fever, encephalitis, and malaria. Usually, though, mosquito bites just cause people to develop raised, red bumps that itch.

This is what happens. Female mosquitoes need blood to nourish their eggs. Consequently, they zero in on living things whose blood they can suck. Once they find a likely victim, the attack begins.

**Cause**
**Effect**
**Cause**
**Signal word**
**Effect**

This attack is not really a bite, since a mosquito isn't able to open her jaws. Instead, she punctures the victim's skin with sharp stylets inside her mouth. The mosquito's saliva then flows into these puncture wounds. Because the saliva keeps the victim's blood from clotting, the mosquito can drink her fill.

Meanwhile, the mosquito's saliva causes the person to have an allergic reaction. As a result, the person develops the itchy swelling we call a mosquito bite. Ironically, if the mosquito finishes eating before the victim slaps her or brushes her off, there will be less saliva left in the skin. Therefore, the redness and itching will not be so severe.

### Practice and Apply

1. Make a graphic organizer like the sample illustrated on page R18 to show the chain of causes and effects described in the text.

2. List three words or phrases that the writer uses to signal cause-effect relationships in the last two paragraphs.

## 4. Compare-and-Contrast Organization

**Compare-and-contrast organization** is a pattern of organization that provides a way to look at similarities and differences in two or more subjects. A writer may use this pattern of organization to compare the important points or characteristics of two or more subjects. These points or characteristics are called **points of comparison.** The compare-and-contrast pattern of organization may be developed in either of two ways:

**Point-by-point organization**—The writer discusses one point of comparison for both subjects, then goes on to the next point.

**Subject-by-subject organization**—The writer covers all points of comparison for one subject and then all points of comparison for the next subject.

### Strategies for Reading

- Look in the text for headings, subheadings, and sentences that may suggest a compare-

and-contrast pattern of organization, such as "Plants Share Many Characteristics," to help you identify where similarities and differences are addressed.

- To find similarities, look for words and phrases such as *like, similarly, both, all, every, also,* and *in the same way.*

- To find differences, look for words and phrases such as *unlike, but, on the other hand, more, less, in contrast,* and *however.*

- Use a graphic organizer, such as a Venn diagram or a compare-and-contrast chart, to record points of comparison and similarities and differences.

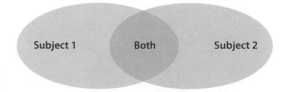

|  | Subject 1 | Subject 2 |
|---|---|---|
| **Point 1** |  |  |
| **Point 2** |  |  |
| **Point 3** |  |  |

Read the following models. As you read, use the signal words and phrases to identify the similarities and differences between the subjects and how the details are organized in each text.

### Model 1
#### Pass the Bread, Please

There are as many varieties of bread as there are countries. Two kinds that you can enjoy today—from Paris, France, to Paris, Texas, and from Cairo, Illinois, to Cairo, Egypt—are the baguette and the bagel. Both baguettes and bagels are made from the same basic ingredients, which may include flour, water, yeast, butter, eggs, and salt. Different methods are used to prepare them, however. In each case, bakers first mix the dough, knead it, and leave it to rise. Unlike baguettes, though, bagels are boiled in water before they are

Comparison word

Subjects

Contrast word

baked. This process makes them heavy and chewy and gives them a very light crust. Baguettes, on the other hand, are soft in the center and have a crisp, crunchy crust.

Another difference between the two types of bread is their shape. The word *baguette* means "wand" or "stick" in French. That describes what the bread looks like, too. Baguettes are thin and usually about two feet long. In some places, you can find shorter and fatter versions as well.

The bagel, in contrast, is shaped like a ring. Some legends say that it was originally created to honor a Polish king. It was made to look like a stirrup as a symbol of his victories in battle on horseback. Although all bagels are round, their size can vary greatly. You can choose from minibagels that are only a couple of inches in diameter to larger bagels six inches or more across.

Standard baguettes and bagels are both made from white flour. Nowadays, you can choose from a whole universe of variations, however. Baguettes come in sourdough, rye, or whole-wheat varieties.

Bagels come in all those varieties, too. In addition, though, they are available in flavors ranging from apple and blueberry to spinach and tomato. Inside, you might find raisins, nuts, or even chocolate chips. And they might be topped with poppy seeds, sunflower seeds, or sesame seeds.

So the next time you get a craving for crispy, light bread, try a baguette. But for chewy bread with tasty flavors and fillings, choose a bagel.

## Model 2
### What Kind of Person Are You?

There are definitely two types of people in the world—cat people and dog people. About the only thing they share is the fact that they like pets. Aside from that, they are as different as the pets they favor. Comparing these pets might help you figure out what kind of person you are.

Cat people tend to be very independent. They don't like to be controlled or to control anything else. So they don't want an animal that needs a lot of attention. Cats are their perfect pets since they almost take care of themselves.

You can leave cats alone for days at a time. Just set out bowls of food and water, and they will eat and drink only what they want.

Cats also groom themselves without your help. They can be quite affectionate, but only on their own terms. A cat will snuggle with you—when and if it feels like it.

Dog people, on the other hand, enjoy feeling needed and don't mind having a pet that is more dependent. Dogs definitely are dependent.

Unlike cats, dogs need a lot of attention daily. They can't be left alone for more than several hours because they have to be fed and walked regularly. You can't just leave food out for them, because they'll eat it all at once. Dogs also generally need a lot of interaction with people. Many of them seem to think their only purpose in life is to please their owners.

As different as cats and dogs are, the good news is that there are plenty of each to go around.

Subjects

Comparison word

Contrast word

Contrast words and phrases

## Practice and Apply

Refer to the preceding models to answer the following questions:

1. Which model is organized by subject? Which model is organized by points of comparison?
2. Identify two words or phrases in each model that signal a compare-and-contrast pattern of organization.
3. List two points that the writer of each model compares and contrasts.
4. For one of the two models, use a Venn diagram or a compare-and-contrast chart to identify two or more points of comparison and the similarities and differences shown.

## 5. Problem-Solution Order

**Problem-solution order** is a pattern of organization in which a problem is stated and analyzed and then one or more solutions are proposed and examined. This pattern of organization is often used in persuasive writing, where an author expresses a specific viewpoint, such as in editorials or proposals.

### *Strategies for Reading*

- Look for an explanation of the problem in the first or second paragraph.
- Look for words, such as *problem* and *reason,* that may signal an explanation of the problem.
- To find the solution, ask: What suggestion does the writer offer to solve the problem?
- Look for words, such as *propose, conclude,* and *answer,* that may signal a solution.

## Model

It happened again last night. Two cars collided at the corner of West Avenue and Beach Street. This is the sixth accident that has taken place at that intersection in the past year. Luckily, no one has been seriously injured or killed so far. But we need to do something before it's too late. How many crashes do there have to be before we make the streets safer for everyone?

This intersection is so dangerous because West Avenue bends around just before it crosses Beach Street. This means that drivers or cyclists aren't able to see traffic approaching on West Avenue until they're entering the intersection. They have to just take their chances and hope they make it to the other side. Too many times, they don't.

One action that would help solve this problem would be to put a stoplight at the intersection. This would allow drivers and cyclists to move safely through the intersection in both directions. It would also slow traffic down and force people to pay more attention to their driving. Although it would cost the community some money to put in the stoplight, think how much it would save in car repairs, personal injuries, and possibly even lives.

Here's what you can do to help solve this problem. First, talk to your friends and neighbors about it. Then, go to the village hall and sign the petition!

## Practice and Apply

Reread the model and then answer the following questions:

1. According to the model, what is the cause of the problem?
2. What solution does the writer offer? What words are a clue?

# Reading Persuasive Texts

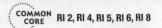 

## 1. Analyzing an Argument

A **persuasive text** is writing that tries to sway its readers' feelings, beliefs, or actions. It typically makes use of an argument and persuasive devices, or tricks. An **argument** is a logical appeal that consists of the following elements:

- A **claim** is the writer's position on an issue or problem. It usually reflects the writer's viewpoint, or attitude, on the issue.
- **Support** consists of the reasons and evidence given to support a claim.
- **Reasons** are declarations made to justify an action, decision, or belief. For example, "I carry an umbrella *because it rains so often.*"
- **Evidence** can be facts, expert opinions, examples, or other details that back up a reason or a claim. For example, "This week, it has rained every day!" (fact)
- A **counterargument** is an argument made to answer likely objections.

| Claim | We get too much homework. |
|---|---|
| Reason | We have no time for other activities. |
| Evidence | We had to quit Eagle Scouts. |
| Counter-argument | Students do need to do a certain amount of homework to learn, but the amount we get is more than necessary. It's overwhelming. |

### Practice and Apply

Use a chart like the one shown to identify the claim, reasons, evidence, and counterargument in the following editorial.

### Our School Needs to Get in the Swim
by Maria Lopez

This school needs a swimming pool. Swimming is an important life skill and one of the best forms of exercise there is. It is one of the few activities that won't harm the body and can actually improve circulation, breathing, and mobility. I believe it is the responsibility of the school to provide this essential part of students' lifelong education.

The school's mission is to educate the whole person—mind and body—and to prepare students to be productive citizens. In addition to our academic subjects, we are taught how to eat right and budget our money. But we don't learn the water safety skills that could someday save our lives.

The community and school board obviously don't feel the same way about this issue as I do, however. They repeatedly have refused to fund the building of a pool. In the opinion of one board member, "Students can take swimming lessons at the local health club." Other school officials think that the school has more important needs, such as repairing the sagging gym floor.

In my opinion, these reasons are not valid. First, most students cannot afford swimming lessons at the health club. Even those who have the money don't have the time. They're busy with homework and other activities during the school year and have to work or go to summer school during vacation.

I agree that the gym floor should be replaced, but I believe that educational needs should come first. Even if knowing how to swim never saves your life, it can improve its quality. Isn't that what an education is all about?

## 2. Recognizing Persuasive Techniques

Persuasive texts typically rely on more than just the **logical appeal** of an argument to be convincing. They also rely on ethical and emotional appeals and other **persuasive techniques**—devices that can convince you to adopt a position or take an action.

**Ethical appeals** establish a writer's credibility and trustworthiness with an audience. When a writer links a claim to a widely accepted value, the writer not only gains moral support for that claim but also establishes him- or herself as a reputable person readers can trust. For example, with the following appeal the writer reminds readers of a value they should accept and aligns himself with the reader: "Most of us think it's important to be informed about current events, but we don't spend much time reading newspapers."

The chart shown here explains several other methods of persuasion.

| Persuasive Technique | Example |
|---|---|
| **Appeals by Association** | |
| **Bandwagon appeal** Suggests that a person should believe or do something because "everyone else" does | Don't be the last person in town to be connected to Neighbor Net. |
| **Testimonial** Relies on endorsements from well-known people or satisfied customers | Start your day with the vitamins recommended by four out of five doctors— Superstrength Vigorvites. |
| **Snob appeal** Taps into people's desire to be special or part of an elite group | You deserve to eat like a king. Join the distinguished diners at Marco's Palace. |
| **Appeal to loyalty** Relies on people's affiliation with a particular group | Show your support for the community by marching in our local parade! |
| **Emotional Appeals** | |
| **Appeals to pity, fear, or vanity** Use strong feelings, rather than facts, to persuade | If you don't see a dentist regularly, your teeth will rot. |

| Practice and Apply |
|---|

Identify the persuasive techniques used in this model.

### Learn While You Sleep

Join the increasing number of with-it people who are making every hour of their day—and night—count. No matter whether they're awake or asleep, they keep going, growing, and improving themselves every minute. Impossible? Not according to college basketball superstar Jordan Navarro, whose grade-point average went from 2.5 to 4.0 after just one month on the program. "As amazing as it sounds, my free-throw average shot up, too," he said. Stop wasting time and start becoming the smart and effective person you always dreamed of being. Just call 555-ZZ-LEARN and sign up right now.

## 3. Analyzing Logic and Reasoning

While persuasive techniques may sway you to side with a writer, they should not be enough to convince you that an argument is sound. To determine the soundness of an argument, you really need to examine the argument's claim and support and the logic or reasoning that links them. To do this, identify the writer's mode of reasoning.

### The Inductive Mode of Reasoning

When a person adds up evidence to arrive at a general idea, or generalization, that person is using **inductive reasoning.** Here is an example.

| Evidence |
|---|
| **Fact 1** Allison's eyes swell and she has trouble breathing when she's around cats. |
| **Fact 2** Roses make her sister Lucy sneeze. |
| **Fact 3** Max gets an allergic reaction from nuts. |
| **Generalization** |
| People can be allergic to animals, plants, and foods. |

**Strategies for Determining the Soundness of Inductive Reasoning**

Ask yourself the following questions to evaluate inductive reasoning.

- **Is the evidence valid?** Inaccurate facts can lead to false conclusions.
- **Does the conclusion follow logically from the evidence?** From the facts listed, the conclusion that *all* animals, plants, and foods cause allergic reactions would be too broad.
- **Is the evidence drawn from a large enough sample?** These three facts are enough to support the generalization. However, if you wanted to support a conclusion that most people are allergic to something, you would need a much larger sample.

### The Deductive Mode of Reasoning

When a person starts with a generally accepted idea and then applies it to a situation or problem in order to reach a conclusion, that person is using **deductive reasoning.** Here's an example.

| | |
|---|---|
| **Many people are allergic to animals.** | Generally accepted idea |
| ▼ | |
| **Allison's eyes swell up and she has trouble breathing when she's around cats.** | Specific situation |
| ▼ | |
| **Allison is allergic to cats.** | Conclusion |

Strategies for Determining the Soundness of Deductive Reasoning

Ask yourself the following questions to evaluate deductive reasoning.

- **What is the generally accepted idea or generalization that the conclusion is based on?** Writers don't always state their general idea. So you may need to begin your evaluation by identifying it.
- **Is the generally accepted idea or generalization something you know is true and agree with?** Sometimes it isn't. Be sure to consider whether you think it is really true.
- **Is the conclusion valid?** To be valid, the conclusion must be the only logical one you can reach by applying the general idea to the specific situation. Here is an example of flawed deductive reasoning.

| | |
|---|---|
| **Many people are allergic to animals.** | Generally accepted idea |
| ▼ | |
| **Allison's eyes are swollen and she's having trouble breathing.** | Specific situation |
| ▼ | |
| **Allison is allergic to cats.** | Conclusion |

While the general idea is true, there is no evidence present in this situation to suggest that Allison's symptoms are the result of an allergy to any animal.

**Practice and Apply**

Identify the mode of reasoning used here.

I was doing my homework in my room last night when the light went out. Going into the hall, I saw that the kitchen lights were still on. That told me the problem was just in my room. The lamp was still plugged in, so I put in a new light bulb. Luckily, that worked.

### Unsupported Inferences

An **inference** is a guess that is based on evidence and, usually, some sort of prior knowledge.

An **unsupported inference** is a guess that is not adequately supported by the evidence that has been provided.

See whether you can spot the unsupported inference in the following paragraph.

> **Model**
>
> My pediatrician says, "When children exercise, they establish a positive pattern for the rest of their lives." That was true for my mom. She danced as a child and now does aerobics as an adult. Clearly, children who exercise regularly are likely to become adults who exercise regularly. They are also more likely to get involved in aerobics classes as adults.

If you guessed that the last sentence in the model was an unsupported inference, you would be right. Although the writer's mother went on to take aerobics classes as an adult, there is certainly not enough evidence present to back up the last statement.

**Practice and Apply**

Identify the unsupported inferences in the following text. Give reasons for your answers.

A good education should include physical fitness classes. The exercise that children get in gym class helps make them strong. It also helps them establish the healthy habit of exercising. My cousin's gym classes have made her the healthy girl she is today. I am sure that we would be healthy, too, if we had physical education at school. We would also get along better.

## Identifying Faulty Reasoning

Have you ever heard or read an argument that struck you as being wrong or faulty but been unable to say just why? If so, chances are good that the argument was based on a **logical fallacy,** or an error in logic. Becoming familiar with common fallacies will give you a better chance of detecting their presence and explaining precisely why an argument is unconvincing. This chart identifies errors in logic that most often find their way into arguments.

| Type of Fallacy | Definition | Example |
|---|---|---|
| **Circular reasoning** | Supporting a statement by simply repeating it in different words | I forgot my lunch because **I didn't remember to bring it.** |
| **Either/or fallacy** | A statement that suggests that there are only two choices available in a situation that really offers more than two options | **Either** you get an A in English this year **or** you'll get an F. |
| **Oversimplification** | An explanation of a complex situation or problem as if it were much simpler than it is | **Just be a good listener** and you'll have lots of friends. |
| **Overgeneralization** | A generalization that is too broad. You can often recognize overgeneralizations by the use of words such as *all, everyone, every time, anything, no one*, and *none.* | I **always** say the wrong thing. |
| **Hasty generalization** | A conclusion drawn from too little evidence or from evidence that is biased | **We all must have done badly on the test,** because Ms. Chen looked angry at the beginning of class today. |
| **Stereotyping** | A dangerous type of overgeneralization. Stereotypes are broad statements about people on the basis of their gender, ethnicity, race, or political, social, professional, or religious group. | **Boys** are better at sports than **girls** are. |
| **Attacking the person or name-calling** | An attempt to discredit an idea by attacking the person or group associated with it | Only **immature** people like animated movies. |
| **Evading the issue** | Responding to an objection with arguments and evidence that do not address its central point | I didn't tell you I broke the statue, **but you said you never liked it anyway.** |
| **False cause** | The mistake of assuming that because one event occurred after another event in time, the first event caused the second one | Ellie studied really hard for the test, **so the teacher cancelled it.** |

Look for examples of logical fallacies in the following argument. Identify each one and explain why you identified it as such.

My parents can't understand me because they just don't get it. Adults are like robots and just keep doing things the way they were taught. For example, all my friends are allowed to stay up as late as they want on weekends, but I have to be in bed by 9:00. Why? Because that's how my parents were raised. I've tried to explain to them that if I can't stay up later, I'll lose all my friends. They just say I'll understand when I'm a parent. Well, I guess I'll never understand, because I'll never have kids.

## 4. Evaluating Persuasive Texts

Learning how to evaluate persuasive texts and identify bias and propaganda will help you become more selective when doing research or just trying to stay informed.

### Strategies for Identifying Bias

**Bias** is an inclination for or against a particular opinion or viewpoint. Journalists usually try to keep their personal biases from affecting their writing, but sometimes a bias shows up anyway. Here are some of the most common signs of bias.

- Presenting just one way of looking at an issue or topic
- The absence of key information
- Stacking more evidence on one side of the argument than the other
- Treating weak or unproven evidence as valid and important
- Using **loaded language,** or words with strongly positive or negative connotations

### EXAMPLE

*This movie insults my intelligence. It was so ridiculous that I walked out before it was done.* (*Insults* and *ridiculous* have very negative connotations.)

### Strategies for Identifying Propaganda

**Propaganda** is any form of communication that is so distorted that it conveys false or misleading information. When a text includes more than one of the following, it is probably propaganda.

- Signs of **bias,** such as the absence of key information
- Inflammatory images that make powerful **emotional appeals**
- **Logical fallacies,** such as name-calling, false cause, and the either/or fallacy
- Lots of **ethical appeals,** or attempts to make readers feel that they and the writer(s) of the text share the same values

### EXAMPLE

*I care about you people. He doesn't. His voting record shows that he really only cares about rich businessmen.* (The candidate does not mention that he voted exactly the same way as his opponent did on the issues.)

### Strategies for Evaluating Evidence

Use the questions below to critically evaluate evidence in persuasive texts.

- **Are the facts presented verifiable?** Facts can be proven by eyewitness accounts, authoritative sources, experts, or research.
- **Are the opinions well informed?** Any opinions offered as support should come from experts on the topic or eyewitnesses to the event.
- **Is the evidence sufficient?** Sufficient evidence leaves no reasonable questions unanswered. If a choice is offered, background for making the choice is provided. If taking a side is called for, all sides of the issue are presented.
- **Is the evidence relevant?** The evidence should come from sources that the text's intended audience respects and regards as suitable. For example, in a report for scientists, evidence should come from scientific journals, experts in the field, and experiments rather than a casual poll of friends, a personal experience, or an expert in some unrelated field.

Read the argument below. Identify the facts, opinions, and elements of bias.

Lewis Middle School doesn't care about students' needs. I know the school board voted to remove our lockers so we can't hide dangerous items there. We don't deserve this lack of respect and suspicion, though. The lockers gave us a place to store our books, jackets, lunches, and other gear when we weren't using them. It's not fair to make us haul our stuff around all day. After all, my textbooks alone weigh over 70 pounds—as much as I do. Would you board members want to carry me around on your back all day?

### Strategies for Determining a Strong Argument

Make sure that all or most of the following statements are true.

- The argument presents a claim or thesis.
- The claim is connected to its support by a general principle that most readers would readily agree with. Valid general principle: *People are responsible for treating others with kindness.* Invalid general principle: *People are responsible for making other people happy.*
- The reasons make sense.
- The reasons are presented in a logical and effective order.
- The claim and all reasons are adequately supported by sound evidence.
- The evidence is adequate, accurate, and appropriate.
- The logic is sound. There are no instances of faulty reasoning.
- The argument offers counterarguments to address possible reader concerns and counterclaims.

Use the preceding criteria to evaluate the strength of the following proposal.

**Model**

## Summary of Proposal

I propose that the town put trash containers at bus stops, train stations, playgrounds, parks, beaches, and all other public areas.

### Need

The community is littered with paper, food and drink containers, and other garbage. This situation doesn't make us feel good about ourselves or where we live.

### Proposed Solution

Making trash containers available in places where people gather will help create a cleaner environment and restore our pride in our community.

Everybody would be willing to throw their bottles, cans, newspapers, gum wrappers, bags, and other garbage in a container if there was one available. Most people aren't willing to carry their trash with them until they find a proper place to throw it, however. Many citizens are such slobs that they won't even walk across the street to throw something away rather than just dropping it on the ground.

I know that installing these trash containers will cost money. Workers also will have to be paid to empty them regularly. Another objection might be that kids sometimes overturn trash containers or enjoy rolling them around.

These objections are ridiculous, though. None of us really believe that having a clean, pleasant community wouldn't be worth the few dollars this would cost. And a simple—and cheap—way to prevent kids from playing with the containers would be to chain them to a pole or fence.

Either the town council votes to approve this proposal and put it into effect right away, or the members should be voted out of office.

# Grammar

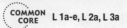 

Writing that has a lot of mistakes can confuse or even annoy a reader. Punctuation errors in a letter might lead to a miscommunication or delay a reply. A sentence fragment might lower your grade on an essay. Paying attention to grammar, punctuation, and capitalization rules can make your writing clearer and easier to read.

## Quick Reference: Parts of Speech

| Part of Speech | Function | Examples |
|---|---|---|
| **Noun** | names a person, a place, a thing, an idea, a quality, or an action | |
| Common | serves as a general name, or a name common to an entire group | subway, fog, puzzle, tollbooth |
| Proper | names a specific, one-of-a-kind person, place, or thing | Mrs. Price, Pompeii, China, Meg |
| Singular | refers to a single person, place, thing, or idea | onion, waterfall, lamb, sofa |
| Plural | refers to more than one person, place, thing, or idea | dreams, commercials, men, tortillas |
| Concrete | names something that can be perceived by the senses | jacket, teacher, caterpillar, aroma |
| Abstract | names something that cannot be perceived by the senses | friendship, opportunities, fear, stubbornness |
| Compound | expresses a single idea through a combination of two or more words | jump rope, paycheck, dragonfly, sandpaper |
| Collective | refers to a group of people or things | colony, family, clan, flock |
| Possessive | shows who or what owns something | Mama's, Tito's, children's, waitresses' |
| **Pronoun** | takes the place of a noun or another pronoun | |
| Personal | refers to the person making a statement, the person(s) being addressed, or the person(s) or thing(s) the statement is about | I, me, my, mine, we, us, our, ours, you, your, yours, she, he, it, her, him, hers, his, its, they, them, their, theirs |
| Reflexive | follows a verb or preposition and refers to a preceding noun or pronoun | myself, yourself, herself, himself, itself, ourselves, yourselves, themselves |
| Intensive | emphasizes a noun or another pronoun | (same as reflexives) |
| Demonstrative | points to one or more specific persons or things | this, that, these, those |

*continued*

| Part of Speech | Function | Examples |
|---|---|---|
| Interrogative | signals a question | who, whom, whose, which, what |
| Indefinite | refers to one or more persons or things not specifically mentioned | both, all, most, many, anyone, everybody, several, none, some |
| Relative | introduces an adjective clause by relating it to a word in the clause | who, whom, whose, which, that |
| **Verb** | expresses an action, a condition, or a state of being | |
| Action | tells what the subject does or did, physically or mentally | run, reaches, listened, consider, decides, dreamed |
| Linking | connects the subject to something that identifies or describes it | am, is, are, was, were, sound, taste, appear, feel, become, remain, seem |
| Auxiliary | precedes the main verb in a verb phrase | be, have, do, can, could, will, would, may, might |
| Transitive | directs the action toward someone or something; always has an object | The storm **sank** the ship. |
| Intransitive | does not direct the action toward someone or something; does not have an object | The ship **sank.** |
| **Adjective** | modifies a noun or pronoun | **strong** women, **two** epics, **enough** time |
| **Adverb** | modifies a verb, an adjective, or another adverb | walked **out, really** funny, **far** away |
| **Preposition** | relates one word to another word | at, by, for, from, in, of, on, to, with |
| **Conjunction** | joins words or word groups | |
| Coordinating | joins words or word groups used the same way | and, but, or, for, so, yet, nor |
| Correlative | used as a pair to join words or word groups used the same way | both . . . and, either . . . or, neither . . . nor |
| Subordinating | introduces a clause that cannot stand by itself as a complete sentence | although, after, as, before, because, when, if, unless |
| **Interjection** | expresses emotion | wow, ouch, hurrah |

# Quick Reference: The Sentence and Its Parts

The diagrams that follow will give you a brief review of the essentials of a sentence and some of its parts.

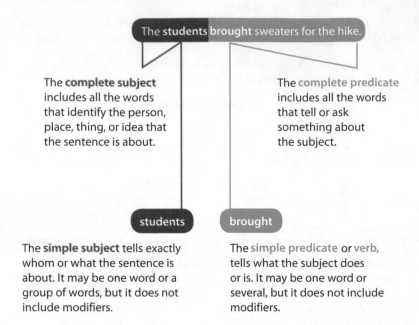

The **complete subject** includes all the words that identify the person, place, thing, or idea that the sentence is about.

The complete predicate includes all the words that tell or ask something about the subject.

The **simple subject** tells exactly whom or what the sentence is about. It may be one word or a group of words, but it does not include modifiers.

The simple predicate or verb, tells what the subject does or is. It may be one word or several, but it does not include modifiers.

Every word in a sentence is part of a complete subject or a complete predicate.

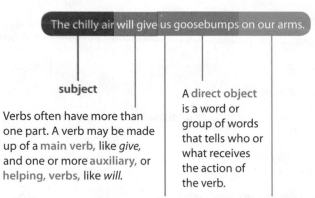

**subject**

Verbs often have more than one part. A verb may be made up of a main verb, like *give*, and one or more auxiliary, or helping, verbs, like *will*.

A direct object is a word or group of words that tells who or what receives the action of the verb.

An **indirect object** is a word or group of words that tells to whom or for whom or to what or for what the verb's action is performed. A sentence can have an indirect object only if it has a direct object. The indirect object always comes before the direct object.

A prepositional phrase consists of a preposition, its object, and any modifiers of the object. In this phrase, *on* is the preposition, *arms* is the object, and *our* modifies *arms*.

# Quick Reference: Punctuation

| Mark | Function | Examples |
|---|---|---|
| **End Marks** period, question mark, exclamation point | ends a sentence | We can start now. When would you like to leave? What a fantastic hit! |
| period | follows an initial or abbreviation **Exception**: postal abbreviations of states | Mrs. Dorothy Parker, Apple Inc., C. P. Cavafy, P.M., lb., oz., Blvd., Dr., NE (Nebraska), NV (Nevada) |
| period | follows a number or letter in an outline or a list | I. Volcanoes   A. Central-vent     1. Shield |
| **Comma** | separates parts of a compound sentence | I had never disliked poetry, but now I really love it. |
| | separates items in a series | She is brave, loyal, and kind. |
| | separates adjectives of equal rank that modify the same noun | The slow, easy route is best. |
| | sets off a term of address | Maria, how can I help you? You must do something, soldier. |
| | sets off a parenthetical expression | Hard workers, as you know, don't quit. I'm not a quitter, believe me. |
| | sets off an introductory word, phrase, or dependent clause | Yes, I forgot my key. At the beginning of the day, I feel fresh. While she was out, I was here. Having finished my chores, I went out. |
| | sets off a nonessential phrase or clause | Ed Pawn, the captain of the chess team, won. Ed Pawn, who is the captain, won. The two leading runners, sprinting toward the finish line, finished in a tie. |
| | sets off parts of dates and addresses | Mail it by May 14, 2010, to the Hauptman Company, 321 Market Street, Memphis, Tennessee. |
| | separates words to avoid confusion | By noon, time had run out. What the minister does, does matter. While cooking, Jim burned his hand. |

continued

| Mark | Function | Examples |
|---|---|---|
| **Semicolon** | separates items in a series that contain commas | We spent the first week of summer vacation in Chicago, Illinois; the second week in St. Louis, Missouri; and the third week in Albany, New York. |
| | separates parts of a compound sentence that are not joined by a coordinating conjunction | The last shall be first; the first shall be last. I read the Bible; however, I have not memorized it. |
| | separates parts of a compound sentence when the parts contain commas | After I ran out of money, I called my parents; but only my sister was home, unfortunately. |
| **Colon** | introduces a list | The names we wrote were the following: Dana, John, and Will. |
| | introduces a long quotation | Abraham Lincoln wrote: "Four score and seven years ago, our fathers brought forth on this continent a new nation. . . ." |
| | follows the salutation of a business letter | To Whom It May Concern: Dear Leonard Atole: |
| | separates certain numbers | 1:28 P.M., Genesis 2:5 |
| **Dash** | indicates an abrupt break in thought | I was thinking of my mother—who is arriving tomorrow— just as you walked in. |
| **Parentheses** | enclose less important material | It was so unlike him (John is always on time) that I began to worry. The last World Series game (did you see it?) was fun. |
| **Hyphen** | joins parts of a compound adjective before a noun | That's a not-so-happy face. |
| | joins parts of a compound with *all-, ex-, self-,* or *-elect* | The ex-firefighter helped rescue him. Our president-elect is self-conscious. |
| | joins parts of a compound number (to ninety-nine) | My bicycle wheel has twenty-six spokes. |
| | joins parts of a fraction | My cup is one-third full. |
| | joins a prefix to a word beginning with a capital letter | Were your grandparents born post-World War II? The mid-April snowstorm surprised everyone. |
| | indicates that a word is divided at the end of a line | How could you have any reason-able expectations of getting a new computer? |

*continued*

| Mark | Function | Examples |
|------|----------|----------|
| **Apostrophe** | used with *s* to form the possessive of a noun or an indefinite pronoun | my friend's book, my friends' books, anyone's guess, somebody else's problem |
| | replaces one or more omitted letters in a contraction or numbers in a date | don't (omitted *o*), he'd (omitted *woul*), the class of '99 (omitted *19*) |
| | used with *s* to form the plural of a letter | I had two A's on my report card. |
| **Quotation Marks** | set off a speaker's exact words | Sara said, "I'm finally ready." "I'm ready," Sara said, "finally." Did Sara say, "I'm ready"? Sara said, "I'm ready!" |
| | set off the title of a story, an article, a short poem, an essay, a song, or a chapter | I like Salisbury's "The Ravine" and Frost's "The Road Not Taken." I like Blake Shelton's "Over You." |
| **Ellipses** | replace material omitted from a quotation | "Early one morning, Mrs. Bunnin wobbled into the classroom lugging a large cardboard box**. . . .** Robert was at his desk scribbling a ballpoint tattoo **. . .** on the tops of his knuckles." |
| **Italics** | indicate the title of a book, a play, a magazine, a long poem, an opera, a film, or a TV series, or the name of a ship | ***Colin Powell: Military Leader***, ***The Prince and the Pauper***, ***Time***, ***After the Hurricane***, ***The Marriage of Figaro***, ***Hatchet***, ***American Idol***, ***Titanic*** |

# Quick Reference: Capitalization

| Category | Examples |
| --- | --- |
| **People and Titles** | |
| Names and initials of people | Maya Angelou, **W.E.B. DuBois** |
| Titles used before a name | Mrs. Price, Scoutmaster Brenkman |
| Deities and members of religious groups | Jesus, Allah, Buddha, Zeus, Baptists |
| Names of ethnic and national groups | Hispanics, Jews, African Americans |
| **Geographical Names** | |
| Cities, states, countries, continents | Philadelphia, Kansas, Japan, Europe |
| Regions, bodies of water, mountains | the South, Lake Baikal, Mount Everest |
| Geographic features, parks | Great Basin, Yellowstone National Park |
| Streets and roads, planets | 318 East Sutton Drive, Charles Court, Jupiter, Mars |
| **Organizations, Events, Etc.** | |
| Companies, organizations, teams | Ford Motor Company, Boy Scouts of America, St. Louis Cardinals |
| Buildings, bridges, monuments | Empire State Building, Eads Bridge, Washington Monument |
| Documents, awards | Declaration of Independence, Stanley Cup |
| Special named events | Mardi Gras, World Series |
| Government bodies, historical periods and events | U.S. Senate, House of Representatives, Middle Ages, Vietnam War |
| Days and months, holidays | Thursday, March, Thanksgiving, Labor Day |
| Specific cars, boats, trains, planes | Porsche, *Carpathia*, *Southwest Chief*, Concorde |
| **Proper Adjectives** | |
| Adjectives formed from proper nouns | French cooking, Spanish omelet, Edwardian age |
| **First Words and the Pronoun *I*** | |
| First word in a sentence or quotation | This is it. He said, "Let's go." I have it. |
| First word of a sentence in parentheses that is not within another sentence | The spelling rules are covered in another section. (Consult that section for more information.) |
| First words in the salutation and closing of a letter | Dear Madam, Very truly yours, |
| First word, last word, and all important words in a title | "Alone in the Nets," *Under the Royal Palms* |

# 1 Nouns

A **noun** is a word used to name a person, a place, a thing, an idea, a quality, or an action. Nouns can be classified in several ways.

For more information on different types of nouns, see **Quick Reference: Parts of Speech,** page R28.

## 1.1 COMMON NOUNS

**Common nouns** are general names, common to entire groups.

## 1.2 PROPER NOUNS

**Proper nouns** name specific, one-of-a-kind people, places, and things.

| Common | Proper |
|---|---|
| volcano, student, country, president | Mount Vesuvius, June, China, President Cleveland |

For more information, see **Quick Reference: Capitalization,** page R34.

## 1.3 SINGULAR AND PLURAL NOUNS

A noun may take a singular or a plural form, depending on whether it names a single person, place, thing, or idea or more than one. Make sure you use appropriate spellings when forming plurals.

| Singular | Plural |
|---|---|
| walrus, bully, lagoon, goose | walruses, bullies, lagoons, geese |

For more information, see **Forming Plural Nouns,** page R58.

## 1.4 POSSESSIVE NOUNS

A **possessive noun** shows who or what owns something.

For more information, see **Forming Possessives,** page R58.

# 2 Pronouns

A **pronoun** is a word that is used in place of a noun or another pronoun. The word or word group to which the pronoun refers is called its **antecedent.**

## 2.1 PERSONAL PRONOUNS

**Personal pronouns** change their form to express person, number, gender, and case. The forms of these pronouns are shown in the following chart.

| | Nominative | Objective | Possessive |
|---|---|---|---|
| **Singular** | | | |
| First Person | I | me | my, mine |
| Second Person | you | you | your, yours |
| Third Person | she, he, it | her, him, it | her, hers, his, its |
| **Plural** | | | |
| First Person | we | us | our, ours |
| Second Person | you | you | your, yours |
| Third Person | they | them | their, theirs |

## 2.2 AGREEMENT WITH ANTECEDENT

Pronouns should agree with their antecedents in number, gender, and person.

If an antecedent is singular, use a singular pronoun.

> EXAMPLE: *That **poem** was fun to read. It rhymed.*

If an antecedent is plural, use a plural pronoun.

> EXAMPLES: ***Poets** choose their words carefully.*
> *I like **poems,** but Mischa doesn't care for them.*

The gender of a pronoun must be the same as the gender of its antecedent.

> EXAMPLE: *Eve Merriam's creativity makes her poems easy to remember.*

The person of the pronoun must be the same as the person of its antecedent. As the chart in Section 2.1 shows, a pronoun can be in first-person, second-person, or third-person form.

EXAMPLES: *We* each have *our* favorite poets.

---

### Grammar Practice

Rewrite each sentence so that the under-lined pronoun agrees with its antecedent.

1. The speaker in Maya Angelou's poem "Life Doesn't Frighten Me" talks about <u>their</u> fears.
2. When I read this poem, <u>we</u> felt braver already.
3. Scary things lose <u>its</u> power.
4. Even frogs and snakes don't seem as bad as <u>you</u> usually do.
5. I want to know how to be unafraid in <u>her</u> life.

---

## 2.3  PRONOUN FORMS

Personal pronouns change form to show how they function in sentences. The three forms are the subject form, the object form, and the possessive form. For examples of these pronouns, see the chart in Section 2.1.

A **subject pronoun** is used as a subject in a sentence.

EXAMPLES: *Steven is my brother. He is the best player on the team.*

Also use the subject form when the pronoun follows a linking verb.

EXAMPLE: *The girl in the closet was she.*

An **object pronoun** is used as a direct object, an indirect object, or the object of a preposition.

SUBJECT    OBJECT
*They locked her in it.*
OBJECT OF PREPOSITION

A **possessive pronoun** shows ownership. The pronouns *mine, yours, hers, his, its, ours,* and *theirs* can be used in place of nouns.

EXAMPLE: *The cat is mine.*

The pronouns *my, your, her, his, its, our,* and *their* are used before nouns.

EXAMPLE: *I found her keys on the floor.*

---

**WATCH OUT!** Many spelling errors can be avoided if you watch out for *its* and *their*. Don't confuse the possessive pronoun *its* with the contraction *it's,* meaning "it is" or "it has." The homonyms *they're* (a contraction of *they are*) and *there* ("in that place") are often mistakenly used for *their*.

**TIP** To decide which pronoun to use in a comparison, such as "He tells better tales than (*I* or *me*)," fill in the missing word(s): *He tells better tales than I tell.*

---

### Grammar Practice

Write the correct pronoun form to complete each sentence.

1. When (he, him) is done with the book, I will give it to you.
2. Mary is going to invite (her, she) to go rollerskating.
3. My friends have lost (their, they) tickets.
4. (We, Us) can cook vegetables on the grill tonight, or we can make a salad.
5. (I, Me) sent an e-mail earlier today to my aunt.

---

## 2.4  REFLEXIVE AND INTENSIVE PRONOUNS

These pronouns are formed by adding *-self* or *-selves* to certain personal pronouns. Their forms are the same, and they differ only in how they are used.

A **reflexive pronoun** follows a verb or preposition and reflects back on an earlier noun or pronoun.

EXAMPLES: *He likes himself too much. She is now herself again.*

**Intensive pronouns** intensify or emphasize the nouns or pronouns to which they refer.

EXAMPLES: *They themselves will educate their children.*

*You yourself did it.*

---

**WATCH OUT!** Avoid using *hisself* or *theirselves.* Standard English does not include these forms.

> NONSTANDARD: *The children congratulated theirselves.*
>
> STANDARD: *The children congratulated themselves.*

## 2.5  DEMONSTRATIVE PRONOUNS

**Demonstrative pronouns** point out things and persons near and far.

|  | Singular | Plural |
|---|---|---|
| Near | this | these |
| Far | that | those |

## 2.6  INDEFINITE PRONOUNS

**Indefinite pronouns** do not refer to specific persons or things and usually have no antecedents. The chart shows some commonly used indefinite pronouns.

| Singular | Plural | Singular or Plural | |
|---|---|---|---|
| another | both | all | none |
| anybody | few | any | some |
| no one | many | more | most |
| neither | | | |

**TIP** Indefinite pronouns that end in *one, body,* or *thing* are always singular.

> INCORRECT: *Did everybody play their part well?*

If the indefinite pronoun might refer to either a male or a female, *his or her* may be used to refer to it, or the sentence may be rewritten.

> CORRECT: *Did everybody play his or her part well? Did all the students play their parts well?*

## 2.7  INTERROGATIVE PRONOUNS

An **interrogative pronoun** tells a reader or listener that a question is coming. The interrogative pronouns are *who, whom, whose, which,* and *what.*

EXAMPLES: *Who is going to rehearse with you?*
*From whom did you receive the script?*

**TIP** *Who* is used as a subject; *whom* is used as an object. To find out which pronoun you need to use in a question, change the question to a statement.

> QUESTION: *(Who/Whom) did you meet there?*
>
> STATEMENT: *You met (?) there.*

Since the verb has a subject (*you*), the needed word must be the object form, *whom.*

> EXAMPLE: *Whom did you meet there?*

**WATCH OUT!** A special problem arises when you use an interrupter, such as *do you think,* within a question.

> EXAMPLE: *(Who/Whom) do you think will win?*

If you eliminate the interrupter, it is clear that the word you need is *who.*

## 2.8  RELATIVE PRONOUNS

**Relative pronouns** relate, or connect, adjective clauses to the words they modify in sentences. The noun or pronoun that a relative clause modifies is the antecedent of the relative pronoun. Here are the relative pronouns and their uses.

|  | Subject | Object | Possessive |
|---|---|---|---|
| Person | who | whom | whose |
| Thing | which | which | whose |
| Thing/ Person | that | that | whose |

Often, short sentences with related ideas can be combined by using a relative pronoun to create a more effective sentence.

> SHORT SENTENCE: *Lucy is an accountant.*
>
> RELATED SENTENCE: *She helped us do our taxes.*
>
> COMBINED SENTENCE: *Lucy is an accountant who helped us do our taxes.*

## 2.9 PRONOUN REFERENCE PROBLEMS

You should always be able to identify the word a pronoun refers to. Avoid problems by rewriting sentences.

An **indefinite reference** occurs when the pronoun *it, you,* or *they* does not clearly refer to a specific antecedent.

UNCLEAR: *They told me how the story ended, and it was annoying.*

CLEAR: *They told me how the story ended, and I was annoyed.*

A **general reference** occurs when the pronoun *it, this, that, which,* or *such* is used to refer to a general idea rather than a specific antecedent.

UNCLEAR: *I'd rather not know what happens. That keeps me interested.*

CLEAR: *I'd rather not know what happens. Not knowing keeps me interested.*

*Ambiguous* means "having more than one possible meaning." An **ambiguous reference** occurs when a pronoun could refer to two or more antecedents.

UNCLEAR: *Jan told Danielle that she would read her story aloud.*

CLEAR: *Jan told Danielle that she would read Danielle's story aloud.*

## 3 Verbs

A **verb** is a word that expresses an action, a condition, or a state of being.

For more information, see **Quick Reference: Parts of Speech,** page R28.

### 3.1 ACTION VERBS

**Action verbs** express mental or physical activity.

EXAMPLE: *Lucy ran several miles every day.*

### 3.2 LINKING VERBS

**Linking verbs** join subjects with words or phrases that rename or describe them.

EXAMPLE: *After a few months, her shoes were worn out.*

### 3.3 PRINCIPAL PARTS

Action and linking verbs typically have four principal parts, which are used to form verb tenses. The principal parts are the **present,** the **present participle,** the **past,** and the **past participle.**

Action verbs and some linking verbs also fall into two categories: regular and irregular. A **regular verb** is a verb that forms its past and past participle by adding *-ed* or *-d* to the present form.

| Present | Present Participle | Past | Past Participle |
|---------|-------------------|------|-----------------|
| jump | (is) jumping | jumped | (has) jumped |
| solve | (is) solving | solved | (has) solved |
| grab | (is) grabbing | grabbed | (has) grabbed |
| carry | (is) carrying | carried | (has) carried |

An **irregular verb** is a verb that forms its past and past participle in some other way than by adding *–ed* or *–d* to the present form.

| Present | Present Participle | Past | Past Participle |
|---|---|---|---|
| begin | (is) beginning | began | (has) begun |
| break | (is) breaking | broke | (has) broken |
| go | (is) going | went | (has) gone |

## 3.4 VERB TENSE

The **tense** of a verb indicates the time of the action or the state of being. An action or state of being can occur in the present, the past, or the future. There are six tenses, each expressing a different range of time.

The **present tense** expresses an action or state that is happening at the present time, occurs regularly, or is constant or generally true. Use the present part.

> NOW: *This apple is rotten.*
> REGULAR: *I eat an apple every day.*
> GENERAL: *Apples are round.*

The **past tense** expresses an action that began and ended in the past. Use the past part.

> EXAMPLE: *They settled the argument.*

The **future tense** expresses an action or state that will occur. Use *shall* or *will* with the present part.

> EXAMPLE: *You will understand someday.*

The **present perfect tense** expresses an action or state that (1) was completed at an indefinite time in the past or (2) began in the past and continues into the present. Use *have* or *has* with the past participle.

> EXAMPLE: *These buildings have existed for centuries.*

The **past perfect tense** expresses an action in the past that came before another action in the past. Use *had* with the past participle.

> EXAMPLE: *I had told you, but you forgot.*

The **future perfect tense** expresses an action in the future that will be completed before another action in the future. Use *shall have* or *will have* with the past participle.

> EXAMPLE: *She will have found the note by the time I get home.*

**TIP** A past-tense form of an irregular verb is not used with an auxiliary, or helping, verb, but a past-participle main irregular verb is always used with an auxiliary verb.

> INCORRECT: *He has did that too many times.* (*Did* is the past-tense form of an irregular verb and shouldn't be used with *has*.)
> INCORRECT: *He done that too many times.* (*Done* is the past participle of an irregular verb and shouldn't be used without an auxiliary verb.)
> CORRECT: *He has done that too many times.*

## 3.5 PROGRESSIVE FORMS

The progressive forms of the six tenses show ongoing actions. Use forms of *be* with the present participles of verbs.

> PRESENT PROGRESSIVE: *Angelo is taking the test.*
> PAST PROGRESSIVE: *Angelo was taking the test.*
> FUTURE PROGRESSIVE: *Angelo will be taking the test.*
> PRESENT PERFECT PROGRESSIVE: *Angelo has been taking the test.*
> PAST PERFECT PROGRESSIVE: *Angelo had been taking the test.*
> FUTURE PERFECT PROGRESSIVE: *Angelo will have been taking the test.*

**WATCH OUT!** Do not shift from tense to tense needlessly. Watch out for these special cases:

- In most compound sentences and in sentences with compound predicates, keep the tenses the same.

> INCORRECT: *She smiled and shake his hand.*
> CORRECT: *She smiled and shook his hand.*

- If one past action happens before another, do shift tenses.

  INCORRECT: *He remembered what he studied.*

  CORRECT: *He remembered what he had studied.*

---

### Grammar Practice

Rewrite each sentence using a form of the verb(s) in parentheses. Identify each form that you use.

1. Helen Keller (become) blind and deaf before she (be) two.
2. A wonderful teacher (change) her life.
3. Anne Sullivan (be) almost blind before she (have) an operation.
4. Even now, Keller (be) an inspiration to everyone with a disability.
5. People (remember) both Helen and her teacher for years to come.

Rewrite each sentence to correct an error in tense.

1. Helen Keller writes a book about her life.
2. She described how she learns to understand language.
3. She felt like she knew it once and forgotten it.
4. Anne Sullivan was a determined teacher and does not give up.
5. Helen had began a life of learning.

---

## 3.6 ACTIVE AND PASSIVE VOICE

The voice of a verb tells whether its subject performs or receives the action expressed by the verb. When the subject performs the action, the verb is in the **active voice.** When the subject is the receiver of the action, the verb is in the **passive voice.**

Compare these two sentences:

ACTIVE: *Nancy Wood wrote "Animal Wisdom."*

PASSIVE: *"Animal Wisdom" was written by Nancy Wood.*

To form the passive voice, use a form of *be* with the past participle of the verb.

**WATCH OUT!** Use the passive voice sparingly. It can make writing awkward and less direct.

AWKWARD: *"Animal Wisdom" is a poem that was written by Nancy Wood.*

BETTER: *Nancy Wood wrote the poem "Animal Wisdom."*

There are occasions when you will choose to use the passive voice because:

- you want to emphasize the receiver: *The king was shot.*
- the doer is unknown: *My books were stolen.*
- the doer is unimportant: *French is spoken here.*

---

## 4 Modifiers

Modifiers are words or groups of words that change or limit the meanings of other words. Adjectives and adverbs are common modifiers.

### 4.1 ADJECTIVES

**Adjectives** modify nouns and pronouns by telling which one, what kind, how many, or how much.

WHICH ONE: *this, that, these, those*

EXAMPLE: *This poem moves along quickly.*

WHAT KIND: *square, dirty, fast, regular*

EXAMPLE: *Fast runners make baseball exciting.*

HOW MANY: *some, few, both, thousands*

EXAMPLE: *Thousands of fans cheer in the stands.*

HOW MUCH: *more, less, enough, as much*

EXAMPLE: *I had more fun watching the game than I expected.*

### 4.2 PREDICATE ADJECTIVES

Most adjectives come before the nouns they modify, as in the examples above. A **predicate adjective,** however, follows a linking verb and describes the subject.

EXAMPLE: *Baseball players are strong.*

Be especially careful to use adjectives (not adverbs) after such linking verbs as *look, feel, grow, taste,* and *smell.*

EXAMPLE: *Exercising feels good.*

### 4.3 ADVERBS

**Adverbs** modify verbs, adjectives, and other adverbs by telling where, when, how, or to what extent.

WHERE: *The children played outside.*

WHEN: *The author spoke yesterday.*

HOW: *We walked slowly behind the leader.*

TO WHAT EXTENT: *He worked very hard.*

Adverbs may occur in many places in sentences, both before and after the words they modify.

EXAMPLE: *Suddenly the wind shifted.*

*The wind suddenly shifted.*

*The wind shifted suddenly.*

### 4.4 ADJECTIVE OR ADVERB?

Many adverbs are formed by adding *–ly* to adjectives.

EXAMPLES: *sweet, sweetly; gentle, gently*

However, *–ly* added to a noun will usually yield an adjective.

EXAMPLES: *friend, friendly; woman, womanly*

### 4.5 COMPARISON OF MODIFIERS

Modifiers can be used to compare two or more things. The form of a modifier shows the degree of comparison. Both adjectives and adverbs have **comparative** and **superlative forms.**

The **comparative form** is used to compare two things, groups, or actions.

EXAMPLES: *Today's weather is hotter than yesterday's.*

*The boy got tired more quickly than his sister did.*

The **superlative form** is used to compare more than two things, groups, or actions.

EXAMPLES: *This has been the hottest month ever recorded.*

*Older people were most affected by the heat.*

### 4.6 REGULAR COMPARISONS

Most one-syllable and some two-syllable adjectives and adverbs have comparatives and superlatives formed by adding *-er* and *-est.* All three-syllable and most two-syllable modifiers have comparatives and superlatives formed with **more** or **most.**

| Modifier | Comparative | Superlative |
|---|---|---|
| messy | messier | messiest |
| quick | quicker | quickest |
| wild | wilder | wildest |
| tired | more tired | most tired |
| often | more often | most often |

**WATCH OUT!** Note that spelling changes must sometimes be made to form the comparatives and superlatives of modifiers.

AWKWARD: *friendly, friendlier* (Change *y* to *i* and add the ending.)

*sad, sadder* (Double the final consonant and add the ending.)

### 4.7 IRREGULAR COMPARISONS

Some commonly used modifiers have irregular comparative and superlative forms. They are listed in the following chart. You may wish to memorize them.

| Modifier | Comparative | Superlative |
|---|---|---|
| good | better | best |
| bad | worse | more |
| far | farther *or* further | farthest *or* furthest |
| little | less *or* lesser | least |
| many | more | most |
| well | better | best |
| much | more | most |

## 4.8 PROBLEMS WITH MODIFIERS

Study the tips that follow to avoid common mistakes.

**Farther and Further** Use *farther* for distances; use *further* for everything else.

**Double Comparisons** Make a comparison by using *-er/-est* or by using *more/most.* Using *-er* with *more* or using *-est* with *most* is incorrect.

> INCORRECT: *I like her more better than she likes me.*

> CORRECT: *I like her better than she likes me.*

**Illogical Comparisons** An illogical or confusing comparison occurs when two unrelated things are compared or when something is compared with itself. The word *other* or the word *else* should be used when comparing an individual member to the rest of a group.

> ILLOGICAL: *I like "A Voice" more than any poem.*
> (implies that "A Voice" isn't a poem)

> LOGICAL: *I like "A Voice" more than any other poem.*
> (identifies that "A Voice" is a poem)

**Bad vs. Badly** *Bad,* always an adjective, is used before a noun or after a linking verb. *Badly,* always an adverb, never modifies a noun. Be sure to use the right form after a linking verb.

> INCORRECT: *I felt badly that I missed the game.*

> CORRECT: *I felt bad that I missed the game.*

**Good vs. Well** *Good* is always an adjective. It is used before a noun or after a linking verb. *Well* is often an adverb meaning "expertly" or "properly." *Well* can also be used as an adjective after a linking verb when it means "in good health."

> INCORRECT: *I wrote my essay good.*

> CORRECT: *I wrote my essay well.*

> CORRECT: *I didn't feel well when I wrote it, though.*

**Double Negatives** If you add a negative word to a sentence that is already negative, the result will be an error known as a double negative. When using *not*

or *-n't* with a verb, use *any-* words, such as *anybody* or *anything,* rather than *no-* words, such as *nobody* or *nothing,* later in the sentence.

> INCORRECT: *The teacher didn't like nobody's paper.*

> CORRECT: *The teacher didn't like anybody's paper.*

Using **hardly, barely,** or **scarcely** after a negative word is also incorrect.

> INCORRECT: *My friends couldn't hardly catch up.*

> CORRECT: *My friends could hardly catch up.*

**Misplaced Modifiers** Sometimes a modifier is placed so far away from the word it modifies that the intended meaning of the sentence is unclear. Prepositional phrases and participial phrases are often misplaced. Place modifiers as close as possible to the words they modify.

> MISPLACED: *We found the child in the park who was missing.*

> CLEARER: *We found the child who was missing in the park.* (The child was missing, not the park.)

**Dangling Modifiers** Sometimes a modifier doesn't appear to modify any word in a sentence. Most dangling modifiers are participial phrases or infinitive phrases.

> DANGLING: *Looking out the window, his brother was seen driving by.*

> CLEARER: *Looking out the window, Josh saw his brother driving by.*

### Grammar Practice

Choose the correct word from each pair in parentheses.

1. According to my neighbor, squirrels are a (bad, badly) problem in the area.
2. The (worst, worse) time of the year to go to India is in the summer.
3. The boy didn't have (any, no) interest in playing baseball.

4. Molly sings really (good, well), though.
5. Tom was (more, most) daring than any other boy scout on the trip.

---

### Grammar Practice

Rewrite each sentence that contains a misplaced or dangling modifier. Write "correct" if the sentence is written correctly.

1. Coyotes know how to survive in the wild.
2. Hunting their prey, we have seen them in the forest.
3. Looking out the window, a coyote was seen in the yard.
4. My brother and I found books about coyotes at the library.
5. We learned that wolves are their natural enemies reading about them.

## 5 The Sentence and Its Parts

A **sentence** is a group of words used to express a complete thought. A complete sentence has a subject and a predicate.

For more information, see **Quick Reference: The Sentence and Its Parts,** page R30.

### 5.1 KINDS OF SENTENCES

There are four basic types of sentences.

| Type | Definition | Example |
|------|-----------|---------|
| Declarative | states a fact, a wish, an intent, or a feeling | Salisbury writes about young people. |
| Interrogative | asks a question | Have you read "The Ravine"? |
| Imperative | gives a command or direction | Find a copy. |
| Exclamatory | expresses strong feeling or excitement | It's really suspenseful! |

### 5.2 COMPOUND SUBJECTS AND PREDICATES

A compound subject consists of two or more subjects that share the same verb. They are typically joined by the coordinating conjunction *and* or *or.*

EXAMPLE: *A short story or novel will keep you interested.*

A compound predicate consists of two or more predicates that share the same subject. They too are usually joined by a coordinating conjunction such as *and, but,* or *or.*

EXAMPLE: *The class finished all the poetry but did not read the short stories.*

### 5.3 COMPLEMENTS

A **complement** is a word or group of words that completes the meaning of a sentence. Some sentences contain only a subject and a verb. Most sentences, however, require additional words placed after the verb to complete the meaning of the sentence. There are three kinds of complements: direct objects, indirect objects, and subject complements.

**Direct objects** are words or word groups that receive the action of action verbs. A direct object answers the question *what* or *who.*

EXAMPLES: *Daria caught the ball.* (Caught what?)
*She tagged the runner.* (Tagged who?)

**Indirect objects** tell to whom or what or for whom or what the actions of verbs are performed. Indirect objects come before direct objects. In the examples that follow, the indirect objects are highlighted.

EXAMPLES: *The audience gave us a standing ovation.* (Gave to whom?)
*We offered the newspaper an interview.* (Offered to what?)

**Subject complements** come after linking verbs and identify or describe the subjects. A subject complement that names or identifies a subject is called a **predicate nominative.** Predicate nominatives include **predicate nouns** and **predicate pronouns.**

> EXAMPLES: *The students were happy campers. The best actor in the play is he.*

A subject complement that describes a subject is called a **predicate adjective.**

> EXAMPLE: *The coach seemed thrilled.*

## 6 Phrases

A **phrase** is a group of related words that does not contain a subject and a predicate but functions in a sentence as a single part of speech.

### 6.1 PREPOSITIONAL PHRASES

A **prepositional phrase** is a phrase that consists of a preposition, its object, and any modifiers of the object. Prepositional phrases that modify nouns or pronouns are called **adjective phrases.** Prepositional phrases that modify verbs, adjectives, or adverbs are **adverb phrases.**

> ADJECTIVE PHRASE: *The central character of the story is a villain.*

> ADVERB PHRASE: *He reveals his nature in the first scene.*

### 6.2 APPOSITIVES AND APPOSITIVE PHRASES

An **appositive** is a noun or pronoun that identifies or renames another noun or pronoun. An **appositive phrase** includes an appositive and modifiers of it. An appositive usually follows the noun or pronoun it identifies.

An appositive can be either **essential** or **nonessential.** An **essential appositive** provides information that is needed to identify what is referred to by the preceding noun or pronoun.

> EXAMPLE: *Longfellow's poem is about the American patriot Paul Revere.*

A **nonessential appositive** adds extra information about a noun or pronoun whose meaning is already clear. Nonessential appositives and appositive phrases are set off with commas.

> EXAMPLE: *The story, a poem, has historical inaccuracies.*

## 7 Verbals and Verbal Phrases

A **verbal** is a verb form that is used as a noun, an adjective, or an adverb. A **verbal phrase** consists of a verbal along with its modifiers and complements. There are three kinds of verbals: infinitives, participles, and gerunds.

### 7.1 INFINITIVES AND INFINITIVE PHRASES

An **infinitive** is a verb form that usually begins with *to* and functions as a noun, an adjective, or an adverb. An **infinitive phrase** consists of an infinitive plus its modifiers and complements.

> NOUN: *To be happy is not easy.* (subject)
> *I want to have fun.* (direct object)
> *My hope is to enjoy every day.* (predicate nominative)

> ADJECTIVE: *That's a goal to be proud of.* (adjective modifying goal)

> ADVERB: *I'll work to achieve it.* (adverb modifying work)

Because *to,* the sign of the infinitive, precedes infinitives, it is usually easy to recognize them. However, sometimes *to* may be omitted.

> EXAMPLE: *No one can help me [to] achieve my goal.*

### 7.2 PARTICIPLES AND PARTICIPIAL PHRASES

A **participle** is a verb form that functions as an adjective. Like adjectives, participles modify nouns and pronouns. Most participles are present-participle forms ending in *-ing,* or past-participle forms ending in *-ed* or *-en.* In the examples below, the participles are highlighted.

> MODIFYING A NOUN: *The waxed floor was sticky.*

> MODIFYING A PRONOUN: *Sighing, she mopped up the mess.*

**Participial phrases** are participles with all their modifiers and complements.

MODIFYING A NOUN: *The girls working on the project are very energetic.*

MODIFYING A PRONOUN: *Having finished his work, he took a nap.*

## 7.3 DANGLING AND MISPLACED PARTICIPLES

A participle or participial phrase should be placed as close as possible to the word that it modifies. Otherwise the meaning of the sentence may not be clear.

MISPLACED: *The boys were looking for squirrels searching the trees.*

CLEARER: *The boys searching the trees were looking for squirrels.*

A participle or participial phrase that does not clearly modify anything in a sentence is called a **dangling participle.** A dangling participle causes confusion because it appears to modify a word that it cannot sensibly modify. Correct a dangling participle by providing a word for the participle to modify.

DANGLING: *Waiting for the show to start, the phone rang.* (The phone wasn't waiting.)

CLEARER: *Waiting for the show to start, I heard the phone ring.*

## 7.4 GERUNDS AND GERUND PHRASES

A **gerund** is a verb form ending in *-ing* that functions as a noun. Gerunds may perform any function nouns perform.

SUBJECT: *Cooking is a good way to relax.*

DIRECT OBJECT: *I enjoy cooking.*

INDIRECT OBJECT: *They should give cooking a chance.*

SUBJECT COMPLEMENT: *My favorite pastime is cooking.*

OBJECT OF PREPOSITION: *A love of cooking runs in the family.*

**Gerund phrases** are gerunds with all their modifiers and complements.

SUBJECT: *Depending on luck never got me far.*

OBJECT OF PREPOSITION: *I will finish before leaving the office.*

APPOSITIVE: *Her hobby, training horses, finally led to a career.*

### Grammar Practice

Rewrite each sentence, adding the type of phrase shown in parentheses.

1. "Fine?" is by Margaret Peterson Haddix. (appositive phrase)
2. Bailey suffered from a migraine headache. (infinitive phrase)
3. Bailey had an MRI. (prepositional phrase)
4. The pediatric wing is full. (gerund phrase)
5. Bailey's mom leaves the hospital. (participial phrase)

## 8 Clauses

A **clause** is a group of words that contains a subject and a predicate. A sentence may contain one clause or more than one. The sentence in the following example contains two clauses. The subject and verb in each clause are highlighted.

EXAMPLE: *Some students like to play sports, but others prefer to play music.*

There are two kinds of clauses: independent clauses and subordinate clauses.

## 8.1 INDEPENDENT AND SUBORDINATE CLAUSES

An independent clause expresses a complete thought and can stand alone as a sentence.

INDEPENDENT CLAUSE: *I read "The Banana Tree."*

A sentence may contain more than one independent clause.

EXAMPLE: *I read it once, and I liked it.*

In the preceding example, the coordinating conjunction *and* joins two independent clauses.

For more information, see **Coordinating Conjunctions,** page R29.

A **subordinate (dependent) clause** cannot stand alone as a sentence because it does not express a complete thought.

By itself, a subordinate clause is a sentence fragment. It needs an independent clause to complete its meaning. Most subordinate clauses are introduced by words such as *after, although, because, if, that, when,* and *while.*

> SUBORDINATE CLAUSE: *Because they worked hard.*

A subordinate clause can be joined to an independent clause to make a sentence that expresses a complete thought. In the following example, the subordinate clause explains why the students did well on the test.

> EXAMPLE: *The students did well on the test because they worked hard.*

### Grammar Practice

Identify the underlined group of words in each sentence as either an independent clause (*IC*) or a subordinate clause (*SC*).

1. He stopped at the library before he came home.
2. You have to arrive early if you want to get a front row seat.
3. She bought a ticket when she boarded the train.
4. I finished my homework while you were gone.
5. Because the test was long, the teacher gave the students extra time to finish it.

## 9  The Structure of Sentences

When classified by their structure, there are four kinds of sentences: simple, compound, complex, and compound-complex.

### 9.1  SIMPLE SENTENCES

A **simple sentence** is a sentence that has one independent clause and no subordinate clauses. Even a simple sentence can include many details.

> EXAMPLES: *Chloe looked for the train.*
> *Seth drove to the station in an old red pickup truck.*

A simple sentence may contain a compound subject or a compound verb. A compound subject is made up of two or more subjects that share the same verb. A compound verb is made up of two or more verbs that have the same subject.

> EXAMPLES: *Seth and Chloe drove to the station.* (compound subject)
> *They waved and shouted as the train pulled in.* (compound verb)

### 9.2  COMPOUND SENTENCES

A **compound sentence** consists of two or more independent clauses. The clauses in compound sentences are joined with commas and coordinating conjunctions (*and, but, or, nor, yet, for, so*) or with semicolons. Like simple sentences, compound sentences do not contain any subordinate clauses.

> EXAMPLES: *We all get older, but not everyone gets wiser.*
> *Some young people don't want to grow up; others grow up too quickly.*

**WATCH OUT!** Do not confuse compound sentences with simple sentences that have compound parts.

> EXAMPLE: *Books and clothes were scattered all over her room.*

Here, the conjunction *and* is used to join the parts of a compound subject, not the clauses in a compound sentence.

### Grammar Practice

Identify each sentence as simple (*S*) or compound (*CD*).

1. Justin and his dad loved bikes.
2. They had their garage set up like a bike shop; they worked there all the time.
3. Justin bought a couple of old bikes and fixed them up.
4. He decided to donate them to a homeless shelter.
5. Many people offered him their old bikes for free.
6. Last year, Justin fixed 250 bikes and gave them all away.

## 9.3 COMPLEX SENTENCES

A **complex sentence** consists of one independent clause and one or more subordinate clauses. Most subordinate clauses start with words such as *when, until, who, where, because,* and *so that.*

EXAMPLES: *While I eat my breakfast, I often wonder what I'll be like in ten years. When I think about the future, I see a canvas that has nothing on it.*

### Grammar Practice

Write these sentences on a sheet of paper. Underline each independent clause once and each subordinate clause twice.

1. Although the Foster Grandparent Program is more than 40 years old, many people do not know about it.
2. This program was established so that children with special needs could get extra attention.
3. Anyone can volunteer who is at least 60 years old and meets other requirements.
4. After a volunteer is trained, he or she works 15 to 40 hours a week.
5. Foster grandparents often help with homework so that the children can improve in school.
6. Since this program was founded In 1965, there have been foster grand-parent projects in all 50 states.

### Grammar Practice

Identify each sentence as compound (*CD*), complex (*C*), or compound-complex (*CC*).

1. In 1998, a hurricane swept through Central America, where it hit Honduras and Nicaragua especially hard.
2. Hurricane Mitch was one of the strongest storms ever in this region; it caused great destruction.
3. People on the coast tried to flee to higher ground, but flooding and mudslides made escape difficult.
4. More than 9,000 people were killed, and crops and roads were wiped out.
5. TV images of homeless and hungry people touched many Americans, who responded generously.
6. They donated money and supplies, which were flown to the region.
7. Volunteers helped clear roads so that supplies could get to villages that needed them.
8. Charity groups distributed food and safe drinking water, and they handed out sleeping bags and mosquito nets, which were needed in the tropical climate.
9. Medical volunteers treated people who desperately needed care.
10. Other volunteers rebuilt homes, and they helped restore the farm economy so that people could earn a living again.

## 9.4 COMPOUND-COMPLEX SENTENCES

A **compound-complex** sentence contains two or more independent clauses and one or more subordinate clauses. Compound-complex sentences are both compound and complex. If you start with a compound sentence, all you need to do to form a compound-complex sentence is add a subordinate clause.

COMPOUND: *All the students knew the answer, yet they were too shy to volunteer.*

COMPOUND–COMPLEX: *All the students knew the answer that their teacher expected, yet they were too shy to volunteer.*

## 10 Writing Complete Sentences

Remember, a sentence is a group of words that expresses a complete thought. In writing that you wish to share with a reader, try to avoid both sentence fragments and run-on sentences.

## 10.1 CORRECTING FRAGMENTS

A **sentence fragment** is a group of words that is only part of a sentence. It does not express a complete thought and may be confusing to a reader or listener. A sentence fragment may be lacking a subject, a predicate, or both.

FRAGMENT: *Didn't care about sports.* (no subject)

CORRECTED: *The lawyer didn't care about sports.*

FRAGMENT: *Her middle-school son.* (no predicate)

CORRECTED: *Her middle-school son played on the soccer team.*

FRAGMENT: *Before every game.* (neither subject nor predicate)

CORRECTED: *Before every game, he tried to teach his mom the rules.*

In your writing, fragments may be a result of haste or incorrect punctuation. Sometimes fixing a fragment will be·a matter of attaching it to a preceding or following sentence.

FRAGMENT: *She made an effort. But just couldn't make sense of the game.*

CORRECTED: *She made an effort but just couldn't make sense of the game.*

## 10.2 CORRECTING RUN-ON SENTENCES

A **run-on sentence** is made up of two or more sentences written as though they were one. Some run-ons have no punctuation within them. Others may have only commas where conjunctions or stronger punctuation marks are necessary. Use your judgment in correcting run-on sentences, as you have choices. You can change a run-on to two sentences if the thoughts are not closely connected. If the thoughts are closely related, you can keep the run-on as one sentence by adding a semicolon or a conjunction.

RUN–ON: *Most parents watched the game his mother read a book instead.*

MAKE TWO SENTENCES: *Most parents watched the game. His mother read a book instead.*

RUN–ON: *Most parents watched the game they played sports themselves.*

USE A SEMICOLON: *Most parents watched the game; they played sports themselves.*

ADD A CONJUNCTION: *Most parents watched the game since they played sports themselves.*

**WATCH OUT!** When you form compound sentences, make sure you use appropriate punctuation: a comma before a coordinating conjunction, a semicolon when there is no coordinating conjunction. A very common mistake is to use a comma without a conjunction or instead of a semicolon. This error is called a **comma splice.**

INCORRECT: *He finished the job, he left the village.*

CORRECT: *He finished the job, and he left the village.*

## 11 Subject-Verb Agreement

The subject and verb in a clause must agree in number. Agreement means that if the subject is singular, the verb is also singular, and if the subject is plural, the verb is also plural.

### 11.1 BASIC AGREEMENT

Fortunately, agreement between subjects and verbs in English is simple. Most verbs show the difference between singular and plural only in the third person of the present tense. In the present tense, the third-person singular form ends in **-s.**

| Present-Tense Verb Forms | |
| --- | --- |
| **Singular** | **Plural** |
| I sleep | we sleep |
| you sleep | you sleep |
| she, he, it sleeps | they sleep |

### 11.2 AGREEMENT WITH *BE*

The verb *be* presents special problems in agreement, because this verb does not follow the usual verb patterns.

| Forms of *Be* | | | |
|---|---|---|---|
| **Present Tense** | | **Past Tense** | |
| **Singular** | **Plural** | **Singular** | **Plural** |
| I am | we are | I was | we were |
| you are | you are | you were | you were |
| she, he, it is | they are | she, he, it was | they were |

## 11.3 WORDS BETWEEN SUBJECT AND VERB

A verb agrees only with its subject. When words come between a subject and a verb, ignore them when considering proper agreement. Identify the subject and make sure the verb agrees with it.

> EXAMPLES: The *poem* I read *describes* a moose.
> The *moose* in the poem *searches* for a place where he belongs.

## 11.4 AGREEMENT WITH COMPOUND SUBJECTS

Use plural verbs with most compound subjects joined by the word *and.*

> EXAMPLE: *My father and his friends play chess every day.*

To confirm that you need a plural verb, you could substitute the plural pronoun *they* for *my father and his friends.*

If a compound subject is thought of as a unit, use a singular verb. Test this by substituting the singular pronoun *it.*

> EXAMPLE: *A bagel and cream cheese [it] is my usual breakfast.*

Use a singular verb with a compound subject that is preceded by *each, every,* or *many a.*

> EXAMPLES: *Each novel and short story seems grounded in personal experience.*

When the parts of a compound subject are joined by *or, nor,* or the correlative conjunctions *either . . . or* or *neither . . . nor,* make the verb agree with the noun or pronoun nearest the verb.

> EXAMPLES: *Cookies or ice cream is my favorite dessert.*
> *Either Cheryl or her parents are being invited. Neither ice storms nor snow is predicted today.*

## 11.5 PERSONAL PRONOUNS AS SUBJECTS

When using a personal pronoun as a subject, make sure to match it with the correct form of the verb *be.* (See the chart in Section 11.2.) Note especially that the pronoun *you* takes the forms *are* and *were,* regardless of whether it is singular or plural.

> **WATCH OUT!** *You is* and *you was* are nonstandard forms and should be avoided in writing and speaking. *We was* and *they was* are also forms to be avoided.
>
> INCORRECT: *You was a good student.*
>
> CORRECT: *You were a good student.*
>
> INCORRECT: *They was starting a new school.*
>
> CORRECT: *They were starting a new school.*

## 11.6 INDEFINITE PRONOUNS AS SUBJECTS

Some indefinite pronouns are always singular; some are always plural.

| Singular Indefinite Pronouns | | | |
|---|---|---|---|
| another | either | neither | one |
| anybody | everybody | nobody | somebody |
| anyone | everyone | no one | someone |
| anything | everything | nothing | something |
| each | much | | |

> EXAMPLES: *Each of the writers was given an award.*
> *Somebody in the room upstairs is sleeping.*

| Plural Indefinite Pronouns | | | |
|---|---|---|---|
| both | few | many | several |

> EXAMPLES: *Many of the books in our library are not in circulation.*
> *Few have been returned recently.*

Still other indefinite pronouns may be either singular or plural.

| Singular or Plural Indefinite Pronouns | | |
|---|---|---|
| all | more | none |
| any | most | some |

The number of the indefinite pronoun *any* or *none* often depends on the intended meaning.

> EXAMPLES: *Any of these stories has an important message.* (any one story)
> *Any of these stories have important messages.* (all of the many stories)

The indefinite pronouns *all, some, more, most,* and *none* are singular when they refer to quantities or parts of things. They are plural when they refer to numbers of individual things. Context will usually give a clue.

> EXAMPLES: *All of the flour is gone.* (referring to a quantity)
> *All of the flowers are gone.* (referring to individual items)

## 11.7 INVERTED SENTENCES

A sentence in which the subject follows the verb is called an **inverted sentence.** A subject can follow a verb or part of a verb phrase in a question; a sentence beginning with *here* or *there*; or a sentence in which an adjective, an adverb, or a phrase is placed first.

> EXAMPLES: *Here comes the scariest part.*
> *There goes the hero with a flashlight.*
> *Then, into the room rushes a big black cat!*

**TIP** To check subject-verb agreement in some inverted sentences, place the subject before the verb. For example, change *There are many people* to *Many people are there.*

## 11.8 SENTENCES WITH PREDICATE NOMINATIVES

In a sentence containing a predicate noun (nominative), the verb should agree with the subject, not the predicate noun.

> EXAMPLES: *Josh's jokes are a source of laughter.* (*Jokes* is the subject—not *source*—and it takes the plural verb *are.*)
> *One source of laughter is Josh's jokes.* (The subject is *source*—not *jokes*—and it takes the singular verb *is.*)

## 11.9 *DON'T* AND *DOESN'T* AS AUXILIARY VERBS

The auxiliary verb *doesn't* is used with singular subjects and with the personal pronouns *she, he,* and *it.* The auxiliary verb *don't* is used with plural subjects and with the personal pronouns *I, we, you,* and *they.*

> SINGULAR: *The humor doesn't escape us.*
> *Doesn't the limerick about Dougal MacDougal make you laugh?*

> PLURAL: *We don't usually forget such funny images.*
> *Don't people like to recite limericks?*

## 11.10 COLLECTIVE NOUNS AS SUBJECTS

**Collective nouns** are singular nouns that name groups of persons or things. *Team,* for example, is a collective name of a group of individuals. A collective noun takes a singular verb when the group acts as a single unit. It takes a plural verb when the members of the group act separately.

> EXAMPLES: *The class creates a bulletin board of limericks.* (The class as a whole creates the board.)
> *The faculty enjoy teaching poetry.* (The individual members enjoy teaching poetry.)

## 11.11 RELATIVE PRONOUNS AS SUBJECTS

When the relative pronoun *who, which,* or *that* is used as a subject in an adjective clause, the verb in the clause must agree in number with the antecedent of the pronoun.

> SINGULAR: *The **myth** from ancient Greece that interests me most is "The Apple of Discord I."*

The antecedent of the relative pronoun *that* is the singular *myth*; therefore, *that* is singular and must take the singular verb *interests.*

PLURAL: *James Berry and Sandra Cisneros are writers who publish short stories.*

The antecedent of the relative pronoun *who* is the plural subject *writers.* Therefore *who* is plural, and it takes the plural verb *publish.*

### Grammar Practice

Locate the subject of each verb in parentheses in the sentences below. Then choose the correct verb form.

1. George Graham Vest's "Tribute to a Dog" (describes, describe) the friend-ship and loyalty canines show humans.

2. Stories about a dog (is, are) touching.

3. Besides dogs, few animals (has, have) an innate desire to please humans.

4. Many traits specific to dogs (bring, brings) their owners happiness.

5. No matter if the owner is rich or poor, a dog, and all canines for that matter, (acts, act) with love and devotion.

6. There (is, are) countless reasons to own a dog.

7. A dog's unselfishness (endears, endear) it to its owner.

8. (Doesn't, Don't) a dog offer its owner constant affection and guardianship?

9. A man's dog (stands, stand) by him in prosperity and in poverty.

10. A dog (guards, guard) his master as if the owner was a prince.

# Vocabulary and Spelling

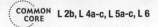 COMMON CORE  L 2b, L 4a-c, L 5a-c, L 6

The key to becoming an independent reader is to develop a tool kit of vocabulary strategies. By learning and practicing the strategies, you'll know what to do when you encounter unfamiliar words while reading. You'll also know how to refine the words you use for different situations—personal, school, and work.

Being a good speller is important when communicating your ideas in writing. Learning basic spelling rules and checking your spelling in a dictionary will help you spell words that you may not use frequently.

## 1 Using Context Clues

The context of a word is made up of the punctuation marks, words, sentences, and paragraphs that surround the word. A word's context can give you important clues about its meaning.

### 1.1 GENERAL CONTEXT

Sometimes you need to determine the meaning of an unfamiliar word by reading all the information in a passage.

*Kevin set out the broom, a dustpan, and three trash bags before beginning the monumental task of cleaning his room.*

You can figure out from the context that *monumental* means "huge."

### 1.2 SPECIFIC CONTEXT CLUES

Sometimes writers help you understand the meanings of words by providing specific clues such as those shown in the chart. When reading content area materials, use word, sentence, and paragraph clues to help you figure out meanings.

### 1.3 IDIOMS, SLANG, AND FIGURATIVE LANGUAGE

Use context clues to figure out the meanings of idioms, slang, and figurative language.

An **idiom** is an expression whose overall meaning differs from the meaning of the individual words.

*The mosquitos drove us crazy on our hike. (Drove us crazy means "irritated.")*

**Slang** is informal language that features made-up words and ordinary words that are used to mean something different from their meanings in formal English.

*That's a really cool backpack you're wearing. (Cool means "excellent.")*

**Figurative language** is language that communicates meaning beyond the literal meaning of the words.

*Like a plunging horse, my car kicked up dirt, moved ahead quickly, and made a loud noise when I hit the gas. (Kicked up dirt, moved ahead, and made a loud noise describe a plunging horse.)*

| Specific Context Clues | | |
|---|---|---|
| **Type of Clue** | **Key Words/ Phrases** | **Example** |
| **Definition or restatement** of the meaning of the word | or, which is, that is, in other words, also known as, also called | In 1909, a French inventor flew a *monoplane*, or a **single-winged plane.** |
| **Example** following an unfamiliar word | such as, like, as if, for example, especially, including | The stunt pilot performed *acrobatics*, such as **dives and wing-walking.** |

*continued*

| Type of Clue | Key Words/ Phrases | Example |
|---|---|---|
| **Comparison** with a more familiar word or concept | as, like, also, similar to, in the same way, likewise | The doctor prescribed a *bland* diet, similar to the **rice and potatoes** he was already eating. |
| **Contrast** with a familiar word or experience | unlike, but, however, although, on the other hand, on the contrary | The moon will *diminish* at the end of the month; however it will **grow** during the first part of the month. |
| **Cause-and-effect** relationship in which one term is familiar | because, since, when, consequently, as a result, therefore | Because their general was *valiant*, the soldiers **showed courage** in battle. |

## 2  Analyzing Word Structure

Many words can be broken into smaller parts. These word parts include base words, roots, prefixes, and suffixes.

### 2.1  BASE WORDS

A **base word** is a word part that by itself is also a word. Other words or word parts can be added to base words to form new words.

### 2.2  ROOTS

A **root** is a word part that contains the core meaning of the word. Many English words contain roots that come from older languages such as Greek and Latin. Knowing the meanings of a word's root can help you determine the word's meaning.

| Root | Meaning | Example |
|---|---|---|
| *auto* (Greek) | self, same | **auto**mobile |
| *hydr* (Greek) | water | **hydr**ant |
| *cent* (Latin) | hundred | **cent**ury |
| *circ* (Latin) | ring | **circ**le |
| *port* (Latin) | carry | **port**able |

### 2.3  PREFIXES

A **prefix** is a word part attached to the beginning of a word. Most prefixes come from Greek, Latin, or Old English (OE).

| Prefix | Meaning | Example |
|---|---|---|
| **dis-** (Latin) | not | **dis**honest |
| **auto-** (Greek) | self, same | **auto**biography |
| **un-** (OE) | the opposite of, not | **un**happy |
| **re-** (Latin) | carry, back | **re**pay |

### 2.4  SUFFIXES

A **suffix** is a word part that appears at the end of a root or base word to form a new word. Some suffixes do not change word meaning. These suffixes are:

- added to nouns to change the number of persons or objects
- added to verbs to change the tense
- added to modifiers to change the degree of comparison

| Suffix | Meaning | Example |
|---|---|---|
| -s, -es | to change the number of a noun | lock + s = locks |
| -d, -ed, -ing | to change verb tense | stew + ed = stewed |
| -er, -est | to indicate comparison in modifiers | mild + er = milder<br>soft + est = softest |

Other suffixes can be added to the root or base to change the word's meaning. These suffixes can also determine a word's part of speech.

| Suffix | Meaning | Example |
|---|---|---|
| **-ion** (Latin) | process of | operat**ion** |
| **-able** (Latin) | capable of | read**able** |
| **-ize** (Greek) | to cause or become | legal**ize** |

### Strategies for Understanding New Words

- If you recognize elements—prefix, suffix, root, or base—of a word, you may be able to guess its meaning by analyzing one or two elements.
- Think about the way the word is used in the sentence. Use the context and the word parts to make a logical guess about the word's meaning.
- Look in a dictionary to see if you are correct.

## 3  Understanding Word Origins

### 3.1  ETYMOLOGIES

**Etymologies** show the origin and historical development of a word. When you study a word's history and origin, you can find out when, where, and how the word came to be.

> **em•per•or**  (ĕm′pər-ər) *n.* **1.** The male ruler of an empire. **2a.** The emperor butterfly. **b.** The emperor moth. [Middle English emperour, from Old French empereor, from Latin imperātor, from imperāre, to command: *in-, in*; see EN–[1] + parāre, to prepare.]

### 3.2  WORD FAMILIES

Words that have the same root make up a word family and have related meanings. The following chart shows a common Greek root and a common Latin root. Notice how the meanings of the example words are related to the meanings of their roots.

| Latin Root | *man:* "hand" |
|---|---|
| English | **manual**  by hand<br>**manage**  handle<br>**manuscript**  document written by hand |

| Greek Root | *phon:* "sound" |
|---|---|
| English | **telephone**  an instrument that transmits sound<br>**phonograph**  machine that reproduces sound<br>**phonetic**  representing sounds of speech |

### 3.3  FOREIGN WORDS IN ENGLISH

The English language includes words from other languages, such as French, Dutch, Spanish, Italian, and Chinese. Many words have stayed the way they were in their original language.

| French | Dutch | Spanish | Italian |
|---|---|---|---|
| ballet | boss | canyon | diva |
| vague | caboose | rodeo | cupola |
| mirage | dock | bronco | spaghetti |

| Practice and Apply |
|---|
| Look up the origin and meaning of each word listed in the preceding chart. Then use each word in a sentence. |

## 4  Synonyms and Antonyms

### 4.1  SYNONYMS

A **synonym** is a word with a meaning similar to that of another word. You can find synonyms in a thesaurus or a dictionary. In a dictionary, synonyms are often given as part of the definition of a word. The following word pairs are synonyms:

satisfy/please          occasionally/sometimes

rob/steal               schedule/agenda

**4.2 ANTONYMS**

An **antonym** is a word with a meaning opposite that of another word. The following word pairs are antonyms.

accurate/incorrect     similar/different

fresh/stale     unusual/ordinary

## 5   Denotation and Connotation

**5.1 DENOTATION**

A word's dictionary meaning is called its **denotation.** For example, the denotation of the word *thin* is "having little flesh; spare; lean."

**5.2 CONNOTATION**

The images or feelings you connect to a word add a finer shade of meaning, called **connotation.** The connation of a word goes beyond its basic dictionary definition. Writers use connotations of words to communicate positive or negative feelings.

| Positive | Negative |
|----------|----------|
| slender  | scrawny  |
| thrifty  | cheap    |
| young    | immature |

Make sure you understand the denotation and connotation of a word when you read it or use it in your writing.

## 6   Analogies

An **analogy** is a comparison between two things that are similar in some way but are otherwise not alike. Analogies are sometimes used in writing when unfamiliar subjects or ideas are explained in terms of familiar ones. Analogies often appear on tests as well. In an analogy problem, the analogy is expressed using two groups of words. The relationship between the first pair of words is the same as the relationship between the second pair of words. Some analogy problems are expressed like this:

in love : hate :: war : _____

**a.** soldier   **b.** peace   **c.** battle   **d.** argument

Follow these steps to determine the correct answer:

- Read the problem as "*Love* is to *hate* as *war* is to . . . ."
- Ask yourself how the words *love* and *hate* are related. (*Love* and *hate* are antonyms.)
- Ask yourself which answer choice is an antonym of *war.* (*Peace* is an antonym of *war,* therefore *peace* is the best answer.)

## 7   Homonyms, Homographs, and Homophones

**7.1 HOMONYMS**

**Homonyms** are words that have the same spelling and sound but have different meanings.

> *The snake shed its skin in the shed behind the house.*

**Shed** can mean "to lose by natural process," but an identically spelled word means "a small structure."

Sometimes only one of the meanings of a homonym may be familiar to you. Use context clues to help you figure out the meaning of an unfamiliar word.

**7.2 HOMOGRAPHS**

**Homographs** are words that are spelled the same but have different meanings and origins. Some are also pronounced differently, as in these examples:

> *Please close the door.* (klōz)

> *That was a close call.* (klōs)

If you see a word used in a way that is unfamiliar to you, check a dictionary to see if it is a homograph.

### 7.3 HOMOPHONES

**Homophones** are words that sound alike but have different meanings and spellings. The following homophones are frequently misused:

it's/its                they're/their/there

to/too/two          stationary/stationery

Many misused homophones are pronouns and contractions. Whenever you are unsure whether to write *your* or *you're* and *who's* or *whose,* ask yourself if you mean *you are* and *who is/has.* If you do, write the contraction. For other homophones, such as *fair* and *fare,* use the meaning of the word to help you decide which one to use.

### 8  Words with Multiple Meanings

Over time, some words have acquired additional meanings that are based on the original meaning.

> *I had to be replaced in the cast of the play because of the cast on my arm.*

These two uses of cast have different meanings, but both of them have the same origin. You will find all the meanings of cast listed in one entry in the dictionary. Context can also help you figure out the meaning of the word.

### 9  Specialized Vocabulary

**Specialized vocabulary** is a group of terms suited to a particular field of study or work. For example, science, mathematics, and history all have their own technical or specialized vocabularies. To figure out specialized terms, you can use context clues and reference sources, such as dictionaries on specific subjects, atlases, or manuals.

### 10  Using Reference Sources

### 10.1  DICTIONARIES

A **general dictionary** will tell you not only a word's definitions but also its pronunciation, syllabication, parts of speech, history, and origin.

**❶** **❷** **❸**

**tan·gi·ble** (tăn´jə-bəl) *adj.* **1a.** Discernible by the touch; palpable. **b.** Possible to touch. **c.** Possible to be treated as fact; **❹** real or concrete. **2.** Possible to understand or realize. **3.** *Law* That can be valued monetarily. **❺** [Late Latin *tangibilis*, from Latin *tangere*, to touch.]

**❶** Entry word syllabication

**❷** Pronunciation

**❸** Part of speech

**❹** Definitions

**❺** Etymology

A **specialized dictionary** focuses on terms related to a particular field of study or work. Use a dictionary to check the spelling of any word you are unsure of in your reading.

### 10.2  THESAURI

A **thesaurus** (plural, *thesauri* ) is a dictionary of synonyms. A thesaurus can be especially helpful when you find yourself using the same modifiers over and over again.

### 10.3  SYNONYM FINDERS

A **synonym finder** is often included in wordprocessing software. It enables you to highlight a word and be shown a display of its synonyms.

### 10.4  GLOSSARIES

A **glossary** is a list of specialized terms and their definitions. It is often found in the back of a book and sometimes includes pronunciations. Many textbooks contain glossaries. In fact, this textbook has three glossaries: the **Glossary of Literary and Informational Terms,** the **Glossary of Academic Vocabulary,** and the **Glossary of Critical Vocabulary.** Use these glossaries to help you understand how terms are used in this textbook.

## 11 Spelling Rules

### 11.1 WORDS ENDING IN A SILENT *E*

Before adding a suffix beginning with a vowel or *y* to a word ending in a silent *e,* drop the *e* (with some exceptions).

**amaze + -ing = amazing**

**love + -able = lovable**

**create + -ed = created**

**nerve + -ous = nervous**

**Exceptions:** *change + -able = changeable; courage + -ous = courageous*

When adding a suffix beginning with a consonant to a word ending in a silent *e,* keep the *e* (with some exceptions).

**late + -ly = lately**

**spite + -ful = spiteful**

**noise + -less = noiseless**

**state + -ment = statement**

**Exceptions:** *truly, argument, ninth, wholly, awful,* and *others*

When a suffix beginning with *a* or *o* is added to a word with a final silent *e,* the final *e* is usually retained if it is preceded by a soft *c* or a soft *g.*

**bridge + -able = bridgeable**

**peace + -able = peaceable**

**outrage + -ous = outrageous**

**advantage + -ous = advantageous**

When a suffix beginning with a vowel is added to words ending in *ee* or *oe,* the final, silent *e* is retained.

**agree + -ing = agreeing**

**free + -ing = freeing**

**hoe + -ing = hoeing**

**see + -ing = seeing**

### 11.2 WORDS ENDING IN *Y*

Before adding most suffixes to a word that ends in *y* preceded by a consonant, change the *y* to *i.*

**easy + -est = easiest**

**crazy + -est = craziest**

**silly + -ness = silliness**

**marry + -age = marriage**

**Exceptions:** *dryness, shyness,* and *slyness* However, when you add *-ing,* the *y* does not change.

**empty + -ed = emptied    but**

**empty + -ing = emptying**

When adding a suffix to a word that ends in *y* preceded by a vowel, the *y* usually does not change.

**play + -er = player**

**employ + -ed = employed**

**coy + -ness = coyness**

**pay + -able = payable**

### 11.3 WORDS ENDING IN A CONSONANT

In one-syllable words that end in one consonant preceded by one short vowel, double the final consonant before adding a suffix beginning with a vowel, such as *-ed* or *-ing.* These are sometimes called 1+1+1 words.

**dip + -ed = dipped**

**set + -ing = setting**

**slim + -est = slimmest**

**fit + -er = fitter**

The rule does not apply to words of one syllable that end in a consonant preceded by two vowels.

**feel + -ing = feeling**

**peel + -ed = peeled**

**reap + -ed = reaped**

**loot + -ed = looted**

In words of more than one syllable, double the final consonant when (1) the word ends with one consonant preceded by one vowel and (2) when the word is accented on the last syllable.

**be·gin´   per·mit´   re·fer´**

In the following examples, note that in the new words formed with suffixes, the accent remains on the same syllable.

**be·gin´ + -ing = be·gin´ning = beginning**

**per·mit´ + -ed = per·mit´ted = permitted**

**Exceptions:** In some words with more than one syllable, though the accent remains on the same syllable when a suffix is added, the final consonant is nevertheless not doubled, as in the following examples.

**tra′vel + er = tra′vel•er = traveler**

**mar′ket + er = mar′ket•er = marketer**

In the following examples, the accent does not remain on the same syllable; thus, the final consonant is not doubled:

**re•fer′ + -ence = ref′er•ence = reference**

**con•fer′ + -ence = con′fer•ence = conference**

## 11.4 PREFIXES AND SUFFIXES

When adding a prefix to a word, do not change the spelling of the base word. When a prefix creates a double letter, keep both letters.

**dis- + approve = disapprove**

**re- + build = rebuild**

**ir- + regular = irregular**

**mis- + spell = misspell**

**anti- + trust = antitrust**

**il- + logical = illogical**

When adding -*ly* to a word ending in *l,* keep both *l's.* When adding -*ness* to a word ending in *n,* keep both *n's.*

**careful + -ly = carefully**

**sudden + -ness = suddenness**

**final + -ly = finally**

**thin + -ness = thinness**

## 11.5 FORMING PLURAL NOUNS

To form the plural of most nouns, just add -*s.*

**prizes   dreams   circles   stations**

For most singular nouns ending in *o,* add -*s.*

**solos halos studios photos pianos**

For a few nouns ending in *o,* add -*es.*

**heroes tomatoes potatoes echoes**

When a singular noun ends in *s, sh, ch, x,* or *z,* add -*es.*

**waitresses   brushes   ditches**
**axes          buzzes**

When a singular noun ends in *y* with a consonant before it, change the *y* to *i* and add -*es.*

**army—armies     candy—candies**

**baby—babies     diary—diaries**

**ferry—ferries   conspiracy—conspiracies**

When a vowel (*a, e, i, o, u*) comes before the *y,* just add -*s.*

**boy—boys          way—ways**

**array—arrays      alloy—alloys**

**weekday—weekdays  jockey—jockeys**

For most nouns ending in *f* or *fe,* change the *f* to *v* and add -*es* or -*s.*

**life—lives        loaf—loaves**

**calf—calves       knife—knives**

**thief—thieves     shelf—shelves**

For some nouns ending in *f,* add -*s* to make the plural.

**roofs   chiefs   reefs   beliefs**

Some nouns have the same form for both singular and plural.

**deer   sheep   moose   salmon   trout**

For some nouns, the plural is formed in a special way.

**man—men           goose—geese**

**ox—oxen           woman—women**

**mouse—mice        child—children**

For a compound noun written as one word, form the plural by changing the last word in the compound to its plural form.

**stepchild—stepchildren     firefly—fireflies**

If a compound noun is written as a hyphenated word or as two separate words, change the most important word to the plural form.

**brother-in-law—brothers-in-law**

**life jacket—life jackets**

## 11.6 FORMING POSSESSIVES

If a noun is singular, add *'s.*

**mother—my mother's car**

**Ross—Ross's desk**

**Exception:** An apostrophe alone is used to indicate the possessive case with the names Jesus and Moses and with certain names in classical mythology (such as Zeus).

If a noun is plural and ends with *s,* add an apostrophe.

**parents—my parents' car**

**the Santinis—the Santinis' house**

If a noun is plural but does not end in *s,* add *'s.*

>  people—the people's choice
>
>  women—the women's coats

## 11.7 SPECIAL SPELLING PROBLEMS

Only one English word ends in *-sede:* supersede. Three words end in *-ceed: exceed, proceed,* and *succeed.* All other verbs ending in the sound "seed" are spelled with *-cede.*

>  concede  precede  recede  secede

In words with **ie** or **ei,** when the sound is long **e** (as in **she**), the word is spelled *ie* except after **c** (with some exceptions).

| *i* before *e* | thief | relieve | field |
|---|---|---|---|
|  | piece | grieve | pier |
| except after *c* | conceit | perceive | ceiling |
|  | receive | receipt |  |
| Exceptions: | either | neither | weird |
|  | leisure | seize |  |

## 11.8 USING A SPELL CHECKER

Most computer word processing programs have spell checkers to catch misspellings. Most computer spell checkers do not correct errors automatically. Instead, they stop at a word and highlight it. Sometimes the highlighted word may not be misspelled; it may be that the program's dictionary does not include the word. Keep in mind that spell checkers will identify only misspelled words, not misused words. For example, if you used *their* when you meant to use *there,* a spelling checker will not catch the error.

## 12 Commonly Confused Words

| Words | Definitions | Examples |
|---|---|---|
| accept/except | The verb *accept* means "to receive" or "to believe." *Except* is usually a preposition meaning "excluding." | Did the teacher **accept** your report? Everyone smiled for the photographer **except** Jody. |
| advice/advise | *Advise* is a verb. *Advice* is a noun naming that which an *adviser* gives. | I **advise** you to take that job. Whom should I ask for **advice**? |
| affect/effect | As a verb, *affect* means "to influence." *Effect* as a verb means "to cause." If you want a noun, you will almost always want *effect*. | How deeply did the news **affect** him? The students tried to **effect** a change in school policy. What **effect** did the acidic soil produce in the plants? |
| all ready/already | *All ready* is an adjective meaning "fully ready." *Already* is an adverb meaning "before" or "by this time." | He was **all ready** to go at noon. I have **already** seen that movie. |
| desert/dessert | *Desert* (dĕz´ərt) means "a dry, sandy, barren region." *Desert* (dĭ-zûrt´) means "to abandon." *Dessert* (dĭ-zûrt´) is a sweet, such as cake. | The Sahara, in North Africa, is the world's largest **desert.** The night guard did not **desert** his post. Alison's favorite **dessert** is chocolate cake. |

*continued*

| Words | Definitions | Examples |
|---|---|---|
| among/between | *Between* is used when you are speaking of only two things. *Among* is used for three or more. | **Between** ice cream and sherbet, I prefer the latter.<br>Gary Soto is **among** my favorite authors. |
| bring/take | *Bring* is used to denote motion toward a speaker or place. *Take* is used to denote motion away from such a person or place. | **Bring** the books over here, and I will **take** them to the library. |
| fewer/less | *Fewer* refers to the number of separate, countable units. *Less* refers to bulk quantity. | We have **less** literature and **fewer** selections in this year's curriculum. |
| leave/let | *Leave* means "to allow something to remain behind." *Let* means "to permit." | The librarian will **leave** some books on display but will not **let** us borrow any. |
| lie/lay | To *lie* is "to rest or recline." It does not take an object. *Lay* always takes an object. | Rover loves to **lie** in the sun.<br>We always **lay** some bones next to him. |
| loose/lose | *Loose* (lo͞os) means "free, not restrained." *Lose* (lo͞oz) means "to misplace" or "to fail to find." | Who turned the horses **loose**?<br>I hope we won't **lose** any of them. |
| passed/past | *Passed* is the past tense of *pass* and means "went by."<br>*Past* is an adjective that means "of a former time." *Past* is also a noun that means "time gone by." | We **passed** through the Florida Keys during our vacation.<br>My **past** experiences have taught me to set my alarm.<br>Ebenezer Scrooge is a character who relives his **past**. |
| than/then | Use *than* in making comparisons. Use *then* on all other occasions. | Ramon is stronger **than** Mark.<br>Cut the grass and **then** trim the hedges. |
| two/too/to | *Two* is the number. *Too* is an adverb meaning "also" or "very." Use *to* before a verb or as a preposition. | Meg had **to** go **to** town, **too.** We had **too** much reading **to** do. **Two** chapters is **too** many. |
| their/there/they're | *Their* means "belonging to them." *There* means "in that place." *They're* is the contraction for "they are." | **There** is a movie playing at 9 P.M. **They're** going to see it with me. Sakara and Jessica drove away in **their** car after the movie. |

# Glossary of Literary and Informational Terms

**Act** An act is a major division within a play, similar to a chapter in a book. Each act may be further divided into smaller sections, called scenes. Plays can have as many as five acts, or as few as one.

**Adventure Story** An adventure story is a literary work in which action is the main element. An **adventure novel** usually focuses on a main character who is on a mission and faces many challenges and choices.

**Alliteration** Alliteration is the repetition of consonant sounds at the beginning of words. Note the repetition of the *d* sound in this line: The *d*aring boy *d*ove into the *d*eep sea.

**Allusion** An allusion is a reference to a famous person, place, event, or work of literature.

**Almanac** *See* Reference Works.

**Analogy** An analogy is a comparison between two things that are alike in some way. Often, writers use analogies to explain unfamiliar subjects or ideas in terms of familiar ones.
*See also* Metaphor; Simile.

**Anecdote** An anecdote is a short account of an event that is usually intended to entertain or make a point.

**Antagonist** The antagonist is a force working against the protagonist, or main character, in a story, play, or novel. The antagonist is usually another character but can be a force of nature, society itself, or an internal force within the main character.
*See also* Protagonist.

**Appeal to Authority** An appeal to authority is an attempt to persuade an audience by making reference to people who are experts on a subject.

**Argument** An argument is speaking or writing that expresses a position on a problem and supports it with reasons and evidence. An argument often anticipates and answers objections that opponents might raise.
*See also* Claim; Counterargument; Evidence.

**Assonance** Assonance is the repetition of vowel sounds within nonrhyming words. An example of assonance is the repetition of the o͞o sound in the following line: Do you like blue?

**Assumption** An assumption is an opinion or belief that is taken for granted. It can be about a specific situation, a person, or the world in general. Assumptions are often unstated.

**Audience** The audience of a piece of writing is the group of readers that the writer is addressing. A writer considers his or her audience when deciding on a subject, a purpose, a tone, and a style in which to write.

**Author's Message** An author's message is the main idea or theme of a particular work.
*See also* Main Idea; Theme.

**Author's Perspective** An author's perspective is the combination of ideas, values, feelings, and beliefs that influences the way the writer looks at a topic. **Tone,** or attitude, often reveals an author's perspective.
*See also* Author's Purpose; Tone.

**Author's Position** An author's position is his or her opinion on an issue or topic.
*See also* Claim.

**Author's Purpose** A writer usually writes for one or more of these purposes: to express thoughts or feelings, to inform or explain, to persuade, or to entertain.
*See also* Author's Perspective.

**Autobiography** An autobiography is a writer's account of his or her own life. In almost every case, it is told from the first-person point of view. An autobiography focuses on the most important events and people in the writer's life over a period of time.
*See also* Memoir; Personal Narrative.

**Ballad** A ballad is a type of narrative poem that tells a story and was originally meant to be sung or recited. Because it tells a story, a ballad has a setting, a plot, and characters. **Folk ballads** were composed orally and handed down by word of mouth from generation to generation.

**Bias** In a piece of writing, the author's bias is the side of an issue that he or she favors. Words with extremely positive or negative connotations are often a signal of an author's bias.

**Bibliography** A bibliography is a list of related books and other materials used to write a text. Bibliographies can be good sources for further study on a subject.

*See also* Works Consulted.

**Biography** A biography is the true account of a person's life, written by another person. As such, biographies are usually told from a third-person point of view. The writer of a biography—a **biographer**—usually researches his or her subject in order to present accurate information. The best biographers strive for honesty and balance in their accounts of their subjects' lives.

**Business Correspondence** Business correspondence is written business communications such as business letters, e-mails, and memos. In general, business correspondence is brief, to the point, clear, courteous, and professional.

**Cast of Characters** In the script of a play, a cast of characters is a list of all the characters in the play, usually in order of appearance. It may include a brief description of each character.

**Cause and Effect** Two events are related by cause and effect when one event brings about, or causes, the other. The event that happens first is the **cause**; the one that follows is the **effect.** Cause and effect is also a way of organizing an entire piece of writing. It helps writers show the relationships between events or ideas.

**Character** Characters are the people, animals, or imaginary creatures who take part in the action of a work of literature. Like real people, characters display certain qualities, or **character traits,** that develop and change over time, and they usually have **motivations,** or reasons, for their behaviors.

> **Main character:** Main characters are the most important characters in literary works. Generally, the plot of a short story focuses on one main character, but a novel may have several main characters.

> **Minor characters:** The less important characters in a literary work are known as minor characters. The story is not centered on them, but they help carry out the action of the story and help the reader learn more about the main character.

> **Dynamic character:** A dynamic character is one who undergoes important changes as a plot unfolds. The changes occur because of the character's actions and experiences in the story. The changes are usually internal and may be good or bad. Main characters are usually, though not always, dynamic.

> **Static character:** A static character is one who remains the same throughout a story. The character may experience events and interact with other characters, but he or she is not changed because of them.

*See also* Characterization; Character Traits.

**Character Development** Characters that change during a story are said to undergo character development. Any character can change, but main characters usually develop the most.

*See also* Character: Dynamic Character.

**Characterization** The way a writer creates and develops characters is known as characterization. There are four basic methods of characterization.

- The writer may make direct comments about a character through the voice of the narrator.
- The writer may describe the character's physical appearance.
- The writer may present the character's own thoughts, speech, and actions.
- The writer may present the thoughts, speech, and actions of other characters.

*See also* Character; Character Traits.

**Character Traits** Character traits are the qualities shown by a character. Traits may be physical (tall) or expressions of personality (confidence). Writers reveal the traits of their characters through methods of characterization. Sometimes writers directly state a character's traits, but more often readers need to infer traits from a character's words, actions, thoughts, appearance, and relationships. Examples of words that describe traits include *brave, considerate,* and *rude.*

**Chronological Order** Chronological order is the arrangement of events in their order of occurrence. This type of organization is used in fictional narratives and in historical writing, biography, and autobiography.

**Claim** In an argument, a claim is the writer's position on an issue or problem. Although an argument focuses on supporting one claim, a writer may make more than one claim in a text.

**Clarify** Clarifying is a reading strategy that helps readers understand or make clear what they are reading. Readers usually clarify by rereading, reading aloud, or discussing.

**Classification** Classification is a pattern of organization in which objects, ideas, and/or information are presented in groups, or classes, based on common characteristics.

**Cliché** A cliché is an overused expression. "Better late than never" and "hard as nails" are common examples. Good writers generally avoid clichés unless they are using them in dialogue to indicate something about a character's personality.

**Climax** The climax stage is the point of greatest interest in a story or play. The climax usually occurs toward the end of a story, after the reader has understood the **conflict** and become emotionally involved with the characters. At the climax, the conflict is resolved and the outcome of the plot usually becomes clear.

*See also* Plot.

**Comedy** A comedy is a dramatic work that is light and often humorous in tone, usually ending happily with a peaceful resolution of the main conflict.

**Compare and Contrast** To compare and contrast is to identify the similarities and differences of two or more subjects. Compare and contrast is also a pattern of organizing an entire piece of writing.

*See also* Pattern of Organization.

**Conclusion** A conclusion is a statement of belief based on evidence, experience, and reasoning. A valid conclusion is one that logically follows from the facts or statements upon which it is based.

**Conflict** A conflict is a struggle between opposing forces. Almost every story has a main conflict—a conflict that is the story's focus. An **external conflict** involves a character who struggles against a force outside him- or herself, such as nature, a physical obstacle, or another character. An **internal conflict** is one that occurs within a character. For example, a character with an internal conflict might struggle with fear.

*See also* Plot.

**Connect** Connecting is a reader's process of relating the content of a text to his or her own knowledge and experience.

**Connotation** A word's connotations are the ideas and feelings associated with the word, as opposed to its dictionary definition. For example, the word *bread,* in addition to its basic meaning ("a baked food made from flour and other ingredients"), has connotations of life and general nourishment.

*See also* Denotation.

**Consumer Documents** Consumer documents are printed materials that accompany products and services. They usually provide information about the use, care, operation, or assembly of the product or service they accompany. Some common consumer documents are applications, contracts, warranties, manuals, instructions, labels, brochures, and schedules.

**Context Clues** When you encounter an unfamiliar word, you can often use context clues to understand it. Context clues are the words or phrases surrounding the word that provide hints about the word's meaning.

**Counterargument** A counterargument is an argument made to oppose another argument. A good argument anticipates opposing viewpoints and provides counterarguments to disprove them.

**Couplet** A couplet is a rhymed pair of lines. A couplet may be written in any rhythmic pattern. For example, Follow your heart's desire/And good things may transpire.

*See also* Rhyme; Stanza.

**Credibility** Credibility is the believability or trustworthiness of a source and the information it provides.

**Critical Essay** *See* Essay.

**Critical Review** A critical review is an evaluation or critique by a reviewer, or critic. Types of reviews include film reviews, book reviews, music reviews, and art show reviews.

**Cultural Values** Cultural values are the behaviors that a society expects from its people.

**Database** A database is a collection of information that can be quickly and easily accessed and searched and from which information can be easily retrieved. It is frequently presented in an electronic format.

**Debate** A debate is an organized exchange of opinions on an issue. In school settings, debate is usually a formal contest in which two opposing teams defend and attack a proposition.

*See also* Argument.

**Deductive Reasoning** Deductive reasoning is a way of thinking that begins with a generalization, presents a specific situation, and then moves forward with facts and evidence toward a logical conclusion. The following passage has a deductive argument embedded in it: "All students in the math class must take the quiz on Friday. Since Lana is in the class, she had better show up." This deductive argument can be broken down as follows: generalization—All students in the math class must take the quiz on Friday; specific situation—Lana is a student in the math class; conclusion—Therefore, Lana must take the math quiz.

**Denotation** A word's denotation is its dictionary definition.

*See also* Connotation.

**Description** Description is writing that helps a reader to picture events, objects, and characters. To create descriptions, writers often use **imagery**—words and phrases that appeal to the reader's senses.

**Dialect** A dialect is a form of a language that is spoken in a particular place or by a particular group of people. Dialects may feature unique pronunciations, vocabulary, and grammar.

**Dialogue** Dialogue is written conversation between two or more characters. Writers use dialogue to bring characters to life and to give readers insights into the characters' qualities, traits, and reactions to other characters. In fiction, dialogue is usually set off with quotation marks. In drama, stories are told primarily through dialogue.

**Diary** A diary is a daily record of a writer's thoughts, experiences, and feelings. As such, it is a type of autobiographical writing. A **journal** is another term for a diary.

**Dictionary** *See* Reference Works.

**Drama** A drama, or play, is a form of literature meant to be performed by actors in front of an audience. In a drama, the characters' dialogue and actions tell the story. The written form of a drama is called a script. A script usually includes dialogue, a cast of characters, and stage directions that give instructions about performing the drama. The person who writes the drama is known as the playwright or dramatist.

**Draw Conclusions** To draw a conclusion is to make a judgment or arrive at a belief based on evidence, experience, and reasoning.

**Editorial** An editorial is an opinion piece that usually appears on the editorial page of a newspaper or as part of a news broadcast. The editorial section of the newspaper presents opinions rather than objective news reports.

*See also* Op/Ed Piece.

**Either/Or Fallacy** An either/or fallacy is a statement that suggests that there are only two choices available in a situation when in fact there are more than two.

**Emotional Appeal** An emotional appeal is a message that creates strong feelings in order to make a point. An appeal to fear is a message that taps into people's fear of losing their safety or security. An appeal.to pity is a message that taps into people's sympathy and compassion for others to build support for an idea, a cause, or a proposed action. An appeal to vanity is a message that attempts to persuade by tapping into people's desire to feel good about themselves.

**Encyclopedia** *See* Reference Works.

**Epic Poem** An epic poem is a long narrative poem about the adventures of a hero whose actions reflect the ideals and values of a nation or a group of people.

**Essay** An essay is a short work of nonfiction that deals with a single subject. There are many types of essays. An **expository essay** presents or explains information and ideas. A **persuasive essay** attempts to convince the reader to adopt a certain viewpoint. A **critical essay** evaluates a situation or a work of art. A **personal essay** usually reflects the writer's experiences, feelings, and personality.

**Ethical Appeal** In an ethical appeal, a writer links a claim to a widely accepted value in order to gain moral support for the claim. The appeal also creates an image of the writer as a trustworthy, moral person.

**Evaluate** To evaluate is to examine something carefully and to judge its value or worth. A reader can evaluate the actions of a particular character, for example. A reader can also form opinions about the value of an entire work.

**Evidence** Evidence is a specific piece of information that supports a claim. Evidence can take the form of a fact, a quotation, an example, a statistic, or a personal experience, among other things.

**Exaggeration** An extreme overstatement of an idea is called an exaggeration. It is often used for purposes of emphasis or humor.

**Exposition** Exposition is the first stage of a typical story plot. The exposition provides important background information and introduces the setting and the important characters. The conflict the characters face may also be introduced in the exposition, or it may be introduced later, in the rising action.

*See also* Plot.

**Expository Essay** *See* Essay.

**External Conflict** *See* Conflict.

**Fable** A fable is a brief tale told to illustrate a moral or teach a lesson. Often the moral of a fable appears in a distinct and memorable statement near the tale's beginning or end.

*See also* Moral.

**Fact Versus Opinion** A **fact** is a statement that can be proved, or verified. An opinion, on the other hand, is a statement that cannot be proved because it expresses a person's beliefs, feelings, or thoughts.

*See also* Generalization; Inference.

**Fallacious Reasoning** Reasoning that includes errors in logic or fallacies.

**Fallacy** A fallacy is an error of reasoning. Typically, a fallacy is based on an incorrect inference or a misuse of evidence.

*See also* Either/Or Fallacy; Logical Appeal; Overgeneralization.

**Falling Action** The falling action is the stage of the plot in which the story begins to draw to a close. The falling action comes after the **climax** and before the **resolution,** also called denouement. Events in the falling action show the results of the important decision or action that happened at the climax. Tension eases as the falling action begins; however, the final outcome of the story is not yet fully worked out at this stage.

*See also* Climax; Plot.

**Fantasy** Fantasy is a type of fiction that is highly imaginative and portrays events, settings, or characters that are unrealistic. The setting might be a nonexistent world, the plot might involve magic or the supernatural, and the characters might have superhuman powers.

**Faulty Reasoning** *See* Fallacy.

**Feature Article** A feature article is an article in a newspaper or magazine about a topic of human interest or lifestyles.

**Fiction** Fiction is prose writing that tells an imaginary story. The writer of a short story or novel might invent all the events and characters or might base parts of the story on real people and events. The basic elements of fiction are plot, character, setting, and theme. Different types of fiction include realistic fiction, historical fiction, science fiction, and fantasy.

*See also* Novel; Novella; Short Story.

**Figurative Language** In figurative language, words are used in an imaginative way to express ideas that are not literally true. "Megan has a bee in her bonnet" is an example of figurative language. The sentence does not mean that Megan is wearing a bonnet, nor that there is an actual bee in it. Instead, it means that Megan is angry or upset about something. Figurative language is used for comparison, emphasis, and emotional effect.

*See also* Metaphor; Onomatopoeia; Personification; Simile.

**First-Person Point of View** *See* Point of View.

**Flashback** In a literary work, a flashback is an interruption of the action to present events that took place at an earlier time. A flashback provides information that can help a reader better understand a character's current situation.

**Folklore** The traditions, customs, and stories that are passed down within a culture are known as its folklore. Folklore includes various types of literature, such as legends, folk tales, myths, trickster tales, and fables.

*See also* Fable; Folk Tale; Myth.

**Folk Tale** A folk tale is a story that has been passed down from generation to generation by word of mouth. Folk tales may be set in the distant past and involve supernatural events. The characters in them may be animals, people, or superhuman beings.

**Foreshadowing** Foreshadowing occurs when a writer provides hints that suggest future events in a story. Foreshadowing creates suspense and makes readers eager to find out what will happen.

**Form** The structure or organization of a written work is often called its form. The form of a poem includes the arrangement of its words and lines on the page.

**Free Verse** Poetry without regular patterns of rhyme and rhythm is called free verse. Some poets use free verse to capture the sounds and rhythms of ordinary speech.

*See also* Rhyme, Rhythm.

**Generalization** A generalization is a broad statement about a class or category of people, ideas, or things based on a study of, or a belief about, only some of its members.

*See also* Overgeneralization; Stereotyping.

**Genre** The term *genre* refers to a category in which a work of literature is classified. The major genres in literature are fiction, nonfiction, poetry, and drama.

**Government Publications** Government publications are documents produced by government organizations. Pamphlets, brochures, and reports are just some of the many forms these publications take. Government publications can be good resources for a wide variety of topics.

**Graphic Aid** A graphic aid is a visual tool that is printed, handwritten, or drawn. Charts, diagrams, graphs, photographs, and maps are examples of graphic aids.

**Graphic Organizer** A graphic organizer is a "word picture"—a visual illustration of a verbal statement—that helps a reader understand a text. Charts, tables, webs, and diagrams can all be graphic organizers. Graphic organizers and graphic aids can look the same. However, graphic organizers and graphic aids do differ in how they are used. Graphic aids help deliver important information to students using a text. Graphic organizers are actually created by students themselves. They help students understand the text or organize information.

**Haiku** Haiku is a form of Japanese poetry in which 17 syllables are arranged in three lines of 5, 7, and 5 syllables. The rules of haiku are strict. In addition to following the syllabic count, the poet must create a clear picture that will evoke a strong emotional response in the reader. Nature is a particularly important source of inspiration for Japanese haiku poets, and details from nature are often the subjects of their poems.

**Hero** A hero is a main character or protagonist in a story. They are typically courageous, strong, honorable, and intelligent. They are protectors of society who hold back the forces of evil and fight to make the world a better place. In modern literature, a hero may simply be the most important character in a story. Such a hero is often an ordinary person with ordinary problems.

**Historical Document** Historical documents are writings that have played a significant role in human events. The Declaration of Independence, for example, is a historical document.

**Historical Fiction** A short story or a novel can be called historical fiction when it is set in the past and includes real places and real events of historical importance.

**How-To Book** A how-to book explains how to do something—usually an activity, a sport, or a household project.

**Humor** Humor is a quality that provokes laughter or amusement. Writers create humor through exaggeration, amusing descriptions, irony, and witty and insightful dialogue.

**Idiom** An idiom is an expression that has a meaning different from the meaning of its individual words. For example, "to let the cat out of the bag" is an idiom meaning "to reveal a secret or surprise."

**Imagery** Imagery consists of words and phrases that appeal to a reader's five senses. Writers use sensory details to help the reader imagine how things look, feel, smell, sound, and taste.

**Implied Main Idea** *See* Main Idea.

**Index** The index of a book is an alphabetized list of important topics covered in the book and the page numbers on which they can be found. An index can be used to quickly find specific information about a topic.

**Inductive Reasoning** Inductive reasoning is the process of logical reasoning that starts with observations, examples, and facts and moves on to a general conclusion or principle.

**Inference** An inference is a logical guess that is made based on facts and one's own knowledge and experience.

**Informational Text** Informational text is writing that provides factual information. Examples include news reports, a science textbook, and lab reports. Informational text also includes literary nonfiction, such as personal essays, opinion pieces, speeches, biographies, and historical accounts.

**Internal Conflict** *See* Conflict.

**Internet** The Internet is a global, interconnected system of computer networks that allows for communication through e-mail, listservs, and the World Wide Web. The Internet connects computers and computer users throughout the world.

**Interview** An interview is a conversation conducted by a writer or reporter in which facts or statements are elicited from another person, recorded, and then broadcast or published.

**Irony** Irony is a contrast between what is expected and what actually exists or happens. Exaggeration and sarcasm are techniques writers use to express irony.

**Journal** A journal is a periodical publication used by legal, medical, and other professional organizations. The term may also be used to refer to a diary or daily record.
*See* Diary.

**Legend** A legend is a story handed down from the past about a specific person, usually someone of heroic accomplishments. Legends usually have some basis in historical fact.

**Limerick** A limerick is a short, humorous poem made up of five lines. It usually has the rhyme scheme *aabba,* created by two rhyming couplets followed by a fifth line that rhymes with the first couplet. A limerick typically has a sing-song rhythm.

**Literary Nonfiction** *See* Narrative Nonfiction.

**Loaded Language** Loaded language consists of words with strongly positive or negative connotations intended to influence a reader's or listener's attitude.

**Logical Appeal** A logical appeal is a way of writing or speaking that relies on logic and facts. It appeals to people's reasoning or intellect rather than to their values or emotions. Flawed logical appeals—that is, errors in reasoning—are called logical fallacies.
*See also* Fallacy.

**Logical Argument**  A logical argument is an argument in which the logical relationship between the support and claim is sound.

**Lyric Poetry**  Lyric poetry is poetry that presents the personal thoughts and feelings of a single speaker. Most poems, other than narrative poems, are lyric poems. Lyric poetry can be in a variety of forms and cover many subjects, from love and death to everyday experiences.

**Main Character**  *See* Character.

**Main Idea**  The main idea, or central idea, is the most important idea about a topic that a writer or speaker conveys. It can be the central idea of an entire work or of just a paragraph. Often, the main idea of a paragraph is expressed in a topic sentence. However, a main idea may just be implied, or suggested, by details. A main idea is typically supported by details.

**Make Inferences**  *See* Inference.

**Memoir**  A memoir is a form of autobiographical writing in which a writer shares his or her personal experiences and observations of important events or people. Often informal in tone, memoirs usually give readers information about a particular person or period of time in the writer's life. In contrast, autobiographies focus on many important people and events in the writer's life over a long period of time.

*See also* Autobiography; Personal Narrative.

**Metaphor**  A metaphor is a comparison of two things that are basically unlike but have some qualities in common. Unlike a simile, a metaphor does not contain the words *like* or *as.*

*See also* Figurative Language; Simile.

**Meter**  In poetry, meter is the regular pattern of stressed (´) and unstressed (˘) syllables. Although poems have rhythm, not all poems have regular meter. Each unit of meter is known as a **foot** and is made up of one stressed syllable and one or two unstressed syllables.

*See also* Rhythm.

**Minor Character**  *See* Character.

**Monitor**  Monitoring is the strategy of checking your comprehension as you read and modifying the strategies you are using to suit your needs.

Monitoring often includes the following strategies: questioning, clarifying, visualizing, predicting, connecting, and rereading.

**Mood**  Mood is the feeling or atmosphere that a writer creates for the reader. Descriptive words, imagery, and figurative language all influence the mood of a work.

**Moral**  A moral is a lesson that a story teaches. A moral is often stated at the end of a fable.

*See also* Fable.

**Motivation**  Motivation is the reason why a character acts, feels, or thinks in a certain way. A character may have more than one motivation for his or her actions. Understanding these motivations helps readers get to know the character.

**Myth**  A myth is a traditional story that attempts to answer basic questions about human nature, origins of the world, mysteries of nature, and social customs.

**Narrative**  Writing that tells a story is called a narrative. The events in a narrative may be real or imagined. Autobiographies and biographies are narratives that deal with real people or events. Fictional narratives include short stories, fables, myths, and novels. A narrative may also be in the form of a poem.

*See also* Autobiography; Biography; Personal Narrative.

**Narrative Nonfiction**  Narrative nonfiction is writing that reads much like fiction, except that the characters, setting, and plot are real rather than imaginary. Narrative nonfiction includes autobiographies, biographies, and memoirs.

**Narrative Poetry**  Poetry that tells a story is called narrative poetry. Like fiction, a narrative poem contains characters, a setting, and a plot. It might also contain such elements of poetry as rhyme, rhythm, imagery, and figurative language.

**Narrator**  The narrator is the voice that tells a story. Sometimes the narrator is a character in the story. At other times, the narrator is an outside voice created by the writer. The narrator is not the same as the writer.

*See also* Point of View.

**News Article** A news article is writing that reports on a recent event. In newspapers, news articles are usually brief and to the point, presenting the most important facts first, followed by more detailed information.

**Nonfiction** Nonfiction is writing that tells about real people, places, and events. Unlike fiction, nonfiction is mainly written to convey factual information. Nonfiction includes a wide range of writing—newspaper articles, letters, essays, biographies, movie reviews, speeches, true-life adventure stories, advertising, and more.

**Novel** A novel is a long work of fiction. Like a short story, a novel is the product of a writer's imagination. Because a novel is considerably longer than a short story, a novelist can develop the characters and story line more thoroughly.

*See also* Fiction.

**Novella** A novella is a work of fiction that is longer than a short story but shorter than a novel. Due to its shorter length, a novella generally includes fewer characters and a less complex plot than a novel.

*See also* Fiction; Novel; Short Story.

**Ode** An ode is a type of lyric poem that deals with serious themes, such as justice, truth, or beauty.

**Onomatopoeia** Onomatopoeia is the use of words whose sounds echo their meanings, such as *buzz, whisper, gargle,* and *murmur.*

**Op/Ed Piece** An op/ed piece is an opinion piece that typically appears opposite ("op") the editorial page of a newspaper. Unlike editorials, op/ed pieces are written and submitted by readers.

**Oral Literature** Oral literature, or the oral tradition, consists of stories that have been passed down by word of mouth from generation to generation. Oral literature includes folk tales, legends, and myths. In more recent times, some examples of oral literature have been written down or recorded so that the stories can be preserved.

**Organization** *See* Pattern of Organization.

**Overgeneralization** An overgeneralization is a statement that is too broad to be accurate. You can often recognize overgeneralizations by the appearance of words and phrases such as *all, everyone, every time, any, anything, no one,* or *none.* An example is "None of the city's workers really cares about keeping the environment clean." In all probability, there are many exceptions. The writer can't possibly know the feelings of every city worker.

**Overview** An overview is a short summary of a story, a speech, or an essay.

**Paraphrase** Paraphrasing is the restating of information in one's own words.

*See also* Summarize.

**Parody** A parody is a humorous imitation of another writer's work. Parodies can take the form of fiction, drama, or poetry. Jon Scieszka's "The True Story of the Three Little Pigs" is an example of a parody.

**Pattern of Organization** The term *pattern of organization* refers to the way ideas and information are arranged and organized. Patterns of organization include cause and effect, chronological, compare and contrast, classification, and problem-solution, among others.

*See also* Cause and Effect; Chronological Order; Classification; Compare and Contrast; Problem-Solution Order; Sequential Order.

**Periodical** A periodical is a magazine or another type of publication that is issued on a regular basis.

**Personal Narrative** A short essay told as a story in the first-person point of view. A personal narrative usually reflects the writer's experiences, feelings, and personality.

*See also* Autobiography; Memoir.

**Personification** The giving of human qualities to an animal, object, or idea is known as personification.

*See also* Figurative Language.

**Persuasion** Persuasion is the art of swaying others' feelings, beliefs, or actions. Persuasion normally appeals to both the mind and the emotions of readers.

*See also* Appeal to Authority; Emotional Appeal; Ethical Appeal; Loaded Language; Logical Appeal.

**Persuasive Essay** *See* Essay.

**Play** *See* Drama.

**Playwright** *See* Drama.

**Plot** The series of events in a story is called the plot. The plot usually centers on a **conflict,** or struggle, faced by the main character. The action that the characters take to solve the problem builds toward a **climax** in the story. At this point, or shortly afterward, the problem is solved and the story ends. Most story plots have five stages: exposition, rising action, climax, falling action, and resolution.

*See also* Climax; Conflict; Exposition; Falling Action; Rising Action.

**Poetry** Poetry is a type of literature in which words are carefully chosen and arranged to create certain effects. Poets use a variety of sound devices, imagery, and figurative language to express emotions and ideas.

*See also* Alliteration; Assonance; Ballad; Free Verse; Imagery; Meter; Narrative Poetry; Rhyme; Rhythm; Stanza.

**Point of View** Point of view refers to how a writer chooses to narrate a story. When a story is told from the **first-person** point of view, the narrator is a character in the story and uses first-person pronouns, such as *I, me,* and *we.* In a story told from the **third-person** point of view, the narrator is not a character in the story. A writer's choice of narrator affects the information readers receive.

*See also* Narrator.

**Predict** Predicting is a reading strategy that involves using text clues to make a reasonable guess about what will happen next in a story.

**Primary Source** *See* Sources.

**Prior Knowledge** Prior knowledge is the knowledge a reader already possesses about a topic. This information might come from personal experiences, expert accounts, books, films, or other sources.

**Problem-Solution Order** Problem-solution order is a pattern of organization in which a problem is stated and analyzed and then one or more solutions are proposed and examined.

**Prop** The word *prop,* originally an abbreviation of the word *property,* refers to any physical object that is used in a drama.

**Propaganda** Propaganda is any form of communication that is so distorted that it conveys false or misleading information to advance a specific belief or cause.

**Prose** The word *prose* refers to all forms of writing that are not in verse form. The term may be used to describe very different forms of writing, such as short stories and essays.

**Protagonist** A protagonist is the main character in a story, play, or novel. The protagonist is involved in the main conflict of the story. Usually, the protagonist undergoes changes as the plot runs its course.

**Public Document** Public documents are documents that were written for the public to provide information that is of public interest or concern. They include government documents, speeches, signs, and rules and regulations.

*See also* Government Publications.

**Pun** A pun is a play on words based on similar senses of two or more words, or on various meanings of the same word. A pun is usually made for humorous effect. For example, the fisherman was fired for playing hooky.

**Radio Play** A radio play is a drama that is written specifically to be broadcast over the radio. Because the audience is not meant to see a radio play, sound effects are often used to help listeners imagine the setting and the action. The stage directions in the play's script indicate the sound effects.

**Realistic Fiction** Realistic fiction is fiction that is set in the real, modern world. The characters behave like real people and use human abilities to cope with modern life's problems and conflicts.

**Recurring Theme** *See* Theme.

**Reference Work** Reference works are sources that contain facts and background information on a wide range of subjects. Most reference works are good sources of reliable information because they have been reviewed by experts. The following are some common reference works: encyclopedias, dictionaries, thesauri, almanacs, atlases, and directories.

**Refrain** A refrain is one or more lines repeated in each stanza of a poem.

**Repetition** Repetition is a technique in which a sound, word, phrase, or line is repeated for emphasis or unity. Repetition often helps to reinforce meaning and create an appealing rhythm.

*See also* Alliteration; Refrain; Sound Devices.

**Resolution** *See* Falling Action.

**Review** *See* Critical Review.

**Rhetorical Question** Rhetorical questions are those that have such obvious answers that they do not require a reply. Writers often use them to suggest that their claim is so obvious that everyone should agree with it.

**Rhyme** Rhyme is the repetition of sounds at the end of words. Words rhyme when their accented vowels and the letters that follow have identical sounds. *Pig* and *dig* rhyme, as do *reaching* and *teaching.* The most common type of rhyme in poetry is called **end rhyme,** in which rhyming words come at the ends of lines. Rhyme that occurs within a line of poetry is called **internal rhyme.**

**Rhyme Scheme** A rhyme scheme is a pattern of end rhymes in a poem. A rhyme scheme is noted by assigning a letter of the alphabet, beginning with *a,* to each line. Lines that rhyme are given the same letter.

**Rhythm** Rhythm is the musical quality created by the alternation of stressed and unstressed syllables in a line of poetry. Poets use rhythm to emphasize ideas and to create moods. Devices such as alliteration, rhyme, and assonance often contribute to creating rhythm.

*See also* Meter.

**Rising Action** The rising action is the stage of the plot that develops the **conflict,** or struggle. During this stage, events occur that make the conflict more complicated. The events in the rising action build toward a **climax,** or turning point.

*See also* Plot.

**Scanning** Scanning is the process used to search through a text for a particular fact or piece of information. When you scan, you sweep your eyes across a page, looking for key words that may lead you to the information you want.

**Scene** In drama, the action is often divided into acts and scenes. Each scene presents an episode of the play's plot and typically occurs at a single place and time.

*See also* Act.

**Scenery** Scenery is a painted backdrop or other structures used to create the setting for a play.

**Science Fiction** Science fiction is fiction in which a writer explores unexpected possibilities of the past or the future, combining scientific information with his or her creative imagination. Most science fiction writers create believable worlds, although some create fantasy worlds that have familiar elements.

*See also* Fantasy.

**Scope** Scope refers to a work's focus. For example, an article about Austin, Texas, that focuses on the city's history, economy, and residents has a broad scope. An article that focuses only on the restaurants in Austin has a narrower scope.

**Script** The text of a play, film, or broadcast is called a script.

**Secondary Source** *See* Source.

**Sensory Details** Sensory details are words and phrases that appeal to the reader's senses of sight, hearing, touch, smell, and taste.

*See also* Imagery.

**Sequential Order** Sequential order is a pattern of organization that shows the order of steps or stages in a process.

**Setting** The setting of a story, poem, or play is the time and place of the action. Sometimes the setting is clear and well-defined. At other times, it is left to the reader's imagination. Elements of setting include geographic location, historical period (past, present, or future), season, time of day, and culture.

**Setting a Purpose** The process of establishing specific reasons for reading a text is called setting a purpose. Readers can look at a text's title, headings, and illustrations to guess what it might be about. They can then use these guesses to figure out what they want to learn from reading the text.

**Short Story** A short story is a work of fiction that centers on a single idea and can be read in one sitting. Generally, a short story has one main conflict that involves the characters and keeps the story moving.

*See also* Fiction.

**Sidebar** A sidebar is additional information set in a box alongside or within a news or feature article. Popular magazines often make use of sidebars.

**Signal Words** In a text, signal words are words and phrases that help show how events or ideas are related. Some common examples of signal words are *and, but, however, nevertheless, therefore,* and *in addition.*

**Simile** A simile is a figure of speech that makes a comparison between two unlike things using the words *like* or *as.*

*See also* Figurative Language; Metaphor.

**Sound Devices** Sound devices are ways of using words for the sound qualities they create. Sound devices can help convey meaning and mood in a writer's work. Some common sound devices include **alliteration, assonance, meter, onomatopoeia, repetition, rhyme,** and **rhythm.**

*See also* Alliteration; Assonance; Meter; Onomatopoeia; Repetition; Rhyme; Rhythm.

**Source** A source is anything that supplies information. **Primary sources** are materials created by people who witnessed or took part in the event they supply information about. Letters, diaries, autobiographies, and eyewitness accounts are primary sources. **Secondary sources** are those made by people who were not directly involved in the event or even present when it occurred. Encyclopedias, textbooks, biographies, and most news articles are secondary sources.

**Speaker** In poetry the speaker is the voice that "talks" to the reader, similar to the narrator in fiction. The speaker is not necessarily the poet.

**Speech** A speech is a talk or public address. The purpose of a speech may be to entertain, to explain, to persuade, to inspire, or any combination of these purposes.

**Stage Directions** In the script of a play, the instructions to the actors, director, and stage crew are called the stage directions. Stage directions might suggest scenery, lighting, sound effects, and ways for actors to move and speak. Stage directions often appear in parentheses and in italic type.

**Stanza** A stanza is a group of two or more lines that form a unit in a poem. Each stanza may have the same number of lines, or the number of lines may vary.

*See also* Couplet; Form; Poetry.

**Stereotype** In literature, characters who are defined by a single trait are known as stereotypes. Such characters do not usually demonstrate the complexities of real people. Familiar stereotypes in popular literature include the absent-minded professor and the busybody.

**Stereotyping** Stereotyping is a dangerous type of overgeneralization. It can lead to unfair judgments of people based on their ethnic background, beliefs, practices, or physical appearance.

**Structure** The structure of a work of literature is the way in which it is put together. In poetry, structure involves the arrangement of words and lines to produce a desired effect. One structural unit in poetry is the stanza. In prose, structure involves the arrangement of such elements as sentences, paragraphs, and events. **Sentence structure** refers to the length and types of sentences used in a work.

**Style** A style is a manner of writing. It involves how something is said rather than what is said.

**Subject** The subject of a literary work is its focus or topic. In an autobiography, for example, the subject is the life of the person telling the story. Subject differs from **theme** in that theme is a deeper meaning, whereas the subject is the main situation or set of facts described by the text.

**Summarize** To summarize is to briefly retell the main ideas of a piece of writing in one's own words.

*See also* Paraphrase.

**Support** Support is any information that helps to prove a claim.

**Supporting Detail** *See* Main Idea.

**Surprise Ending** A surprise ending is an unexpected plot twist at the end of a story. The surprise may be a sudden turn in the action or a piece of information that gives a different perspective to the entire story.

**Suspense** Suspense is a feeling of growing tension and excitement experienced by a reader. Suspense makes a reader curious about the outcome of a story or an event within a story. A writer creates suspense by raising questions in the reader's mind. The use of **foreshadowing** is one way that writers create suspense.

*See also* Foreshadowing.

**Symbol** A symbol is a person, a place, an object, an animal, or an activity that stands for something beyond itself. For example, a flag is a colored piece of cloth that stands for a country. A white dove is a bird that represents peace.

**Synthesize** To synthesize information means to take individual pieces of information and combine them in order to gain a better understanding of a subject.

**Tall Tale** A tall tale is a humorously exaggerated story about impossible events, often involving the supernatural abilities of the main character. Stories about folk heroes such as Pecos Bill and Paul Bunyan are typical tall tales.

**Teleplay** A teleplay is a play written for television. In a teleplay, scenes can change quickly and dramatically. The camera can focus the viewer's attention on specific actions. The camera directions in teleplays are much like the stage directions in stage plays.

**Text Feature** Text features are elements of a text, such as boldface type, headings, and subheadings, that help organize and call attention to important information. Italic type, bulleted or numbered lists, sidebars, and graphic aids such as charts, tables, timelines, illustrations, and photographs are also considered text features.

**Theme** A theme is a message about life or human nature that the writer shares with the reader. In many cases, readers must infer the writer's message. One way to infer a theme is to note the lessons learned by the main characters.

> **Recurring themes:** Themes found in a variety of works. For example, authors from different backgrounds might express similar themes having to do with the importance of family values.

> **Universal themes:** Themes that are found throughout the literature of all time periods. For example, Cinderella stories contain a universal theme relating to goodness being rewarded.

*See also* Moral.

**Thesaurus** *See* Reference Works.

**Thesis Statement** A thesis statement, or controlling idea, is the main proposition that a writer attempts to support in a piece of writing.

**Third-Person Point of View** *See* Point of View.

**Title** The title of a piece of writing is the name that is attached to it. A title often refers to an important aspect of the work.

**Tone** The tone of a literary work expresses the writer's attitude toward his or her subject. Words such as *angry, sad,* and *humorous* can be used to describe different tones.

*See also* Author's Perspective.

**Topic Sentence** The topic sentence of a paragraph states the paragraph's main idea. All other sentences in the paragraph provide supporting details.

**Tragedy**  A tragedy is a dramatic work that presents the downfall of a character or characters. The events in a tragic plot are set in motion by a decision that is often an error in judgment on the part of the hero. Events are linked in a cause-and-effect relationship and lead to a disastrous conclusion, usually death.

**Traits**  *See* Character.

**Treatment**  The way a topic is handled in a work is referred to as its treatment. Treatment includes the form the writing takes as well as the writer's purpose and tone.

**Turning Point**  *See* Climax.

**Universal Theme**  *See* Theme.

**Unsupported Inference**  A guess that may seem logical but that is not supported by facts.

**Visualize**  Visualizing is the process of forming a mental picture based on written or spoken information.

**Voice**  The term *voice* refers to a writer's unique use of language that allows a reader to "hear" a human personality in the writer's work. Elements of style that contribute to a writer's voice can reveal much about the author's personality, beliefs, and attitudes.

**Website**  A website is a collection of "pages" on the World Wide Web that usually covers a specific subject. Linked pages are accessed by clicking hyperlinks or menus, which send the user from page to page within a website. Websites are created by companies, organizations, educational institutions, government agencies, the military, and individuals.

**Word Choice**  The success of any writing depends on the writer's choice of words. Words not only communicate ideas but also help describe events, characters, settings, and so on. Word choice can make a writer's work sound formal or informal, serious or humorous. A writer must choose words carefully depending on the goal of the piece of writing. For example, a writer working on a science article would probably use technical, formal words; a writer trying to establish the setting in a short story would probably use more descriptive words. Word choice is sometimes referred to as diction.

*See also* Style.

**Workplace Document**  Workplace documents are materials that are produced or used within a work setting, usually to aid in the functioning of the workplace. They include job applications, office memos, training manuals, job descriptions, and sales reports.

**Works Cited**  The term *works cited* refers to a list of all the works a writer has referred to in his or her text. This list often includes not only books and articles but also Internet sources.

**Works Consulted**  The term *works consulted* refers to a list of all the works a writer consulted in order to create his or her text. It is not limited just to those works cited in the text.

*See also* Bibliography.

# Using the Glossary

This glossary is an alphabetical list of vocabulary words found in the selections in this book. Use this glossary just as you would a dictionary—to determine the meanings, parts of speech, pronunciation, and syllabication of words. (Some technical, foreign, and more obscure words in this book are not listed here but are defined for you in the footnotes that accompany many of the selections.)

Many words in the English language have more than one meaning. This glossary gives the meanings that apply to the words as they are used in the selections in this book. Words closely related in form and meaning are listed together in one entry (for instance, *consumption* and *consume*), and the definition is given for the first form.

The following abbreviations are used to identify parts of speech of words:

*adj.* adjective    *adv.* adverb    *n.* noun    *v.* verb

Each word's pronunciation is given in parentheses. A guide to the pronunciation symbols appears in the Pronunciation Key below. The stress marks in the Pronunciation Key are used to indicate the force given to each syllable in a word. They can also help you determine where words are divided into syllables.

For more information about the words in this glossary or for information about words not listed here, consult a dictionary.

# Pronunciation Key

| Symbol | Examples | Symbol | Examples | Symbol | Examples |
|---|---|---|---|---|---|
| ă | pat | m | mum | ûr | urge, term, firm, word, heard |
| ā | pay | n | no, sudden* (sud'n) | | |
| ä | father | ng | thing | **Symbol** | **Examples** |
| âr | care | ŏ | pot | v | valve |
| b | bib | ō | toe | w | with |
| ch | church | ô | caught, paw | y | yes |
| d | deed, milled | oi | noise | z | zebra, xylem |
| ĕ | pet | ŏŏ | took | zh | vision, pleasure, garage |
| ē | bee | ōō | boot | | |
| f | fife, phase, rough | ŏŏr | lure | ə | about, item, edible, gallop, circus |
| g | gag | ôr | core | | |
| h | hat | ou | out | ər | butter |
| hw | which | p | pop | | |
| ĭ | pit | r | roar | | |
| ī | pie, by | s | sauce | **Sounds in Foreign Words** | |
| îr | pier | sh | ship, dish | KH | *German* ich, ach; *Scottish* loch |
| j | judge | t | tight, stopped | | |
| k | kick, cat, pique | th | thin | N | *French,* bon (bôn) |
| l | lid, needle* (nēd'l) | th | this | œ | *French* feu, œuf; *German* schön |
| | | ŭ | cut | ü | *French* tu; *German* uber |

*In English the consonants *l* and *n* often constitute complete syllables by themselves.

### Stress Marks

The relevant emphasis with which the syllables of a word or phrase are spoken, called stress, is indicated in three different ways. The strongest, or primary, stress is marked with a bold mark (´). An intermediate, or secondary, level of stress is marked with a similar but lighter mark (´). The weakest stress is unmarked. Words of one syllable show no stress mark.

# Glossary of Academic Vocabulary

**achieve** (ə-chēv´) *v.* to perform or carry out with success; accomplish

**appropriate** (ə-prō´prē-ĭt) *adj.* suitable or acceptable for a particular situation, person, place, or condition

**authority** (ə-thôr´ĭ-tē) *n.* an accepted source, such as a person or text, of expert information or advice

**benefit** (bĕn´ə-fĭt) *n.* something that provides help or improves something else

**circumstance** (sûr´kəm-stăns´) *n.* a condition or fact that affects an event

**consequence** (kŏn´sĭ-kwĕns´) *n.* something that logically or naturally follows from an action or condition

**constraint** (kən-strānt´) *n.* something or someone that limits or restricts another's actions

**distinct** (dĭ-stĭngkt´) *adj.* easy to tell apart from others; not alike

**emphasize** (ĕm´fə-sīz´) *v.* to give something special importance or attention

**environment** (ĕn-vī´rən-mənt) *n.* surroundings; the conditions that surround someone or something

**evident** (ĕv´ĭ-dənt) *adj.* easily seen or understood; obvious

**factor** (făk´tər) *n.* someone or something that has an affect on an event, a process, or a situation

**illustrate** (ĭl´ə-strāt´) *v.* to show, or clarify, by examples or comparing

**impact** (ĭm´păkt´) *n.* something striking against another; also, the effect or impression of one thing on another

**indicate** (ĭn´dĭ-kāt´) *tr.v.* to point out; also, to serve as a sign or symbol of something

**individual** (ĭn´də-vĭj´ōō-əl) *n.* a single human being apart from a society or community

**injure** (ĭn´jər) *tr.v.* to hurt or cause damage

**instance** (ĭn´stəns) *n.* an example that is cited to prove or disprove a claim or illustrate a point

**justify** (jŭs´tə-fī´) *v.* to demonstrate or prove to be just, right, reasonable, or valid

**legal** (lē´gəl) *adj.* permitted by law; of, related to, or concerned with law

**occur** (ə-kûr´) *v.* to take place; happen

**outcome** (out´kŭm´) *n.* a natural result or consequence

**period** (pîr´ē-əd) *n.* a particular length of time, often referring to a specific time in history or in a culture

**principle** (prĭn´sə-pəl) *n.* a rule or standard, especially of good behavior

**relevant** (rĕl´ə-vənt) *adj.* important to, connected to, or significant to an issue, event, or person in some way

**respond** (rĭ-spŏnd´) *v.* to make a reply; answer

**significant** (sĭg-nĭf´ĭ-kənt) *adj.* meaningful; important

**similar** (sĭm´ə-lər) *adj.* alike in appearance or nature, though not identical; having features that are the same

**specific** (spĭ-sĭf´ĭk) *adj.* concerned with a particular thing; also, precise or exact

**tradition** (trə-dĭsh´ən) *n.* the passing down of various elements of a culture from generation to generation; a custom

# Glossary of Critical Vocabulary

**activate** (ăk´tə-vāt´) *v.* To *activate* something means to cause it to start working.

**aggression** (ə-grĕsh´ən) *n.* Angry, violent behavior or action is called *aggression*.

**alley** (ăl´ē) *n.* An *alley* is a narrow street or passage behind or between city buildings.

**allure** (ə-lŏŏr´) *n.* An *allure* is a power of attraction, an ability to interest or entice others.

**ambush** (ăm´bŏŏsh) *v.* Some animals *ambush* their prey by hiding and then attacking as the prey comes near them.

**amiable** (ā´mē-ə-bəl) *adj.* To be *amiable* is to be good-natured and friendly.

**antibiotic** (ăn´tĭ-bī-ŏt´ĭk) *n.* An *antibiotic* is a drug used in medicine to kill bacteria and to cure infections.

**aptitude** (ăp´tĭ-tōōd´) *n.* An *aptitude* for something is an ability to easily and quickly learn how to do it.

**attribute** (ə-trĭb´yōōt) *tr.v.* If you *attribute* something to a person, thing, or event, you believe that they cause it or have it.

**banquet** (băng´kwĭt) *n.* A *banquet* is a huge, elaborate feast with many kinds of food and drink.

**bore** (bôr) *v.* (past tense of *bear*) If you say a person *bore* something, you mean they carried it or had it on them; it is visible in some way.

**brood** (brōōd) *v.* If you *brood,* you are deep in thought, maybe worrying or feeling depressed about something.

**cascade** (kăs-kād´) *v.* Something that can *cascade* will fall, pour, or rush in stages, like a waterfall over steep rocks.

**claustrophobic** (klô´strə-fō´bĭk) *adj.* A *claustrophobic* place feels uncomfortably closed or crowded.

**collapse** (kə-lăps´) *v.* If you *collapse,* you fall down suddenly.

**complexity** (kəm-plĕk´sĭ-tē) *n. Complexity* is the state of having many different parts that are connected in a tangled or layered way.

**conceal** (kən-sēl´) *v.* If you *conceal* something, you hide it and keep it from being found or seen.

**confidence** (kŏn´fĭ-dəns) *n.* A person who has *confidence* believes in his or her abilities or ideas.

**conscientious** (kŏn´shē-ĕn´shəs) *adj.* If someone is *conscientious,* that person is very careful and thorough.

**criticize** (krĭt´ĭ-sīz´) *v.* To *criticize* is to tell someone what you think is wrong with them.

**degradation** (dĕg´rə-dā´shən) *n.* Damage done to something in nature, by weather or water for example, is called *degradation*.

**despair** (dĭ-spâr´) *n.* Feeling defeated, with a complete loss of hope, is called *despair*.

**dialect** (dī´ə-lĕkt´) *n.* A *dialect* is a regional language variation, characterized by differences in pronunciation, grammar, or vocabulary.

**dictate** (dĭk´tāt´) *v.* To *dictate* something is to require it to be done or decided.

**distract** (dĭ-străkt´) *v.* To *distract* is to pull attention away from something or someone.

**eavesdrop** (ēvz´drŏp´) *intr.v.* To *eavesdrop* is to listen secretly to others' private conversations.

**embrace** (ĕm-brās´) *n.* An *embrace* is a hug or encirclement, showing acceptance.

**emphatic** (ĕm-făt´ĭk) *adj.* If something is *emphatic,* it is expressed in a definite and forceful way.

**entrance** (ĕn-trăns´) *v.* To *entrance* is to fill with delight or wonder.

**evolve** (ĭ-vŏlv´) *v.* When animals and plants *evolve,* they gradually change and develop into different forms.

**exotic** (ĭg-zŏt´ĭk) *adj.* Something that is *exotic* is from another part of the world.

**foil** (foil) *tr.v.* If you *foil* someone, you stop that person from being successful at something.

**gauge** (gāj) *tr.v.* To *gauge* something is to measure it or judge it, as in to make an estimate.

**glisten** (glĭs´ən) *v.* An object that *glistens* is sparkly and shiny.

**gnarly** (när´lē) *adj.* Something that is *gnarly* has many knots and bumpy areas on its surface.

**grimace** (grĭm´ĭs) *v.* If you *grimace,* you twist your face in an unattractive way because you are unhappy, disgusted, or in pain.

**immaturity** (ĭm´ə-tyŏor´ĭ-tē) *n. Immaturity* is the state of not being fully developed or grown.

**immortal** (ĭ-môr´tl) *adj.* If someone or something is *immortal,* it will never die.

**inconsistency** (ĭn´kən-sĭs´tən-sē) *n.* If something shows *inconsistency,* it does not always behave or respond the same way every time.

**indignity** (ĭn-dĭg´nĭ-tē) *n.* An *indignity* is something that offends, insults, or injures one's pride or dignity.

**indomitable** (ĭn-dŏm´ĭ-tə-bəl) *adj.* Something or someone that is *indomitable* is unable to be tamed or defeated.

**indulge** (ĭn-dŭlj´) *v.* If you *indulge* in something, you allow yourself to do or have something you want.

**intercept** (in´tər-sĕpt´) *v.* To *intercept* is to stop or interrupt something.

**invisible** (ĭn-vĭz´ə-bəl) *adj.* If something is *invisible,* you cannot see it.

**isolate** (ī´sə-lāt´) *v.* To *isolate* something is to set it apart or separate it from others.

**jar** (jär) *n.* A *jar* can be a jolt or shock, as well as a harsh, scraping sound.

**knot** (nŏt) *n.* A *knot* is a unit of speed used by ships. One knot is equal to one nautical mile, or about 1.85 kilometers per hour.

**lament** (lə-mĕnt) *v.* If you *lament,* you are wailing or crying as a way of expressing grief.

**lethargy** (lĕth´ər-jē) *n.* In a state of *lethargy,* a person experiences drowsiness, inactivity, and a lack of energy.

**linger** (lĭng´gər) *v.* To *linger* means to leave slowly and reluctantly, not wanting to go.

**magnitude** (măg´nĭ-tōod´) *n. Magnitude* is a measure of the amount of energy released by an earthquake.

**malice** (măl´ĭs) *n. Malice* is a desire to harm others or to see someone suffer.

**mandate** (măn´dāt´) *n.* A *mandate* is an authoritative command or instruction.

**menagerie** (mə-năj´ə-rē) *n.* A *menagerie* is a collection of live wild animals, often kept for showing to the public.

**mock** (mŏk) *v.* To *mock* someone is to treat them with scorn or contempt.

**monumental** (mŏn´yə-mĕn´tl) *adj.* A *monumental* event is one that is of outstanding significance.

**mope** (mōp) *intr.v.* To *mope* is to be gloomy, miserable, and not interested in anything.

**morbid** (môr´bĭd) *adj.* A *morbid* quality or feeling is one that is unhealthy or unwholesome, like an illness or disease.

**ominous** (ŏm´ə-nəs) *adj.* Something that is *ominous* is frightening or threatening.

**perseverance** (pûr´sə-vîr´əns) *n.* To have *perseverance* is to stay focused on a plan, a belief, or a purpose.

**pestilence** (pĕs´tə-ləns) *n.* A *pestilence* is often a fatal illness or evil influence that spreads quickly to many people.

**phenomenon** (fĭ-nŏm´ə-nŏn´) *n.* A *phenomenon* is an unusual or remarkable fact or event.

**plummet** (plŭm´ĭt) *v.* If you *plummet,* you fall straight down, suddenly and steeply.

**poised** (poizd) *adj.* To be *poised* means to be calm and assured, showing balanced feeling and action.

**precarious** (prĭ-kâr´ē-əs) *adj.* If something is done in a *precarious* manner, it is done in a dangerously unstable or insecure way.

**precipice** (prĕs´ə-pĭs) *n.* A *precipice* is an overhanging or extremely steep area of rock.

**predator** (prĕd´ə-tər) *n.* A *predator* is an animal that survives by eating other animals.

**prestigious** (prĕ-stē´jəs) *adj.* If something is *prestigious,* it has a greater level of people's respect or honor than others like it.

**priority** (prī-ôr´ĭ-tē) *n.* A *priority* is the thing that is most important to a person in a particular situation or relationship.

**prosperity** (prŏ-spĕr´ĭ-tē) *n. Prosperity* means having success, particularly having enough money.

**raggedy** (răg´ĭ-dē) *adj.* Something that is *raggedy* is worn out, torn, or frayed.

**rattle** (răt´l) *v.* If you hear something *rattle,* it is making short, fast knocking sounds as it moves.

**recoil** (rĭ-koil´) *intr. v.* To *recoil* from something is to shrink back, as if in fear.

**regulate** (rĕg´yə-lāt´) *v.* If you *regulate* something, you control or direct it according to a rule, principle, or law.

**reminisce** (rĕm´ə-nĭs´) *v.* When you *reminisce,* you remember past experiences or events.

**repress** (rĭ-prĕs´) *v.* If you *repress* something, you hold it back or try to stop it from happening.

**resentment** (rĭ-zĕnt´mənt) *n.* If you feel *resentment*, you feel anger or irritation.

**revolutionary** (rĕv´ə-lōo´shə-nĕr´ē) *adj.* Something that is *revolutionary* causes important and sometimes sudden changes in a situation.

**rivulet** (rĭv´yə-lĭt) *n.* A *rivulet* is a small brook or stream.

**rupture** (rŭp´chər) *v.* To *rupture* means to break open or burst.

**serene** (sə-rēn´) *adj.* If you are *serene,* you are calm and unflustered.

**shudder** (shŭd´ər) *n.* A *shudder* is a strong shiver or tremor.

**stake** (stāk) *n.* A *stake* is something that can be gained or lost in a situation, such as money, food, or life.

**stealthily** (stĕl´thə-lē) *adv.* To do something *stealthily* means doing it quietly and secretly so no one notices.

**summons** (sŭm´ənz) *n.* A *summons* is a call or a notice by an authority to appear somewhere or to do something.

**surfeit** (sûr´fĭt) *n.* A *surfeit* is an excessive amount of something, such as food or drink.

**technician** (tĕk-nĭsh´ən) *n.* A *technician* is a person who does skilled practical work using specific equipment.

**timid** (tĭm´ĭd) *adj.* To act in a *timid* manner is to act shyly, fearfully, or hesitantly.

**traumatize** (trô´mə-tīz´, trou´-) *tr.v.* To *traumatize* means to upset or shock someone, causing emotional and mental pain.

**treacherous** (trĕch´ər-əs) *adj.* A *treacherous* person is untrustworthy and likely to betray others.

**trigger** (trĭg´ər) *v.* To *trigger* something means to cause it to begin.

**turbulence** (tûr´byə-ləns) *n.* In flying, *turbulence* is an interruption in the flow of wind that causes planes to rise, fall, or sway in a rough way.

**undaunted** (ŭn-dôn´tĭd) *adj.* An *undaunted* person is someone who is strongly courageous, not discouraged or disheartened.

**venture** (vĕn´chər) *n.* A *venture* is a dangerous, daring, or poorly planned task or activity.

**vigil** (vĭj´əl) *n.* A *vigil* is an act or a time of watching, often during normal sleeping hours.

**wallop** (wŏl´əp) *v.* To *wallop* is to hit or strike with a hard blow.

**weary** (wîr´ē) *adj.* If you are growing *weary,* you are getting tired of something, either physically or mentally.

# Index of Skills

## A

Academic Vocabulary, 2, 63, 67, 72, 133, 138, 201, 210, 247, 252, 303, 307, 312, 373, 377. *See also* Glossary of Academic Vocabulary
adjectives, R29, R40
  comparative forms, R41
  phrases, R40, R44
  predicate, R40, R44
  proper, 128
  versus adverbs, R41
adventure stories, R61
adverbs, R29, R41, R44
alliteration, 169, R61
allusions, R61
almanacs, R61
analogies, 231, 269, 329, R55, R61
analyzing
  arguments, 95, 226, 230, R22, R61
  biographies, 266, 267
  cause-and-effect organization, 153, R18
  characterization, 237
  dramas, 361
  editorials, 226
  folk tales, 341
  informational texts, 55, 125, 153
  logic and reasoning, R23
  media, 59, 293, 301
  memoirs, 259, 267
  mood, 277
  myths, 327
  narrative nonfiction texts, 193
  newspaper articles, 299
  parodies, 333
  persuasive techniques, 95, 229. *See also* appeals; loaded language
  poems, 39, 165, 168, 283, 291
  point of view, 33, R70
  style, 193, 237
  text features, 47
  theme, 219, 283, 327
  tone, 193, 237, 245
  word choice, 237
Analyzing the Media, 62, 200, 299, 301, 302
Analyzing the Text, 14, 34, 40, 48, 56, 90, 96, 104, 114, 125, 126, 154, 165, 168, 170, 182, 194, 220, 226, 229, 230, 238, 246, 259, 266, 268, 278, 284, 292, 328, 334, 342, 362, 370
anecdotes, 55, 125, R61
animation, 61, 199

Annotate It!, 14, 34, 40, 48, 56, 90, 96, 104, 114, 126, 154, 165, 168, 170, 182, 194, 220, 226, 229, 230, 238, 246, 259, 266, 268, 278, 284, 292, 299, 328, 334, 342, 362, 370
antagonists, R61
antecedents, pronoun agreement with. *See* pronouns
antonyms, R55
appeals
  emotional, 95, R26, R64
  ethical, R22, R26, R65
  logical, R22, R67
  to authority, R61
arguments, 95, 226, R22, R61
  analyzing, 95, R22, R61
  claims in, 95, 226, R2, R22, R63
  comparing and contrasting, 230
  counterarguments, 95, R22, R63
  counterclaim in, R2
  evaluating, 95, 226, R26–R27, R65
  evidence in, 95, 226, R2, R22, R65
  loaded language in, 229, R67
  logical, R68
  persuasive techniques in, 95, 229
  reasons in, 95, 226, R2, R22
  support in, 95, 226, R2, R22
  tracing, 95, 226
  writing, R1
assonance, R61
assumptions, R61
As You View, 60, 198, 300
audience
  considering your, 64, 68, 130, 134, 202, 206, 248, 304, 308, 374, 378
  for argument in a speech, 248
  for essay, 308
  for expository essay, 68, 134
  for literary analysis, 130, 374
  for multmedia presentation, 202
  for narrative nonfiction, 206
  for personal narrative, 304
  for play, 378
  for short story, 64
audiences, media target, R61
author's message, R61
author's perspective, R61
author's position, R61
author's purpose, 113, R61
autobiographies, 267, R61

## B

ballads, R61
bias, R26, R62
bibliographies, R62

biographies, 266, 267
  analyzing, 266, 267
  chronological order in, 266, R17, R63
  primary sources in, 267, R70
  quotations in, 266
  secondary sources in, 267, R71
  sequence in, 266
  third-person point of view in, 266
business correspondence, R62

## C

capitalization, R34
  of proper adjectives, 128
  of proper nouns, 184
cause-and-effect organization, 153, R18
central idea, 55, 113, 369. *See also* main idea
  determining, 55
  implied, 55, R16
  organization of, 369
  summarizing, 113
characters, 89, R62
  characterization of, 237, R62
  development of, 13, R62
  dynamic, R62
  main, R62
  minor, R62
  motivation of, 13, R62
  responses of, 89, 237
  static, R62
  traits of, 13, R62
chronological order, 266, R17
citations, MLA guidelines, R10–R11
Cite Text Evidence, 14, 34, 40, 48, 56, 62, 90, 96, 104, 114, 126, 154, 165, 168, 170, 182, 194, 200, 220, 229, 230, 238, 246, 266, 268, 278, 284, 292, 299, 301, 302, 328, 334, 342, 362, 370
claims, in argument, 95, 226, R2, R63
clarifying, R63
classification, R63
clauses, R45–R46
cliché, R63
climax, of a plot, 33, 64, R63
Collaborative Discussion, 12, 32, 38, 46, 54, 60, 88, 94, 102, 112, 124, 152, 167, 180, 192, 198, 218, 228, 236, 244, 265, 276, 282, 290, 298, 300, 326, 340, 360, R12–R13
comedies, R63
commas, 36, 240, R31
commentaries, 227–228, 302
compare-and-contrast organization, R19
Compare Media, 293
Compare Texts, 157, 223, 253

myth, 313–326, 327, R68
short stories, 33, R72
figurative language, 103, 245,
R52, R65
metaphors, 221, 245, R68
onomatopoeia, R69
personification, 103, 181, 221, R69
similes, 221, 238, 245, R72
folklore, R66
folk tales, 335–340, 341, R66
footage, 199, 301
*fyi*, 2, 72, 138, 210, 252, 312

## G

generalizations, R66
genre, R66
biographies, 260–265
commentaries, 227–228
documentaries, 197–198
dramas, 345–360
editorials, 223–225
essays, 363–368
folk tales, 335–340
informational texts, 51–54,
117–124, 139–152
memoirs, 253–258
myths, 313–326
news articles, 294–298
online articles, 41–46
online science exhibit, 59–60
plays, 345–360
poems, 37–38, 157–164, 166–167,
241–243, 244, 281–282,
285–290, 331–332
science writing, 105–112
short stories, 3–12, 17–32, 73–88,
171–180, 211–218, 233–236,
271–276
speeches, 93–94
TV newscasts, 300
gerunds, R45
glossaries, 343, R56, R75
Glossary of Academic Vocabulary,
R76
Glossary of Critical Vocabulary,
R77–R79
Glossary of Literary and
Informational Terms, R61–R74
government publications, R66
grammar. *See also* Language
Conventions
adjectives, 128, R29, R40–R41
adverbs, R29, R41
clauses, R45–R46
conjunctions, R29
interjections, R29
modifiers, R41–R43
nouns, 184, R28, R35
objects, R30, R43
parts of speech, quick reference
guide, R28–R29

phrases, R44–R45
predicates of a sentence, R30,
R43–R44
prepositions, R29, R30
pronouns, 50, 58, 92, 98, 156,
R28–R29, R35–R38
punctuation, 36, 240, 372, R31–R33
sentences and their parts, R30,
R43–R44, R46–R51
subjects of a sentence, R30, R43
verbs, R29, R30, R38–R40
graphic aids, R66
graphic organizers, R66
5 *W*s and *H* charts, 299
cause-and-effect charts, R18
charts, 15, 115, 155, 195, 301,
302, R19
controlling idea charts, 374
hierarchy charts, 134, 248, 308
outlines, 202
storyboards, 202
story maps, 304, 378
Venn diagrams, R19
webs, 35, 371
graphics, in media, 299

## H

haiku, R66
headings, 47
hero, R66
historical document, R67
historical fiction, R67
historical writing, 185–192
HISTORY®, 41, 73, 139, 197, 285
hmhfyi.com. *See* fyi
homographs, R55
homonyms, R55
homophones, R55
how-to books, R67
humor, 333, R67

## I

idioms, R52, R67
imagery, 103
independent clauses, R45
indexes, R67
inductive reasoning, R23, R67
inferences, making, 13, 245, R24, R67
about a poem's tone, 245
evidence for, 13
supported, 13
unsupported, R24
informational texts, 51–54, 117–124,
139–152, R67
organization of, R16–R21
Interactive Lessons, 63, 129, 133, 201,
205, 247, 303, 307, 373, 377
interjections, R29
internal conflict. *See* conflict
interviews, 199, 301, R67
irony, 89, R67

## J

journals, R67

## L

Language Conventions
capitalization, 128, 184
commas and dashes, 36
common nouns, 184
dialect, 16, 181
expression, improving, 222
parentheses, 372, R32
pronoun number, 116
pronoun person, shifts in, 156
pronouns, correcting vague, 270
pronouns, intensive, 92
pronouns, possessive, 58
pronouns, subjective and objective,
50
pronouns *who* and *whom*, 98
proper adjectives, 128
proper nouns, 184
punctuating dialogue, 240
punctuation, 372
recognizing variations from
Standard English, 16
sentence patterns, varying, 280
spelling words correctly, 232,
330, 344
style and tone, consistency in, 196
legend, R67
limerick, R67
literary devices, 193
literary nonfiction, R67
loaded language, 229, R67
lyric poetry, 39

## M

main idea, 55, 369, R68. *See also*
central idea
determining, 55
implied, 55
organization of, 369
making inferences. *See* inferences
media. *See also* media elements and
techniques; media genres and
types
analyzing, 62, 200, 299, 301, 302
analyzing structure of, 299
comparing, 293, 302
integrating information in,
199, 302
interpreting diverse forms of, 199
interpreting information in, 61, 301
purpose of, 61
media activity
commentaries, 302
multimedia presentations, 126, 200
podcasts, 62
slideshow presentations, 126
media elements and techniques
animation, 61, 199

# Index of Titles & Authors

# Acknowledgments

Excerpt from "After the Hurricane" by Rita Williams-Garcia from *Free? Stories About Human Rights* by Amnesty International. Text copyright © 2009 by Rita Williams-Garcia. Reprinted by permission of Rita Williams-Garcia.

Excerpt from *The American Heritage Dictionary of the English Language, Fifth Edition.* Text copyright © 2011 by Houghton Mifflin Harcourt. Adapted and reprinted by permission of Houghton Mifflin Harcourt Publishing Company.

Excerpt from *Animal Snoops: The Wondrous World of Wildlife Spies* by Peter Christie. Text copyright © 2010 by Peter Christie. Reprinted by permission of Annick Press, Ltd. All rights reserved.

"Animal Wisdom" from *Sacred Fire* by Nancy Wood. Text copyright © 1998 by Nancy Wood. Reprinted by permission of Nancy Wood.

"The Apple of Discord I" from *Voices of the Trojan War* by Kate Hovey. Text copyright © 2004 by Kate Hovey. Reprinted by permission of Margaret K. McElderry Books, an imprint of Simon & Schuster Children's Publishing Division, and Kate Hovey.

"The Banana Tree" from *A Thief in the Village and Other Stories* by James Berry. Text copyright © 1987 by James Berry. Reprinted by permission of Penguin Books Ltd. and Peters Fraser & Dunlop (www.petersfraserdunlop.com) on behalf of James Berry.

Excerpt from *Black Ships Before Troy: The Story of the Iliad* by Rosemary Sutcliffe. Originally published by Frances Lincoln, Ltd., 1993. Text copyright © 1993 by Anthony Lawton. Reprinted by permission of Delacorte Press, a division of Random House, Inc. and Frances Lincoln, Ltd. Any third party use of this material, outside of this publication, is prohibited. Interested parties must apply directly to Random House, Inc. for permission.

Excerpt from *Colin Powell: Military Leader* by Warren Brown. Text copyright © 1992 by Chelsea House Publishers, a division of Main Line Book Co. Reprinted by permission of Chelsea House Publishers.

"Eleven" from *Woman Hollering Creek and Other Stories* by Sandra Cisneros. Text copyright © 1991 by Sandra Cisneros. Published by Vintage Books, a division of Random House, Inc. Reprinted by permission of Susan Bergholz Literary Services, New York, NY and Lamy, NM and Bloomsbury. All Rights Reserved.

"Fears and Phobias" from *kidshealth.org.* Text copyright © 1995-2012 by The Nemours Foundation/KidsHealth®. Reprinted by permission of The Nemours Foundation.

"Fine?" by Margaret Peterson Haddix from *On the Edge: Stories at the Brink* edited by Lois Duncan. Text copyright © 2000 by Margaret Peterson Haddix. Reprinted by permission of Adams Literary.

"The First Day of School" from *The Happy Marriage and Other Stories* by R.V. Cassill. Text copyright © 1966 by R.V. Cassill. Reprinted by permission of R.V. Cassill.

Excerpt from *Greek Mythology* by Simone Payment. Text copyright © 2006 by The Rosen Publishing Group, Inc. Reprinted by permission of The Rosen Publishing Group, Inc.

Excerpt from *How Smart Are Animals?* by Dorothy Hinshaw Patent. Text copyright © 1990 by Dorothy Hinshaw Patent. Reprinted by permission of Houghton Mifflin Harcourt Publishing Company.

"In the Spotlight" from *Stuff that Scares Your Pants Off* by Glenn Murphy. Text copyright © 2011 by Glenn Murphy. Reprinted by permission of Roaring Brook Press, an imprint of Macmillan Children's Publishing Group.

Excerpt from *It Worked for Me: In Life and Leadership* by Colin Powell with Tony Kolz. Text copyright © 2012 by Colin Powell. Reprinted by permission of HarperCollins Publishers.

"The Last Wolf" by Mary TallMountain. Text copyright © 1994 by the TallMountain Estate. Reprinted by permission of the TallMountain Estate. All rights reserved.

"Let People Own Exotic Animals" by Zuzana Kukol from *USA Today*, March 3, 2003. Text copyright © 2003 by Gannet. Reprinted by permission of PARS International on behalf of USA Today. All Rights Reserved.

"Life Doesn't Frighten Me" from *And Still I Rise* by Maya Angelou. Text copyright © 1978 by Maya Angelou. Reprinted by permission of Random House, Inc. and Virago, an imprint of Little, Brown Book Group. Any third party use of this material, outside of this publication, is prohibited. Interested parties must apply directly to Random House, Inc. for permission.

"Mammoth Shakes and Waves, Disaster in 12 Countries" from *Disasters: Natural and Man-Made Catastrophes Through the Centuries* by Brenda Guiberson. Text copyright © 2010 by Brenda Guiberson. Reprinted by permission of Macmillan Children's Publishing Group.

"The Midnight Ride of Paul Revere" by Henry Wadsworth Longfellow, read by c-david cotrill, sound editing by Shaelyn Hall. Text copyright © 2011 by The Funny Farm Studios. Reprinted by permission of Ron Hall/Evans-Hall, Inc.

Excerpt from "My Wonder Horse" from *Tierra Amarilla: Stories of New Mexico* by Sabine Ulibarrí, translated by Thelma Campbell Nason. Text and English translation copyright © 1971 by University of New Mexico Press. Reprinted by permission of University of New Mexico Press and the Estate of Sabine Ulibarrí.

Excerpt from *A Night to Remember* by Walter Lord. Text copyright © 1955, 1983 by Walter Lord. Reprinted by permission of Henry Holt and Company, LLC.

"On Doomed Flight, Passengers Vowed to Perish Fighting" by Jodi Wilgoren and Edward Wong from *The New York Times*, September 13, 2001. Text copyright © 2001 by The New York Times. Reprinted by permission of

PARS International on behalf of The New York Times. All Rights Reserved.

"The Prince and the Pauper" by Mark Twain, adapted by Joellen Bland, in *Plays, The Drama Magazine for Young People* © 2012 and *Stage Plays from the Classics* © 1987. Text copyright © 1987 by Joellen Bland. Reprinted by permission of Plays/Sterling Partners, Inc. Performance rights must be obtained in writing from the publisher.

"The Ravine" by Graham Salisbury from *On the Edge: Stories at the Brink* edited by Lois Duncan. Text copyright © 2000 by Graham Salisbury. Reprinted by permission of Jennifer Flannery Literary Agency.

"The Road Not Taken" from *Mountain Interval* by Robert Frost. Text copyright © 1916 by Henry Holt and Company, LLC. Reprinted by permission of Henry Holt and Company, LLC.

"A Voice" from *Communion* by Pat Mora. Text copyright © 1991 by Arte Público Press - University of Houston. Reprinted by permission of Arte Público Press - University of Houston.

"Watcher (After Katrina, 2005)" from *Beyond Katrina: A Meditation on the Mississippi Gulf Coast* by Natasha Trethewey. Text copyright © 2010 by Natasha Trethewey. Reprinted by permission of the University of Georgia Press.

"Wild Animals Aren't Pets" from *USA Today*, October 20, 2011. Text copyright © 2011 by Gannett. Reprinted by permission of PARS International on behalf of USA Today. All Rights Reserved.

"Words Like Freedom" from *The Collected Works of Langston Hughes* by Langston Hughes, edited by Arnold Rampersad with David Roessel. Text copyright © 1994 by the Estate of Langston Hughes. Reprinted by permission of Random House, Inc. and Harold Ober Associates Inc. as given by Random House. Any third party use of this material, outside of this publication, is prohibited. Interested parties must apply directly to Random House, Inc. for permission.

*Yeh-Shen: Cinderella Story from China* retold by Ai-Ling Louie. Text copyright © 1982 by Ai-Ling Louie. Reprinted by permission of Philomel Books, a division of Penguin Group (USA) Inc. and McIntosh & Otis, Inc.